The American Steel Navy

The American Steel Navy

A Photographic History of the U.S. Navy from the Introduction of the Steel Hull in 1883 to the Cruise of the Great White Fleet, 1907−1909

By John D. Alden, Commander, U.S. Navy (Retired)

Photographic Research
and Editorial Supervision by Ed Holm

Fifty Warship Profiles by Arthur D. Baker III

Naval Institute Press, Annapolis, Maryland

American Heritage Press, New York

Revised printing, 1989

Library of Congress Catalogue Number 76-163111
ISBN 0-87021-681-3

Printed in the United States of America

Photograph on half-title page: *Liberty—the figurehead of the
protected cruiser* Cincinnati, *1901.*

Two-page photograph: *A forecastle view on board the battleship*
Indiana, *circa 1898.*

Photograph opposite title page: *The armored cruiser* Washington
*on the day of her launching at Camden, New Jersey,
18 March 1905.*

Photograph on this page: *A view from the fighting top of
the battleship* Oregon, *nearing the Straits of Magellan,
April 1898*

Design by Gerard A. Valerio and Ed Holm.

Preface to the Reprinted Edition

All those interested in the rebirth of the U.S. Navy at the end of the nineteenth century will welcome this reprinting of Commander John D. Alden's *The American Steel Navy*. This work impressed the naval historical community when it first appeared in 1972 because of the outstanding quality and variety of its photographs. Readers also discovered a succinct yet comprehensive text, which discussed nearly every aspect of the Navy's transition from wood to steel. As a summary of a period of tumultuous change in naval affairs, this volume remains unsurpassed more than a decade and a half after it was first published.

Four years' research went into the preparation of this book and especially into the choice of its 345 photographs. Ed Holm, himself a professional photographer, selected and edited them from 25,000 prints and original glass negatives in the National Archives, the Library of Congress, and a dozen other major museums and collections in the United States and abroad. The exceptional photo quality results above all from the use of large-format glass negatives for many of the photographs, as well as from the photographers' ability to see beauty in the products of the machine age. These maritime photos are second to none as monuments to the photographer's art.

The Navy in those days allowed commercial photographers to roam its ships. These photographers printed and sold photo albums as mementos. Their work therefore captured not only the ships themselves but also the crews showing off their weapons, engine rooms, living quarters, mascots, and recreations. We see officers, deckhands, coal passers, cooks, bakers, and many others, pictured in a world that has vanished forever.

Alden integrated the photos into a concise text that synopsizes an important period in U.S. naval history. Since his work appeared, only a few scholars have looked in greater depth at certain parts of the story, and in general their works do not change the major themes or conclusions in *The American Steel Navy*.

Alden has been a precedent-setter in his other naval writings as well. One of his earlier writings, a two-part series called "A New Fleet Emerges," published in the U.S. Naval Institute's *Naval Review* of 1964 and 1965, helped open the way for historical study of post–World War II U.S. Navy shipbuilding policy by making available previously unpublished data on the earlier annual building programs. Alden's *Flush Decks and Four Pipes* (1965, reissued in 1989) was an early example of a new type of book, the technical and operational analysis of a specific ship class or type, which has since become extremely popular. His *The Fleet Submarine in the U.S. Navy* (1979) is a particularly noteworthy example of this genre.

Another important contributor to *The American Steel Navy* was Arthur Davidson Baker III, who produced almost fifty ship profiles for the technical appendix. He has since drafted detailed ship plans for many other books, and has earned a reputation as an expert on contemporary navies by editing the English-language edition of *Combat Fleets of the World*.

Hidden in the photo credits are some comments that deserve attention. The photographic record in this book exists today largely because a few public and private repositories acquired and preserved the original negatives of some key naval photographers. Ed Holm noted that an additional valuable source of photographs was a number of personal albums compiled by men serving in the Navy, and he expressed the hope that publication of *The American Steel Navy* would bring more to light. This reprint is issued with the same hope.

Stephen S. Roberts, 1989
Editor, *The Development of a Modern Navy*

The armored cruiser New York *salutes the return of Admiral George Dewey to New York from the Philippines, 29 September 1899.*

Foreword

The influence of American sea power as a significant factor in world politics is a phenomenon of relatively recent origin, commencing roughly with the entry into service of the Navy's pioneer steel ships in the late 1880s. This volume therefore deals with the seagoing instruments of national policy whose appearance, chronologically, signalized the first tentative moves of the United States into the larger field of international commitments and responsibilities. Within a decade these vessels were engaged in the defense of American overseas trade and possessions, the inevitable development of which Mahan foresaw and for which he endeavored to prepare his fellow naval officers and his countrymen.

It should be noted, too, that the photographic history of the new steel Navy was compiled in amazing detail. E. H. Hart, Enrique Muller, and their lesser known contemporaries among marine photographers found few prohibited areas in ships of the predreadnought age. They therefore were able to reveal the innermost life of the new ships, beginning with the Squadron of Evolution, producing in the process thousands of glass negatives and a veritable flood of prints. Working with cumbersome equipment and hazardous flash powder, they peered into mess deck, turret, and fireroom, and produced some masterpieces of American photographic art. A surprisingly large portion of their output has been preserved. No other nation indeed offers the historical researcher so abundant a store of naval photographs. The illustrations accompanying the text of this book attest to its richness.

The American Steel Navy deals with the period in American history when *"Olympia," "Oregon,"* " 'Fighting Bob' Evans," and "Great White Fleet" were household words. Technology, war, and politics combined in these years of the late nineteenth and early twentieth centuries to popularize the Navy in unusual degree.

There was, first, the impact on the nation of a wholly new weapons system in an age made receptive to change by reason of rapid economic growth. The advent of the steel protected cruiser, followed shortly by the armored cruiser and the battleship in the United States Navy, relegated the *Hartford,* the *Kearsarge,* and their wooden-walled sisters to the limbo of "Old Ironsides," or indeed of the caravels of Columbus. Then again, the Steel Navy in its first battle trials, at Manila Bay and Santiago, had achieved victories of annihilation. Most fundamentally, the course of world politics itself affected popular attitudes towards the Navy in these years, for the United States, burdened with new and unaccustomed responsibilities of empire in the western Pacific, simultaneously sensed a naval threat from a new quarter—the expanding German empire. Navies themselves moreover, were becoming independent factors in the world power balance, as the Anglo-German construction race gathered momentum.

Fairly involved, after 1900, in world power politics, Americans looked to their navy and to the leadership of their navy-minded President, Theodore Roosevelt. The national mood recalled Decatur's era, and Congress responded with appropriations on unprecedented scale to expand the fleet proportionately to the requirements of the changing international situation.

To percipient officers, the Navy's growth during the period from 1883 to 1909 was basically uneven, however spectacular. After 1895 battleship and heavy cruiser requirements received generally adequate recognition; in construction of light cruisers, the "eyes of the fleet," the nation lagged; and as the period drew to a close, the destroyer arm became increasingly neglected relative to strategic requirements. Ship design likewise progressed, but unevenly.

But to the average citizen the fleet testified, as few other symbols did, to the industrial capability of the United States and to its economic, no less than scientific, progress. Above all else, he viewed it as the most tangible—and visible—embodiment of national power in a rapidly changing and uncertain world.

Neville T. Kirk
Department of History
United States Naval Academy

Sailors on board the protected cruiser Cincinnati *retrieve their clothes from the wash line, circa 1903.*

Contents

"The condition of the Navy imperatively demands the prompt and earnest attention of Congress. Unless some action be had in its behalf it must soon dwindle into insignificance."

Secretary of the Navy William H. Hunt, 1881.

Officers and bluejackets muster in marching order on board the sloop-of-war Trenton, *1880.*

Moored alongside a circular crane, the 1,900-ton wooden sloop Swatara *lends a note of life to an almost deserted New York Navy Yard, circa 1876.*

Prologue

The United States Navy had been slowly deteriorating since the end of the Civil War. The fleet that had existed in 1865 had commanded universal respect. The Navy's prewar wooden sailing frigates, ship for ship the finest in the world, had been succeeded by powerful steam vessels and ironclads. U.S. cruisers, among the world's fastest, had been thought capable of sweeping the seas of merchant shipping. The introduction of the monitor with its supposedly invulnerable armor and irresistible big guns had shaken the science of naval warfare to its roots.

As the decade of the 1880s opened, however, the great Civil War fleet had long since been dispersed. The big ironclads had been laid up or sold out of service. Those monitors not broken up for scrap iron were left to rust in obscure backwaters. The fast cruiser-raiders laid down in the large building programs of the war were abandoned or gutted for ignominious service as hulks or storeships. Skeleton frames of unfinished ships stood "ghastly and discouraging" on the stocks of run-down navy yards whose shops and warehouses were cluttered with "old machinery and condemned stores."

The fleet itself was scattered on faraway stations, out of sight and out of mind. Obsolete ships bravely showed the flag in the ports of China, on the Barbary coast, along the troubled reaches of South America, and among the whaling fleets in the fog-shrouded waters off Alaska. They were low-lying, black-hulled, sullen-looking ships—steam frigates, sloops, and gunboats, mostly—with broadside muzzle-loading cannon glowering through the ports in their wooden walls. The fleet was one still operated largely by the sheer brawn of rough manpower—pulling boats, massive hand-steering wheels, capstans hove round to the stamping of feet and the boatswain's call.

It was a fleet of sailing ships into which had been dropped the incongruous and ill-tolerated engines and boilers of the uncouth engineers. Rakish bowsprits and full sail rigs dominated the squat, telescopic stacks as completely as sail dominated steam in the thinking of the officers of the line. Penny-pinching economizers had insisted that inefficient two-bladed propellers be installed to produce less drag when under sail, which was most of the time. Some ships even had demountable shafts and hoisting gear to lift the screws completely out of the water, for regulations discouraged use of any but the most niggardly ration of coal.

The soundest ships were the oldest, those built in the 1840s and '50s when live oak and craftsmanship were still plentiful. That their low-pressure engines were now wheezing relics was considered a technical detail of little significance to the commanders of sail. The newer ships, although equipped with more modern engines and boilers, were infected with accelerated rot due to their hasty wartime construction from unseasoned or inferior grades of oak. Of the twenty-one ships added to the Navy since the end of the Civil War programs, only one exceeded 3,000 tons in measurement and only the five smallest were of iron. The rest were little more than duplicates of the wrecked, worn-out, and rotten craft they were intended to replace. Seven of the twenty-one ostensibly were old vessels "repaired," repair appropriations being the only funds available to the harassed administrators of the Navy Department. No new construction whatever had been authorized since 1874.

Former Civil War generals dominated political life, and national policy was focused on internal expansion. No real external threat to the nation's security was in evidence. The prevailing post-Civil War strategic view, founded on experience with massed armies in that conflict, was that Americans were entirely capable of defending themselves on land if any invader should be rash enough to come over. U.S. maritime commerce had been practically wiped out by the war and there was little sentiment for spending money on a large merchant marine or the warships to protect it. The action lay in the railroads, the land, and the mineral resources of the great inland empire. Under the circumstances there was little pressure to seek colonies or establish footholds for trade overseas. In the eyes of Congress the mission of the Navy was to show the flag, to protect American commerce from outright piracy, to defend American citizens from harm or insult, and to spend as little money as possible.

The Navy's officer corps was controlled by Civil War heroes whose strategic concepts hinged on a combination of coast defense and commerce raiding. Admiral David Dixon Porter—proud, self-righteous, and mercurial—held undisputed sway on the quarterdeck. His hand was in firm control of the engine order telegraph, but the pointer, most of the time, read "All Engines Stop."

The United States Navy of 1880 was not a second-rate or even a third-rate force. It was twelfth-rate. Even the navies of Chile and China exceeded it in ironclad strength. Therefore it is not surprising that foreign naval progress far outmatched even the most optimistic programs suggested in the United States. Among the navies of Europe the period was one of transition, experimentation, discovery, and confusion. The battle lines of the world consisted of a mixture of war-ships, carrying guns in a variety of calibers mounted broadside, in turrets, or in barbettes. Full sail rig was still the vogue but was occasionally omitted entirely in the most radical ironclads. Ram bows of extreme size and shape were in style one year and out of fashion the next. High-freeboard cruising ships alternated with monitor types whose decks were practically awash in a calm. New developments in projectiles and propellants were matched by constant changes in gun caliber and design.

Although foreign progress outclassed U.S. ambitions in nearly all areas, the situation prevailing abroad at the beginning of the 1880s was, in a way, auspicious for the Americans, for the experimentation and rapid changes tended to create obsolescence among ships only a few years old. A navy starting out almost from scratch could anticipate that its new warships would hold their own against foreign opponents to a greater extent than a mere comparison of numbers might indicate. It was in this era of turbulence that the Steel Navy of the United States had its conception and birth.

Marines and sailors aboard the sloop-of-war Mohican *stand at quarters for inspection. Laid down in 1872, the* Mohican *was more than a decade under construction and was not commissioned until 1885.*

Civil War Veterans

For more than twenty years following the Civil War, U.S. naval strength abroad was represented almost exclusively by proud and graceful—but obsolete—wooden sail and steam vessels of an earlier era. One of the most notable of these was the 2,900-ton steam frigate Hartford *of Mobile Bay fame, seen above at Hong Kong while flagship of the old Asiatic Station during 1872–74. Also visible in the photograph, just beyond the* Hartford's *stern, is the 1,575-ton American steam corvette* Iroquois. *Most of the other vessels in the harbor are British men-of-war.*

Bluejackets of the 1880s pass an idle hour aboard the old Ericsson monitor Montauk, *laid up in ordinary at League Island since 1865. The* Montauk's *turret, built up from inch-thick iron plates, shows the scars of some of the more than fifty Confederate shot that struck her at Charleston in 1863. U.S. armored warship strength during the early 1880s was limited to fourteen of these Civil War monitors—all out of service—and five others of more modern design, laid down during the mid-1870s but still uncompleted.*

Iron Guns and Iron Men

Crewmen of the steam frigate Pensacola *exercise her forward pivot gun for the Navy Board of Inspection in 1888. The gun, a Civil War cast-iron Parrott rifle, was one of a number modernized for breech-loading operation in 1878. The* Pensacola *carried four of the big Parrotts—two 60- and two 80-pounders—in addition to a broadside battery of twelve old 9-inch smoothbore muzzle loaders.*

Berth-deck cooks aboard the Pensacola, *attended by their canine mascot, present fork and ladle for a souvenir photograph during the late 1880s. Versed from youth in the ways of sail and representing a multitude of nationalities, such old-time sailors were doomed to extinction a decade or two later, as wood and iron construction slowly gave way to the modern hulls, high-powered guns, and complex machinery of the American Steel Navy.*

"It is therefore the opinion of the Board that these . . .
vessels should be built throughout of steel."

Report of the First Naval Advisory Board, 1881.

Ships of the American Steel Navy

Her hull painted black in the style of the Old Navy, the protected cruiser Chicago
awaits finishing touches at the New York Navy Yard in early 1889.

The ABCD Ships

When Secretary of the Navy William H. Hunt took office at the beginning of the James A. Garfield administration in the spring of 1881, he knew that something urgently needed to be done to rehabilitate the Navy. Convinced that past legislative inaction was due, at least in part, to the lack of a comprehensive and unified program for warship construction, Hunt appointed Rear Admiral John Rodgers to head a board of officers to advise the Department on all particulars of the number and types of vessels needed by the Navy.

Unfortunately, during weeks of debate the fifteen members of the First Naval Advisory Board found there was little on which they could agree. The choice of hull material—iron or steel—for the proposed warships soon emerged as a major point of conflict. Although steel warship construction had been successfully introduced abroad and had several significant advantages, including the combination of light weight and great strength, some members feared that these benefits would be more than offset by the difficulties of developing large-scale steel production in the United States, by delays in delivery of material, and by high costs. Finally, since there were unyielding differences of opinion on this and nearly every other specification that had been taken under consideration, the Board was forced to submit both a majority and a minority report. The report of the majority was notable for its ambitious proposed building program of sixty-eight new vessels and for its conclusion that the major warships "should be built throughout of steel."

It was soon apparent that the extravagance of the Board's program and the divided counsel of its members had played into the hands of the Navy's opponents. Secretary Hunt, upset by such disunity and realizing that a divided plan stood little chance in Congress, tried to bridge the gap between the naval factions and to lubricate the gears of legislative machinery. Every form of persuasion that might expedite passage of a Navy bill was brought to bear, but at the height of his campaign, in the fall of 1881, Hunt fell victim to a turn of fate. President James A. Garfield died from the effects of an assassin's bullet and his successor, Chester A. Arthur, paid off a political debt by naming William E. Chandler to head the Navy Department. Hunt was removed from the scene by being appointed Minister to Russia, where he died in 1884.

Meanwhile, the Advisory Board's plan was encountering stiff opposition in Congress. The best that the Navy's friends could come up with was a bill providing for six steel cruisers and nine smaller ships. Then even this was whittled down. When the long-awaited law emerged in 1882 it authorized only two cruisers and allocated no funds except as might be left over from the Department's regular budget. Moreover, the cautious Congress provided that all work on the new ships must be overseen by another Naval Advisory Board of five officers and two civilians.

The second Board, headed by Commodore Robert W. Shufeldt, was much more conservative—and politically realistic—than its predecessor. It recommended revision of the building program to include the smaller of the two cruisers previously authorized, three even smaller ones, and a dispatch vessel. This time the program slipped through Congress nearly intact, only one of the smaller cruisers being deleted, and $1,300,000 was appropriated for construction of the ships. On 3 March 1883, the bill that would give birth to the Steel Navy was signed into law by President Arthur.

These first four vessels authorized for the New Navy were later named the *Atlanta, Boston, Chicago,* and *Dolphin,* and would become popularly known as the "ABCD ships."

Secretary Chandler, who viewed the existing U.S. fleet as "a subject of ridicule at home and abroad," was anxious to get the new warships under construction quickly. Although the general designs for the vessels had been drawn under the direct supervision of the Second Naval Advisory Board, preparation of the detailed drawings and specifications had to be fragmented between several bureaus, and inevitable delays and confusion resulted. When the Department advertised for bids in May 1883, the plans were still far from complete. The final hull design for the *Dolphin* was approved by the Advisory Board just one hour before the opening of bids, and the machinery plans for the *Atlanta* and *Boston* were not completed until four days after the contracts had been awarded. Thus it was hardly surprising that several potential builders were frightened off.

Of the eight firms finally submitting proposals, only William Cramp and Sons of Philadelphia and John Roach of Chester, Pennsylvania, bid on all four. Roach, the owner of an integrated facility capable of rolling the steel plates, fabricating the hulls, and erecting the machinery, was the low bidder in every case. Over the angry protests of the losers, led by Charles H. Cramp, he was awarded all four contracts. This was clearly the procedure prescribed by law, but nevertheless the award was open to criticism, for John Roach and Secretary Chandler were old cronies. Furthermore, Roach had been deeply involved in some scandalous dealings with George Robeson (now a member of the House Appropriations Committee) when the latter had been Secretary of the Navy during the Grant administration. "Roach, Robeson, Robbers" became the war cry of the Democratic opposition and their journalistic supporters.

As criticism mounted, Roach's shipyard ran into the inevitable problems and delays that had been foreseen by the pessimistic minority of the First Naval Advisory Board. Fabrication of the steel plates took longer than anticipated and many of them had to be remade after failing to meet the exacting Navy requirements. A fire destroyed vital shipyard equipment, and worse yet, the bureaus kept changing details of the plans and specifications even as the first of the ships, the *Dolphin*, took shape on the ways. In spite of great efforts by the Roach yard, the *Dolphin* was two months late for her first sea trials. Then, just after the voters had elected Grover Cleveland and the Democrats into office in November 1884, the *Dolphin*'s steel propeller shaft fractured during speed trials. Roach and the ABCD program were in deep trouble.

Cleveland's Secretary of the Navy, William C. Whitney, came into office in 1885 convinced that "there is something radically wrong with the Department." Seizing on minor deficiencies as an excuse to avoid accepting the *Dolphin* and paying Roach the balance due on his contract, Whitney persuaded the Attorney General to declare the contract invalid. Work on all four ships ground to a halt as Roach was beset by creditors and threatened with suit by the government to return the money he had already been paid. In steadily worsening health, Roach threw his company into receivership. "John Roach's career as a naval barnacle is ended," chortled the *New York World*. Two years later the heart-broken builder would be dead.

Secretary Whitney now found Roach's problems dropped into his own hands in the form of the rejected *Dolphin* and the still-uncompleted *Atlanta*, *Boston*, and *Chicago*. Chagrined to discover that even the big navy yard at New York was incapable of finishing the cruisers' hulls and engines, Whitney was forced to seize Roach's shipyard at Chester, Pennsylvania, and have most of the remaining work completed there under the direction of naval constructors.

In such circumstances it was understandable that the last of the ABCD ships, the *Chicago*, did not join the fleet until 1889. As for the *Dolphin*, Whitney soon realized that his high-handed rejection of the ship would not hold up in court. A *sub rosa* compromise was arranged and the dispatch vessel was quietly commissioned in December 1885.

The smallest of the ABCD ships, the 1,485-ton *Dolphin* was designed to carry messages rapidly to off-lying stations and to the commanders at sea—a vital role in an era of primitive naval communications—though there were some who charged that she was really meant to serve as a yacht for the dignitaries of the day. Although not a fighting ship, the *Dolphin* was given a gunboat armament of one 6-inch breech-loading rifle (soon replaced by a pair of 4-inchers) and two 6-pounder rapid-fire guns. The dispatch vessel's unprotected machinery extended above the waterline and her designed speed of sixteen knots would not be considered very fast just a few years later, but nevertheless she had been a good project for introducing steel warship construction to the Navy. The stoutness of her hull and machinery, so harshly condemned by Secretary Whitney, was vindicated by a 58,000-mile world cruise in 1888–89, during which the *Dolphin*'s engine was inoperative for adjustments for less than two hours, a performance hailed by a later Secretary of the Navy, Benjamin F. Tracy, as being "probably without parallel in the history of naval vessels."

The designs for the two 3,189-ton protected cruisers, the *Atlanta* and *Boston*, were mainly the work of the secretary to the Second Naval Advisory Board, Assistant Naval Constructor Francis T. Bowles, who had recently studied naval architecture in Greenwich, England. Bowles' British training was reflected in the vessels' plans, which in several important features emulated the pace-setting "Elswick Cruisers" built by Sir W. G. Armstrong, Mitchell, and Company of Newcastle-on-Tyne. The two ships, which were nearly identical, each mounted a main armament of two 8-inch and six 6-inch breech-loading rifles. Forecastle and stern were cut away, providing a wide arc of fire for the 8-inch guns but also making the ships wet in a seaway and giving them a humpbacked appearance. Full brig rigs and single-screw propulsion—concessions to the advocates of sail—and a maximum speed of only about fifteen knots further compromised their design.

With crew manning yards and boat booms in time-honored fashion, the protected cruiser
Atlanta *salutes a reunion of the Grand Army of the Republic at Boston, 11 August 1890.*

As such the cruisers were inadequate for really effective coastal defense or commerce raiding, and their main value, as in the *Dolphin*, was in having taken the first steps into a new era of American warship construction.

At 4,500 tons, the protected cruiser *Chicago* was the largest ABCD ship and in fact, the biggest warship considered practicable for the fledgling U.S. steel shipbuilding industry. With high sides, a bowsprit, and a well-proportioned three-masted bark rig, she was generally regarded as the handsomest of the four ships. The *Chicago*'s heavy armament of four 8-inch, eight 6-inch, and two 5-inch breech-loading rifles was the equal of that in foreign contemporaries, but her power plant was a mixture of contradictions. Twin-screw propulsion was a modern departure for the U.S. Navy, but the compound overhead-beam engines and cylindrical boilers perched on top of brick fireboxes "similar to the crude boilers used to power sawmills" were distinctly old-fashioned.

Unremarkable in comparison to foreign naval practice, the ABCD ships nevertheless represented a great stride forward for the U.S. Navy. Its most recently built iron ships— the *Alert, Huron,* and *Ranger*—had been completed in the mid-1870s and had displaced only about 1,100 tons each. The much larger new steel cruisers incorporated double bottoms and watertight compartmentation, and although their main engines were of familiar design, had all kinds of new auxiliary machinery. Electric power plants—introduced experimentally aboard the sloop-of-war *Trenton* in 1883—were also included for the first time as standard equipment. The adoption of modern steel breech-loading rifles in these warships was another major advance, necessitating much experimental work by the Bureau of Ordnance and helping to create a heavy steel forging capability in U.S. industry.

One feature that the cruisers necessarily lacked was side armor. Such protection would have been too heavy for the ships' assigned displacements, and furthermore, the fabrication of large quantities of such heavy plate was still beyond the capacity of the domestic steel industry. Instead, as "protected" cruisers they employed the English system of incorporating a three-quarters- to one-and-one-half-inch thick watertight steel deck into the hull (above the waterline at the centerline but curving below at either side), along with whatever depth of coal that could be bunkered above it, to protect the engine spaces and magazines from enemy projectiles.

All of the ABCD ships, whatever their conceptual shortcomings, went on to provide "conclusive testimony to the high skill of American artisans and the excellence of their work." Organized into the "Squadron of Evolution" in 1889, the ships served for several years as a valuable tactical and operational training school for a new generation of Navy men. Subsequently left behind in the technological ferment of the 1890s, they were rearmed with rapid-fire guns and stripped of their awkward and little-used sails, to serve after the turn of the century in what were essentially gunboat roles. The *Atlanta* was sold out of the service in 1912, but the little *Dolphin* remained on the Navy list until 1922 and the *Chicago* (as a barracks ship) lasted until 1936. The *Boston*, which had fought in Dewey's squadron at Manila in 1898, survived to the ripe old age of fifty-nine, serving her twilight years in the role of a receiving ship on San Francisco Bay before finally being towed to sea and sunk in 1946.

In retrospect, such faults as existed in the ABCD ships were the inevitable consequence of suddenly introducing the complexities of steel construction and a host of other new features into the mainstream of U.S. naval development, and of the rapid pace of technological innovation which soon rendered obsolete nearly every warship laid down in any country during the last two decades of the nineteenth century.

The dispatch vessel Dolphin—*first ship completed for the Steel Navy—pays a visit to Yokohama, Japan, in February 1889 during an extraordinary 58,000-mile voyage around the world.*

The ABC Cruisers

The Boston *swings at anchor in New York waters in October 1889, during the first rendezvous of the newly formed Squadron of Evolution. Shortly thereafter the squadron, commanded by acting Rear Admiral John G. Walker and consisting of the cruisers* Chicago, Boston, *and* Atlanta, *and the gunboat* Yorktown, *embarked on a cruise to European ports, during which U.S. naval officers received their first real experience in modern fleet operations. An almost exact duplicate of the* Atlanta, *the* Boston *was 270 feet long on the load-waterline and had a normal displacement of slightly over 3,000 tons. Like the other early ships of the Steel Navy, she carried an auxiliary sail rig for economical operation on long voyages.*

The Chicago *lies moored off Gravesend, England, during the summer of 1894, while serving as flagship of the U.S. European Squadron. At this time her commanding officer was Captain Alfred Thayer Mahan, later recognized as the nineteenth century's leading theorist on sea power. Largest of the ABCD ships, the* Chicago *measured 325 feet on the load-waterline and displaced 4,500 tons. Her main armament of four 8-inch, eight 6-inch, and two 5-inch rifles was considered very powerful for a vessel of this class. Beginning in 1889 the* Chicago *and other new ships of the Navy were painted white, following the example set by the* Dolphin *on her world cruise.*

Steel Ships to Launch a New Era

This wooden pilothouse and chartroom aboard the Atlanta was for peacetime cruising. Basic piloting and control facilities included a binnacle, a helm to control the steam-operated steering gear, and a simple engine-order telegraph. In time of battle the watch officers and helmsmen moved a few feet forward into the protection of an armored conning tower.

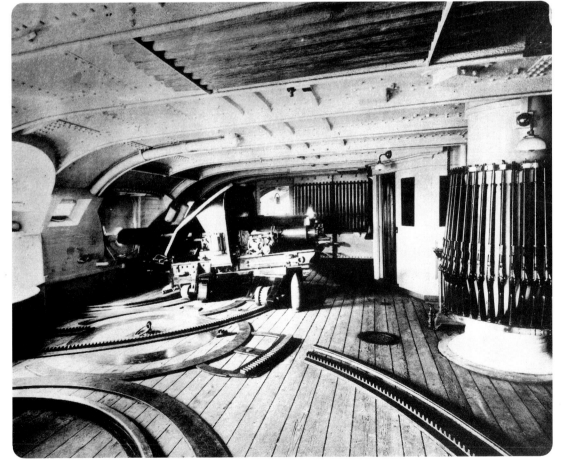

Although bearing a superficial resemblance to the cast-iron guns of Civil War days, this 6-inch breech-loading rifle—one of six aboard the Boston—was a great improvement over previous U.S. designs. It was built up from machined steel forgings, burned slow-burning prismatic powder, and fired armor-piercing steel shells. The carriage was a cumbersome affair, however, and the gun had to be aimed by simply sighting down the top of the barrel.

When the Boston *was underway, this forward berthing compartment was often wet from seas washing over the cruiser's low forecastle. The mess table and benches were triced to the overhead between meals, and at night the crew's hammocks were slung from hooks on the deck beams. The* Boston *had accommodations for a crew of 265 enlisted men and 19 officers.*

The chief engineer's station aboard the Atlanta—*gleaming with polished brass throttles, pressure gauges, and stanchions—controlled a single 4,000-horsepower horizontal compound engine. Steam working pressure was ninety pounds per square inch, and the cruiser had a designed operating speed of only about fourteen knots. Steam also powered the ship's auxiliary machinery—pumps, blowers, ash hoists, and a rudimentary electric plant.*

Officers and bluejackets aboard the Boston *show off the variety of guns in their ship's armament. On the port side of the forecastle, sailors cluster around one of the cruiser's two biggest guns, an 8-inch breech-loading rifle.*
To starboard, a 6-inch rifle peers from a gun-deck hatch. On the spar deck—just above the 8-incher—gunners aim a Hotchkiss revolving cannon, while on the other side of the armored conning tower sailors man a Gatling gun. Also included in the Boston's *armament were several 1-, 3-, and 6-pounder rapid-fire guns.*

The newly commissioned Charleston *lies moored at Mare Island, California. The two 6-inch guns on the quarterdeck were temporary substitutes, pending delivery of 8-inch armament from the East Coast.*

Second-Generation Protected Cruisers

President Grover Cleveland's Secretary of the Navy, William C. Whitney, was a man of strong party loyalties, but he also had a deep respect for the advances of science and technology and for efficient organization and management. Whitney's political partisanship had led him to condemn the ABCD ships so intemperately that it would have been unthinkable for him to allow their designs to be repeated in subsequent warships. He was thus left in the embarrassing position of having to temporarily postpone construction of two protected cruisers authorized in 1885, under the previous administration, in order to develop new plans incorporating the essential characteristics that he felt were lacking in the earlier warships.

Just as Whitney had been chagrined to find that his navy yards were incapable of finishing John Roach's cruisers, so was he now disappointed in the limited capacity of his bureaus to produce modern warship designs. Construction of the first of the new cruisers, the *Newark*, was postponed a full year while the Bureau of Construction and Repair prepared her hull plans. A delay of an additional year occurred when bids for her construction exceeded the funds authorized. Finally in 1887 the contract for the cruiser was awarded to William Cramp and Sons of Philadelphia—the recent archrivals of John Roach. The *Newark* was completed in 1891, later than any of the other second-generation cruisers.

The *Newark* somewhat resembled the protected cruiser *Chicago,* but her three-masted bark rig lacked the anachronistic bowsprit of the earlier ship and, having a displacement of 4,083 tons, she was slightly smaller. A homogeneous battery of twelve 6-inch rifles, all mounted in sponsons on the gun deck, comprised her main armament. The Navy had originally specified obsolete compound engines for the *Newark* but the Cramp yard substituted horizontal triple-expansion ones, and with this more modern plant she attained nineteen knots on trials. In the *Newark,* and subsequent protected cruisers, auxiliary machinery was also improved over that in the ABCD ships, and the steel protective deck was increased in thickness and extended throughout the entire length of the hull.

Meanwhile, in an effort to expedite construction, Secretary Whitney had turned to Sir W. G. Armstrong, Mitchell and Company of Newcastle-on-Tyne, England, for the design of the second of the new cruisers, the 4,040-ton *Charleston.* Supposedly the purchased plans were the same as those for the *Naniwa,* a cruiser built by Armstrong for the Japanese Navy. It was soon discovered, however, that the engine drawings also included details from the Italian cruisers *Etna* and *Giovanni Bausan* and the Chilean cruiser *Esmeralda* as well! The contract for the *Charleston* was awarded to the Union Iron Works of San Francisco, and the builder had to make many adjustments to reconcile the mixed plans.

The *Charleston* was similar to the *Atlanta* and *Boston* in armament and to some extent in appearance, mounting a main battery of two 8-inch and six 6-inch rifles, and having a low freeboard fore and aft. A mechanical innovation in the *Charleston* was the use of hydraulic steering equipment instead of steam-operated gear, a feature that would become a trademark of Union-built ships. The obsolete inclined compound engines specified in the English plans were the last of this type installed in a U.S. warship.

During the Spanish-American War in 1898 the *Charleston*'s crew captured the Spanish possession of Guam, the inhabitants of that isolated Pacific island being unaware until arrival of the American ship that a state of war had even existed. Later in the same cruise she became one of the few warships of the Steel Navy to meet an untimely end, being wrecked without loss of life on an uncharted reef in the Philippines in November 1899.

In August 1886, before construction had even begun on the first two ships, Congress authorized another protected cruiser. Again the Navy Department purchased plans from the Armstrong company, these particular ones having been previously entered in a competition before the Spanish government, but not accepted. The contract for this ship, the *Baltimore*, was awarded to the Cramp yard. The 4,600-ton cruiser had a high freeboard and a rounded cruiser stern, making her stand out noticeably from her counter-stern contemporaries. She mounted a main armament of four 8-inch rifles high on the forecastle and poop and six 6-inch rifles in sponsons along the gun deck. The *Baltimore*'s horizontal triple-expansion engines produced over 10,000 horsepower, giving her a speed of nearly twenty knots.

In 1887 Congress authorized two additional protected cruisers. The hull and machinery of one, the *Philadelphia*, were near-duplicates to those of the *Baltimore*. Her armament, however, consisted of twelve 6-inch rifles, four mounted on the forecastle and quarterdeck and eight on the gun deck. The *Philadelphia*'s contract was appropriately awarded to the Cramp shipyard in the city for which she was named. With her high battery and freeboard the cruiser turned out to be unstable and a heavy roller, and it was necessary always to carry water in her double bottoms as ballast. Her heavy steel masts were also soon removed and replaced by lighter wooden ones. (The old masts were saved and later installed in the second-class battleship *Maine*, and survive to this day at the Arlington National Cemetery and at Annapolis as memorials to that ill-fated vessel.)

The remaining new protected cruiser, the 4,083-ton *San Francisco*, was built at the Union Iron Works. She was basically an improved *Newark*, with sail rig reduced to that of a three-masted schooner and four of her twelve 6-inch rifles raised one deck to the forecastle and poop like the *Philadelphia*'s. This combination of a homogeneous main battery with pairs mounted high on the bow and stern proved to be a happy arrangement, having the advantages of simplicity of ammunition handling and a heavy end-on and broadside fire. The *San Francisco* was regarded as one of the most useful of the first- and second-generation protected cruisers.

Secretary Whitney's penchant for administrative improvement led to the introduction of an early version of the fixed-price, performance-type contract with a built-in incentive clause for these cruisers. For the ships authorized in 1885 and 1886 the Department required a guarantee based on indicated horsepower during contract trials, the builders receiving bonuses if they delivered more than the specified figures or suffering penalties if they failed to meet them. On later contracts the guarantee was revised to depend on actual trial speed, the premium or penalty amounting to $50,000 for each quarter-knot in excess of or short of the contract speed. In the cases of the *Baltimore, Philadelphia*, and *San Francisco*, trial speeds exceeding the contract requirements earned the builders bonuses totaling more than $300,000.

The Navy now had five new protected cruisers under construction before it had the benefit of any operating experience with the long-delayed ABCD ships. These cruisers formed an oddly mixed assortment, it is true, but in them the Navy had increased speed by nearly five knots, drastically reduced the appurtenances of sail, introduced modern machinery, begun the standardization of armament, and manufactured all of it domestically. It had used foreign plans as a stopgap, introduced incentive provisions into its contracts, and cultivated two new building yards, one on each coast, to construct its ships. The groundwork had been laid for the next major step forward in protected cruiser development.

The Newark, *seen backing away from her pier, was the last U.S. protected cruiser to be fitted with a full sail rig. Later cruisers carried a few lighter sails for steadying purposes as well as for tradition's sake, however.*

In full dress, the San Francisco *takes part in an international naval rendezvous which was held at Hampton Roads as part of the Columbian Celebrations of 1893. The* San Francisco *was a near-sister to the* Newark, *each ship having a length of 310 feet, displacing slightly over 4,000 tons, and carrying a homogeneous battery of twelve 6-inch rifles. The disposition of the guns was different in the two cruisers, however, and the* San Francisco *carried only a light schooner rig.*

With a leadsman taking soundings from a gun sponson, and with the Presidential flag at the main indicating that Benjamin Harrison is on board, the 4,600-ton Baltimore *arrives at Boston for the 1890 reunion of the Grand Army of the Republic. One of the few Steel Navy warships to see three wars, the* Baltimore *fought in Commodore George E. Dewey's squadron at Manila Bay in 1898, helped lay the North Sea Mine Barrage during World War I, and on 7 December 1941, although a decommissioned hulk, was present during the Japanese attack on Pearl Harbor.*

Miss Alice Tracy Wilmerding—with her bearded grandfather, Secretary of the Navy Benjamin F. Tracy, at her side—raises the traditional champagne bottle to launch the armored warship Maine, *18 November 1890.*

The Debut of the Armored Ship

The Naval Advisory Boards of 1881–83 had considered proposals for armored warships of up to 8,500 tons in displacement, but had stopped short of recommending such construction. Large steel battleships and armored cruisers were still considered beyond the reach of U.S. technology, and moreover, American navy yards and drydocks could not yet accommodate them.

By 1886, however, it appeared that the domestic steel industry's capabilities and the Navy's shipbuilding know-how had developed to the point where such construction was practicable, and the naval appropriations bill submitted to Congress that year therefore included provision for two seagoing armored vessels of about 6,000 tons displacement each. As a means of encouraging the continued development of U.S. industry and the improvement of government shipyards, the bill—enacted into law 3 August 1886—stipulated that domestic steel and machinery be employed in the vessels and that at least one of the ships be built in a navy yard.

Because the bureaus had limited resources for developing the complex plans required, particularly for classes of warships with which they had no previous experience, the Navy Department sponsored a $15,000 international competition for the design of one of the new vessels, and that submitted by the Naval Construction and Armaments Company of Barrow-in-Furness, England, was purchased. The resulting second-class battleship, the *Texas*, was perhaps best described as an "isolated type," having a displacement of only 6,315 tons—far less than most foreign battleships—and an unusual main battery of two 12-inch rifles in single turrrets. The turrets were arranged *en echelon* and were sponsored well out over the sides of the ship, one slightly forward of amidships on the port side and the other slightly aft to starboard. The intent of this odd disposition was to provide a wide arc of fire for both, each being able to fire nearly dead ahead or astern, as well as to broadside. Inboard of each turret the ship's superstructure was reduced to a skeletonized flying deck for boat stowage, permitting the guns also to be fired

across the centerline through a substantial arc. Additional armament included six 6-inch guns and four torpedo tubes. An armored redoubt of twelve-inch-thick steel extended diagonally across the hull to protect the turret handling rooms, and a waterline belt of equal thickness shielded the battleship's engine and boiler spaces. The engines of the *Texas*, as would be those in all of the Steel Navy battleships, were of the modern, twin-screw, vertical triple-expansion type.

Construction of the *Texas* was assigned by the Department to the Norfolk Navy Yard. The time required to fabricate the necessary shipbuilding facilities at Norfolk, as well as a heated controversy over the merits of the ship's unusual design, resulted in such delays that her keel was not laid until 1889. Belated delivery of the engines and armor plate by civilian contractors further slowed construction and, by the time the *Texas* was commissioned in August 1895, she had become something of an anachronism.

The designs for her turrets were particularly awkward because the rammers were situated outside of the barbettes, allowing the guns to be loaded only when trained directly ahead or abeam. About seven minutes were thus required to load, elevate, train, aim, and fire a single round from either gun. Just before the Spanish-American War, however, the ship's gunnery officer devised a modification employing a telescoping rammer inside of each turret, enabling the guns to be loaded regardless of their degree of train. This improvement reduced the firing interval to less than two minutes and stood the *Texas* in good stead at the Battle of Santiago.

A series of minor mishaps dogged the *Texas* during her early operations and she acquired somewhat the reputation of a "hoodoo." Nevertheless, she was a very steady gun platform and her top speed of nearly eighteen knots substantially exceeded that of any other U.S. battleship until after the turn of the century.

The second of the armored vessels, the 6,682-ton *Maine*,

was even more a hybrid. Originally designated Armored Cruiser No. 1, she was reclassified a second-class battleship during construction, but in fact did not really fit into either category. Her main armament of four 10-inch and six 6-inch guns was unique, lighter than carried by any other battleship, but heavier than would be mounted in any U.S. armored cruiser for another decade.

The *Maine*'s designs, although prepared by the Navy Department, were in many respects similar to those for various foreign armored ships, and were probably inspired by them. The *Maine* also bore a superficial resemblance to the *Texas* in that her two turrets were mounted *en echelon,* in this instance the forward turret being to starboard and the after one to port. Each turret's two 10-inch guns could be fired over an arc extending from directly ahead to directly astern, as well as across the centerline.

Both the *Maine* and *Texas* shared the weakness of carrying inadequate topside protection, having been designed before the destructive effects of rapid-fire guns and high-explosive shells were fully recognized. Also, it was discovered that when the main guns were fired inboard across the centerline, the muzzle blasts tended to spring the deck plating badly out of shape and to damage the adjacent superstructure and fittings. The off-center arrangement of the turrets did not prove to have enough practical advantages to be repeated in any subsequent U.S. warships.

Another feature common to the two ships was that each was designed to carry a pair of small "third-class" torpedo boats, to be launched against the enemy at the scene of battle. Although the two sixteen-ton, sixty-one-foot craft for the *Maine* were completed, they were found much too slow for the intended purpose and were instead eventually employed as practice boats at the Naval Torpedo Station in Newport.

Laid down at the New York Navy Yard, the *Maine* was also subject to delays in the delivery of armor plate. Nearly seven years under construction, she was far outdated by the time of her commissioning in September 1895. She was considered a smart ship, however, and her service career in the North Atlantic Squadron might have passed uneventfully had not rioting broken out in Havana, the capital of Spain's rebellious and strife-torn colony of Cuba, in January 1898. A garbled press dispatch led officials in Washington to believe that the U.S. consulate at Havana was in danger, and to protect American lives and property the Navy Department ordered Rear Admiral Montgomery Sicard, commanding the fleet off Key West, to send a warship posthaste. The *Maine,* under command of Captain Charles D. Sigsbee, got underway immediately and dropped anchor in Havana harbor on 25 January. Although U.S.-Spanish relations were tense, this was ostensibly a friendly visit, and the Spanish government reciprocated by ordering one of its armored cruisers to New York.

Swinging quietly at a buoy in Havana harbor on the evening of Sunday, 15 February 1898, the *Maine* was suddenly rocked by two violent explosions in the vicinity of her forward magazines, and immediately sank. Two hundred and fifty-one crewmen were killed outright or drowned in the ensuing confusion, and seven more later succumbed to their injuries. The Spanish cruiser *Vizcaya,* steaming into New York harbor four days later for her "friendly" visit, found there instead a city buzzing with rumors and preparations for war.

In the subsequent U.S. Navy inquiry into the disaster, examination of the *Maine*'s wreckage by divers produced evidence that the keel had been blown in, and the Board of Inquiry concluded that an external explosion had detonated the ship's forward magazines. The Spaniards, however, maintained that the explosions had been entirely due to internal causes, and some U.S. and European experts have held similar views. To this day no positive proof of Spanish or Cuban sabotage has come to light, and it is unlikely that the full story of the *Maine* tragedy will ever be known.

Immaculate in buff and white, the Maine *anchors at Bar Harbor during a courtesy visit to the waters of her namesake state in 1897.*

The Ill-Fated *Maine*

Laid down as an armored cruiser but commissioned as a second-class battleship, the 6,682-ton Maine
*was remarkable for the off-centerline arrangement of her two turrets, a design permitting all four
of the 10-inch guns to fire directly ahead or astern, as well as to either beam. The forward turret
was offset well to starboard, while the after one, as seen on the opposite page, was to port.
The* Maine's *destruction with heavy loss of life at Havana, Cuba, in February 1898 was the immediate
cause of the Spanish-American War. In 1912 she was refloated and towed to sea for a deep-ocean
burial with honors.*

"Old Hoodoo"—The Battleship *Texas*

Like the Maine, *the English-designed second-class battleship* Texas *was noteworthy for the en echelon arrangement of her two turrets. At right, barefoot sailors pose by the squat forward turret with its single 12-inch rifle, which aboard this ship was located to port. Dogged by minor accidents during her early years and considered a bad-luck ship, the 6,315-ton* Texas *nevertheless turned in one of the most creditable performances of all of the U.S. warships at the Battle of Santiago in 1898. Her relatively short career as the Navy's first battleship ended in 1911 when, as the* San Marcos, *she was sunk in Chesapeake Bay as an experimental gunnery target.*

Spectators in rowboats, part of an enthusiastic crowd of twenty thousand, obtain a choice view as the gunboat Yorktown *takes to the water at the Cramp shipyard in Philadelphia, 28 April 1888.*

Gunboats and Peace Cruisers

Probably no class of warship in the New Navy received less glory or performed more actual service than the gunboat. Often dismissed as a type with negligible fighting value, it nevertheless turned up practically everywhere there was active or incipient fighting, and showed the flag in more far-flung areas than did the larger and more glamorous armored and protected cruisers. As the Steel Navy's counterpart to the old wooden gunboat and steam sloop, it was designed to cruise for long periods on distant stations, to be inexpensive to operate, and to be formidable enough to deal with native uprisings and with minor incidents provoked by third- and fourth-rate nations.

The gunboat's small size and displacement precluded the use of armor for the protection of its vital areas against gunfire. As in the protected cruiser, a steel deck was worked over the machinery spaces and magazines, but this plating—here called a "watertight" deck—had to be very thin, usually not exceeding three-eighths of an inch on the slopes. The gunboat's real protection lay in the minute subcompartmentation of the hull along the waterline and in the thickness of the coal bunkered there.

Although the dispatch vessel *Dolphin* of the ABCD ships was eventually classified as a gunboat, U.S. steel gunboat construction really commenced with authorization of the *Petrel* and *Yorktown* in 1885. The little *Petrel,* only 176 feet long on the load-waterline and displacing 892 tons, carried an unusually heavy armament of four 6-inch rifles in sponsons on her open well deck. Her antiquated single-screw, horizontal back-acting compound engine provided a top speed of only eleven and one-half knots, making her one of the slowest ships in the Steel Navy, and her watertight deck extended over only the most important lower-deck spaces.

The *Yorktown* displaced 1,710 tons and mounted six 6-inch rifles, four on the forecastle and stern and two in sponsons amidships. She was designed as a torpedo gunboat, a type popular in Europe during the 1880s and intended to cruise with the fleet to protect it against the threat of torpedo boats—the same role that torpedo boat destroyers would later assume. Her top speed of sixteen knots turned out to be much too slow for combating the torpedo boats of the day, however, and the concept of the torpedo gunboat was soon dropped in the U.S. Navy. The *Yorktown*'s draft of fourteen feet was also a bit deep for an ideal cruising gunboat, but before these deficiencies were recognized two sisters, the *Concord* and *Bennington,* were authorized and built under the 1887 program. The *Yorktown* and her sisters were powered by twin-screw, horizontal triple-expansion engines. Each had hull openings for six torpedo tubes, but the U.S. Navy was not to introduce torpedoes into general fleet use until about 1894, several years after the class had been commissioned. The watertight deck in these and subsequent gunboats extended through the entire length of the hull.

In 1888 Congress authorized two additional gunboats, the *Machias* and *Castine.* Although reminiscent of the *Petrel,* these were larger, mounted more conservative main batteries of eight 4-inch rapid-fire guns, and had modern, twin-screw, vertical triple-expansion engines. Following trials and acceptance, the Navy Department belatedly discovered that the ships were lacking in stability and each had to be hauled back out of the water, cut in two, and fitted with an additional fourteen-foot midsection. The masts and stack of each were also shortened, armor plate removed from the gun sponsons, and ballast added. One benefit of the extensive alterations was a marked increase in cruising range, the new midsection being devoted mainly to coal bunkers.

To keep displacement low, all of these early Steel Navy gunboats were designed with an open well deck amidships. This was necessarily at the expense of accommodations and the small ships were often overcrowded, since on outlying stations they were frequently called upon to carry extra detachments of Marines, to transport soldiers, or to house refugees.

The 1888 naval construction program also provided for three cruisers of absolute minimum characteristics, displacing only 2,094 tons each, and actually described in the authorizing act as "gunboats, or cruisers." The engine and boiler spaces of these, the *Montgomery, Detroit,* and *Marblehead,* were protected by watertight steel decks less than one-half inch in thickness, barely heavier than in a gunboat and far thinner than carried in any protected cruiser. These ships performed all of the duties of a gunboat and led to the concept of the "peace cruiser," a ship deliberately designed for optimum service in peacetime with little pretense of meeting wartime requirements. As such each featured a schooner sail rig to save on coal, a relatively low speed with a generous bunker capacity for endurance, a broad beam and shallow draft for safe navigation in coastal waters and rivers, and spacious, airy berth decks for habitability in tropical regions. The ships were at first each fitted with a main battery of two 6-inch rifles—one each on the forecastle and poop—and eight 5-inch rifles in sponsons along the gun deck. The *Montgomery* and her sisters were soon discovered to have the same poor stability characteristics as the *Machias* class, however, and in order to increase the metacentric height it was necessary to remove the after 6-inch gun, replace the forward one with a lighter 5-inch rifle, and add ballast.

Nearly all of these ships had varied and useful careers. The *Yorktown* operated with the ABC cruisers in the well-known Squadron of Evolution from 1889 to 1891. The *Concord* and *Petrel* were in Dewey's battle line at Manila Bay in 1898, and the *Montgomery* and *Marblehead* fought in Cuban and Puerto Rican waters. The *Castine* served as a submarine tender from 1908 to 1913, during which period Lieutenant Chester W. Nimitz flew his flag from her as Commander, Atlantic Submarine Flotilla. The *Machias* had the distinction of serving the last fifteen years of her sea-life in the Mexican Navy as the *Agua Prieta.* One ship, the *Bennington,* came to an unhappy and premature end at San Diego in July 1905, being wrecked by a boiler explosion with a loss of sixty lives.

When Benjamin Tracy became Secretary of the Navy in 1889, he ordered that gunboat construction be deferred in favor of more powerful additions to the fleet; and several years would elapse before any new gunboats would be authorized for the U.S. Navy.

With boilers generating a full head of steam, the Yorktown *makes 16.7 knots over the measured mile during contract trials in February 1889.*

Steel Navy Gunboats

Bluejackets man the yards of the 892-ton gunboat Petrel *in August 1890. Although one of the smallest and slowest vessels in the fleet, she was very heavily armed for her size with a main battery of four 6-inch rifles and an assortment of smaller rapid-fire guns, revolving cannon, and machine guns, and was known among the sailors of the fleet as the "baby battleship."*

The Machias, *pictured here in Boston Harbor in 1901, and her sister* Castine *were launched in the early 1890s as 190-foot gunboats. Before being placed in service, however, they were discovered to have poor stability and were cut in two and lengthened to 204 feet, thereby being increased in displacement to 1,177 tons. Gunboats of this and later classes were armed with 4-inch rapid-fire guns.*

"Peace Cruisers"

Officially listed as "unprotected cruisers," the Marblehead—*seen above steaming out of an East Coast port during the 1890s, and at right moored off Seattle after the turn of the century—and her sisters* Montgomery *and* Detroit *were in essence enlarged gunboats designed for peacetime foreign cruising. In spite of inadequate protection over the engine and boiler spaces, which made the 2,094-ton ships ill-suited for combat roles, both the* Montgomery *and* Detroit *took part in spirited engagements in Caribbean waters during the Spanish-American War.*

The armored ram Katahdin—*her slender proportions foreshortened by an end-on view—
awaits launching ceremonies at Bath, Maine, on a frigid 4 February 1893.*

Dynamite Gun and Ram

In 1886 a powerful new instrument of destruction made its appearance on the horizon of naval weapons technology—the pneumatic dynamite gun.

Ordnance experts were well aware that dynamite—and its relative nitrocellulose, or guncotton—had a destructive energy far exceeding that of the traditional black powder that had been used as a bursting charge in projectiles for decades past. But shells containing the unstable newer explosive were so sensitive to shock, and hence liable to explode prematurely and disastrously if fired from ordinary guns, that the Navy had thus far been unable to employ them. Guncotton warheads were fitted in the self-propelled torpedoes of the day, but the range, accuracy, and usefulness of these weapons were still very limited.

During the early 1880s, however, an innovative Army lieutenant, Edmund L. G. Zalinski, had undertaken the development of a gun which could fire guncotton-loaded shells. Zalinski's invention employed compressed air as the propelling agent and imparted a much smoother acceleration to the sensitive projectiles than could be achieved with conventional gunpowder. A group of investors, convinced of the system's practicability, had formed the Pneumatic Dynamite Gun Company of New Jersey to build and market the new guns and shells.

Proponents of the Navy urged adoption of the unique weapon and in 1886 Congress was duly persuaded to appropriate $350,000 for one "dynamite-gun cruiser," the contract to be awarded to the Pneumatic Dynamite Gun Company. Construction of the warship herself was in turn subcontracted to William Cramp and Sons, who designed and built in the aptly-named *Vesuvius* an early, if imperfect, example of a "weapons system" in which ship and armament were inseparably related.

The rakish and yacht-like *Vesuvius* did not really qualify as a cruiser for she was only 252 feet long, displaced only 929 tons, and was completely without protection. Powerful twin-screw, vertical triple-expansion engines gave her a speed of over twenty-one knots on trials, but peculiarities of design made the *Vesuvius* difficult to steer and gave her the largest turning radius in the fleet. The dynamite guns—her real distinguishing feature—consisted of three fifteen-inch diameter, fifty-four-foot long smoothbore tubes, projecting a few feet above her forecastle at a fixed angle of eighteen degrees. The breech of each gun, located below the waterline, was simply a hinged section of the tube that could swing down to mate with one of three revolving chambers or magazines, which held a total of twenty-seven projectiles. The guns were controlled by a complex arrangement of machinery and valves, and firing was accomplished by the sudden admittance of air into the breeches of the guns from giant cast-iron air storage flasks at a pressure of 1,000 pounds per square inch. Unfortunately, the sophistication of these components was outweighed by the over-simplicity of the remainder of the system. Since the guns could be neither trained nor elevated, they had to be aimed by pointing the entire ship at the target, and the range had to be adjusted by varying the duration of the air blasts or the weight of the projectiles. A more unwieldy arrangement would be hard to find.

Three sizes of dynamite shells were produced, the largest nearly seven feet long and containing five hundred pounds of guncotton. The two smaller designs—for use when maximum range was required—were sub-caliber in diameter and fitted with wooden sabots in order to fit snugly into the gun barrels. Since the gun tubes were smoothbore to minimize friction, the shells had to be spin-stabilized by vaned fins. Fired with an initial velocity of more than four hundred miles an hour, they had effective ranges varying from about five hundred to more than two thousand yards. Although the operation of the pneumatic guns themselves was almost noiseless, the detonation and effect of their projectiles upon striking the target was spectacular. During tests on the Delaware River in 1890, explosions from dynamite shells fired by the

Vesuvius rattled windows five miles distant and produced great geysers of mud and water towering some two hundred feet into the air.

Commissioned in June 1890, the *Vesuvius* was held in high esteem by press and public. She was a special favorite at local celebrations or "flower shows," her shallow draft enabling the dynamite cruiser to visit a number of ports inaccessible to larger warships. Her deficiencies as a fighting ship, however, made the *Vesuvius* less popular within the Navy. Problems in addition to those already described included great difficulty in obtaining consistent ranges with the guns—since the firing valves had to operate within tolerances of a few thousandths of a second—and failure of many of the projectiles to explode during tests due to faulty fuzes. A complete lack of armor was one of the *Vesuvius'* most serious shortcomings, rendering the vessel and her high-explosive cargo vulnerable to destruction from even small-caliber gunfire.

By the mid-1890s the Pneumatic Dynamite Gun Company had drifted into bankruptcy and the *Vesuvius* herself had become largely discredited. Funds that had been authorized for a sister ship were diverted to other uses, stocks of projectiles were allowed to dwindle, and plans were made for converting the dynamite cruiser into a torpedo boat.

The arrival of the Spanish-American War rescued the *Vesuvius* from oblivion, however, and in June 1898 she was sent to join the blockading squadron off Santiago. Hiding behind the battleships and cruisers during daylight hours, the little warship would creep inshore at night to belch dynamite shells at the fortifications. To the fascinated sailors of the blockading fleet the firing of her guns had the "strange sound of a giant's cough" issuing from the darkness. The blindly aimed projectiles splashed near some of the Spanish warships in Santiago harbor and gouged several impressive scars in the surrounding hillsides—badly frightening the defenders—but the final effect, in the words of Secretary of the Navy John D. Long, "was materially unimportant though morally great."

If the *Vesuvius* was intended as a technological leap forward, it must be admitted that the 2,155-ton armored ram *Katahdin* represented a retrogression to concepts of a bygone era. Die-hard advocates of the harbor-defense strategy, led by Rear Admiral Daniel Ammen, had pushed for a fleet of rams ever since the First Naval Advisory Board. The British Navy had in fact constructed a vessel of the ram type, the *Polyphemus,* during the early 1880s. In 1889 one example of the type—based on designs by Ammen—was finally authorized. Although the practical value of the ram in warfare was disputed by many U.S. naval officers, its lethal qualities were convincingly demonstrated during the *Katahdin's* construction in 1893 when the British battleship *Victoria* was acci-

dentally rammed and sunk by the battleship *Camperdown.*

In spite of the antiquated concept, the green-painted *Katahdin* was an innovative craft, presaging the development of the submarine in several features. Her lower hull, dish-shaped and curving gracefully upwards at each end, was fitted with a double bottom throughout and could be partially flooded to bring the ship to fighting trim. Along each side, just below the waterline, the hull formed a sharp knuckle which was packed with wood and heavily armored. Protective plating, varying from two to six inches in thickness, then continued over the deck to form a huge turtleback. The entire structure was framed with longitudinal girders which converged at the bow to support a massive cast-steel stem. The few appurtenances above the *Katahdin's* deck included a heavily armored conning tower and stack, a signal mast, ventilators, four 6-pounder rapid-fire guns in tub-like shields, and a framework of skid beams for the ship's boats.

The *Katahdin* was built at the Bath Iron Works in Maine and was completed in 1895. Although the ram's twin-screw, horizontal triple-expansion engines exceeded their design horsepower, the 16.1 knots achieved on trials was still nearly a knot short of the contract speed and the Navy was prevented by law from accepting her. However, the Department concluded that in view of the unique hull form "it would probably be impossible to make a ship of this kind run at seventeen knots with engines of any horsepower that could be put in her," and a special bill was enacted in Congress in 1896 to authorize her acceptance.

Below-deck arrangements in the *Katahdin* were necessarily unorthodox. Ventilation was inadequate and habitability in the cramped, condensation-dripping compartments and head-bumping passageways was miserable. Temperatures in the wardroom commonly ran to 110° F. and the heat in the fire-rooms was almost insufferable. Moreover, in any kind of a seaway the *Katahdin* had to be buttoned up like a submarine, for she ran, in the words of commanding officer George F. Wilde, "half-seas under."

After a year's shakedown the *Katahdin* was decommissioned, only to be resuscitated by the Spanish-American War. Like the old Civil War monitors that she vaguely resembled, the harbor defense ram's mission was to reassure nervous inhabitants of East Coast ports that they were safe from raids by Spanish cruisers. In late June 1898 her commanding officer, who had great faith in the ram's capabilities, managed to obtain orders dispatching his warship to the blockading force off Cuba, but en route word was received that Cervera's squadron had been destroyed. The *Katahdin* was hurriedly decommissioned, this time permanently, and thereafter lay in reserve as a curious monument to an obsolete concept, until sunk as a gunnery target off Virginia in 1909.

The three 15-inch pneumatic guns of the dynamite cruiser Vesuvius *point menacingly over the rooftops of Philadelphia. As integral parts of the ship's hull, they could neither be trained nor elevated.*

The Dynamite Cruiser *Vesuvius*

Resembling a pleasure yacht, the 929-ton Vesuvius *was indeed no cruiser, but rather a lightly constructed test platform for the pneumatic dynamite guns. Although a very fast vessel for her size, she was unseaworthy and had poor steering characteristics, was completely lacking in armor protection, and was unable to control the range or direction of her guns with accuracy.*
Her popular reputation as a fearsome secret weapon was never shared within the service.

The heart of the dynamite cruiser Vesuvius' *weaponry—a complex assemblage of air compressors, giant storage flasks, firing valves, and hydraulic fittings—was located below the ship's waterline. The breech mechanisms for the pneumatic guns, photographed above, could be aligned either with the gun tubes or with rotary magazines forward. The gun nearest the officer is ready for firing, while the breech assembly at right has been lowered for reloading.*

"Old Half-Seas Under"—The Ram *Katahdin*

Out of her native element and not yet fitted with topside encumbrances, the Katahdin *had a sleek, menacing appearance worthy of a Jules Verne creation. Her massive steel beak, backed by an almost-solid network of girders, would have torn through any warship afloat—in the unlikely event that the harbor defense ram could have come within striking distance.*

In the water the 2,155-ton Katahdin *took on the sullen appearance of an enormous, half-submerged rock—bearing fitting tribute to the mountain of granite in Maine for which she was named. Because her freeboard of less than five feet required that the ram be sealed tight much of the time, the cramped vessel was a stifling, dismal home for her crew of Jonahs.*

*The slim and rakish Minneapolis—pictured shortly after commissioning—became the
fastest cruiser afloat in 1894 when she exceeded twenty-three knots on trials.*

The Craze for Speed

American cruiser design, which had at first developed along conventional lines, began to branch in several new directions in 1888 when Congress approved Secretary of the Navy William C. Whitney's request for seven cruisers representing four new classes. Two of these designs, for an armored cruiser and a small cruiser-gunboat or "peace cruiser," are described in other chapters. The other two were for protected cruisers incorporating recent advances in ordnance and engineering. One of the most serious deficiencies of the early U.S. steel warships, in the eyes of Secretary Whitney, had been their low speed in comparison with foreign naval vessels, and for the next several years "a perfect craze for high speed" would dominate U.S. cruiser development.

In the largest of the new protected cruisers, the 5,870-ton *Olympia,* the Department achieved a highly successful and widely acclaimed balance of armament, protection, speed, and endurance. The *Olympia*'s powerful main battery of four 8-inch rifles was housed in a pair of cylindrical armored turrets, an arrangement unique among U.S. protected cruisers, and her secondary battery of ten new 5-inch rapid-fire guns represented a substantial increase in efficiency over the heavier, but much slower-firing, secondary batteries of previous classes. She also carried a number of 1- and 6-pounder rapid-fire guns and mounted six torpedo tubes.

The cruiser's heavy protective deck, measuring nearly five inches in thickness on the slopes, was supplemented by a cellular structure of coal bunkers and cofferdams containing water-excluding cellulose. Watertight integrity was further enhanced by a minimum of hull openings, the only guns mounted below the main deck being several 6-pounders in inconspicuous sponsons. The *Olympia*'s modern twin-screw, vertical triple-expansion engines generated over 17,300 horsepower for a trial speed of 21.7 knots—higher than any previously authorized U.S. protected cruiser—and she had a cruising range of over six thousand miles.

Built by the Union Iron Works of San Francisco, the *Olympia* was ordered to the Far East soon after completion in 1895. There in 1897 she became the flagship of Commodore George E. Dewey, and with him during the Spanish-American War she earned lasting fame at Manila Bay. Following the war she operated off the U.S. East Coast, serving as flagship of the Caribbean Squadron and later as a midshipman cruise ship. At the end of World War I the *Olympia* led an expedition to Murmansk, Russia, and in 1921 bore the body of America's Unknown Soldier home across the Atlantic. Decommissioned in 1922, she serves today as a floating memorial at Philadelphia, the last survivor of her colorful era.

Less successful were the designs for the remaining protected cruisers of the 1888 program, the *Cincinnati* and *Raleigh.* Because of congressional resistance to escalating costs of construction, the Navy attempted to limit these ships to a displacement of slightly over 3,000 tons while retaining the nineteen-knot speed of earlier, much larger cruisers. A respectable armament was provided—including one 6-inch breech-loading rifle, ten 5-inch rapid-fire guns, and four torpedo tubes—but heavy penalties were exacted in other areas. The customary cellular structure of coal bunkers had to be all but abandoned; the protective deck measured only two and one-half inches on the slopes; and with the exception of a light bridge, masts, ventilators, and funnels, the upper deck was left practically bare.

In order to squeeze a 10,000 horsepower, twin-screw vertical triple-expansion propulsion plant into the slender hull, it was necessary to design two small low-pressure cylinders for each engine in place of the usual single large-diameter one, and coal capacity was so limited that the class had a cruising range of only three thousand miles.

Construction of the *Cincinnati* and *Raleigh* was assigned to the New York and Norfolk Navy Yards as a means of further strengthening the Navy's in-house capability to fabricate steel hulls. As is so often the case when design is ruled by economy, the completed ships proved unpopular among the officers who had to sail them. Critics such as Rear Admiral Richard W. Meade judged them good only for short-range operations, uncomfortable, and having "so much power that the ships haven't got room for anything else." Although the cruisers were able to reach their designed speed for brief periods, temperatures in the crowded and inadequately ventilated engineering spaces routinely soared to more than 200° F., and the Navy Department was forced to conclude that "the heat below is such that they will never be efficient...." Following the Spanish-American War both ships were refitted with smaller, but far more satisfactory, power plants and thereafter served useful careers in "peace cruiser" roles.

The epitome of fast protected cruiser development was reached with the 7,375-ton *Columbia*, authorized in 1890, and the *Minneapolis,* approved the following year. Designed to destroy the enemy's commerce and to engage his converted merchant cruisers, these ships embodied Navy Secretary Benjamin F. Tracy's most advanced concepts of unmatched power and technological sophistication. An expansion of the *Olympia*'s design—they were, at 412 feet, the longest warships in the Navy—they had large coal capacities for sustained speed and endurance, and engines producing more than 18,000 horsepower. So much power could not be safely borne at that time by two propeller shafts and Engineer-in-Chief George W. Melville designed an unusual triple-screw, three-engine plant, which had the added advantage of economical operation during normal steaming through use of the central engine and shaft alone. As might be expected, the quest for high speed led to the sacrifice of other important qualities, and in these ships offensive power suffered, the main armament being limited to a single 8-inch rifle and two 6-inch and eight 4-inch rapid-fire guns.

Construction of the *Columbia* was awarded to William Cramp and Sons of Philadelphia. Dubbed the "Pirate" during construction, she received much attention from the press and after entering service was widely hailed as the "Gem of the Ocean." During contract trials in 1893 the big cruiser attained a speed of 22.8 knots, making her the fastest ship of her class afloat. The *Minneapolis* was also built at the Cramp yard, and although nearly identical in specifications to the *Columbia,* differed in appearance in having two large funnels instead of four slender ones. On her trials in 1894 the *Minneapolis* surpassed her sister ship's speed record, exceeding twenty-three knots and earning a bonus of $414,600 for her builders.

Even during the Whitney and Tracy regimes the emphasis on speed had its critics. Complaints were openly pressed after the Presidential election of 1892 had returned Grover Cleveland to office and Hilary A. Herbert had assumed the helm of the Navy Department. "The craze for speed is the curse of modern naval architecture," declared Lieutenant Albert P. Niblack before the Society of Naval Architects and Marine Engineers in 1895. Other authorities denounced the triple-screw warships as an expensive experiment and charged that they would be unable to steam for long periods at the high speeds for which they had been designed. To settle the controversy, Secretary Herbert ordered the *Columbia* to cross the Atlantic at full speed on her return to New York from Southampton, England, in July 1895. The fast Hamburg-American liner *Augusta-Victoria* followed her in a well-publicized race. The *Columbia* won decisively, averaging more than eighteen knots without forced draft and completing the voyage in just under seven days, a record that was bettered by only a few of the speediest commercial greyhounds running under forced draft with picked fireroom crews.

The naval engineers, led by their chief, George Melville, defended the efficiency of their designs. He had been asked to design a fast ship, Melville complained, "and now we have beaten our foreign friends, and we are told that fast ships are useless...." But the critics were to carry the day. Less than three years after their completion, the *Columbia* and *Minneapolis* were laid up in reserve. Hastily recommissioned for the war with Spain, they were used for patrol, scouting, and transport duties but were given little opportunity for employment in their designed capacity as commerce raiders. Indeed, the growing power of the U.S. Navy was to render such a role largely unnecessary. As in the *Wampanoag* class of Civil War cruisers, the Navy had committed its most significant technological advances to ships whose function was out of step with the strategic requirements of their era.

Still triumphant from her victory at Manila Bay, the protected cruiser Olympia *anchors off Boston in 1899, flying the pennant of Admiral Dewey at the main and the crew's laundry at the fore.*

The *Olympia*—Cruiser Design *Par Excellence*

With her admirable blend of heavy armament, thick protective deck, high speed, and great endurance,
the 5,870-ton Olympia marked a high point in U.S. protected cruiser design. Just a few years after
her completion, however, naval authorities decided that a protective deck alone was inadequate defense
against the new rapid-fire guns and high-explosive shells of the day, and belt armor thereafter became
indispensable in new cruisers—except for unarmored scouts and semi-gunboat "peace cruisers."
In the photograph above, the Olympia is seen leaving Boston in 1902 following a long refit.
Extensive alterations included removal of her torpedo tubes and fighting tops, relocation of the
anchor hawsepipes, and replacement of the simple bow ornament with ornate gilt scrollwork
and a bronze figurehead.

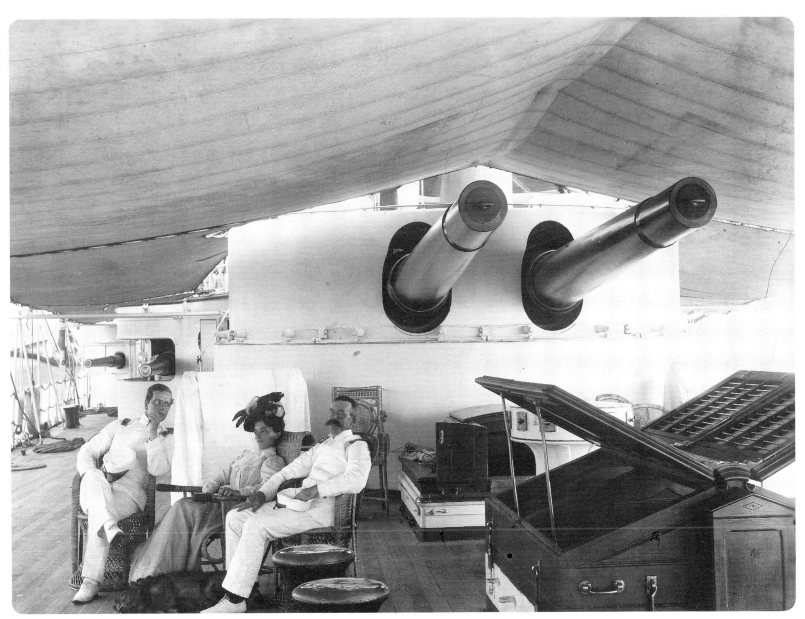

Officers relax with one of their ladies under the quarterdeck awning of the Olympia *soon after the famous warship's return to the United States in 1899. Two 5-inch rapid-fire guns of the secondary battery project from the superstructure at left, while 8-inch rifles of the main battery loom overhead. The main battery in the* Olympia *was the only one aboard a U.S. protected cruiser to be mounted in turrets. During a World War I rearming, however, the turret installations were removed and replaced by open mounts. The* Olympia's *career as an active unit of the fleet ended in 1922, but she is still afloat today, under the sponsorship of the Cruiser* Olympia *Association, as a naval relic at Philadelphia.*

An attempt to economize by crowding an inordinate amount of machinery and armament into too small a hull made the 3,213-ton protected cruisers Cincinnati *and* Raleigh *uncomfortable, unpopular, and unsuited for their designed roles. Nevertheless the* Raleigh—*photographed above in 1895—rendered distinguished service at Manila Bay in 1898, and after the war both ships were refitted with more conservative engineering plants for peace-cruiser service. During her reconstruction the* Cincinnati—*seen on the opposite page at New York in December 1901—lost her mainmast, received new guns, had her stacks lengthened, and was fitted with a magnificent gilt figurehead representing the goddess Liberty.*

Commerce Raiders

The two-stacked Minneapolis, *seen above in English waters in 1896, and her four-funneled sister* Columbia *were deliberately designed as commerce destroyers..The stern view of the* Columbia *on the opposite page—photographed in about 1899—shows the stern walk on which commanding officers could take their air, a feature common in British warships but seldom seen in the U.S. Navy. A single 8-inch rifle, left, was mounted on the after deck to fend off more powerful warships, while a pair of 6-inchers on the forecastle was primarily for commerce destruction. In spite of their imposing appearance, the 7,375-ton cruisers were thin-sided, underarmed, and expensive to man and operate, and their careers as commerce raiders were short-lived.*

Tugs stand by as the new armored cruiser New York *enters the waters of the Delaware at William Cramp and Sons of Philadelphia, 2 December 1891.*

Enter the Armored Cruiser

The most notable achievement of the 1888 naval construction program—which had also included the highly regarded *Olympia*—was the introduction of the Navy's first real armored cruiser, the *New York*. A type originated by the French Navy, the armored cruiser was distinguished from the somewhat smaller protected cruiser in that it carried belts of side armor in addition to the usual internal protective steel deck. Although the armored cruiser's protection and armament still fell short of those in a battleship, its speed and cruising range were usually greater. Armored cruisers were popular with most major foreign powers, and some navies even built them as less expensive (but unsuccessful) substitutes for battleships. The motive for adoption of the class in the U.S. Navy seems simply to have been a desire to match the best that Europe had to offer, for there appears to have been no clearly defined policy to differentiate between subsequent U.S. armored cruiser and protected cruiser employment. In any event, cruisers during this stage of U.S. naval development were intended to serve as commerce destroyers. With its speed, range, and good protection, the new type was admirably suited for such work, as well as for engaging hostile commerce raiders and, indeed, anything short of a battleship.

Of Bureau design, the *New York* was laid down by William Cramp and Sons in 1890 and was completed in 1893. With a load-waterline length of 380 feet and a displacement of 8,200 tons she was the largest U.S. warship up to that time, even exceeding the still uncompleted second-class battleships *Texas* and *Maine*. She was armed with a main battery of six 8-inch rifles, four mounted forward and aft in a pair of cylindrical turrets, and two amidships in single open mounts as in older cruisers. Her secondary armament included twelve 4-inch rapid-fire guns—a caliber that was soon recognized as inappropriate, being too small for fighting an armored opponent and too unwieldy for effective employment against fast torpedo boats. In accordance with current practice the cruiser was fitted with three above-surface torpedo tubes, one in the bow and two amidships. The *New York*'s protective deck, which extended through the entire length of her hull, had a maximum thickness of six inches, and the armor belts, running the length of the machinery spaces, were of four-inch steel.

The big warship had twin screws but was powered by four vertical triple-expansion engines, two driving each shaft. With over 17,000-horsepower her engines were for a time the most powerful in the Navy, driving her at a top speed of twenty-one knots. For economical cruising at speeds of less than sixteen knots the forward engines could be disconnected and the ship run on the after pair alone. A generous 1,290-ton coal capacity gave her a cruising range of well over ten thousand miles.

The *New York* was highly praised by U.S. and foreign naval authorities and was regarded as one of the handsomest examples of nineteenth-century American warship design. Up to the time of the Spanish-American War she was probably the most popular and well-known vessel in the fleet.

In 1892 a second ship of the type, the *Brooklyn*, was authorized and also awarded to the Cramp yard. The *Brooklyn* was twenty feet longer than the *New York* and her increased displacement of 9,215 tons permitted installation of additional armament. This included a main battery of eight 8-inch rifles in twin turrets—distributed in a lozenge arrangement, in which a pair of turrets were mounted forward and aft, and a second pair amidships—and a secondary battery of twelve 5-inch rapid-fire guns. Although the *Brooklyn*'s armor belts were only three inches in thickness, they were of a harder alloy than those in the *New York* and consequently were more effective. The addition of a forecastle deck, raised nearly thirty feet above the waterline, gave the forward turret a more commanding prospect, made the ship dryer at sea, and added to the already commodious berthing accommodations. The *Brooklyn*'s engines were essentially the same as those in her predecessor but several minor refinements, including increased heating surface under the boilers and her longer hull, made her nearly a knot faster. Cruising range was extended to more than fourteen thousand miles by a bunker capacity of 1,400 tons.

The *Brooklyn* was especially remarkable for the extreme tumble home of her sides and the height of her three stacks, which measured one hundred feet from the grate bars to the funnel caps. The former characteristic—like her huge ram bow, borrowed from the French—gave the wing turrets a wide arc of fire, enabling them to be trained from dead ahead to directly astern. The high stacks, a trademark of Engineer-in-Chief George W. Melville, provided a strong natural draft to the furnaces, thereby reducing the requirement for forced-draft steaming and reducing the attendant wear and tear on boilers and fireroom personnel.

During the mid-1890s the Navy was beginning to devote increased attention to the use of electricity for powering auxiliaries, and as a competitive experiment two turrets aboard the new armored cruiser were fitted with electrically-operated training machinery and the remaining pair with conventional steam-operated gear. The subsequent reliability and smooth and precise operation of the electrical system, and the inherent disadvantages of steam (including heat and danger from ruptured steam lines), were to lead to increased employment of electricity for this purpose in later warships.

As the Navy's only armored cruisers up to 1905, the *New York* and *Brooklyn* were rivals for the choicest flagship assignments and numbered some of the Navy's most illustrious names among their commanding officers, including Robley D. Evans, French E. Chadwick, and Francis A. Cook. During the Spanish-American War both cruisers served in the block-ading fleet off Cuba, the *New York* as flagship of Rear Admiral William T. Sampson, who had overall command of the American fleet, and the *Brooklyn* as flagship of Commodore Winfield S. Schley, commander of the romantic but short-lived Flying Squadron. Although Admiral Sampson's planning and leadership were in large part responsible for the resounding U.S. victory over Spanish Admiral Cervera's squadron on 3 July 1898, the *New York* herself had the bad luck to be a few miles beyond gunnery range during the battle. The *Brooklyn* played a leading role in the destruction of the enemy cruisers off Santiago that day and received much of the glory, but a controversial maneuver ordered by Commodore Schley early in the action was severely criticized, and subsequent bitterness between Sampson and Schley—and a Court of Inquiry into the latter's conduct—later tarnished the careers of both officers.

Although more powerful armored cruisers eventually eclipsed the *New York* and *Brooklyn*, their spacious living accommodations continued to make the two cruisers useful as flagships on distant stations, and the reputations earned during their early years served them well in showing the flag on a number of diplomatic missions. The *Brooklyn* was relegated to the scrappers in 1921, but her older rival—subsequently under the names of *Saratoga* and *Rochester*, and in the roles of convoy escort, troop transport, and finally, administrative flagship—served actively until 1933, when she was a full forty years of age. But even then her story had not quite ended. Consigned to rust in the back waters of her last duty station, at Subic Bay in the Philippines, the old *New York-Saratoga-Rochester* stubbornly remained afloat until December 1941, when U.S. forces evacuating the station towed her into the Subic Bay channel and scuttled her.

The armored cruiser Brooklyn *prepares to drydock at the New York Navy Yard, circa 1902.*
The extreme tumble home of her sides provided the wing turrets with clearance for fore-and-aft fire.

The Proud *Brooklyn*

Examples of the ages of sail and steam pass in review in a fine turn-of-the-century portrait of the
Brooklyn. *With her high freeboard, towering stacks, and extreme ram bow, the 9,215-ton armored*
cruiser had one of the most distinctive profiles in the Steel Navy. In a photograph of the Brooklyn's
shipshape forecastle, opposite, bluejackets stand by the forward 8-inch turret, which was situated
one deck higher than those amidships and aft. Sailors in the fighting top man a pair of rapid-fire guns,
used for defense against torpedo boats, while signal boys on the open bridge pose by the big ship's-wheel.
At sea the cruiser was usually conned from the enclosed pilothouse just below, while in time of battle
the watch moved down still another level into the armored conning tower.

Spic and span in fresh white and buff, the Brooklyn *presents an imposing appearance alongside a New York Navy Yard quay wall. Idlers watch as a sailor in a bos'n's chair adjusts an overboard discharge. The long shore rigged at left keeps the cruiser's hull from scraping against the rough wall, while an old muzzle-loading cannon in the foreground serves as a bollard for mooring lines. At the next pier, a crew's laundry dries above an* Indiana-*class battleship.*

The Popular *New York*

A handsome ship in her own right, the 8,200-ton armored cruiser New York *was less extreme in all particulars than her younger rival the* Brooklyn. *The arrangement of her main-battery guns was transitional, with pairs of 8-inch rifles in turrets forward and aft, but also with a single older-style open mount at either beam, as photographed at right. The numerous mixed-caliber, rapid-fire guns of her secondary battery—4-inchers and 6-pounders—provided all-round coverage from sponsons on her gun deck, as is evident in the bow view, opposite page.*

Bluejackets, visitors, and a lone Marine pass a quiet afternoon in port aboard the New York. A big windsail, rigged just forward of the 8-inch turret, directs a current of fresh air to the berthing spaces below. The field gun parked near the lady guest was for use by landing parties ashore.

With temporary anchors ready for letting go if necessary to check her momentum, the new battleship Iowa *enters her element at the Cramp shipyard at Philadelphia, 28 March 1896.*

Real Bone and Sinew

Secretaries Hunt, Chandler, and Whitney had laid the foundations of the Steel Navy, but it would take yet another administrator to create the modern battleships that would really bring the fleet into being. Before the fact few Navy men might have selected Benjamin F. Tracy—a lawyer, Civil War general, and Republican party stalwart—for a strong secretary. Certainly President Benjamin Harrison, on taking office in 1889, selected Tracy more for reasons of practical politics than for any strategic views he may have held.

Tracy, however, turned out to be an outstanding administrator with an open mind. Within a few months he had absorbed and adopted Captain Alfred Thayer Mahan's doctrine that control of the sea is the key to national power, and the capital ship the key to control of the sea. "We must have armored battleships," he strongly emphasized in his first annual report to the President, and Navy men vigorously supported him. The argument for the battleship as "the real bone and sinew of any naval force" was perhaps best stated later by Rear Admiral Philip Hichborn of the Bureau of Construction and Repair when he pointed out that "it is only through battleships that an enemy can be met and vanquished before he has even sighted our coast."

In his 1889 report, Tracy urged the immediate construction of two fleets of battleships—eight ships to be assigned to the Pacific and twelve to the Atlantic and Gulf coasts. So ambitious a program was obviously more than could be accepted in Congress, however. The Navy's legislative supporters dared ask for no more than three ships, and bowed to coast-defense strategists by labeling the vessels "sea-going coast-line battleships" and limiting their size and endurance. On 3 June 1890 Congress duly authorized construction of the three battleships.

Designs for the class were prepared by the Navy Department under the supervision of Lieutenant Lewis Nixon, a brilliant young naval constructor who as a civilian would later head his own shipyard. William Cramp and Sons of Philadelphia was low bidder on two of the vessels, and the Union Iron Works of San Francisco received the remaining contract in accordance with a provision of the authorizing act which directed that one of the ships be built on the West Coast. The Cramp bid proposed a battleship twelve feet longer than that envisioned by the Department, and this 348-foot-long hull was subsequently adopted for all three vessels.

The 10,288-ton battleships *Indiana, Massachusetts,* and *Oregon* proved to be of outstanding design. Although displacing considerably less than many contemporary foreign battleships, each mounted a heavy main battery of four 13-inch rifles in a pair of turrets, an intermediate battery of eight 8-inch rifles in four wing turrets, a secondary battery of four 6-inch rifles on the main deck, and six torpedo tubes. The added weight of fire provided by the intermediate battery—a feature not adopted by the British Navy for another decade—made these the most powerful battleships in the world.

Complementing each vessel's armament was a defensive shield of more than 2,700 tons of steel armor. Waterline armor belts, seven feet high and eight to eighteen inches in thickness, protected the battleship's vitals between her main turrets. The powder and ammunition handling rooms below the turrets were encased in barbettes seventeen inches thick, and the turrets themselves were of fifteen-inch armor. Five inches of steel plating also shielded much of the hull and superstructure above the main belts, including the 6-inch batteries, and the wing turrets had six inches of armor protection. The Harvey steel face-hardening process was perfected during construction of the class and for much of the armor in the *Indiana* and *Oregon* the Navy was able to substitute superior "Harveyized" steel in place of the conventional nickel-steel originally specified.

For additional protection the hull along the waterline forward and aft of the main armor belts was fitted with cofferdams packed with cocoa fiber cellulose, which was supposed to swell and plug any leak caused by a shell penetrating the ship's skin. It would take the Department a number of years to learn that this scheme was in fact ineffective as well as being terribly messy whenever the cellulose got wet and rotted, or had to be removed during repairs.

Preliminary plans had specified conical-shaped turrets with thick, sloping sides, based on an old design by famed Civil War engineer James Eads. The Bureau of Ordnance soon realized, however, that such turrets would not provide enough space for working the guns and that they would be difficult to manufacture, and large cylindrical turrets with vertical faces were substituted. Even these created some unforeseen problems. To obtain adequate elevation of the 13-inch rifles without making the port openings too large, the gun mountings had to be placed near the front of the turrets, thus moving each turret's center of balance nearly four feet forward of its axis. Whenever the big guns were trained to either beam, the resulting shift in mass caused the ship to list several degrees toward the engaged side, making gun-pointing difficult, straining the turret-turning machinery, and submerging the armor belt on that side. During a storm at sea in 1896 the unbalanced main turrets aboard the *Indiana* broke free from their stops and, swinging wildly to and fro, required the combined efforts of over a hundred of the crew to lash them down.

The 8-inch guns were mounted a full twenty-six feet above the waterline, giving them a commanding fire and permitting each pair to be trained across the top of the adjacent 13-inch turret, as far as fourteen degrees beyond the ship's centerline. In practice, however, it was discovered that when fired any closer than ten degrees from the centerline their muzzle blasts rendered the sighting hoods of the larger turrets untenable. A similar interference was discovered to exist between the 13- and 6-inch guns when the big turrets were trained abeam.

So many heavy guns and so much armor on a limited displacement naturally exacted compromises in other areas, and in this class the top speed was only about sixteen knots—less than that of either the *Texas* or *Maine*—and the berth deck accommodations and the capacity of the coal bunkers were somewhat limited. (Although 1,800 tons of coal could be taken on if necessary, the "normal" supply was only 400 tons, an amount deemed adequate for coastal-defense operations.) The ships had a freeboard of only twelve feet, making them wet in a seaway, and in some conditions·they were heavy rollers, since the limited capacity of existing U.S. drydocks delayed for several years installation of the bilge keels specified in their designs.

In 1892 a fourth battleship, the *Iowa*, was authorized and awarded to the Cramp yard. An increase of twelve feet in length and of about 1,000 tons in displacement over the *Indiana* class permitted designers to incorporate a higher freeboard forward, greater coal and berth-deck capacity, and generally better sea-keeping qualities. The new battleship also had a top speed of more than seventeen knots.

In the *Iowa* the caliber of the main-battery guns was reduced from thirteen to twelve inches, but a more rapid rate of fire helped to compensate for the reduced weight of projectile. The lighter guns could also be elevated or depressed by hand power in the event of machinery failure, a desirable precautionary feature. An oval-shaped balanced turret of new design was adopted, which could also be trained by hand in an emergency. The *Iowa*'s 8-inch and main-battery guns were placed farther apart than in her predecessors, reducing blast interference, and six 4-inch rapid-fire guns replaced the heavier 6-inch rifles of the *Indiana* class. Use of "Harveyized" steel permitted the main armor belts to be reduced to fourteen inches in thickness and they were consequently extended to protect more than three-fourths of the battleship's waterline.

The Sino-Japanese Battle of the Yalu in 1894 demonstrated the havoc wrought by wood splinters from hits by rapid-fire guns, and in the *Iowa* and succeeding battleships much of the traditional woodwork was replaced by joiner steel, while that which remained was fireproofed.

Probably the most striking features of the *Iowa* were her two towering hundred-foot stacks. As in the armored cruiser *Brooklyn*, these served to give the boilers a superior natural draft, reducing the need for operations with pressurized firerooms.

These four battleships provided the backbone for the Navy's blockading force during the Spanish-American War. The *Oregon* achieved perhaps the greatest fame, particularly for her dramatic 14,000-mile dash around South America from the West Coast to join the fleet off Cuba. She also outraced the other battleships, including the speedier *Iowa*, during the chase after Cervera's fleeing warships at the Battle of Santiago. This feat was mainly due to her engineering officer's foresight in keeping fires spread thin under all boilers during blockade duty—in contrast to the other warships' policy of "cold iron" under half of the boilers in accordance with normal practice—and in storing the best coal near the firerooms, under lock, for use at the time of supreme need.

After the turn of the century all four ships became completely outclassed by newer and faster battleships, but the weight of an *Indiana*-class broadside would not be exceeded until introduction of the dreadnought *Michigan* in 1910. The United States had been slow in entering the battleship race, but its first entries took second place to none.

The battleship Massachusetts *fits out at New York for a midshipmen's cruise in 1904. In the background the floating derrick* Hercules *lifts guns from her sister ship* Indiana, *out of commission for a long overhaul.*

Coast-Line Battleships

The low-freeboard Oregon, *above, and her 10,288-ton sisters* Indiana *and* Massachusetts *were wet at sea and were slower than many contemporary foreign battleships, but their heavy armament of 6-, 8-, and 13-inch guns was the most powerful afloat. Each of the four 60½-ton, thirteen-inch-caliber main-battery rifles—like that photographed in a turret aboard the* Oregon *at right—could lob a 1,100-pound projectile to a range of two to four miles with fair accuracy.*

Battleship Armament

An Indiana *crewman in casual working uniform poses between two gleaming 8-inch rifles of the battleship's intermediate battery. Eight of these guns, mounted in twin turrets and firing 250-pound projectiles, boosted the weight of an* Indiana-*class broadside above that of any contemporary foreign warship.*

The secondary battery in Indiana-*class battleships included four 6-inch rifles in casemates at the corners of the superstructure. This gun aboard the* Massachusetts *was manned by members of the ship's Marine detachment. The big wooden tub below the gun's breech received the residue of partially burned brown powder that had to be swabbed out of the barrel after every round.*

This unshielded six-pounder rapid-fire gun, one of twenty aboard the Massachusetts, was a key element in the battleship's defense against torpedo boat attack. Six one-pounders (the designation indicating the weight of projectile fired) were also carried.

Six tubes for launching Whitehead torpedoes were mounted above the waterline amidships and in the bow and stern of the Indiana and her sisters. This tube in the Massachusetts' broadside battery could be aimed by means of the training ring on the deck and a ball joint in the hull armor. The more lightly protected—and highly vulnerable—bow and stern tubes were removed from all of the new battleships soon after completion.

The High-Stacked *Iowa*

A raised forecastle made the 11,340-ton Iowa's *deck dryer and her forward guns more effective in heavy seas than those of her predecessors. She also boasted more complete armor protection, higher speed, and a greater cruising range than the* Indiana-*class battleships. Her rounded sides and hundred-foot stacks were trademarks of warships laid down for the Navy in 1893.*

Iowa *crewmen pose under the battleship's forward turret guns for a visiting commercial photographer. The 12-inch main-battery rifles, which fired 850-pound projectiles, had somewhat less destructive power than the heavier 13-inchers of the previous class, although their lighter weight enabled them to be trained and elevated by hand in the event of machinery breakdown.*

By the mid-1890s the Navy's major warships had grown into fighting machines of remarkable complexity. The Iowa had a crew of over five hundred; was armed with forty-six guns of various calibers; and in addition to her main engines, had some 150 auxiliary steam or electric engines, pumps, winches, turbines, motors, and blowers. This view facing aft from one of her bridge wings includes a few of the fourteen boats carried, which ranged from a punt for side cleaning to a forty-foot vedette steam launch.

The slab-sided battleship Kearsarge, *the only U.S. battleship not named after a state, towers over launch-day visitors at Newport News, Virginia, on 24 March 1898. Her sister ship* Kentucky *was launched on the same day from adjacent ways to the right.*

The Superposed-Turret Battleship

Following authorization of the *Iowa* in 1892, a hiatus of several years ensued during which no battleships were added to the Navy. The tide of expansionism which had begun during the administration of President Benjamin Harrison slackened during that of Grover Cleveland, who returned to the presidency for a second term in 1893. His new Secretary of the Navy, Hilary A. Herbert, came into office as something of an opponent to the battleship theory of sea power, but he was soon converted to the doctrines of Captain Mahan. However, an economic depression precluded any opportunity for large shipbuilding appropriations, and it was not until 1895 that Congress was persuaded to authorize two additional battleships.

In February 1894 the steam sloop *Kearsarge* had run aground off Central America and, despite salvage efforts, was lost. Sentimental attachment to the famous veteran of the Civil War was so strong that Congress legislated that "one of said battleships shall be named *Kearsarge*." The other ship was named for the state of Kentucky in accordance with traditional practice. Both contracts were awarded to a new builder for the Steel Navy, the Newport News Shipbuilding and Dry Dock Company of Virginia.

In size, displacement, and speed the *Kearsarge* and *Kentucky* were quite conventional, and they suffered from almost as low a freeboard as the *Indiana*-class battleships. Aspects of their armament and machinery were highly innovative, however. For the main-battery guns, designers returned to four 13-inch rifles, tests at the Navy Proving Ground having revealed that 12-inch guns of the type mounted in the *Iowa* were incapable of penetrating the armor carried in most new battleships. An intermediate battery of 8-inch rifles was also specified, but the interference problems discovered in the *Indiana*-class guns ruled out a duplication of their arrangement. Naval constructors recommended placing a smaller turret above and behind each of the main-battery ones, but they were overruled by ordnance experts who devised the radical scheme of mounting an 8-inch turret directly on top of each 13-inch turret.

This daring departure stirred up a controversy that would continue for years. Those in favor of the superposed turret arrangement argued that the problem of blast interference was overcome, that the efficiency of the intermediate batteries was greatly improved (two turrets doing essentially the same work as four in the *Indiana class*), and that several sets of heavy turret-turning machinery were eliminated. Those objecting to the system pointed out that a single hit could disable four guns, that both the 8- and 13-inch guns would have to be pointed at the same target even though tactical requirements might dictate otherwise, and that their combined firing rate would be reduced because of one set of guns having to wait for the other to fire.

Each of the battleships also carried a huge broadside secondary battery of fourteen 5-inch rapid-fire guns, a substantial advance over both the light 4-inchers of the *Iowa* and the slow-firing 6-inch rifles of the *Indiana* class.

The ships' main propulsion systems were conventional in design, but in the widespread employment of electricity for the operation of auxiliary machinery the *Kearsarge* and *Kentucky* were a great step forward. Gun-elevation and turret-turning machinery, ammunition hoists, deck winches, boat cranes, and ventilation systems were all electrically powered.

During the excitement of the Spanish-American War, construction work on the new battleships surged ahead, but with the arrival of peace work slowed again, and they were not completed until 1900. Both served for several years as flagships and participated in the world cruise of the Great White Fleet in 1907–09. By that time they were outclassed, however, and thereafter served mainly as training ships. The *Kentucky* was scrapped in 1924, but the *Kearsarge* survived until 1955, serving her last thirty-five years in the unique capacity of the Navy's only crane ship.

Double-Decked-Turret Battleships

Two-story turrets with pairs of 8- and 13-inch rifles, and an imposing secondary battery of fourteen 5-inch rapid-fire guns in casemates, gave the 11,540-ton Kearsarge, *above, and her sister* Kentucky *an appearance of massive firepower. Some naval authorities were highly critical of the superposed-turret arrangement and the housing of the large secondary battery on either side of the main deck in a single compartment, because several guns could be put out of action by the explosion of a single enemy shell. The large and vulnerable gun-port openings in the main-battery turrets, as seen aboard the* Kentucky *on the opposite page, were such an embarrassment that officers aboard the two battleships finally rigged wood and canvas screens in them to resemble armored port shields.*

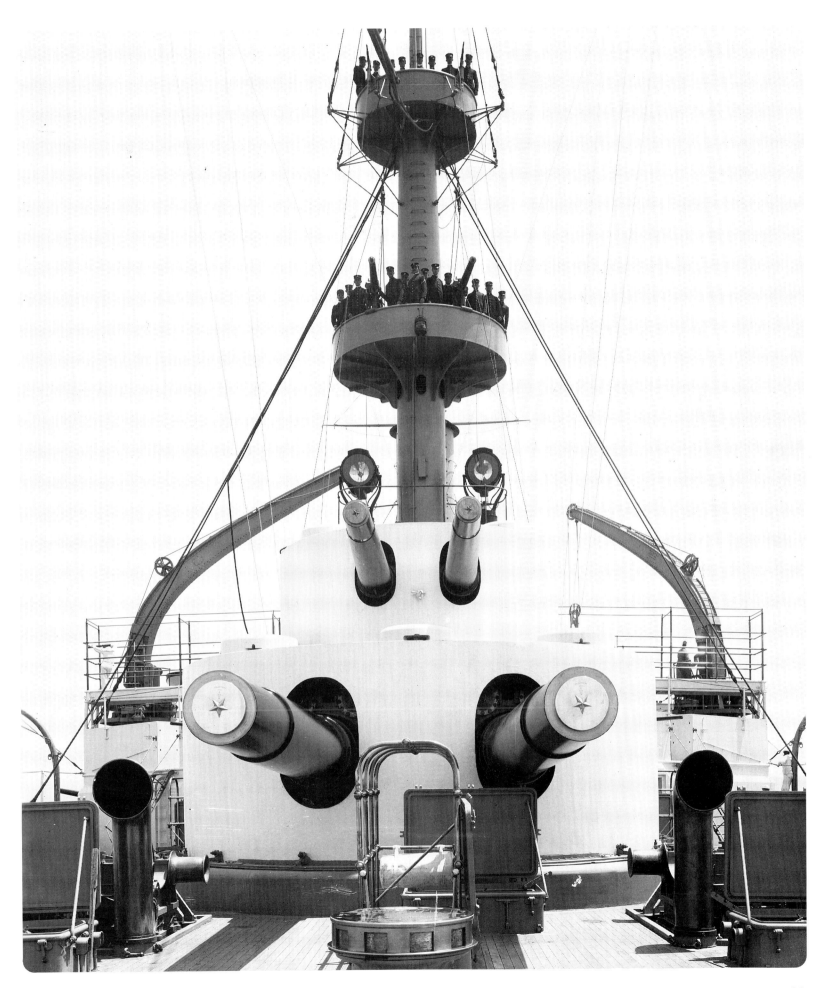

The monitor Miantonomoh, *with ground tackle and canvas-sheltered heads cluttering her forecastle, lies at anchor in an East Coast port during the late 1890s.*

Floating Flatirons and Galoshes

I am a great monitor man," declared Captain William C. Wise in 1898. His enthusiasm for this class of warship was shared by many others, and over the years the Steel Navy acquired ten of these wallowing curiosities under the delusion that they were ideal harbor- and coast-defense vessels, and under the even greater misconception that harbor and coast defense was a fitting strategy for a world power.

Five of the monitors were holdovers from the Old Navy, twenty years in the building and constructed with iron hulls instead of steel. The *Puritan* and the four ships of the *Amphitrite* class (*Amphitrite, Miantonomoh, Monadnock,* and *Terror*) had all been laid down surreptitiously in 1874–75 under the guise of repairing Civil War monitors of the same names, this deception being the only way that funds for construction could be obtained. Work on these monitors proceeded at a snail's pace during the years of naval stagnation, although considerable sums of money were dribbled into them under some cloudy contractual dealings.

In his annual report for 1881, Secretary of the Navy William H. Hunt roundly damned the still uncompleted monitors as "simply bad copies of old models . . . to continue these vessels on the original plans . . . would be to introduce a worthless class of vessels into the Navy." Nevertheless it was decided to finish them "solely as a choice of evils."

The original "repair" contracts had been awarded to several civilian builders, including John Roach and his rival Charles H. Cramp, but after new funds were appropriated during the 1880s to complete the ships, most of the remaining work on them was carried out at navy yards. During these years the ordnance designs for the monitors were updated and steel was specified for their armor protection. One monitor, the *Miantonomoh,* was fitted with obsolete compound armor purchased in England, but in 1887 armor requirements for the other four were combined into a single order large enough to induce U.S. industry to build the necessary steel forging and rolling facilities. Although delivery of the armor was much delayed as a result, the Navy Department considered this an acceptable price to pay for rendering itself independent of foreign steel suppliers. The *Miantonomoh* was briefly commissioned in 1882 for trials (without her armament) and was finally completed in 1891, but the other monitors did not enter service until 1895–96.

Like the Civil War ironclads from which they had descended, these ships were characterized by low speed; heavy armor protection; broad, flat hull design; shallow draft; and an extremely low freeboard, which made them terribly wet at sea but also inconspicuous as targets. The largest of the five, the *Puritan,* displaced 6,060 tons and had a main armament of four 12-inch rifles in a pair of cylindrical turrets. Her twin-screw, horizontal compound engines were essentially those specified in the original plans drawn in the 1870s, and in 1897—just a year after her commissioning—they were described by Assistant Engineer Frank M. Bennett as presenting "one of the earliest examples of compound practice in this country . . . interesting chiefly as objects for antiquarian investigation . . ."

The 3,990-ton monitors of the *Amphitrite* class were in essence smaller editions of the *Puritan* but differing in detail. Each was armed with a main battery of four 10-inch rifles. The turrets of the *Amphitrite* and *Monadnock* were mounted on barbettes; those of the other two were not. The *Miantonomoh* had almost no superstructure while that of her sisters was quite extensive, containing a pilothouse, wardroom, officers' cabins, and heads. The *Terror* had an innovative pneumatic system for the operation of her guns, turrets, and steering gear; the corresponding equipment in the *Amphitrite* was powered hydraulically, and in the remaining ships was operated by steam. The *Monadnock* was completed with efficient horizontal triple-expansion engines; the old inclined compound engines in the other three monitors were, like those in the *Puritan,* practically floating marine museum pieces and were notable mainly for their compact arrangement, with the cylinders of each engine being positioned athwartships over the propeller shaft of its companion.

The engineering spaces in these monitors were among the most poorly ventilated in the Navy. Temperatures in the engine room of the *Amphitrite* frequently exceeded 150° F., and one official inspection party was only able to measure the 205° temperature recorded near her fire-room steam valves by attaching a thermometer onto the end of a long fishpole. During one short cruise off the Atlantic coast in 1895 so many firemen aboard the *Amphitrite* were prostrated by heat exhaustion that the monitor eventually lost steam pressure, drifted to a complete halt, and had to be anchored! Additional ventilators installed in the monitors eventually improved habitability in the engineering spaces and, in the case of the *Amphitrite,* resulted in an increase in cruising speed from a plodding four or five knots to about eight.

While these ships were still under construction monitor enthusiasts added a sixth one, the 4,084-ton *Monterey,* for service on the West Coast. Authorized in 1887 and built by the Union Iron Works, she was an updated version of the older ships and had modern, twin-screw, vertical triple-expansion engines. An unusual feature resurrected from Civil War days was her ability to "submerge" to fighting trim, tanks in her double bottoms being flooded before battle until only a few inches of freeboard remained. The *Monterey*'s armament designs at first included one 16-inch and one 12-inch rifle, a 15-inch dynamite gun, and a total of sixteen smaller rapid-fire guns, but it turned out that all of these, along with adequate armor protection, would be far too heavy for her assigned displacement. The armament specifications were subsequently reduced to include two 12-inch rifles forward and a pair of 10-inchers aft, to be mounted in Eads-type conical turrets, and a few 1- and 6-pounder rapid-fire guns. Later the Eads design was dropped in favor of more practical cylindrically-shaped turrets. In an additional effort to reduce displacement, two types of boilers were installed, one pair being of the usual cylindrical type for normal steaming, and four other supplementary boilers being of a lightweight coil design, for use in attaining maximum speed. The *Monterey* was thus a compromise in nearly every respect, but she was designed, altered, and completed by 1893, earlier than any of the other monitors except the *Miantonomoh.*

During the Spanish-American War the *Amphitrite, Miantonomoh, Puritan,* and *Terror* performed bombardment and blockade duty in Caribbean waters, and the *Monadnock* and *Monterey* sailed all the way across the Pacific to augment Commodore George Dewey's squadron in the Philippines. All were insufferably hot in the tropics and impossible to keep dry at sea, and their gunnery suffered from the ships'

low freeboard and tendency to roll heavily. Rear Admiral William Sampson was not enamored of those assigned to his fleet, complaining that they caused him "endless trouble and delay," especially since the monitors' limited coal capacities required that they frequently be taken under tow by the larger warships.

Nevertheless the grip of the "monitor men" was hard to break and the public viewed these obsolete craft as powerful insurance against invasion. Not only were several Civil War veterans of the *Passaic* and *Canonicus* classes reboilered and overhauled in 1898 to "guard" East Coast ports with their smoothbore cannon, but in May of that year Congress even appropriated funds for four additional monitors of modern design. The authorizing legislation provided for either single- or double-turreted vessels, but the cost limitation was such that the Navy Department chose to adopt the single-turret design. These 3,200-ton warships were built with powerful 12-inch rifles, fully balanced turrets, efficient water-tube boilers, and extensive electrical auxiliary machinery. They were given state names like battleships—*Arkansas, Connecticut* (renamed *Nevada* during construction), *Florida,* and *Wyoming*—but these would be exchanged for city names in 1908–09.

In 1898 Captain Wise had boasted that the *Puritan* was the strongest ship in the Navy and his former command the *Amphitrite* "a most perfect sea boat," but just six years later Secretary of the Navy Charles J. Bonaparte was able to state that while "it was thought that vessels of a special type were needed for coast defense . . . this idea is now outgrown . . . an old heresy in our naval policy." The concept of monitors as first-line fighting ships had finally died, and they would thereafter be relegated to service as fleet auxiliaries.

The peculiar vessels, dubbed "floating flatirons and galoshes" by their detractors, were yet to render some contributions to naval progress, however. In 1908 the *Florida*—although manned by her crew and retained in commission—was employed as an experimental target in Chesapeake Bay to determine the effects of modern large-caliber projectiles and torpedoes on contemporary armor and hull construction. In another major experiment the following year, the West Coast monitor *Cheyenne* (ex-*Wyoming*) was converted into the Navy's first successful fuel-oil-burning warship.

After about 1913 the single-turreted monitors were pressed into service as submarine tenders, although their low freeboard was about the only feature making them suitable for such duty. The older monitors were used as station, receiving, gunnery training, militia, and target ships until being sold during the early 1920s, but the *Cheyenne*'s modern engineering plant kept her on the active Navy list until 1937 as a Naval Reserve drill ship.

The Monterey, *her deck submerged to "fighting trim," buries her nose in a San Francisco Bay swell during trials in January 1893. A temporary shed roof seals the forward battle hatch.*

Old-Navy Holdovers

The 3,990-ton monitor Terror, *above, and her three near-sisters of the* Amphitrite *class were supposedly reconstructed Civil War veterans, but in fact retained only the names of the wooden-hulled, Ericsson-designed warships of the 1860s. Laid down under questionable circumstances in 1874–75, during the administration of Navy Secretary George Robeson, they were decades under construction and by the time of their completion in 1891–96 were completely outmoded. Although fitted with steel armor protection and breech-loading rifles, they were of old-fashioned wrought-iron hull construction and three of the four had antiquated compound engines.*

A large awning provides shade for the forecastle and forward 10-inch guns of the Amphitrite *on a summer day at around the turn of the century. Round gratings in the deck shielded glass ports which allowed a little daylight to filter down to the berthing spaces below. The turrets aboard the* Amphitrite *and* Monadnock *were raised on armored barbettes, giving the two ships better protection and keeping them drier below decks than the* Miantonomoh *and* Terror. *However, with a freeboard of only slightly over two feet and a tendency to roll heavily, none of the monitors proved very successful as gun platforms.*

Bad Copies of Old Models

The 6,060-ton Puritan, opposite, was the largest of the monitors and, like the vessels of the Amphitrite class, was a hand-me-down from the Old Navy. More than twenty years from keel-laying to commissioning, she was a hodgepodge of obsolete engines, iron-hulled construction, steel armor, and relatively modern 12-inch rifles. The 4,084-ton Monterey, photographed above during an 1893 visit to Portland, Oregon, was an updated steel-hulled version of the older monitors. She also carried 12-inch rifles in her forward turret, but the after-turret guns were limited to ten inches in caliber in order to reduce weight.

New-Navy Monitors

The 3,200-ton Wyoming, *destined to survive as the* Cheyenne *until the late 1930s as the last U.S. Navy monitor, swings at anchor in San Francisco Bay in about 1905. Four of these anachronistic single-turreted craft mounting pairs of 12-inch rifles were included in the Spanish-American War expansion program by monitor enthusiasts. However, limitations of the Arkansas-class monitor design, along with maturing attitudes regarding the Navy's mission on the seas, soon resulted in these vessels' being transferred from their harbor- and coast-defense duties to noncombatant roles as tenders, training ships, and auxiliaries.*

In a remarkable action photograph, the experimental wooden torpedo boat Stiletto
launches a flywheel-driven Howell torpedo during tests on Narragansett Bay in 1893.

Rise and Decline of the Torpedo Boat

The modern torpedo boat was slow in coming to the U.S. Navy, but primitive versions of this type of war vessel were employed by Americans as far back as the Civil War. In 1864 Union Navy Lieutenant William Cushing braved a hail of fire to sink the ironclad *Albemarle,* using a steam launch armed with an explosive charge or "torpedo" mounted on the end of a long spar. In the Confederate Navy several semi-submersible "Davids" equipped with similar devices were directed against Union warships. Immediately after the war the Navy tested the sophisticated spar-torpedo boat *Spuyten Duyvil,* and during the 1870s it experimented with the torpedo ram *Intrepid* and the high-speed torpedo launch *Lightning.* Nevertheless, the suicidal propensities of the spar torpedo—which sometimes proved as devastating to the attacker as to his victim—and the introduction of small rapid-fire guns for defense limited the offensive value of these early torpedo craft.

It was the perfection of the self-propelled or "automobile" torpedo by British engineer Robert Whitehead during the late 1860s and early '70s that really made the torpedo boat practical, since with this invention high explosives could be released and sent to their targets from a reasonably safe distance. The British Navy was quick to recognize the advantages of the potent new weapon and in 1877 built its first modern high-speed torpedo boat, the *Lightning.* Within a few years European navies were building torpedo boats by the hundreds; in 1892 France had 220 of them afloat, England 186, Russia 152, Germany 143, and Italy 129.

As early as 1881 the Naval Advisory Board had recommended the construction of torpedo boats, but despite mounting agitation it was not until 1886 that Congress appropriated funds for the first real U.S. torpedo boat, which was appropriately named the *Cushing.* Designed and built by the Herreshoff Manufacturing Company of Bristol, Rhode Island—world-famous for its sail and steam yacht designs—the *Cushing* was of galvanized steel construction, had a fifteen-foot beam, was 139 feet long, and displaced 105 tons.

Lightweight water-tube boilers and twin-screw quadruple-expansion engines provided a top speed of 22.5 knots. Armament consisted of three eighteen-inch diameter Whitehead torpedoes mounted in a pair of trainable launch tubes on deck and in a fixed tube in the bow, and three 1-pounder rapid-fire guns. Armor protection was limited to thin shielding on the conning tower. Twenty enlisted men and two officers comprised the crew. Commissioned in 1890 and employed mainly in experimental duties at the Naval Torpedo Station in Newport, the *Cushing* set the pattern for the principal line of U.S. torpedo boat construction to follow.

The *Cushing* was preceded into service, however, by the *Stiletto,* another Herreshoff-built craft purchased by the Navy in 1887. She was of wooden construction and displaced only thirty-one tons. During the early 1890s the *Stiletto* carried out pioneer torpedo experiments with the American-designed Howell torpedo, and later she served as a test-bed for such schemes as the use of dark olive green paint for reducing detectability at night, and the employment of oil for fuel.

Development proceeded at a slow pace for several more years, perhaps because torpedo boats were considered to be coast-defense weapons and the isolation of the United States made the likelihood of an attack seem remote. One more boat, the 120-ton *Ericsson,* was authorized in 1890 and was awarded to an inland builder, the Iowa Iron Works of Dubuque, Iowa. This vessel was built to Navy designs but completion was delayed until 1897 by endless construction problems and machinery breakdowns.

During this period some foreign and U.S. naval authorities concluded that armored warships would benefit from carrying small third-class torpedo boats on davits to be launched for use in battle or to serve as picket boats when at anchor. Two sixteen-ton boats of this type were built for the second-class battleship *Maine,* but failed to attain their design speeds and were never seriously employed.

Construction of larger craft finally began in earnest in

1894 with authorization of the 142-ton boats *Foote, Rodgers,* and *Winslow,* all awarded to the Columbian Iron Works of Baltimore. Three more torpedo boats were begun in 1895: the 165-ton sisters *Porter* and *Du Pont* at the Herreshoff plant and the 210-ton *Rowan* at the Moran Brothers Company in Seattle. All but the last of these entered service in time to participate in Caribbean operations during the Spanish-American War.

In spite of taking part in some spectacular engagements, the torpedo boat as a type was badly discredited by the war. Some officers blamed the lack of success on the unenterprising Spanish, who afforded no real combat opportunities to U.S. torpedo boat skippers. Others pointed out that the Navy had little prior experience in employing such craft and few trained crews. And there was no question but that the boats were misused in jobs for which they were poorly fitted— mainly patrol and dispatch assignments—as they were simply too small to stay at sea for any extended period and too delicate to stand rough handling. Owing to a shortage of qualified engineers only a few experienced officers could be provided to supervise the machinery of all of the boats in service, and the compact high-powered engines—which were precision instruments demanding special care—were frequently placed in the rough hands of crudely skilled mechanics. Boats were sent on overextended cruises and sometimes even had to steam with salt water in the boilers in order to reach port. The inevitable overall result, as described by Engineer-in-Chief George Melville, was that "the machinery in some at the close of the war was in a condition which can only be described as horrible, where boilers were burnt, cylinder covers broken, pistons and valves stuck, and everything in bad shape."

Torpedo boat duty, while considered glamorous by some, was of the most rigorous sort. At sea the boats pounded unmercifully and their endless rolling (as fast as twenty-five oscillations per minute) tended, in the words of one officer, "to wear out the crews in a very few days." Accommodations were cramped, provisions spoiled quickly without refrigeration, drinking water turned rusty and became contaminated by seawater, and berthing compartments were either oven-hot from the adjacent firerooms or Arctic-cold because of faulty radiators. Seas flooded in through open hatches and ventilators, and condensation constantly dripped down the thin hull plating onto bunks and clothing, making rheumatism a chronic malady. Moreover, torpedo boats were dangerous. At high speeds vibration wracked the fast-turning machinery and loosened high-pressure steam lines, to the jeopardy of engineers and firemen, while on deck crewmen were always in danger of being washed overboard. In combat

against larger warships the torpedo boat was afforded virtually no odds for survival except when making a surprise attack at night.

Unfortunately, most of this experience was absorbed too late to be of much value during the continuing fleet expansion, which already included ten new torpedo boats in the 1896 program, three in 1897, and twelve more in 1898, to which were added two others purchased abroad for the war. Designers came up with a hodge-podge of types and sizes that ranged from the 99½-foot, 46-ton sisters *Talbot* and *Gwin* to the 225-foot, 340-ton *Stringham*. In speed the boats varied from under twenty knots in the 65-ton *McKee* to more than thirty as in the 279-ton *Farragut*. Indeed, the *Stringham* and *Farragut* were more or less officially referred to as torpedo boat destroyers because of their large size, high speed, and heavy armament of 6-pounder guns. Nine of the final group of twelve boats were generally patterned on the Navy-designed *Winslow* type, but so much latitude was allowed the individual builders that little homogeneity resulted.

Contracts for the boats authorized in 1897 and 1898 were apportioned among a number of smaller yards to encourage the development of the shipbuilding industry, but some of the builders turned out to be ill-prepared for such demanding precision work, and had little concept of the real construction costs involved. To further add to the builders' ultimate grief, prices of steel and other materials jumped astronomically soon after the contracts were awarded. Most of the boats were overweight when completed, great difficulty was experienced in meeting speed requirements, nearly every builder losts tens of thousands of dollars, and three shipyards went bankrupt. The last torpedo boat finally straggled into commission in 1908.

During peacetime most of the bottle-green-colored torpedo boats were laid up in reserve flotillas with skeleton crews, occasionally to be recommissioned for brief periods of training. After 1910 several boats were stripped for use as target rafts in fleet battle practice, and during World War I most of the remaining ones were pressed into coastal patrol service and then scrapped immediately after the armistice.

In retrospect the steam torpedo boat in the U.S. Navy was a dismal failure. The boats did, however, provide valuable experience to designers, builders, and crews in developing the equipment and tactics leading up to the creation of the destroyer, whose material lineage can be traced directly through the more successful torpedo boat designs. Many years later the original torpedo boat concept would be revived in the World War II "PT" or motor torpedo boat, but because of the ensuing revolution in technology the two types had little more in common than the name.

The forty-six ton Talbot, *photographed in New York in 1900, proved too small and too slow for effective torpedo boat service; however, she performed useful duty in pioneer experiments with oil fuel.*

Giant Killers

The newly commissioned torpedo boats Du Pont, *in the foreground, and* Ericsson *receive touch-up work in a New York Navy Yard drydock in 1897. The 165-ton Herreshoff-built* Du Pont *was regarded as one of the best constructed and most seaworthy of the early U.S. torpedo boats, and in 1898 cruised more than nine thousand miles without incident during Cuban blockade duty. The 120-ton* Ericsson *was plagued by machinery breakdowns during the war, but nevertheless was the only U.S. torpedo boat off Santiago on the day of the big naval battle, where she rescued more than one hundred sailors from the burning Spanish warships.*

Sailors ease a grease-coated Whitehead torpedo into their boat's stern tube. The big weapon was powered by compressed air driving a three-cylinder engine, and had a maximum range of about a thousand yards. A small charge of gunpowder launched it from the tube. Most U.S. torpedo boats were armed with two or three torpedoes and three or four 1-pounder rapid-fire guns. The boats were designed primarily to engage major warships such as battleships and cruisers, but such attacks were generally ruled out except under the cover of darkness, when the little craft had some hope of closing to within torpedo-launching range before being shot to pieces.

Built for Speed

The 175-ton Bagley, *above, was one of five torpedo boats built by the Bath Iron Works, all of which were based on purchased French designs. Their construction featured extensive use of aluminum to reduce weight and the* Bagley *had a top speed of more than twenty-nine knots, considered quite respectable for a U.S. torpedo boat. Here she is seen loafing along with the after fireroom secured for economy. Reckless speed had its hazards: on the opposite page New York Navy Yard officers contemplate repairs to the telescoped bow of the Newport-based* Du Pont, *which had been permitted to "run into the slip at too high a speed" in June 1900. In spite of the damage, the* Du Pont *managed to limp from Newport to the Brooklyn yard under her own power.*

High in the water and with engineering plant secured, the protected cruiser New Orleans *awaits drydocking during a post-Spanish-American War overhaul at the New York Navy Yard.*

The Foreign War Purchases

When war with Spain began to appear imminent in early 1898, the Navy Department, concerned by an imagined inferiority in naval fighting strength, began scouring foreign markets for warships that could be bought in a hurry. The most promising prospect turned out to be the *Amazonas,* a 3,437-ton protected cruiser nearly completed for the Republic of Brazil at the yard of Sir W. G. Armstrong, Whitworth, and Company at Newcastle-on-Tyne, England. A sister ship, the *Almirante Abreu,* was also at the yard in an early stage of construction. Negotiations were carried out with Brazil and on 16 March 1898 the United States purchased the two cruisers. By this time the *Amazonas* had already been commissioned in the Brazilian Navy and had her crew on board, ready to depart for South America. The U.S. naval attaché from London promptly recommissioned her as the USS *Amazonas* and a pickup crew from the cruiser *San Francisco* took over. To their dismay, the Americans discovered that the living spaces were without provision for heat and that all of the machinery labels and operating instructions were printed in Portuguese! After several days of hectic improvisation the *Amazonas* departed for New York, where she was subsequently renamed the *New Orleans* and fitted for service with the Cuban blockading squadron. The *Almirante Abreu* was not completed until 1900 and thus missed the war. Altered in some details during construction to better meet the needs of U.S. naval service, she was completed as the *Albany.*

The *New Orleans* and *Albany* were the first steel cruisers in the U.S. Navy to have wood-sheathed and coppered hulls. Each was armed with a main battery of six 6-inch and four 4.7-inch rapid-fire guns and three torpedo tubes. The two ships somewhat resembled *Cincinnati*-class cruisers in having unusually light protective decks and inordinately powerful engines, and were subject to some of the same criticisms. They were not very highly regarded by U.S. naval authorities, who considered them "show" vessels designed "purely for speed and the heaviest battery the law would allow" at the expense of other qualities. Freeboard was low, making them wet at sea; berthing arrangements were inadequate by U.S. standards; magazine capacity was limited; and auxiliary machinery, where not omitted entirely, was often unsatisfactory. In 1906–07 the ships were rearmed with U.S. 5- and 6-inch rapid-fire guns, and both continued to serve in typical cruiser-gunboat capacities until the 1920s.

Brazil also provided the Navy with one auxiliary cruiser, the 6,888-ton *Nictheroy.* Completed at Newport News in 1893 as the fast merchant liner *El Cid,* she had been purchased and armed the same year for service with the Brazilian government against that country's rebellious navy. After her incorporation into the U.S. Navy in May 1898, the *Nictheroy* was refitted with 4- and 5-inch rapid-fire guns, renamed the *Buffalo,* and sent out with the other merchant auxiliary cruisers on patrol duty.

Two torpedo boats were also purchased abroad; the 150-ton *Somers,* a vessel built in Germany in 1893 as a private speculation but never accepted by the German Navy, and the 30-ton *Manley* (sometimes spelled *Manly*), a similar product from England. Following three unsuccessful attempts to tow the *Somers* across the Atlantic, the outbreak of war and the neutrality laws marooned her in England for the duration. She was later found to be of little value to the Navy, being ill-matched for operations with domestically built craft. The *Manley* also missed the war and was so small that she ended up serving as a noncommissioned launch at Annapolis.

A final foreign purchase was the 1,800-ton *Diogenes,* built in Kiel, Germany, about 1883 for Portugal and acquired from private interests in an unarmed condition. Renamed the *Topeka,* she was fitted out as a gunboat in time to take part in operations off Cuba. Considered a very comfortable ship for service in tropical waters, the *Topeka* turned out to be one of the most useful of the war purchases, not being stricken from the register of U.S. naval vessels until 1930.

"Show" Vessels

In full dress—and with a large dent in her forward gun sponson—the 3,437-ton New Orleans, above, celebrates victory over Spain at the Philadelphia Peace Jubilee in October 1898. Pictured a few years later in peacetime colors, opposite, she shows off her fancy stern ornament, a souvenir of brief service in the Brazilian Navy. The New Orleans and her sister Albany were both built in England and were fitted with British armament, including the 6-inch rapid-fire gun at right. The foreign guns employed cordite ammunition and had longer barrels and produced higher muzzle velocities than did contemporary American weapons. An earlier ship of the class—the Barrozo—was completed in 1897 and remained in the Brazilian Navy.

Foreign War Purchases

In spite of the 4- and 5-inch guns glowering from her forecastle and gun deck, the 6,888-ton auxiliary cruiser Buffalo's *merchant origin is apparent in this turn-of-the-century photograph. Designed as the fast cargo steamer* El Cid, *she had already seen naval service under the Brazilian flag when purchased by the U.S. Navy in 1898. As the warship* Nictheroy *in 1893 her armament had included a 15-inch Zalinski dynamite gun, an improved version of those fitted in the U.S. dynamite cruiser* Vesuvius. *Patrol duty along the East Coast during the Spanish-American War was followed by a long and varied career as a training ship, destroyer tender, and transport.*

The 1,800-ton gunboat Topeka, *seen here off Boston, was a contemporary of the old ABCD ships, having been built in Germany in about 1883 as the* Diogenes. *Although intended for service in the Portuguese Navy she was not accepted. After purchase by the U.S. Navy in 1898 she was rearmed in time to see action along the coast of Cuba. When photographed above, in September 1900, the* Topeka *had just exchanged her light schooner rig for square sails, for service as a training ship for landsmen. In later years she proved a useful vessel for flag-showing duties in the tropics. A sister ship, the* Lima (ex-Socrates), *served in the Peruvian Navy.*

In postwar white and gilt, the Scottish-built Yankton (ex-Penelope) *lies alongside a quay wall at Portsmouth, New Hampshire. The 185-foot yacht accompanied the Battle Fleet on its world cruise in 1907–09.*

The Pleasure Yacht Is Enlisted

Along with the merchant vessels and foreign-built warships that were hurriedly mobilized during 1898, a number of steam yachts were recruited for service in the Spanish-American War. Because the Navy had almost no regularly assigned auxiliaries, the pleasure craft of the rich were earmarked for three roles: harbor patrol, offshore picket duty, and service with the larger warships as tenders and shallow-water gunboats. Most of the twenty-eight yachts sold or loaned to the Navy were assigned to the first two functions, but the latter role was where the glory lay.

During March of 1898 the sleek craft began reporting into East Coast navy yards, most frequently to New York. In short order their green boot-tops, jet-black topsides, rich brown deckhouses, yellow spars, and gilt cove- and trail-boards were covered with coats of lead-colored war paint. Masts were stripped, bowsprits sawed off, fancy steam and naptha launches sent ashore, and dining saloons gutted to accommodate war crews twice the size of those needed for peaceful pursuits. Rapid-fire guns were mounted on forecastles and quarterdecks, and Colt automatic machine guns bristled from upper works. Soon the once-luxurious pleasure boats were at sea performing the tedious and unglamorous chores of the Naval Auxiliary Force.

The smaller yachts were assigned to harbor patrol along the East Coast, where they guarded minefields and halted incoming merchantmen for inspection. Others operated with the offshore picket fleet, the purpose of which was simply, in the words of a naval officer, "to make a string along the coast, and if Cervera's fleet comes along, they will make so much noise we will know something has happened and will send a big ship out there." This Spanish threat never materialized, however, and when the Navy Department realized that Admiral Cervera's cruisers would stay bottled up in Santiago Harbor, the barrier was disbanded and the yachts were diverted to other duties.

The most interesting service was enjoyed by the larger and faster ships that were sent to Cuban waters with the fleet, where they served as jacks-of-all-trades. Many of these yachts proved overloaded or too fragile for their demanding new war roles. Boilers broke down under the unskilled care of hastily mobilized Naval Militiamen, decks buckled from the shock of gunfire, and thin hulls gave out from rough use and the constant pushing and hauling around larger warships and piers. Nevertheless, several yachts—including the *Vixen, Yankton, Scorpion,* and *Hist*—earned excellent service reputations. The 434-ton *Eagle,* sent with the cruiser *Marblehead* to patrol the southern coast of Cuba, proved to be one of the fastest vessels in the fleet. At the signal *"Eagle,* chase" she would dash off to challenge "any bit of smoke or cloud that appeared on the horizon," leaving her nominally speedier consort far behind.

The largest and one of the most sumptuously appointed of the Spanish War yachts was the 2,690-ton *Mayflower,* built in 1896. Following her purchase for $430,000, the 273-foot vessel was heavily armed as a torpedo gunboat with two 5-inch rapid-fire guns in the waist, two torpedo tubes in the former dining room, and twelve 6-pounders and four Colt automatic machine guns. As with a number of the other converted yachts, plates of seven-eighths-inch steel were worked over her sides amidships to protect the boilers and engines against small-caliber gunfire. Although workmen removed most of the *Mayflower's* lavish furnishings—including gilt French decor and a grand piano—one of four bathtubs hewn from solid marble was left aboard for the comfort of her officers. During the war the *Mayflower* took part in the blockade off Cuba and captured several merchant prizes.

Probably the greatest renown achieved by any of the yachts during the Spanish-American War was that of the 786-ton *Gloucester.* Under the command of Lieutenant Commander Richard Wainwright, who had been executive officer of the *Maine* when that battleship was lost, the *Gloucester,* with the smaller 545-ton *Vixen,* tackled the Spanish destroyers

Pluton and *Furor* at the Battle of Santiago, sinking the *Pluton* and driving the *Furor* ashore a wreck. This exploit was grist for the journalists' mills and Wainwright was hailed as a hero of the day.

Recognizing the need for large numbers of small auxiliary warships to round out the great postwar naval expansion, and realizing that funds would not be forthcoming to build such craft in addition to the battleships, cruisers, and destroyers needed to provide bone and sinew for the new fleet, the Navy Department decided to retain the best of the war-acquired yachts for peacetime service as submarine tenders, supply ships, miscellaneous auxiliaries, and training vessels for the state Naval Militias.

The longest-lived of these vessels was the *Mayflower*, which, following the war, served briefly as a floating headquarters for the American governor of Puerto Rico at San Juan, and later as Admiral Dewey's flagship. In 1904 the *Mayflower* was refitted as the presidential yacht, and for the next quarter-century took part in nearly every major U.S. naval ceremonial function. The delegates who met to end the Russo-Japanese War gathered on her decks at Oyster Bay, Long Island, in 1905, and the following year President Theodore Roosevelt journeyed in her to Panama to view progress on the new canal. In 1907 he reviewed the departing Great White Fleet from aboard the *Mayflower,* and in her in 1909 welcomed its battleships back to Hampton Roads. President William H. Taft loved the palatial yacht, and on her decks Woodrow Wilson courted the woman who would become his second wife. Finally, in 1929, the *Mayflower* was retired from presidential duty. During subsequent reconstruction as a gunboat she caught fire, burned, and sank. The hull was salvaged, however, and after passing through a succession of owners was rebuilt to serve the U.S. Coast Guard in World War II as a convoy escort and radar training ship. In 1948 the old veteran reappeared for a final burst of glory as the Panamanian-flag vessel *Malla,* transporting Jewish refugees to Palestine.

Another yacht, the *Hawk,* served until the eve of World War II as a militia and training vessel, but most of the Spanish-War conversions were phased out much earlier as more suitable vessels—submarine chasers, patrol craft, and minesweepers—were added to the fleet. During two World Wars, however, the need for small and handy craft sent the Navy back to the yacht squadrons, and pleasure boats continued to perform well the duties for which they were never designed, just as they had during the heyday of the Steel Navy.

The 850-ton Scorpion, *stripped down and painted lead gray, receives her Spanish War armament of four 5-inch and six 6-pounder rapid-fire guns at the New York Navy Yard.*

Pleasure Craft at War

In a May 1898 photograph, the newly commissioned Viking *gets underway at New York while another converted yacht just astern receives finishing touches. Displacing only 218 tons, the* Viking *was armed with a single 1-pounder on the forecastle and three Colt automatics. She had a regular Navy crew and later saw duty off Cuba. Most of the smaller yachts, however, were manned by Naval Militiamen and served on harbor patrol or coastal picket duty out of East Coast ports. After hostilities ended a few were retained as tenders, training ships, and miscellaneous auxiliaries, but most were sold or returned to their owners.*

The 786-ton Gloucester, *originally financier John Pierpont Morgan's* Corsair, *was typical of the larger converted yachts. Armed with 3- and 6-pounder rapid-fire guns, she earned a dashing reputation under the command of brilliant Lieutenant Commander Richard Wainwright. At Santiago she guarded the shoreward flank of the blockading squadron and was commended for successfully engaging the Spanish destroyers* Furor *and* Pluton. *Like most of the other big yachts, the* Gloucester *continued to serve the Navy for many years following the Spanish-American War in a variety of roles, including duty as a Naval Academy school ship, tender, militia training ship, and patrol vessel.*

The clipper-bowed Glacier, *built in England in 1891 as the 8,300-ton merchantman* Port Chalmers,
served as one of the U.S. Navy's first refrigerated storeships from 1898 to 1922.

Auxiliaries of the Steel Navy

Although a few specialized auxiliary ships had been improvised during the Civil War, about the only types to see regular service with the Navy up to the outbreak of the Spanish-American War were a few supply ships and tugs. Such material and personnel as could not be transported on board warships en route to and from foreign stations were usually carried commercially by regular merchantmen. The only new auxiliary craft built during the early years of the Steel Navy were seven tugs laid down beginning in 1891, all of which subsequently had long and useful careers.

During the 1890s the Navy's preoccupation with commerce raiding led to an interest in the employment of big, fast passenger steamers as auxiliary cruisers in time of war. In 1891 Congress was persuaded to authorize the use of mail contracts to stimulate the construction of vessels incorporating features that would facilitate their conversion into warships, and by 1898 more than twenty such subsidized U.S. steamers were in commercial service. During the Spanish-American War several of the best of these—the *El Norte, El Rio, El Sol, El Sud, Venezuela,* and *Yumuri* (renamed the *Yankee, Dixie, Prairie, Yosemite, Panther,* and *Badger*)—were hastily purchased by the Navy, armed with respectable batteries of 4-, 5-, and 6-inch guns, and sent out on patrol in the Atlantic and Caribbean. Another vessel of the type, the *Nictheroy* (formerly *El Cid,* renamed *Buffalo*), was obtained from Brazil (see photo on page 114). Four larger subsidized U.S. steamers, the *St. Louis, St. Paul, New York* (renamed *Harvard*), and *Paris* (renamed *Yale*), were also leased from their owners for war use at rates of up to $2,500 per day.

During the Caribbean campaign the auxiliary cruisers captured or destroyed several merchant vessels, and the *St. Paul* even succeeded in putting the Spanish torpedo boat *Terror* out of action during an enagagement off San Juan, Puerto Rico. Several of the cruisers also served part of the time as scouts and as transports for Marines and Army troops. Probably the most outstanding exploits were those of the crew of the big 17,000-ton *St. Louis,* which successfully located and cut several submarine telegraph cables along the southern coast of Cuba in spite of heavy hostile fire.

A somewhat different situation prevailed in the Pacific, where the Spanish posed no direct threat to U.S. shores. Commodore George Dewey, operating independently far from home, purchased the small transport *Zafiro* and the collier *Nanshan* just before the outbreak of hostilities and thus freed his cruisers for operations away from shore bases, of which the United States had none in the Far East until after the capture of the Philippines. Thereafter the big problem lay in getting troops and supplies all the way from the U.S. West Coast to Manila, and for this purpose several merchant ships, including the *City of Pekin,* were chartered but not actually taken into the Navy.

Seventeen colliers, mostly of English or Scottish origin, were purchased by the Navy for the vital role of keeping its war fleet supplied with fuel. One of these ships, the *Merrimac,* was scuttled at Santiago in June 1898 in a daring but unsuccessful attempt to trap Admiral Cervera's squadron in the harbor. Another collier, the *Pedro* (renamed *Hector*), was captured as a prize from Spain.

The Navy also purchased twenty-seven tugs, intended primarily to serve with the converted yachts as auxiliary gunboats on the coastal picket line. Some, however, joined their Navy sisters in traditional tugboat duties, and several of these were retained in service for many years after the war.

Also requisitioned for the duration were fifteen Revenue Service cutters, four lighthouse tenders, three Coast Survey ships, and two Fish Commission vessels. These served as auxiliary gunboats and patrol vessels until returned to their respective agencies when they could be spared.

"Special class" vessels formed the most interesting group of auxiliaries. The *Arctic,* an ice boat loaned by the city of Philadelphia for one dollar, saw little service. Two Boston ferryboats, the *East Boston* and *Governor Russell,* and a pilot boat, the *Peoria,* were armed for the picket force. The *Zafiro* and *Supply,* which were classified as supply ships, also proved invaluable to Dewey as dispatch vessels and small transports. The refrigerator ships *Celtic, Glacier,* and *Culgoa* shuttled beef, mutton, and ice from Australia to Manila Bay. The *Resolute* and *Manila* were transports, and the *Arethusa* was the Navy's first oil tanker.

Two other vessels, the *Iris* and *Rainbow,* were outfitted as distilling ships, blockade-force·operations in warm southern waters having demonstrated that evaporator facilities aboard most U.S. warships were unable to meet demands for fresh water for boilers and personnel. The two auxiliaries were each equipped with evaporators capable of producing up to 60,000 gallons of fresh water per day, but the conversion was completed too late for their use in the war.

Most of the colliers and supply ships were manned by merchant seamen, with only a nucleus of naval personnel on board. The *Iris,* for example, carried a commissioned line officer as commanding officer in addition to her merchant master, and a paymaster, a yeoman, and an apprentice for signal duties.

The *Solace,* formerly the *Creole,* was employed as a Navy ambulance ship. The Army also used its own ships *Relief* and *Bay State* in hospital service during the war. Experience with the *Solace* was so promising that in 1902 the Secretary of the Navy asked (but was denied) authorization to build two specially designed hospital ships. Instead the *Relief* was turned over to the Navy and refitted at Mare Island. Although work was completed by 1904, a general shortage of officers prevented her commissioning until 1908.

Much interest was shown in the repair ship *Vulcan* (ex-steamer *Chatham*), which during the war was hurriedly equipped with forges, a foundry, pattern and coppersmith shops, machine tools, stores of spare parts, and a skilled force of about a hundred mechanics, and which performed yeoman service at Guantanamo Bay in keeping U.S. warships in operation without their having to leave the blockading force. At times fully a third of the force was in need of major repairs, and the Navy's chief engineer later observed that "with the exception of the battleship *Oregon,* there was not a vessel on the south side of Cuba that contributed indirectly more [than the *Vulcan*] to the destruction of Admiral Cervera's squadron." This first Navy repair ship was, however, judged too small and too slow for ideal performance. Experience with her showed that a proper vessel of the type should have high decks, large hatches, a wide beam, enough speed to keep up with the fleet, and plenty of commodious storerooms for parts. Many years would elapse before the Navy would ob-

tain authorization to build its first repair ship from the keel up, but in 1904 a floating repair shop, the *Alpha,* was completed at the New York Navy Yard to service ships at Tompkinsville, Staten Island.

Immediately after the war many of the purchased ships were converted to other uses. The tools of the *Vulcan* were removed and installed in the collier *Marcellus,* and one of the auxiliary cruisers, the *Panther,* was also subsequently equipped as a repair ship. (During 1907–09 the *Panther* and the refrigerator ships *Culgoa* and *Glacier* provided support to the Battle Fleet on its around-the-world cruise.) Another auxiliary cruiser, the *Buffalo,* became in effect the first destroyer tender when she escorted the First Torpedo Flotilla to Manila in 1904. The conversion was made official in 1918. Other familiar veterans which ultimately served as submarine or destroyer tenders included the *Rainbow, Dixie,* and *Prairie.*

Some of the colliers also saw varied careers. These former merchantmen were essentially big, slow, floating coal bins, and the job of loading bunkers from them was the curse of every warship's crew. Experiments with early coaling-at-sea rigs emphasized the deficiencies in the converted ships, and a number of new naval colliers were subsequently authorized, beginning with the *Vestal* and *Prometheus* in 1904 (both of which were later converted to fleet repair ships). After 1910 these were followed by vessels of the *Jupiter* type —huge ships with their boilers and engines far aft and with a veritable forest of derricks and kingposts. As these big fleet colliers entered service the ex-merchantmen were gradually phased out or used to haul coal from port to port. A few of the old colliers were also converted to other auxiliary roles and served with the Navy on into the 1920s. Among the better known of these were the *Leonidas,* which became a destroyer tender; *Pompey,* a refrigerated store ship; *Southery,* the notorious prison ship; *Hannibal,* a surveying ship and miscellaneous auxiliary; and several, including the *Abarenda, Ajax, Lebanon,* and *Nanshan,* which became station ships.

It is beyond the scope of this account to trace the later careers of all of the Spanish-American War purchased auxiliaries, but their influence on the New Navy was far greater than their humble origins would have indicated. From them sprang a long line of specially designed fleet colliers and oilers, refrigerated store ships, distilling ships, tenders and repair ships, surveying ships, and hospital ships that formed the Base Force of the fleet, and ultimately the great mobile forward bases that supported the World War II advance across the Pacific.

The 4,800-ton Badger *was outfitted with six 5-inch guns and, along with ten other large ex-merchantmen, was employed as an auxiliary cruiser and transport during the Spanish-American War.*

Ships of the Auxiliary Force

The 3,100-ton Relief, *a former coastal passenger-cargo steamer, served as an Army hospital ship during the war with Spain. Later transferred to the Navy, she was refitted and commissioned in 1908 under the command of a medical officer, whose appointment precipitated a major intraservice controversy over line versus staff relationships. During the world cruise of the Great White Fleet, the* Relief *accompanied the battleships from Hawaii to the Philippines, where she was left behind for repairs. In November 1908 she nearly foundered in a Pacific typhoon and thereafter served as an immobile floating dispensary at Olongapo. Another hospital ship, the* Solace, *was manned by the Navy during the Spanish-American War.*

The 6,200-ton naval auxiliary Rainbow *was the former merchantman* Norse King. *Purchased in 1898 for conversion to a distilling ship, she missed war service but was sent to the Asiatic Fleet in 1902. For the next twenty-six years the* Rainbow *served variously as a flagship, torpedo boat tender, transport, general auxiliary, and finally submarine tender. Of the many similar merchant vessels taken into the Navy during the Spanish-American War, most served as colliers, but others became repair ships, supply ships, tenders, and other useful auxiliaries to the growing fleet of warships that entered service just after the turn of the century.*

The ex-Spanish gunboats Isla de Cuba *and* Isla de Luzon, *salvaged from the shallows of Manila Bay, wear temporary thatched roofs to provide shade during their refit for U.S. naval service.*

Prizes of War

Soon after the outbreak of war in 1898 the Navy began capturing Spanish vessels off Cuba and in the Philippines. Most were unarmed merchantmen of no particular interest, but several warships also fell into American hands, either through outright capture or as wrecks sunk in action or scuttled by their crews. As was the custom in those days, most of these captured or salvaged prizes were incorporated directly into their captor's navy as legitimate spoils of war.

The largest haul came with the U.S. occupation of the Philippines. On 2 May a boarding party from Commodore George E. Dewey's newly victorious squadron commandeered the 1,900-ton transport *Manila,* which had been run aground and abandoned just off Cavite. Ten days later the 200-ton gunboat *Callao* was intercepted while attempting to escape the U.S. blockade and was quickly placed in service against her erstwhile owners. During the next few months a total of eighteen small gunboats, one torpedo boat, four tugs, a lighthouse tender, and six yard craft were taken over by the Army or Navy. In several cases the Army purchased vessels and, after operating them for a while, gave them to the Navy.

The major prizes in the Philippines were the 1,000-ton gunboats *Don Juan de Austria, Isla de Cuba,* and *Isla de Luzon,* all sunk during the naval battle off Manila and later raised and repaired for the U.S. Navy by a commercial salvage firm. The *Arayat,* a small iron gunboat that had been scuttled in the Pasig River, was also restored to operation.

Although most war prizes in Cuban waters were merchant vessels, two 100-ton gunboats—the *Alvarado* and *Sandoval*—were captured for later U.S. naval use. Three of the four Spanish armored cruisers driven ashore during the 3 July battle off Santiago were beyond salvage, but the 6,400-ton *Infanta Maria Teresa* was found to be nearly intact. After many setbacks, a salvage company managed to get the cruiser afloat and she was taken under tow for Norfolk. During a storm en route the *Teresa* had to be cut loose, however, and when found several days later in the Bahamas she was so hard aground that salvage efforts had to be abandoned.

One other Spanish cruiser at Santiago, the 3,090-ton *Reina Mercedes* (a contemporary of the ABCD ships), had been in such poor condition that she was unable to sortie with Cervera's squadron, and had instead been scuttled in an attempt to block the harbor entrance. The old cruiser was refloated and towed to Norfolk, where she was housed over for use as a receiving ship. In 1912 the *Reina Mercedes* was shifted to Annapolis, where she would serve for forty-five years as a station ship and brig for errant midshipmen.

The ex-Spanish gunboats in the Philippines were kept busy for several years helping suppress an insurrection that flared under guerrilla general Emilio Aguinaldo in 1899. One gunboat, the *Urdaneta,* ran aground and was temporarily overrun by the insurgents, who killed her captain and several of the crew.

Most of the Philippine gunboats were inherited in poor condition and some were always being laid up at Cavite for repairs while their crews moved on to others. Nevertheless, their shallow draft made the craft useful for navigating the narrow channels and rivers of the archipelago to deliver supplies to the Army and to bring their own rapid-fire guns to bear on guerrilla positions ashore. Typically commanded by a youthful and ambitious lieutenant and manned by one or two even more junior officers and about thirty-five enlisted men, the little ships provided glamorous and challenging independent duty. The gunboat officers later banded together as "The Ancient and Honorable Sons of Gunboats" to perpetuate the memory of these romantic and often dangerous operations.

By 1902 the rebellion was well enough in hand to permit a reduction in gunboat strength, and a number of the boats were laid up or disposed of. The *Elcano, Pampanga,* and *Villalobos* remained in use until 1928, however, and a few of the old Spanish tugs and launches were still on hand when the Japanese captured the Philippines in 1942.

Trophies from Manila Bay

The 1,000-ton Isla de Cuba—*seen above off Cavite in 1903—and her near-sister* Isla de Luzon *were built in England for Spain during the late 1880s. Both were scuttled and partially burned out at the Battle of Manila Bay. Following reconstruction at Hong Kong they helped suppress guerrilla forces during the Philippine Insurrection, and later served in the United States as militia training ships. The* Isla de Cuba *ultimately sailed under a third navy's flag as the Venezuelan gunboat* Mariscal Sucre. *The Spanish-built gunboat* Don Juan de Austria, *opposite, was also sunk at Manila and salvaged for the Navy. In addition to peace-keeping duty in the Philippines, she later saw service protecting U.S. interests along the China coast.*

Cuban War Prizes

Sailors from a New York newspaper's press boat pick their way across the capsized hull of the 6,800-ton armored cruiser Cristobal Colon, defeated at the Battle of Santiago. Sent into battle without her main battery, the Colon *struck her flag and was beached after a fifty-mile chase by U.S. warships. Although the finest vessel in the Spanish squadron—and the least damaged by U.S. naval gunfire—she was so effectively scuttled that no serious attempts were ever made to refloat her. Of the five Spanish cruisers at Santiago, only the old* Reina Mercedes *was ultimately salvaged.*

The little 100-ton English-built gunboat Alvarado, *above, was captured by the U.S. Army at Santiago.
Turned over to the Navy, she was recommissioned in time to take part in several engagements in
Cuban waters. A sister ship, the* Sandoval, *was scuttled by the Spanish at Guantanamo Bay and salvaged
by the Navy. Both gunboats were subsequently refitted in the United States and served for a number
of years as training ships with various state Naval Militias. One other Cuban war prize, the merchant
steamer* Pedro, *was also commissioned briefly into the U.S. Navy as the collier* Hector.

With the navigating party on the bridge and leadsmen in the chains, the battleship
Illinois *is about to pass under the Brooklyn Bridge in this 1902 photograph.*

Continued Battleship Expansion

The impetus gained with authorization of two battleships in 1895 continued the following year when Congress approved funds for three more. Building contracts for these new 11,565-ton battleships—the *Illinois, Alabama,* and *Wisconsin*—were awarded, respectively, to the Newport News Shipbuilding and Dry Dock Company, William Cramp and Sons, and the Union Iron Works. Although the *Illinois* was assigned the lowest hull number of the three, her subsequent construction at Newport News was slowed by concurrent work on the *Kearsarge* and *Kentucky,* and the battleships completed by the other two yards preceded her into commission by nearly a year.

These vessels bore somewhat the same design relationship to the *Kearsarge*-class battleships that the *Iowa* had shared with the *Indiana* class. General hull form and dimensions were the same as in the *Kearsarge,* but freeboard was increased by the addition of a long forecastle and spar deck extending aft for nearly three-quarters of the length of each ship. As in the *Iowa,* this refinement gave the forward turret a more commanding prospect, improved the seakeeping qualities, and provided more spacious berthing facilities for the crew. There was almost no increase in displacement, however, and the draft, as in previous U.S. battleships, was necessarily limited to less than twenty-four feet by the shallow depth of most principal U.S. harbors. In armament and boiler arrangement the ships were strikingly similar to contemporary British battleships, but they were smaller, slower, and had shorter cruising ranges, reflecting the differing strategic and operational requirements of the two navies.

A major departure in battleship armament was made by discarding the 8-inch intermediate battery of the previous three classes—to the dismay of many fleet officers—and adopting a heavy secondary battery of fourteen 6-inch rapid-fire guns mounted in sponsons in the hull and casemates on the upper decks. Although the greater penetrating power of the 8-inch rifles was thus sacrificed, the much higher firing rate

of the new 6-inch guns resulted in an overall increase in weight of fire, and simplicity was served by the employment of fewer calibers of ammunition.

As in the *Kearsarge* class, the main-battery guns were of thirteen-inch caliber, but in these ships the turrets were elliptical in shape, with an inclined front and an overhang at the rear. This design provided a turret that was fully balanced for ease of train under all conditions of roll or list; one that had substantially smaller gun-port openings and much greater resistance to penetration; and which was lighter and more efficient than the traditional cylindrical turret, which had working room to spare at the sides of the guns but too little at the breeches, and which presented an unnecessarily large target to the enemy.

Although the propulsion machinery in the *Illinois* and her sisters was essentially the same as in the previous class, the steam-plant arrangement was completely revised, all of the boilers being mounted fore-and-aft with the firerooms outboard of them to either side. This disposition, which was intended to provide easier access to the coal bunkers and better communications between firerooms, necessitated placing the two stacks side by side, a common British practice but unique in the U.S. Navy.

No new battleships were provided for by Congress in 1897, but three more were authorized in 1898 as part of the major fleet expansion program stemming from the Spanish War crisis. These new ships were at first intended to be near-repeats of the *Illinois* class, but subsequently, in hopes of bringing U.S. battleship speed and endurance more in line with contemporary foreign practice, the Department invited bidders to submit their own proposals for designs. The resulting accepted plans were for a battleship twenty feet longer than its predecessors, over seven hundred tons greater in displacement, and having increased bunker capacity and a top speed in excess of eighteen knots. The unusual athwartships fireroom arrangement of the *Illinois*-class battleships was dropped, modern water-tube boilers were adopted and their number increased, and a third stack was added to accommodate them.

The lead ship of the new class was named the *Maine* and her keel was laid on 15 February 1899, one year to the day after the loss of her namesake at Havana. The other two battleships were named the *Missouri* and *Ohio*. As before, one ship was awarded to each major private shipyard.

A new 12-inch rifle, designed expressly for use with newly developed smokeless powder, was employed for the first time in these ships, and in spite of the projectiles' being considerably lighter than those for 13-inch guns (850 pounds versus 1,100 pounds), a substantial increase in muzzle velocity resulted in greater over-all destructive power. The increased length of the *Maine*-class battleships permitted designers to add two 6-inch rapid-fire guns to the secondary battery, increasing the number of these guns to sixteen.

Armor hardened by the Krupp process was also introduced with this class of battleships, and its great toughness allowed the thickness of the armor belt to be reduced from the more than sixteen inches of Harveyized steel in the *Maine* class to eleven inches without a sacrifice in protection. Another new development was the use of submerged torpedo tubes in place of above-surface mountings, which had been found dangerously vulnerable to shellfire. Because of the relative complexity of underwater launch tubes the United States had been late in adopting them, but henceforth this type would be a standard battleship feature in the Steel Navy.

Both the *Illinois* and *Maine* classes were well-conceived and well-executed battleships for the turn of the century, but their heyday was to be a brief one. Really designed for the war just fought, the new ships were soon left behind by the rapid pace of naval progress. The great cruise around the world in 1907–09 came just in time for them to display their apparent power to nations which did not yet realize that new developments had already doomed such vessels to second-line, utilitarian, service for the remainder of their allotted span.

Massive 13-inch rifles dominate a forecastle view on the Alabama, *a sister to the* Illinois. *Modern inclined-face turrets were introduced to the U.S. Navy with this class of battleship.*

Turn-of-the-Century Battleships

The 11,565-ton Illinois, *seen above in a 1903 photograph, and the* Alabama *and* Wisconsin *were easily recognized by their side-by-side stacks, necessitated by the unorthodox athwartships layout of the boilers and fire rooms. With these ships the Navy temporarily abandoned the 8-inch intermediate battery and increased the size of the secondary battery to include fourteen 6-inch rapid-fire guns of new design. Although the forward pair of 6-inchers—mounted in sponsons on the main deck—proved miserably wet at sea and consequently was of little fighting value, the general seakeeping qualities of the ships were improved over those of the previous class by the addition of a forecastle deck.*

The three 12,370-ton battleships of the Maine *class were stretched versions of their predecessors in which the additional length was employed for extra boilers and secondary-battery guns. The caliber of the main-battery rifles once again reverted to twelve inches, but the modern guns created for use with smokeless powder were more powerful than those of any previous U.S. design. The* Maine, *pictured above in about 1907, was easily distinguished from the* Missouri *and* Ohio *by the somewhat larger diameter of her three stacks. Fitted with twenty-four Niclausse boilers, she was notorious as one of the Navy's most greedy coal burners, and on long voyages frequently almost exhausted her fuel supply.*

The Marine detachment in spiked helmets musters on the Alabama's *quarterdeck in the summer of 1903, probably in anticipation of visiting dignitaries. Protection for the casemated rifles of the formidable-appearing broadside battery, at far right, was improved over that in previous battleships by the addition of steel splinter shields between each pair of guns. However, the light shields mounted on the exposed quick-firing guns of the anti-torpedo battery, high on the superstructure, were considered by many gunnery officers to be more of a hazard than a protection under fire.*

With topsides nearly completed and steam temporarily rigged up to her whistle,
the new battleship Georgia *salutes her own launching at Bath, Maine, 11 October 1904.*

Resurgence of the Two-Story Turret

Battleship construction continued apace during the expansionist years following the Spanish-American War, as the United States moved to acquire the trappings of empire in the Pacific and Caribbean. In 1899 Congress appropriated funds for three new battleships and the following year, before work had even begun on these, construction of two more of identical size was approved. The designs for these warships abandoned all pretense of a limited coast-defense mission—they were to be first-class battleships in every respect, with a length of 435 feet, displacement of nearly 15,000 tons, and a speed of nineteen knots.

In 1900 a special Board of Construction, composed of senior officers from the various concerned bureaus, convened to determine the final specifications for the new battleships. The members were in agreement on the selection of 12- and 6-inch guns for the main and secondary batteries, and also upon the reintroduction of an intermediate battery of 8-inch guns, which had been omitted from the last two classes. There were strong differences of opinion, however—particularly between the heads of the Bureaus of Ordnance and Construction and Repair—regarding the most suitable disposition of the four two-gun turrets of the intermediate battery. In a compromise solution the Board finally recommended that two of the ships should have 8-inch turrets in a quadrilateral arrangement as in the *Indiana* class, while in the other three ships a pair of turrets should be superposed on the main-battery turrets, as in the *Kearsarge* class, with the remaining pair flanking the superstructure amidships. Arguments pro and con flared anew a few months later, however, and the Secretary of the Navy appointed a new board with firm instructions to settle on one design for all five battleships. As a result the superposed arrangement plus wing turrets was ultimately adopted for the entire class.

Construction of the lead ship, the *Virginia,* was entrusted to the experienced Newport News Shipbuilding and Dry Dock Company, but other major civilian yards were already busy with existing contracts and new builders had to be found. The *Nebraska* was thus awarded to the Moran Brothers of Seattle, Washington; the *Georgia* to the Bath Iron Works of Bath, Maine; and the *New Jersey* and *Rhode Island* to the Fore River Shipbuilding Company of Quincy, Massachusetts.

Torpedo armament was improved over that in previous classes, each ship having four launch tubes designed for new turbine-driven models having long range and great destructive power. Armor protection was also more extensive, with the main waterline belts extending the full length of the hull. It was at first planned that three of the battleships would have wood-sheathed and coppered bottoms for resistance to fouling, but this idea was later dropped.

The *Virginia* was fitted with inward-turning propellers on the theory that this would improve her steering qualities, but in fact she was found to be most difficult to manage at low speeds or when docking. Her screws sucked a passing steamer into a sideswiping collision at Hampton Roads in 1906, and the scheme was so unsatisfactory that conventional outward-turning screws were installed after the *Virginia* returned from the world cruise of the Great White Fleet in 1909.

The superposed turrets also turned out to be much less effective than had been hoped. Improvements in loading arrangements and fire control, along with emphasis on target practice, soon increased the firing rate of the 12-inch batteries so much that the 8-inch rifles above could not be employed at their best rate without disrupting the aim or delaying the firing of the larger guns. As a result of this and other problems, the double-decked turret was never repeated again.

All of the *Virginia*-class battleships were relegated to training, transport, or convoy escort roles during World War I, and most were sold for scrap a few years later, but the *Virginia* and *New Jersey* were sunk as targets during Army General William L. "Billy" Mitchell's spectacular demonstration of air power in 1923.

Virginia-Class Battleships

Superposed turrets, introduced in the Kearsarge *and* Kentucky, *enjoyed a brief revival in the five ships of the* Virginia *class. The 14,948-ton* Virginia—*seen above at Hampton Roads in 1907—and her sisters were considerably larger and a full knot faster than the previous class of battleships, and boasted such refinements as a high freeboard from bow to stern, a large coal supply, modern watertube boilers, and full-length waterline armor belts. Statistically speaking the armament was impressive and included four 12-inch, eight 8-inch, and twelve 6-inch guns, but the superposed-turret concept lost favor almost as soon as it was tried in actual service. Secondary armament also included a dozen new 3-inch rapid-fire guns; armor-plated embrasures of four of these may be seen in the stern view of the* Georgia *on the opposite page.*

Officers and enlisted men of the Georgia *gather for a formal portrait on the forecastle of their battleship during the Jamestown Exposition of 1907.*

The new destroyer Worden *awaits a tow to the fitting-out pier at the Maryland Steel Company in Sparrows Point, Maryland, after being launched with her sisters* Truxtun *and* Whipple *on 15 August 1901.*

Introducing the Destroyer

Just as the U.S. Navy lagged far behind the fleets of Europe in torpedo boat design and construction, so was it late in adopting the destroyer. As early as 1885 the British had begun the development of torpedo boat "catchers, hunters, or destroyers" to protect their squadrons from torpedo craft, and by 1892 they had produced successful designs in the *Havock* and *Daring*—triple-screw, twenty-seven-knot boats displacing 240 and 260 tons. In 1898, when the first U.S. destroyers were authorized, the British already had ninety of the type in service or under construction and were working on their first turbine-drive ships.

In the U.S. Navy the first attempts to produce torpedo boat catchers were in the form of large experimental torpedo boats. The first of these, the *Farragut* of the 1896 program, was 214 feet long, displaced 279 tons, mounted four 6-pounder rapid-fire guns and a pair of torpedo tubes, and had a top speed of thirty knots. Perhaps the fact that the *Farragut* was a West Coast boat and was thus out of the mainstream of torpedo operations—which centered at Newport, Rhode Island—had something to do with her relatively insignificant career.

Three more large torpedo boats were authorized in 1897. Unfortunately all were awarded to relatively inexperienced builders. The 280-ton *Bailey*, built by a combination known as the Gas Engine and Power Company and Charles L. Seabury and Company Consolidated, of Morris Heights, New York, was completed and accepted in 1901 but had to spend the next two years in a navy yard having her hull strengthened. The other two were beset by even worse problems. The 340-ton *Stringham*, awarded to the Harlan and Hollingsworth Company of Wilmington, Delaware, suffered four accidents between 1899 and 1902 which thoroughly crippled her machinery. The company finally abandoned efforts to complete the required speed trials and turned the ship over to the government to finish as best it could. The 255-ton *Goldsborough* was built by Wolff and Zwicker of Portland, Oregon. In spite of fifteen major attempts over a two-year period she never made a successful speed trial. Her engines were wrecked, the builders forfeited the contract, and the ship was consigned to the Puget Sound Navy Yard for what was practically a rebuilding, finally to be commissioned in 1908.

Thus none of these early "destroyers" could be regarded as having any positive effect on U.S. destroyer development. They merely confirmed a lesson learned by the Royal Navy in the early 1890s—that the design and construction of destroyers was a job for specialists, such as the well-known Thornycroft and Yarrow firms of Great Britain.

In the absence of operational experience, the first group of true U.S. destroyers—sixteen of which were authorized in the expansion program of 1898—had to be patterned after foreign ships of the period or evolved from native torpedo boat designs. Actually, there were four distinct types in this so-called "class" of destroyers. Seven of the ships were built to three different designs produced by private builders. The *Hopkins* and *Hull* were built by the Harlan and Hollingsworth Company, which apparently had profited from its unhappy experience with the *Stringham*. The *Lawrence* and *Macdonough* were awarded to the Fore River Engine Company of East Braintree, Massachusetts, and launched in 1900; the *Truxtun, Whipple,* and *Worden* went to the Maryland Steel Company. All three of these private designs were essentially four-stacked enlargements of earlier torpedo boats with the characteristic sloping whaleback forecastle that was also a feature of British destroyers up to 1901.

The other nine destroyers were built to government plans developed by the Bureau of Construction and Repair, and apparently incorporated elements of British, French, and U.S. design. The *Bainbridge, Barry,* and *Chauncey* were awarded to Neafie and Levy of Philadelphia; the *Dale* and *Decatur* to the William R. Trigg Company of Richmond, Virginia; the *Paul Jones, Perry,* and *Preble* to the Union Iron Works of San Francisco; and the *Stewart* to the Gas Engine and Power Company of Morris Heights.

The sixteen destroyers ranged in length from 239 feet to

248 feet on the load-waterline with a twenty-four-foot beam, and their design displacements varied from 408 to 433 tons. Twin-screw, vertical triple-expansion engines generating 8,000 horsepower provided speeds of about twenty-nine knots. Armament in each included a pair of powerful 3-inch rapid-fire guns, five or six 6-pounders, and two torpedo tubes for a new longer version of the Whitehead torpedo. The complement numbered three officers and sixty-nine enlisted men.

All of the destroyers incorporated bilge keels to reduce the awful rolling that had so demoralized torpedo boat crews. Torpedo boat experience also showed that the traditional turtleback bow had more drawbacks than advantages, and the government-designed destroyers were instead built with high, flat forecastles to provide added deck room and improved seakeeping qualities. Midway during their construction, tests at the new model basin at the Washington Navy Yard disclosed that a modification to the hull lines was desirable, and a number of frames in the afterbody of each of the Navy-designed ships were removed and replaced. Other changes later found necessary included strengthening of the conning towers to withstand the shock of firing the 3-inch guns, and the relocation of the galleys in small deckhouses to improve habitability. The government-designed ships proved slightly slower than their sisters but set a successful pattern for U.S. destroyers up to the flush-deckers of World War I.

Even while these ships were building, however, experienced observers recognized that they would be too small for satisfactory service with the fleet, especially in the Pacific where the annexation of Hawaii had effectively extended the U.S. coastline several thousand miles westward. Nevertheless the little coal burners served the Navy long and well. In 1903 the old Torpedo Flotilla was reorganized into two units and the new First Flotilla (*Bainbridge, Barry, Chauncey, Dale,* and *Decatur*) was ordered to duty on the Asiatic Station. Accompanied by the converted tender *Buffalo* and sailing by way of Suez, the flotilla made the four-month, 15,000-mile voyage without serious incident, although several of the destroyers ran out of coal while crossing the Atlantic and had to be fueled at sea. In 1907–08 six remaining East Coast destroyers (*Hopkins, Hull, Lawrence, Stewart, Truxtun,* and *Whipple*) preceded the Battle Fleet around South America to San Francisco, and remained in West Coast waters for most of the next decade. All of the *Bainbridge*-class destroyers were pressed into arduous service against the German submarine force during the World War, a mission that was completely unthought of when they were designed to chase and destroy torpedo boats. One ship, the *Chauncey*, was accidentally rammed during night convoy operations west of Gibraltar and was lost along with her captain and twenty of the crew. All of the remaining destroyers were sold out of the service in 1920. Three of these—the *Truxtun, Whipple,* and *Worden*—were re-engined with diesels and spent many more years ferrying cargoes of bananas to market.

Sailors in the huge warships we call destroyers today would be aghast at the conditions of service in these frail cockleshells of the turn of the century, with their primitive living arrangements, bone-shaking reciprocating machinery, and smoke-spewing coal-burning boilers. Yet the path of evolution is clear, and these were the first of the line.

Destroyer No. 1, the Bainbridge, *nears completion at the Neafie and Levy yard in Philadelphia in 1902. The partially fitted-out warship alongside is the unarmored "peace" cruiser* Denver.

Pioneer Destroyers

Armed with rapid-fire guns of up to three inches in caliber, the Navy's first destroyers were designed as seagoing escorts to the fleet to protect it against torpedo boat attack. However, they also carried torpedo tubes for operations against larger warships. The Macdonough—*pictured above steaming out of Norfolk on two boilers in about 1907—and her sister* Lawrence *were built by the Fore River Ship and Engine Building Company of Massachusetts. In common with five other ships of private design they inherited the whaleback forecastle typical of most U.S. torpedo boats, but were unique in the closely spaced arrangement of their four stacks, all of the boilers having been installed forward of the engine rooms.*

Nine of the first sixteen U.S. torpedo boat destroyers—including the Paul Jones, *a West Coast ship seen above in about 1905—were built to Navy plans. Their designs featured a high forecastle cut away at the sides to provide firing clearance for the 6-pounder waist guns, an arrangement which proved superior at sea and which was perpetuated in several later classes. Although planned to displace 420 tons, most of the government-designed ships were about forty tons overweight when completed, and with a full load of stores, ammunition, and coal, they displaced nearly 700 tons. When thus loaded down for a long cruise the top speed was reduced from twenty-nine knots to less than twenty-five.*

The Torpedo Flotilla in Upkeep

Torpedo boat destroyers photographed in various stages of upkeep at the Norfolk Navy Yard in 1907 include (in the foreground, from left to right) the Hull, Lawrence, Hopkins, Whipple, *and* Truxtun. *The government-designed* Stewart *is moored to the pierhead at right. Torpedo boats of many classes occupy berths on both banks of the Elizabeth River, while the veteran Steel Navy cruiser* Atlanta—*used as a barracks ship for the torpedo boat crews—is moored on the far side. Later in the year all of the destroyers pictured here embarked on a five-month voyage around South America to the West Coast.*

The armored cruiser North Carolina, *still incomplete, works up to speed during contract trials off the coast of Maine in January 1908.*

The Armored Cruiser Squadron

Two developments in the late 1890s led to a revival of U.S. armored cruiser construction after a lapse of several years. One was a decision by Britain to build a large number of the type, beginning with the *Cressy* class in 1898. The other was the spectacular success achieved by the armored cruisers *New York* and *Brooklyn* during the war with Spain.

Curiously, there seemed to be no clearly defined concept of why this type of warship was needed by the Navy or how it was to be employed. The dominant British school looked on the armored cruiser as sort of a second-class battleship to be used as a fast arm of the battle fleet. Other European navies tended to regard it as a bigger and better version of the protected cruiser—a ship to show the flag on distant stations in time of peace and to destroy enemy commerce during war. Subsequent U.S. practice with the so-called "Big Ten" ships of the armored cruiser squadron appeared to combine elements of both theories.

Three armored cruisers were authorized in 1899: the *Pennsylvania,* awarded to William Cramp and Sons; the *West Virginia,* to the Newport News Shipbuilding and Dry Dock Company; and the *California,* to the Union Iron Works. An identical order the following year produced the *Colorado, Maryland,* and *South Dakota.* Each cruiser displaced 13,680 tons, was 502 feet in length—longer than any battleship—and had a battleship-size complement of more than eight hundred officers and enlisted men. A huge engineering plant, generating over 28,000 horsepower, provided a top speed of twenty-two knots. Protection and armament were far below battleship quality, however, with armor belts only six inches thick and main ordnance consisting of four 8-inch rifles in small turrets and fourteen 6-inchers in casemates.

The naval authorization bill of 1900 also included three curious hybrids which represented a legislative attempt to reverse the tide of warship growth. The "semi-armored" cruisers *Charleston, Milwaukee,* and *St. Louis*—essentially small *Pennsylvania*s and having about the same speed—dis-placed 9,700 tons each and were officially rated as protected cruisers. These ships had no turrets, carried unusually weak main batteries of fourteen 6-inch rapid-fire guns, and had only partial belts of 4-inch armor. They were severely criticized while still on paper, denounced as obsolete even before being placed in commission, and were employed in cruiser roles for only about five years before being relegated to duty as submarine tenders, administrative flagships, or receiving ships.

In 1902 a final class of armored cruiser was introduced with authorization of the *Tennessee* and *Washington,* awarded to the Cramp and New York Shipbuilding yards. Two additional ships of the class, the *North Carolina* and *Montana,* were approved in 1904 and awarded to the Newport News shipyard. In these 14,500-ton vessels, representing the highest plane of U.S. armored cruiser development, the twenty-two-knot speed of the *Pennsylvania* class was retained, the armor belts were extended to cover more area, and the armament was strengthened to near-battleship quality with four 10-inch rifles and sixteen 6-inch rapid-fire guns.

During much of their careers the "Big Ten" armored cruisers were assigned to detached service on stations in the Far East, Europe, and South America, but for several years after establishment of the Pacific Fleet, in 1908, two divisions of the big ships comprised the major U.S. naval strength on the West Coast. About this time, however, the armored cruiser type became eclipsed by the appearance in the Royal Navy of the first battle cruisers, fast counterparts of the dreadnought battleship. During the First World War U.S. armored cruisers served in secondary roles as convoy escorts and troop transports, and the *San Diego* (ex-*California*) was the only large U.S. warship lost, being sunk by a German submarine-laid mine off Fire Island. After the war the majority of the armored cruisers were placed in reserve and by the early 1930s were scrapped. Only the *Seattle* (ex-*Washington*) survived as a receiving ship at New York until 1946.

"Big Ten" Armored Cruisers

Four towering stacks amidships gave all of the later U.S. armored cruisers a distinctive silhouette. The 13,680-ton Colorado, *seen above off Tompkinsville, New York in 1905, was one of six sisters of the* Pennsylvania *class. Their development generally followed practice in the Royal Navy, where the armored cruiser type had become quite popular a few years earlier. Armament included four 8-inch rifles in turrets, a broadside battery of fourteen 6-inch rapid-fire guns, and a pair of submerged tubes for 18-inch torpedoes.*

The four 14,500-ton ships of the Tennessee *class were the same length as the* Pennsylvania *but with their 10-inch main guns were practically second-class battleships. Armor protection was also more extensive than in the previous class, the number of guns in the broadside battery was increased to sixteen, and the torpedo armament was strengthened to four 21-inch tubes. Later in their careers all of the ships of the armored cruiser squadron lost their names to new battleships. The* Tennessee, *seen above in a 1908 photograph, was renamed the* Memphis. *In August 1916 she was washed ashore and wrecked by a huge seismic wave at Santo Domingo in the Caribbean.*

"Semi-Armored" Cruisers

The second Charleston—*seen on the opposite page at Bremerton in 1907, and above off San Francisco the following year—and her sisters* St. Louis *and* Milwaukee, *were 9,700-ton semi-armored hybrids bearing a superficial resemblance to the "Big Ten" cruisers. The main battery of fourteen 6-inch rapid-fire guns, which included a pair of exposed mounts on the main deck, right, was puny armament for such a big ship. The armor belts were also inadequate, being only four inches thick and extending for less than two hundred feet abreast the engine and boiler spaces. The* Milwaukee *was wrecked in January 1917 when, during an attempt to pull the grounded submarine H-3 off a northern California beach, she swung broadside into the breakers.*

The gunboat Nashville *was distinguished by slender smoke pipes towering nearly sixty feet above the waterline. Her quadruple-expansion power plant was one of the most sophisticated of the era.*

Gunboat Diplomacy and Banana Wars

Gunboat construction, temporarily halted by Secretary of the Navy Benjamin Tracy in 1889, was resumed four years later when Congress authorized funds for three 1,400-ton craft for service in the Far East. Experience on the Asiatic Station with existing gunboats, as well as with the old side-wheel steamer *Monocacy*, had demonstrated a need for ships especially designed to suit the peculiar requirements of that vast region. Commanders had learned that a large cruising radius was required in Far Eastern waters because naval bases and coaling stations were few and scattered. A shallow draft was also necessary, since the rivers along the China coast were shallow and poorly charted, frequently shifting their courses. Finally, spacious, well-ventilated berth decks were needed to preserve the health of the crew in tropical climates and to shelter refugees or to transport troops during times of political unrest.

The design for the first of the new ships, the *Nashville*, incorporated a full spar deck in place of the usual well deck amidships, increasing room for living accommodations and making the ship dryer at sea. The gunboat's unique power plant, which was designed for economical operation both at higher speeds and when cruising, consisted of a pair of four-cylinder engines and a combination of traditional cylindrical fire-tube boilers and lightweight high-pressure water-tube boilers of advanced design. At full power the engines were quadruple expansion, but during normal cruising their low-pressure cylinders were disconnected for efficient triple-expansion operation.

Because the *Nashville* was intended for general service in coastal and offshore waters, she was given a moderately shallow draft of eleven feet as a compromise between the requirements for river navigability and seaworthiness. Navy designers specified that her hull be of composite construction (wood planking over steel frames) to reduce marine fouling, but in a frustrating example of legalism triumphing over efficiency, it was discovered that since the authorizing act had stipu-

lated "steel vessels," composite construction would not be within the letter of the law and the plan had to be dropped.

The other new ships, the *Wilmington* and *Helena*, were designed expressly for river operations in China. Each drew only nine feet of water, was fitted with twin-screw propulsion and a pair of oversize rudders for positive control in swift-moving river currents, and had spacious personnel accommodations. A peculiar combination military mast and armored conning tower was designed to give the gunboat officers a commanding view over the fifty-foot-high banks and dikes of the Yangtze. A spiral staircase inside the six-foot-diameter mast provided access to the elevated conning tower in time of battle without exposure to small-arms fire. The high mast and tall, thin stack typical of Chief Engineer Melville's designs gave these ships an imposing, if somewhat top-heavy, appearance. Their engines were of the conventional triple-expansion type and were served by cylindrical boilers. Both river gunboats had generous coal bunkers and were fitted with inner bottoms under the engineering spaces for protection in the event of grounding.

All three ships were delayed in reaching their intended station by combat duty during the Spanish-American War. The *Nashville* had the distinction of firing the first shot of the war, capturing a merchant steamer during the initial hours of the Cuban naval blockade. She also was one of the longest-lived ships of the Steel Navy era, her stout hull surviving into the mid-1950s in the humble role of a lumber barge bearing the name *Richmond Cedar Works No. 4.*

Congress authorized six additional gunboats in 1895, and in these the Bureau of Construction and Repair was finally able to obtain composite hull construction. For economy of operation and to extend the cruising range, the 1,000-ton vessels *Annapolis, Vicksburg, Newport,* and *Princeton* were each given a single-screw power plant and a full barkentine rig spreading more than 11,000 square feet of canvas. The other two ships, the *Wheeling* and *Marietta*, were of about the same displacement but had more powerful twin-screw power plants and steadying sails only. The two types represented a compromise between contending schools of thought since, as Secretary of the Navy Hilary A. Herbert explained it, "one cannot have speed, endurance, and offensive power at the same time."

In 1898 Congress authorized another gunboat, Number 16, to replace the aged side-wheel steamer *Michigan* on the Great Lakes. However, State Department lawyers subsequently concluded that such construction would be in violation of the 1817 Rush-Bagot agreement limiting the size of warships on U.S.-Canadian waters, and the project was quietly abandoned. In 1914 the hull number was reassigned to the new Asiatic gunboat *Palos*.

Two final gunboats of the era, the *Dubuque* and *Paducah*, were authorized in 1902. Although notable in appearance for their rounded, spoon-shaped bows, these 1,085-ton ships were otherwise generally similar in characteristics and performance to their predecessors. Both served in the Caribbean prior to the First World War, keeping peace among the "Banana Republics" of Central America.

All of the gunboats of this period had main batteries of 4-inch rapid-fire guns, usually six or eight in number; speeds of thirteen to fifteen knots; and cruising ranges of 8,000 to 12,000 miles (except for the river gunboats, which were shorter-legged). Each was manned by a crew of 150 to 165 officers and enlisted men.

In the aftermath of the Spanish-American War, in 1899, Congress authorized a new class of six 3,191-ton "peace cruisers." Although about the same size as the protected cruisers of the *Cincinnati* class, the *Denver* and her sisters (*Des Moines, Chattanooga, Galveston, Tacoma,* and *Cleveland*) were designed along more conservative lines, having only about two-thirds the horsepower and two knots less speed at full power. Their more efficient plants gave the ships a higher sustained speed than in the *Cincinnati* class, however, and an increase in bunker capacity gave them much greater endurance. Their steel hulls were sheathed with pine and coppered for long service in tropical waters, and the vessels were furnished with roomy quarters for the crews. Each had a two-and-one-half-inch-thick protective deck and was armed with a main battery of ten 5-inch rapid-fire guns.

Construction of this class suffered from a low priority in comparison with the major battleship and armored cruiser programs, and several of the contracts were awarded to marginal builders. Two ships, the *Chattanooga* and *Galveston*, finally had to be towed to navy yards for completion because of the failure of their contractors. The Navy Department could not seem to make up its mind whether these vessels were cruisers or gunboats—both classifications were used at various stages of their careers—but their actual service was mainly as gunboats in Asiatic and Central American waters, where their enforcement of U.S. foreign policy came to epitomize the phrase "gunboat diplomacy."

The yachtlike Newport, *representative of a four-ship class of composite (wood plank on steel frame) gunboats, gets a tow out of the New York Navy Yard at the beginning of an 1897 cruise to Nicaragua.*

165

Light-Draft Gunboats

The 1,397-ton gunboat Helena *shows the flag in Asiatic waters some time after the turn of the century. The heavy military mast with armored conning tower in this ship and her sister, the* Wilmington, *was especially designed for visibility and protection during operations on high-banked Chinese rivers. The* Helena *spent most of her thirty-five-year career in the Far East, principally on the Yangtze and South China patrols. Built with an extremely shallow draft, the river gunboats were uncomfortable at sea and were notorious for their frequent fifty- to sixty-degree rolls.*

Although built with a composite steel and wood hull for service in tropical waters, the spoon-bowed Dubuque, *above, spent most of her service career operating off the U.S. East Coast and on the Great Lakes. In 1940 the 1,085-ton gunboat and her sister* Paducah *were recalled from reserve and modernized for patrol and training duty. Along with their cousin* Wheeling, *the ships were among the few veterans of the Steel Navy to serve through both World Wars.*

Wood-Sheathed Cruisers

The 3,191-ton Galveston, *above, was one of a class of six so-called "peace cruisers" of the* Denver *class laid down shortly after the war with Spain. Their design was deliberately optimized for peacetime service on remote stations, with sails—an anachronism after 1900—to extend their cruising range while economizing on coal, and with wood-sheathed and coppered hulls for long service without drydocking. Although they were too slow to accompany the fleet and too weakly armed and lightly protected to be of much military value in time of war, the peace cruisers were well suited for showing the flag and protecting American interests in Caribbean, Mediterranean, and Far Eastern waters.*

Galveston *crewmen prepare to fire her forecastle 5-inch gun during short-range target practice in the Philippines in about 1906. Primitive fire-control aids include the flexible speaking tube one sailor is holding to his ear at left, and the range-indicator box held aloft by a bluejacket on the opposite side of the gun.*

In a rare display of studding sails, the old apprentice training ship Monongahela *leaves Narragansett Bay under light airs in August 1901 to begin a six-month cruise to Europe.*

The Training Squadrons

The Navy has always needed training ships of various kinds, and the era of the Steel Navy was no exception. Then as now, older vessels of reduced military value were generally relegated to such duty. Some were assigned to the reserve units (then organized as state Naval Militias) for use as floating armories and as drill ships. These included such old-line sail and steam vessels as the *Dale, Minnesota, Portsmouth,* and *St. Louis,* and the Civil War monitors *Ajax, Nantucket,* and *Wyandotte.* After the Spanish-American War a number of newer monitors, gunboats, and converted yachts were also so employed. Other obsolete warships, including the *Enterprise, Saratoga,* and *St. Mary's,* were loaned to various states as training ships for their "nautical schools," counterparts to the modern state maritime academies. Then there were the receiving ships, floating barracks where men were enlisted into the Navy and billeted until detailed to the fleet or to training stations. These were mainly old hulks, some even ancient wooden ships-of-the-line, immobilized and housed over with great barn-like superstructures, and included such well-known veterans as the *Constitution, Franklin, Independence, Richmond, Vermont,* and *Wabash.* In a later era, several Steel Navy warships—notably the *Boston, Chicago, Illinois,* and *Washington*—would also serve in this role.

The main need for training ships, however, stemmed from the apprentice system and the later landsman-for-training system, under which newly enlisted boys and men received several months to a year of basic training at sea in ships especially detailed for the purpose. The Navy's apprentice training squadron during the 1880s and early '90s consisted of the sailing vessels *Jamestown, Portsmouth,* and *Saratoga,* which operated out of the naval training station on Coaster's Harbor Island at Newport, Rhode Island. Before embarking in these ships, which usually made two six-month cruises each year, apprentices received instruction aboard the old double-decked ship-of-the-line *New Hampshire,* which re-

mained alongside a pier at Newport as a drill and berthing ship. Towards the turn of the century these older vessels were replaced by the *Alliance, Essex,* and *Monongahela* in the Atlantic, and by the *Adams,* which operated out of a new training station on Yerba Buena Island in San Francisco Bay, in the Pacific.

Cruising ships assigned to the landsman program, which was inaugurated in 1899, included the *Hartford* and *Lancaster* in the Atlantic and the *Alert* and *Mohican* in the Pacific. Although training under sail was regarded by many authorities as ideal for developing the desired mental, physical, and moral qualities in new seamen, several steel warships were also pressed into training service after the turn of the century as increasing numbers of men were enlisted. These included the purchased gunboat *Topeka* and the auxiliary cruisers *Dixie, Prairie,* and *Yankee.*

Other vessels were needed to take Naval Academy cadets on their annual summer training cruises. Chief among these during the 1880s and '90s were the sailing ships *Constellation* and *Monongahela.* Warships also served year-around at Annapolis as drill ships, and before the turn of the century these included the old monitor *Passaic* and the sail and steam vessels *Wyoming, Enterprise,* and *Essex.* Later a number of more up-to-date vessels were assigned as Academy drill ships, and at various times between 1900 and 1909 these included the torpedo boats *Bagley, Gwin,* and *Talbot;* the gunboats *Alvarado* and *Sandoval;* the converted yacht *Gloucester;* the protected cruisers *Atlanta, Chicago, Newark,* and *Olympia;* and the monitors *Arkansas, Florida, Nevada, Puritan,* and *Terror.* The submarine torpedo boat *Holland* also was stationed there for a time to familiarize the midshipmen with the new mode of undersea warfare.

As the technology of the Steel Navy grew increasingly complex, several warships were also detailed for the specialized training of certain enlisted rates. Just after the turn of the century these included the monitor *Amphitrite* for seaman gunners, the fast cruisers *Columbia* and *Minneapolis* for engineers, and the protected cruiser *Cincinnati* for firemen.

In addition to all of these, the Steel Navy's training requirements were considered to be of sufficient importance to justify the construction of four brand-new training ships. The first of these, the 839-ton *Bancroft*, was authorized in 1888 and commissioned in 1893 as a practice and cruise vessel for cadets at the Naval Academy. Basically a steel gunboat similar to the *Petrel*, she incorporated a peculiar combination of modern vertical triple-expansion engines and an auxiliary barkentine sail rig, and for training purposes mounted four 4-inch rapid-fire guns and a pair of torpedo tubes. Because the *Bancroft* had accommodations for only about forty cadets in addition to the crew, she proved too small for efficient employment at the Naval Academy and after the 1896 summer cruise was transferred to conventional gunboat duties with the European and North Atlantic Squadrons. After the Spanish-American War she served as a survey vessel and station ship in the West Indies, and in 1906 was transferred to the Revenue Cutter Service and renamed *Itasca*.

In 1897 a replacement for the *Bancroft,* the full-rigged 1,175-ton *Chesapeake,* was authorized. Her birth in Congress was attended by considerable confusion, for although the *Chesapeake* had been designed for sail power alone, the words "steam and sail" were inadvertently placed in the authorizing legislation. When a subsequent bill was passed to delete the unwanted specifications, half of the $250,000 appropriation was also cut! It was not until the following year that the necessary funds for construction were restored. The *Chesapeake*'s hull was of steel, sheathed with yellow pine and coppered (making her the first vessel of the New Navy so outfitted), and her lower masts were of steel. She was armed with an up-to-date cruising-gunboat battery of six 4-inch rapid-fire guns; featured a complete installation of auxiliary machinery including generators, steam pumps, distilling plant, reefer, and steam heat; and had ample accommodations for more than 250 crewmen and naval cadets. Although appropriately bearing the name of the bay adjacent to the Naval Academy, the *Chesapeake* also coincidentally commemorated an older *Chesapeake,* the unfortunate frigate that had been twice captured by the British, in 1807 and 1813. To some Navy officers this seemed hardly appropriate for a Naval Academy vessel, and with presidential approval the ship's name was changed to *Severn* in 1905. The *Severn* trained midshipmen at Annapolis until 1910, after which she served as a submarine berthing ship, and in 1916 she was sold into merchant service as the sailing bark *John J. Phillips.*

In 1903 the advocates of sail succeeded in having three more unusual training ships authorized along with the major fleet expansion programs. Two, the *Cumberland* and *Intrepid,* were identical 1,800-ton steel barks, constructed at the Boston and Mare Island Navy Yards for service with the enlisted training squadrons. Like the *Chesapeake,* they had steam power for auxiliaries but sail power alone for propulsion. Each was fitted with generous accommodations for more than 330 officers and enlisted men, and was armed with six 4-inch and several smaller guns. The third ship, the 345-ton sailing brig *Boxer,* was even more of an anachronism. Intended for short training cruises out of Newport, she was entirely of wooden construction and had no machinery at all.

These three ships saw only limited employment in their intended roles, for in 1904—before they had even been completed—the Navy's training squadrons were disbanded along with the apprentice and landsman systems in favor of shore-based training followed by on-the-job experience in ships of the active fleet. The *Boxer* served at Newport and Annapolis until 1920, when she was transferred to the Interior Department for service in Alaskan waters. The *Intrepid* was used as a drill ship, receiving ship, and submarine crew barracks in San Francisco Bay until 1921, and was later cut down into a commercial barge which was wrecked on the coast of Washington in 1954. The *Cumberland* remained at Newport until 1912, then served as a training ship at Guantanamo and Norfolk, and in 1919 became a fixture at the Naval Academy where she survived as a barracks ship until 1947.

Monuments to the dying age of sail, the training ships of the Steel Navy provided a strange contrast to the modern battleships, cruisers, torpedo boat destroyers, and submarines that were their contemporaries.

Admiral Farragut's famous Civil War flagship Hartford, *photographed here after a complete reconstruction in 1895–99, served as an apprentice, landsman, and midshipman training ship during the early years of the new century.*

Steel Training Ships

The steam- and sail-powered Bancroft, *seen here in about 1895, was designed especially for training cadets at the Naval Academy. For instructional purposes she was fitted with four 4-inch rapid-fire guns and a pair of torpedo tubes, one in the bow and one athwartships on the berth deck. The 839-ton vessel's cadet accommodations proved too limited, however, and after a few years she was shifted to ordinary gunboat duties.*

The anachronistic Cumberland, *an 1,800-ton steel-hulled bark commissioned in 1907, served as a drill ship for apprentice seamen at Newport, Rhode Island. She had sail propulsion only— the thin stack served donkey boilers that powered a steam windlass, generators, and other auxiliaries. The* Cumberland *saw little cruising service, being (as seen here) chained securely to the dock most of the time. A sister ship, the* Intrepid, *was stationed at the Yerba Buena Training Station in San Francisco Bay.*

The 1,175-ton Naval Academy practice ship Chesapeake, *commissioned in 1899, had a wood-sheathed steel hull and was powered entirely by sail. In a photograph made soon after the turn of the century, above, she is seen carrying most of her 19,975 square feet of canvas, while opposite, midshipmen perch on the fore topgallant yard, more than one hundred feet above the sea, to "learn the lead of all the running gear." To this day many mariners believe that only sail can teach seamen the real feel of the sea.*

Lieutenant Harry H. Caldwell, the first captain of the Steel Navy's first submarine, watches as Naval Academy midshipmen squeeze aboard the tiny Holland *for an orientation tour in about 1901.*

The Submarine Torpedo Boat

The United States was slow in beginning its Steel Navy and it lagged far behind other maritime powers in adopting such innovations as the torpedo boat and destroyer, but in the development of the modern submarine the Americans showed the way. This did not come about through any special foresight on the part of U.S. naval authorities, nor was it because other navies were not trying. Rather, U.S. dominance in submarine design was mainly due to the genius and perseverance of Irish immigrant and inventor John P. Holland, who—after many others had failed—successfully combined in one boat all of the necessary elements for reliable undersea navigation.

In contrast to the more or less orderly military development of other warship types during the late nineteenth century, the designing of submarine torpedo boats in the United States and abroad was left almost exclusively in the hands of individual inventors. Progress tended to be haphazard, with designers of varying talents and theories often repeating the mistakes of predecessors or relearning, after much trial and error, lessons already assimilated by others.

By the late 1880s the navies of France, Greece, Russia, Spain, and Turkey had all purchased or built experimental submarines, but so formidable were the technical obstacles to be overcome that every one of these early boats fell short of satisfactory performance in one or more major characteristics. Particularly troublesome were the development of a suitable power plant and the control of submarine inclination and depth when submerged.

In the United States, John P. Holland approached the Navy Department with a proposal for a submarine boat as early as 1875, but "authorities" responded that his scheme would be unworkable. Undeterred by Navy skepticism and indifference, Holland had a crude, fifteen-foot, one-man experimental craft built which he tested in New Jersey's Passaic River in 1878. Later he moved on to more ambitious designs, the most noteworthy of which were the thirty-one-foot "Fenian Ram" of 1881, a boat powered with a gasoline engine, built with the financial aid of the Irish patriot Fenian Society, and the fifty-foot "Zalinski boat," a wood-and-steel submarine constructed in cooperation with Army officer and dynamite-gun inventor Edmund L. G. Zalinski. Unlike many of his contemporaries, Holland went in for dynamic submarine control, boldly angling his boats up or down by means of diving planes to attain the desired depth of submergence. With this method he was able to retain a slight reserve of buoyancy at all times, a real safety feature in view of the hazards of underwater navigation.

Official interest, finally whetted by a few enthusiasts, led Secretary of the Navy William C. Whitney to advertise for bids for an experimental submarine torpedo boat in 1888, and Holland and three rivals submitted designs. Holland's proposal was adjudged the best, but because the Cramp shipyard of Philadelphia—which represented him as a builder—could not guarantee the proposed boat's performance, no contract was awarded. Competition was reopened the following year and Holland was again declared winner, but this time a change in administration led to a reversal of Navy Department policy and funds that had been set aside for the submarine were diverted to other construction. In 1893 still another competition was initiated and a Holland design was once again selected. More delays followed, but finally in 1895 the Navy Department awarded a $150,000 building contract to the John P. Holland Torpedo Boat Company and a year later the long-awaited boat was laid down at the Columbian Iron Works of Baltimore under subcontract. Christened the *Plunger* at her launching in 1897, the eighty-five-foot submarine mounted two torpedo tubes and was designed to run on electricity when submerged. For surface propulsion, however, only a triple-screw steam plant could deliver the 1,500 horsepower required to achieve the fifteen-knot speed demanded by the government, and this in turn ultimately led to so many complications that the boat became a monstrosity. When her steam engines were tested at dockside in 1898 the fireroom temperature sizzled at 137 degrees F. at only two-thirds of rated power.

Having in the meantime realized that the overly ambitious *Plunger* was doomed to failure, Holland shifted his efforts to the design and construction of a smaller, less complex submarine employing a gasoline engine for surface power. This fifty-four-foot craft, built for the Holland company at the Crescent Shipyard at Elizabethport, New Jersey, was launched in 1897 and extensively tested during the next two years.

In 1896 Congress had authorized the procurement of two more Navy submarines, contingent on the successful completion of the *Plunger,* and in 1899 friends of the Holland company had this bill amended to permit the funds to be used instead to buy the smaller privately financed boat, which had turned out to be a spectacular success. Thus on 11 April 1900 the Navy purchased its first modern submarine, the *Holland,* for the sum of $150,000 and simultaneously contracted for an improved version, later named the *Plunger.* As for the old *Plunger,* the company returned the $93,000 advanced by the government and the boat was quietly abandoned.

The press loved to refer to the *Holland* as the "Monster War Fish," "Uncle Sam's Devil of the Deep," and even the "Naval Hell Diver," but she was actually a warship of the most primitive sort when compared to most naval vessels. Circular in cross section and displacing just sixty-four tons on the surface, the cigar-shaped boat was limited to a depth of submergence of seventy-five feet. Her armament consisted of a small (and seldom employed) Zalinski-type pneumatic gun and a single eighteen-inch-diameter launch tube with three Whitehead torpedoes. When on the surface she was powered by a forty-five-horsepower Otto gasoline engine, and when underwater by an electric motor of about equal power. A sixty-cell, twenty-one-ton battery nominally gave the *Holland* a submerged range of about forty miles at five knots, but because she had no periscope and was completely blind underwater, she seldom actually remained below the surface for more than a few minutes at a time, having to "porpoise" at intervals in order for the captain to get his bearings through small eyeports in the diminutive conning tower. On the surface the *Holland* had a top speed of about eight knots and a theoretical range of 1,500 miles. Her endurance was severely limited by the absence of accommodations for the seven-man crew, however, and cruises of more than a few hours were infrequent. Moreover, the submarine had a freeboard of only eighteen inches and seldom ventured far to sea.

Nevertheless, the Navy was sufficiently impressed with the *Holland*'s performance to obtain funds for six more submarines in June 1900. The previously authorized *Plunger*

and the *Adder, Moccasin, Porpoise,* and *Shark* were subcontracted by the Holland company to the Crescent Shipyard, and the *Grampus* and *Pike* to the Union Iron Works of San Francisco. Enlarged and improved versions of the *Holland,* these boats each measured sixty-four feet in length, displaced 107 tons, and were capable of diving to one hundred feet. Their underwater performance was enhanced by the addition of periscopes, but these instruments were initially of poor quality and fixed in the forward direction only.

The crews of these early Navy submarines worked in an atmosphere of excitement, thrills, and danger. The massive wet-cell battery installations in the boats were a source of special concern as they generated explosive hydrogen gas and, when contaminated by seawater, toxic chlorine gas. With their limited visibility and low freeboard the submarines were in constant danger of being run down by surface craft or swamped through an open hatch. Nearly all suffered actual or potentially serious casualties. In 1899 all of the *Holland*'s civilian crewmen were almost killed by fumes from a gasoline leak in the boat, and in 1902 both the *Holland* and the *Fulton*—a civilian prototype for the *Adder* and her sisters—were damaged and their crews injured by hydrogen explosions. During a dive in 1904, the *Porpoise* lost her reserve buoyancy and sank to the bottom in 125 feet of water, but finally returned to the surface after the crew pumped out the ballast tanks by hand. A few months later the *Shark* had a similar narrow escape, and on another occasion she sank alongside the pier. In 1908 one sailor was killed and several injured by a gasoline explosion while fueling the *Grampus* and *Pike.* Much later, in 1917, all eight crewmen aboard the *A-7* (ex-*Shark*) were killed by another gasoline explosion, as was one crewman aboard the *A-2* (ex-*Adder*).

In spite of such hazards, Congress saw fit to authorize four more submarines in 1904. The Holland company, which by this time had been reorganized as the Electric Boat Company, continued its virtual monopoly in submarine construction and was awarded the contract for all four, which was in turn subcontracted to the Fore River Shipbuilding Company of Quincy, Massachusetts. The *Viper, Cuttlefish,* and *Tarantula* were eighty-two-foot, 145-ton models, while the *Octopus* was the prototype for a class of 105-foot, 238-ton submarines. These were vastly improved sea boats, as was demonstrated during trials in 1907 when the *Viper* remained underway off the East Coast for four days.

For many more years submarines would be scorned by battleship sailors as "pigboats" and "submersible cigars," inhabited by the "Green Death and the Fiery Devil" (chlorine gas and hydrogen gas), and they were really just a sideshow to the Great White Fleet. Only a few zealots could foresee their ultimate rise to dominance of the sea lanes.

Crewmen of the Adder warm up their boat's engine at the Naval Torpedo Station in Newport, Rhode Island, in 1903. A sister craft, the Moccasin, *is moored astern.*

Primitive but Streamlined

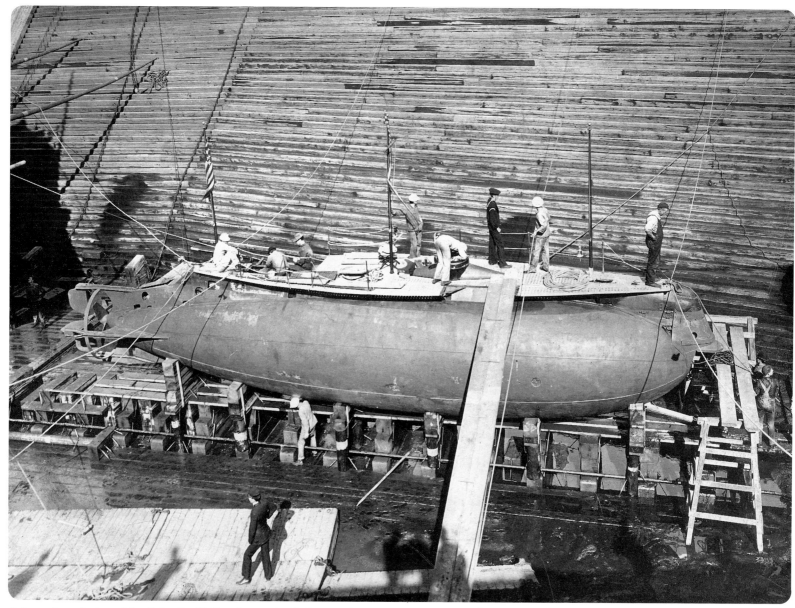

Submarines designed by John P. Holland were built for maximum performance underwater and were more streamlined than any built during the next fifty years. The fifty-four-foot Holland, *photographed above during an overhaul at New York in 1901, was commissioned in October 1900 and spent most of her ten-year career training submarine crews and indoctrinating officers and midshipmen in underseas warfare. A gasoline engine propelled the* Holland *when on the surface and an electric motor drove her when submerged. When turned by the engine, the motor also served as a dynamo for charging the submarine's battery. The* Plunger, *shown on the opposite page at Oyster Bay, Long Island, in 1905, was ten feet longer than her predecessor and shared her design with six boats of the* Adder *class.*

Rapid Submarine Development

Crewmen pose atop the 107-ton submarines Porpoise *and* Shark *at the New York Navy Yard, after they had been lifted out of the water by a floating crane in June 1905. The cap for the single bow torpedo tube opened like a fish's mouth. These boats had a surface speed of eight knots, a submerged speed of seven, and were equipped with simple periscopes. The* Porpoise *and* Shark *were transferred to the Philippines aboard a collier in 1908, and the next year the* Adder *and* Moccasin *followed. In 1911 the* Plunger, Adder, Grampus, Moccasin, Pike, Porpoise, *and* Shark *were reclassified as the* A-1 *through* A-7.

The 145-ton Viper *cruises in New York's East River in 1909. Among many improvements introduced in her design were twin torpedo tubes, a rudimentary bridge fairwater, and an improved periscope. She was also a knot faster than the previous class, had about twice the range, and could dive twice as deep. The* Viper *and two sisters, the* Cuttlefish *and* Tarantula, *were subsequently reclassified* B-1 *through* B-3 *and were shipped to the Philippines in 1912. Another submarine completed during the Steel Navy era, the 238-ton* Octopus *(later* C-1*), had twin-screw propulsion and was more than a knot faster than the boats of the* Viper *class.*

With her ram bow throwing up a huge wave, the Connecticut *makes a trial run off the coast of Maine in 1907. Moments after this picture was taken, photographer Enrique Muller's boat was nearly swamped by the onrushing battleship.*

The Final Flowering

Development of the pre-dreadnought battleship reached its zenith with creation of the *Connecticut* class, for which two ships were authorized in 1902. Under the supervision of model-testing pioneer David W. Taylor, the hull form for these ships was worked out in a new test basin at the Washington Navy Yard, the first time such a method had been employed in the calculations for a major class of U.S. naval vessels. Results of the experiments showed that at high speeds a long hull form was more efficient than a short one and consequently the new battleships were designed with a load-waterline length of 450 feet, 15 feet longer than that of the preceding class. Displacement was also significantly increased over that of earlier U.S. battleships, to 16,000 tons, and the previous limitation on draft was eased to 24½ feet. Although the design speed of eighteen knots was the same as in the *Virginia* class, this was actually to be achieved with less expenditure of power, and the cruising range was to be greater.

In choosing the armament for the proposed battleships the Navy Board of Construction was divided by the same strong differences of opinion that had hampered the selection of guns for the *Virginia* and her sisters. During the summer of 1901 its members were unable to reach agreement, the majority recommending a main battery of four 12-inch rifles and a secondary battery of twenty 7-inch rapid-fire guns, with a single member holding out for a near-repeat of the superposed-turret mixed-battery arrangement of the *Virginia* class. During new deliberations a few months later, however, a third design was unanimously agreed upon, consisting of four 12-inch rifles in a pair of turrets, eight 8-inch rifles in four wing turrets, and twelve 7-inch rapid-fire guns in casemates. This arrangement was somewhat reminiscent of that employed in the much smaller ships of the *Indiana* class.

The 12-inch rifles of the main battery were of the same general design as in the preceding *Maine* and *Virginia* classes but were made five feet longer to provide a modest increase in muzzle velocity and to reduce the effects the muzzle blasts would have on the crews of the smaller guns below when fired to either beam. The 7-inch rapid-fire guns of the secondary battery were of an entirely new design and were considered the largest ones for which powder and projectile could be loaded by hand.

In 1902 the Navy Department decided to omit torpedo tubes from all future battleships and armored cruisers, but in light of new increases in torpedo ranges and accuracy this decision was soon reversed, and the new battleships each received four underwater launch tubes. Armor protection included full-length waterline belts with a maximum thickness of eleven inches, tapering to four inches at the ends.

Innovations in the class included the first use of centrifugal pumps for auxiliary purposes and an attempt to speed construction by providing builders with more detailed plans and specifications than heretofore, and by designing the plates and shapes used in the ships to conform to standard commercial sizes of steel material.

The *Connecticut* was assigned to the New York Navy Yard for construction and was thus the first battleship since the old *Maine* and *Texas* to be built in a government facility. Her sister ship, the *Louisiana,* was awarded to the Newport News Shipbuilding and Dry Dock Company. The Navy Department observed the progress on these two vessels with special interest in order to determine the relative efficiency and cost of construction in the two types of yards. Although government workers had shorter workdays and costs in the Navy yards were generally higher, construction of the *Connecticut* was unexpectedly competitive, and the quality of work was excellent. Navy yards would be regularly involved in battleship construction from this time on.

Three additional battleships of the type were authorized by Congress in 1903. The *Vermont* was awarded to the Fore River Shipbuilding Company, the *Kansas* to the New York Shipbuilding Company of Camden, New Jersey, and the *Minnesota* to Newport News. These battleships were identical to the *Connecticut* in most respects, but the maximum thickness of the waterline armor belts was reduced to only nine inches, an amount of protection that was clearly substandard for 12-inch-gun battleships. Finally in 1904 a sixth ship, the *New Hampshire,* was authorized and awarded to the Camden shipyard. Although a sister to the other five, her hull number did not fall in sequence because of the introduction in the meantime of two other battleships of a new class.

In 1903 the rapid growth in the size and cost of warships led to one of those periodic reactions whereby an attempt is made to limit technological progress by legislative action. In that year Congress authorized two additional first-class battleships, decreeing however, that neither should exceed 13,000 tons in displacement or $3,500,000 in cost. (The *Vermont, Kansas,* and *Minnesota,* authorized in the same act, were budgeted at $4,212,000 each.) Thus in the *Mississippi* and *Idaho* the Department was forced to regress to battleships seventy-five feet shorter and 3,000 tons lighter than current standard practice. Nevertheless, in them the Navy's designers managed to repeat essentially the entire armament of the *Connecticut,* less only four broadside guns. This was necessarily accomplished at the expense of horsepower, speed, and cruising range at a time when tactical and strategic requirements demanded exactly the opposite.

As was to be expected, the *Mississippi* and *Idaho* were first-class battleships in name only and were thoroughly unpopular in the fleet. With limited endurance and a top speed of only seventeen knots they were unable to keep up with the main battle squadrons, and after about four years of service were placed in reserve. The *Mississippi* was recommissioned in 1914 for pioneer work with the Navy's new air arm, but

soon thereafter the government sold both ships to Greece. There they served in the Greek Navy as coast defense battleships long after their contemporaries had disappeared, finally to be destroyed by German bombers in 1941.

To the *Connecticut* fell the honor of leading the Great White Fleet on its cruise around the world in 1907–09 under the flags of Rear Admirals Robley D. Evans and Charles S. Sperry. She and her class formed the backbone of the U.S. fleet for a few short years, but their status was really little more than that of caretakers. Even while they had been under construction, the United States was initiating a naval revolution with the design of the *South Carolina* and *Michigan,* to introduce the concept of all-big-gun, centerline-mounted battleship armament. The British were independently reaching similar conclusions with their *Dreadnought,* laid down in secrecy and rushed to completion with unprecedented haste to give her name to a new battleship era.

When the ships of the *Connecticut* class returned to Hampton Roads and paraded in triumphant review in early 1909, they were already on the verge of obsolescence. Stripped of their graceful bow ornaments and painted a businesslike gray, the six battleships gradually slipped into second-line roles during the decade that followed, as successively larger and more powerful dreadnought-type battleships of the *South Carolina, Delaware, Florida, Wyoming, New York, Pennsylvania,* and *New Mexico* classes entered service. At the end of World War I the once-proud veterans of an era of white-and-gilt naval elegance were even pressed briefly into duty as improvised troop transports, and in 1923 they were sold for scrap in accordance with the Washington Treaty for the limitation of naval armaments.

Officer of the Deck in bridge coat scans the anchorage with his long glass from the quarterdeck of the Kansas, one of six battleships of the Connecticut class.

The Pre-Dreadnought Battleship Design Reaches Its Zenith

In the United States the pre-dreadnought battleship achieved its highest plane of excellence in the 16,000-ton vessels of the Connecticut *class, of which the* Louisiana, *pictured above in 1906, was the first actually completed. With their eighteen-knot speed, long cruising range, extensive armor protection, and heavy mixed-battery armament of 7-, 8-, and 12-inch guns, these were formidable warships, but new developments in fire control and the appearance of the dreadnought design with its all-big-gun main armament made them obsolete within just a few years of entering service.*

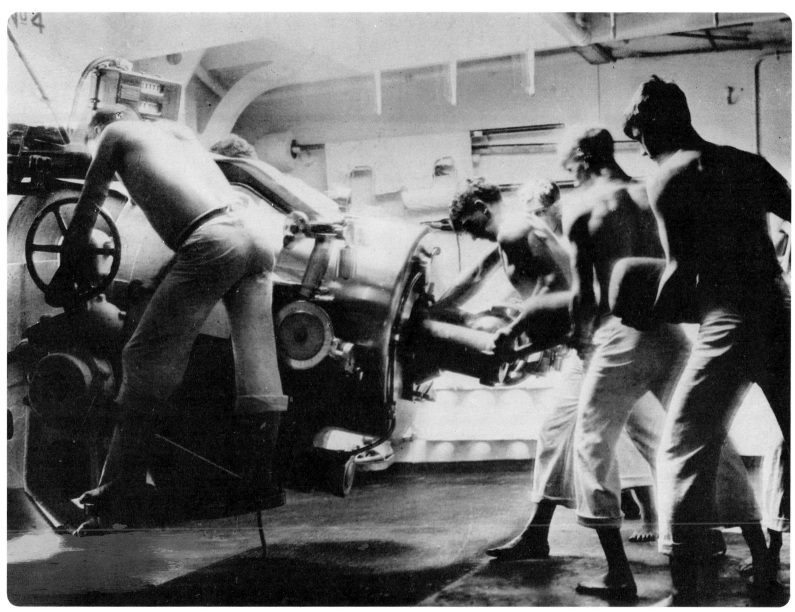

The broadside battery in ships of the Connecticut *class included twelve rapid-fire guns of seven-inch caliber, a size not previously employed in the Steel Navy. This photograph of a crew working one of the casemate-mounted 7-inchers was probably taken aboard the* New Hampshire *in 1909. One sailor is hefting a 165-pound projectile into the gun's breech while companions stand ready with bags of smokeless powder. Visible at left, just above the gun pointer's head, is an electric data transmitter by which estimates of the target's range and bearing could be forwarded from the gunnery officer.*

The *Mississippi* Class—False Economy

A legislative attempt to reduce the costs of new battleships led to construction of the 13,000-ton Mississippi, *photographed above in 1908, and her sister* Idaho. *Although heavily armed and well protected, these two 375-foot abbreviated versions of the* Connecticut *proved to be unpopular misfits because of their low speed and limited endurance. In 1914 both were sold to Greece, where they became the coast defense battleships* Lemnos *and* Kilkis.

A forecastle view of the Mississippi, *above, shows the hatches of the forward 12-inch turret open for ventilation. The assemblage of long rods and counterweights on the turret top was part of the "ping-pong" device used to simulate firing of the guns during aiming practice. The* Mississippi *and* Connecticut *classes were the last U.S. battleships to be fitted with these oval turrets and turret-top sighting hoods.*

"The ship of war must be allowed to follow out its lines of highest development, and the seamen must be trained to suit the development of the machine."

Lieutenant Richard Wainwright in the *Army and Navy Journal,* 1890.

Forging a Modern Steel Navy

The battleship Nebraska *steams at maximum speed during trials in Puget Sound, 1906.*

Two years after the laying of her keel, the armored ship Maine *protrudes through an old shiphouse at the New York Navy Yard in 1889. She so taxed the yard's antiquated facilities that completion required six more years.*

Construction and Repair

The major problem facing the Navy during the early 1880s was steel itself, without which a powerful fleet could not come into being. American mills had proved capable of rolling mild steel plates for the hulls of the Navy's first unarmored cruisers, but heavy steel armor and massive forgings for guns and engines were another problem altogether. Until a domestic manufacturing capability could be developed such material would have to be ordered from Europe. It was a situation which many who wanted to see the United States become a first-class power considered humiliating if not intolerable.

Steel, a refined iron-carbon alloy, had been manufactured in the United States since the 1850s but early batches, which were produced in crucibles, were limited in size from about sixty to ninety pounds each. Later, Bessemer converters were developed which produced lots up to eight tons. By the 1880s the open hearth process had been perfected, and while there had not previously been any incentive for the U.S. iron industry to expand into full-scale steel production, the technology to do so was at hand. Before the manufacturing of armor and gun forgings could begin, however, steps had to be taken to develop the necessary industrial base. The Navy Department set out to accomplish this by combining its steel requirements into large enough orders to entice private industry to build steel-making facilities, and in 1887 the Bethlehem Iron Company of Pennsylvania was awarded a contract for 1,300 tons of gun forgings and 6,700 tons of steel armor plate, which Secretary of the Navy William C. Whitney had put together by pooling orders for four of the iron-hulled monitors and the second-class battleships *Texas* and *Maine*. Later Secretary Benjamin F. Tracy brought in the Carnegie interests of Pittsburgh to establish a second source of supply, and by 1891 domestic steel was in quantity production. A logjam of delays continued to plague the Navy for several more years, but by 1900 U.S. steel manufacturers had produced some 35,000 tons of armor plate and gun forgings, and had orders for about 75,000 tons more.

Naval architecture flowered during this period, when such great names as Sir William H. White and William Froude of England and David W. Taylor of the United States were in their prime. In the U.S. Navy the major responsibility for the designing of warships and the supervision of their construction and repair was vested in a small corps of naval constructors which usually numbered fewer than fifty officers. Between 1879 and 1900 most new candidates for this select group—usually two or three of the top-ranking students from each graduating class at the Naval Academy—were sent abroad to such noted schools as the Royal Naval College at Greenwich and the Ecole d'Application du Genie Maritime in Paris for advanced degrees in naval architecture. As a result, U.S. steel warship design owed a large debt to European developments of the 1880s and 1890s. After the turn of the century, new officers entering the Construction Corps were sent to the Massachusetts Institute of Technology to study under famous naval architect William Hovgaard.

A few of the Steel Navy's ships were built in navy yards, notably at New York and Norfolk, but most warship construction was carried out at about a dozen major commercial shipyards, the most important of which were William Cramp and Sons of Philadelphia, the Newport News Shipbuilding and Dry Dock Company of Virginia, and the Union Iron Works of San Francisco. The building of a warship, while similar in technique to that for a merchant vessel, was much more involved because of the fighting ship's greater complexity, requiring thousands of man-years of labor by an army of artisans. The construction of a battleship of the *Indiana* class, for example, required the manufacture, assembly, and installation of 4,400 tons of mild steel for the hull and superstructure, 2,700 tons of nickel-steel armor plate, 875 tons of boilers, engines, and auxiliary machinery, 400 tons of armament, and 700 tons of rivets to hold everything together. Armor plate was finished to size by the steel manufacturer and most of the guns were built at the Naval Gun Factory, but almost everything else that went into a warship was usually fabricated in the builder's own shops. While the major calculations for the hull and machinery were the responsibility of the Navy's Bureaus of Construction and Repair and Steam Engineering, most of the detailed construction drawings were left to the builder to complete. Thus for the *Indiana,* 400 additional drawings for the hull and 250 for the engines had to be prepared, enough to occupy a staff of more than fifty draftsmen for over a year.

At the outset of construction a large wooden model of the warship's hull was usually built to scale, from which the location and size of each of the hull plates could be precisely determined and measured. The hull lines were also laid out full-size on the floor of a giant mold loft and wooden templates or patterns constructed to correspond to each of the frames in the hull structure.

In the builder's shops steel angle bars for hull frames were heated in glowing furnaces, then laid on "bending slabs" into which huge steel pins had been set to conform to the curve of the wooden patterns. Sweating artisans, swinging heavy sledges and straining at long-handled "moon bars," then forced the cherry-red frames into the proper curvature. In other shops brawny workers manhandled the big hull plates, often twenty feet or more in length and weighing several tons, through giant rollers to bend them to the proper degree of roundness. Later huge punching machines bit rivet holes out of the frames and plates and they were milled and planed to exact size.

On the building ways the hull was erected piece by piece, beginning with the keel, then the ribs or frames extending out to either side, followed by stiffeners and girders, inner bottoms, floors, the protective deck, platforms, decks, bulkheads, and shell plating for the sides. Everything was joined together by sledgehammer-wielding teams of riveters who pounded tens of thousands of red-hot rivets through matching holes in the frames and plates and smashed the heads down to expand them. Boilers and engines were lowered into place by huge cranes and thick slabs of armor belting were bolted onto the hull.

Once the hull was completed, building activity paused briefly for the critical launching operation—attended by impressive ceremonies and thousands of cheering visitors— and then was resumed alongside a fitting-out pier. The superstructure and military masts were erected, turrets placed on their roller paths, and guns eased onto their trunnions. Finally, after a myriad of smaller items had been installed, the warship was ready for an informal builder's trial, then the official four-hour contract trial, acceptance by the Navy Department, delivery to a navy yard for manning by her crew, and commissioning into the active fleet.

Along with its many advantages, steel warship construction had its special problems. Whereas rot had been a major worry in wooden ships, rust took its place in steel hulls. Electrolytic corrosion due to contact between dissimilar metals in sea water was also a nuisance, and builders soon learned not to use bronze or copper fittings in ferrous hulls. Fouling by marine growth was another worry. Many antifouling formulations were tried but none were consistently effective, and steel ships had to be drydocked about every six months to have their hulls cleaned.

After the sinking of the British battleship *Victoria* in 1893, constructors took a new interest in watertight doors and hatches. Designers went to great lengths to eliminate bulkhead penetrations below the waterline, and the black gangs cursed the ladders every time they had to go "up and over." A related idea was the use of cellulose material to fill voids and cofferdams for protection against shell hits and collision. The cellulose (usually coconut husk extract or corn pith) was supposed to swell up on exposure to water and seal shot holes automatically, but in practice water seeped into the spaces prematurely and caused the material to swell when it shouldn't have, and it often deteriorated into a rotten mess under which rust ate away unseen and unchecked. Everyone was happy when the scheme was finally abandoned.

U.S. naval architecture made a big leap forward in 1900, when a million-gallon model-testing tank was completed and put into operation at the Washington Navy Yard. For the first time, Navy designers could scientifically determine the relative efficiency of various hull forms. After the turn of the century attention also began to be paid to making shipboard equipment more uniform. Ships' boats were standardized in design, and hatches, hull fittings, valves, and auxiliary machinery were brought under better control by the preparation of standard plans, the first forty-four of which were issued in 1903.

The Spanish-American War and the massive expansion that came in its wake disclosed all of the inadequacies of the old establishment, and led to a major improvement program for the navy yards. Repair facilities were enlarged, several huge granite and concrete drydocks were completed, and three floating drydocks were purchased. New construction also began to be assigned to several government yards on a regular basis, and soon became competitive with civilian work in spite of the shorter navy yard workday.

By 1909 the outlines of the Navy's construction and repair facilities were well established and shipbuilding technology had hit a plateau. There would be few major changes until the introduction of electric arc welding many years in the future.

The 16,000-ton battleship Connecticut *fits out at the New York Navy Yard in 1905. By this time the speed and quality of Navy construction work was on a par with that of the best commercial shipyards.*

The Construction Stage

The Connecticut, pride of the Brooklyn Navy Yard, was the first armored warship to be laid down in a government facility since 1888. In this photograph, three months after her keel laying in March 1903, the battleship's double bottom and frames are beginning to take shape on the building ways. The arched girders will support the watertight armored deck over the Connecticut's vitals. According to the supervising naval constructor's monthly report, the ship is about ten percent completed.

Surrounded by a forest of staging, the battleship's hull is almost plated-in after fourteen months of shipfitting work. She is nearly forty percent completed, but practically all of the internal fittings are still in the shops.

The Connecticut *slides off the building ways and into the East River at a gala launching ceremony attended by 30,000 visitors on 29 September 1904. With forty-five percent of the work remaining, including installation of most of the superstructure, armor, and machinery, the battleship rides high in the water.*

More than a year after launching, work continues alongside a fitting-out pier. The Connecticut *is ninety percent completed, and a workman has begun installation of the decorative bow crest. A number of time-consuming details remain, however, and commissioning is still eleven months in the future.*

Fitting-Out Activity

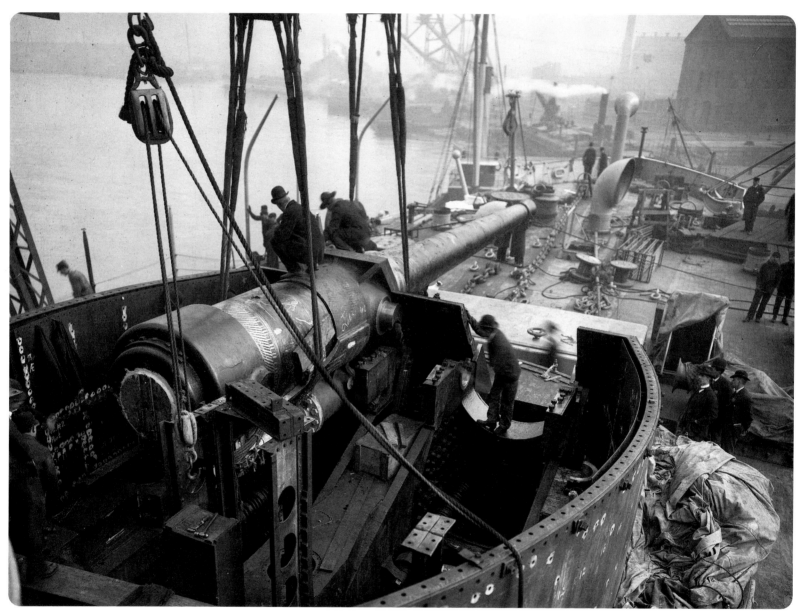

With eight months to go, mechanics ease a new twelve-inch-caliber, forty-five-ton rifle into the still-roofless forward main turret. Before arrival of the ordnance, which was manufactured at the Naval Gun Factory in Washington, D.C., the yard had already conducted preliminary sea trials to test the battleship's main propulsion plant.

*With the commissioning crew mustered on the quarterdeck and guests crowding the superstructure,
Old Glory is hoisted above the* Connecticut's *stern on 29 September 1906, marking the successful
conclusion to three and one-half years of work by more than a thousand artisans and engineers,
at a cost for labor and materials of $6,340,247.63.*

Because U.S. industry did not yet have the capacity to produce them, the steel forgings for this 8-inch breech-loading rifle aboard the protected cruiser Atlanta *had to be imported from England.*

Arms and Armor

The era of the American Steel Navy was especially a period of rapid evolution in the powers of naval offense and defense. On the defensive side there was one major element —armor—while for the offense, advocates of the gun, the torpedo, the dynamite shell, and even the marine ram each had their day. The gun remained the principal weapon of the period, however, and it was in the contest between gun and armor that developments were most dramatic.

On the eve of the U.S. naval renaissance in the early 1880s nearly every aspect of ordnance design and gunnery practice in the Navy was ripe for major improvement. Miserly naval appropriations during the previous decade and a half had left U.S. developments in this, as in other spheres of naval science, far behind those achieved by naval powers abroad. In fact, between 1865 and 1878 there was almost no progress at all. Most of the ordnance handed down from the Old Navy consisted of antiquated cast-iron smooth-bores and Parrott rifles of Civil War vintage, while the show-pieces of the fleet's arsenal were 8-inch muzzle-loading rifles converted from 11-inch smoothbores by the addition of wrought-iron liners. All of these weapons employed traditional black powder and fired cast-iron projectiles.

In 1878, however, the first real step towards a new age in U.S. naval armament was made by Commodore William Jeffers, head of the Bureau of Ordnance, when he prepared designs for a six-inch-caliber, built-up, steel breech-loading rifle, employing slow-burning brown or "cocoa" gunpowder —a new development from Germany having much greater power than fast-burning black powder. A working model of this gun, constructed from imported forgings and tested at the Naval Proving Grounds at Annapolis in 1882, became the basic prototype for the Steel Navy's modern ordnance.

Under Rear Admiral Montgomery Sicard, Jeffers' successor, the Bureau established a gun factory at the Washington Navy Yard in 1882–85 and began limited production of a family of steel breech-loading rifles. Forgings for 6-inch and

smaller guns for the ABCD ships and monitors then building were obtained from the Midvale Steel Company of Philadelphia, but those for larger calibers were beyond the capabilities of the fledgling U.S. steel industry and had to be ordered from England. In 1887, however, the Bethlehem Iron Company of Pennsylvania expanded its facilities and was awarded a contract for forgings in all major calibers.

By the end of the decade the Naval Gun Factory was manufacturing breech-loading rifles in four-, five-, six-, eight-, and ten-inch calibers. Typical of these was the first production 6-inch rifle, which was thirty calibers (fifteen feet) in length and weighed 4.8 tons. It burned a forty-five-pound charge of brown powder and fired a one-hundred-pound steel armor-piercing projectile at a muzzle velocity of 2,000 feet per second. The projectile and powder bags were loaded separately, firing was by percussion, and aiming was accomplished by peering over open sights. Although the cumbersome gun carriage still resembled those used with Civil War ordnance, it incorporated an efficient new hydraulic recoil cylinder. Three separate movements were required to open or close the interrupted-screw breech mechanism, and the gun had a firing rate of about one round per minute.

During the next few years new models equipped with pedestal mountings and spring-return mechanisms were developed. Gun barrels were made longer, thus increasing muzzle velocities and providing increased range and accuracy. Firing by electricity was introduced and in larger guns replaced percussion fire. Rapid-fire guns, employing brass powder cases and breech mechanisms which opened in a single movement, were developed for four-, five-, and six-inch calibers. Rangefinders and telescopic sights, devised by Navy inventor Bradley A. Fiske, achieved limited acceptance.

By the mid-1890s, main-battery guns had grown to thirteen-inch-caliber giants weighing 60½ tons apiece. The model employed in *Indiana*-class battleships fired a 1,100-pound projectile at a muzzle velocity of 2,100 feet per second, producing a muzzle energy of over 33,000 foot-tons. (The latter value, a measure of the projectile's kinetic energy, was the equivalent of lifting 33,000 tons one foot into the air.)

In 1899–1900 the Bureau achieved a major breakthrough with the wholesale adoption of smokeless powder and the design of a new family of guns to use it most effectively. Brown prismatic powder had the characteristic of wastefully expending most of its energy during the first few feet of the projectile's travel down the gun barrel, and produced great quantities of obscuring smoke and residue. The new powder burned more slowly, imparting a much higher velocity to the projectile without a significant increase in chamber pressure, and was almost smokeless. (The black powder primer used to ignite it produced more smoke than the main charge.) So great was the increase in energy with smokeless powder that the Navy was able to reduce the caliber of its new battleship guns to twelve inches while simultaneously increasing their destructive power. The first of these new models produced a muzzle energy of over 40,000 foot-tons.

Meanwhile, attention was focusing on other aspects of the gunnery problem. For decades past, the universal system of gun pointing had been to let the gun roll with the ship, firing as the sights crossed the target at the top of the roll. During 1898–1900, however, Captain Percy Scott of the British Navy had developed a new system known as "continuous-aim" firing—in which the gun pointer held sights and gun on the target continuously, regardless of the oscillations of the vessel—and warships under his command had achieved remarkable records at practice. In contrast, U.S. naval gunnery had been highly unreliable. Of some 8,000 U.S. shells fired at the Battle of Santiago in 1898, only 123 had been confirmed as hits, and during target practice in 1901 the battleships of the North Atlantic Fleet had been unable to make more than a few ineffectual hits on an obsolete wooden lightship at close range.

About this time Lieutenant William S. Sims, an American officer who was familiar with Scott's work, launched a crusade to introduce continuous-aim firing into the U.S. Navy. Although some officers were hostile to Sims' harsh criticism of existing U.S. gunnery methods, he also attracted many supporters, including President Theodore Roosevelt, and the new system was adopted. Because continuous-aim firing required considerable skill, its employment led to a new emphasis on target practice, and in 1902 the energetic Lieutenant Commander Albert P. Niblack was placed in charge of the fleet's gunnery training. The next year Sims was appointed Inspector of Target Practice for the Navy, an assignment he would hold until 1909. Semiannual fleetwide target practice was instituted and more than $200,000 a year was expended on ammunition. Gun crews competed on an individual basis each spring at short-range "record" practice (at a 1,600-yard range from the target), while in the fall each warship's guns operated together under simulated battle conditions at long range (7,000–9,000 yards).

Although the old major-caliber turret guns were too cumbersome to be modified for continuous-aim fire, the development of accurate telescopic sights, the introduction of tracer ammunition, and the use of improved training methods led to greatly increased accuracy with these guns as well as with the smaller mounts. Gunnery training devices such as the "dotter," in which a miniature target suspended just beyond the gun barrel was maneuvered by guy wires while a solenoid-operated pencil marked the pointer's "fall of shot," and the related "Morris tube," which used a shooting gallery rifle instead of the pencil enabled gun pointers to practice without actually firing the big guns.

By 1908 the rate and accuracy of fire in the fleet had increased to about double that achieved in 1903. At record practice the crews of some 6-inch guns were achieving more than thirteen hits per minute on a seventeen by twenty-one foot target, and at battle ranges the big guns often registered better than fifty-percent hits on the thirty by sixty foot targets. By this time the Navy was also developing new concepts of fire control, and range-keepers, wide-base range-finders, and improved interior communications facilities were installed in its major warships. The Russo-Japanese War of 1904–05 had demonstrated that battleships could be put out of action before their intermediate and broadside batteries could be brought into range, and observers were noting that greatly increased firing rates were making it almost impossible to distinguish the fall of shot from mixed-caliber armaments. Technical improvements were laying the foundation for the all-big-gun, single-caliber, salvo-firing warship.

Closely related to improvements in ordnance and gunnery were advances in armor protection. Civil War armor had been built up from inch-thick plates of wrought iron, so limited was the industrial capability of that period. Soon after the birth of the New Navy the monitor *Miantonomoh*'s compound armor (steel bonded to iron) was purchased from England, but in 1887 the steel armor requirements for her sisters were consolidated into a single competitive contract—which was awarded to the Bethlehem Iron Company—as a means of "rendering us independent" of foreign industry.

In September 1890 the Bureau of Ordnance conducted a notable series of trials at the Annapolis proving ground, firing 8-inch projectiles under controlled conditions into plates of English compound, plain steel, and new nickel-steel armor. The compound and ordinary steel plates shattered dramatically but the nickel-steel did not even crack. Tests at the new Indian Head, Maryland, site the following year proved a new

One of the four 10-inch rifles of the monitor Miantonomoh—possibly this one, being mounted in about 1890— was the first modern gun of large caliber to be entirely forged and manufactured in the United States.

carbon face-hardened steel, developed by American industrialist Hayward A. Harvey, even better. By 1891 Bethlehem was producing nickel-steel plates, reforged and face-hardened. In 1895 the Krupp process (whereby chromium-nickel-steel was face-hardened in a gas atmosphere) was developed in Germany, and three years later was introduced into the United States. Thus the early Steel Navy monitors, battleships, and armored cruisers represented the full gamut of armor development: compound, untreated nickel-steel, face-hardened ("Harveyized"), and finally nickel-chrome (Krupp). These improvements enabled naval architects to design equal or better protection into successive ships with less and less thickness of armor. The weight saved was reinvested in more and heavier guns, greater areas of armor protection, larger engines and boilers, and more extensive coal bunkers for increased endurance. The price paid was a chronic delay in the receipt of armor for the new ships.

Projectiles too were vastly improved over the old cast-iron shells of the early 1880s. As armor was toughened, successively stronger steel shells were developed to penetrate it, culminating in 1897 with the introduction of the Johnson soft-steel cap, which protected the point of the projectile to keep it from breaking or ricocheting off the armor plate.

Unfortunately, the rapid pace of ordnance design in the U.S. Navy resulted in the introduction of several serious defects. Early American battleship turrets—unlike those in the most advanced European navies—had open shafts connecting the guns and the ammunition handling rooms below, rendering the powder stored there and in the adjacent magazines extremely vulnerable to any fire or explosion in the turrets. Equally serious was the lack of a reliable means of expelling the combustible gases and smoldering residue that sometimes lingered in the chambers of the guns after firing.

During fleet target practice in April 1904, burning gases caused a "flareback" in a 12-inch rifle aboard the battleship *Missouri*, igniting more than three hundred pounds of smokeless powder being loaded into the gun. Burning powder grains cascaded into the handling rooms below, igniting two more charges. All thirty officers and enlisted men in the turret and handling rooms died of burns or asphyxiation. Two years later, in April 1906, a gunner extracting an unused charge from a 13-inch gun aboard the battleship *Kearsarge* accidentally shorted out an electrical circuit, igniting the powder. Eight of the twelve men in the turret died.

As a result of these disasters and other accidents, partitions were fitted between the turrets and ammunition handling rooms, and doors with automatic shutters were installed to allow the projectiles and powder to be hoisted to the guns. Nonessential electrical equipment was moved out of the turrets and gas ejectors employing high-pressure blasts of air were installed at the gun breeches.

That these measures were still inadequate was tragically demonstrated in July 1907, when a flareback occurred in one of the turrets of the battleship *Georgia*, killing ten men. This last accident finally resulted in formation of a Navy "Turret Board," whose recommendations led to installation of closed two-stage ammunition hoists in new battleships and additional modifications and safety precautions in existing ones.

U.S. employment of the modern torpedo, as with the steel breech-loading rifle, initially lagged far behind that of most foreign naval powers. As early as 1866 Robert Whitehead, a British engineer, had developed a self-propelled or "automobile" torpedo, but twenty years later the U.S. fleet was still limited to the primitive spar torpedo of Civil War days.

Initial U.S. interest, during the late 1880s and '90s, centered on native inventions, including the wire-controlled, electric-powered Edison "dirigible" torpedo, and the flywheel-driven Howell torpedo. In 1888 an order was placed with the Hotchkiss Ordnance Company for torpedoes of the Howell type, but technical problems and subsequent production delays prompted the Department to award an additional contract in 1891 to the E. W. Bliss Company for domestically manufactured Whitehead torpedoes. By 1894 both types had entered the fleet and above-water launch tubes were fitted in most battleships, cruisers, larger gunboats, and torpedo boats. (The Howell torpedo was soon phased out of service.)

The U.S. Mark I Whitehead torpedo was 17.7 inches in diameter, weighed 845 pounds, and had a range of about 1,000 yards. Its counter-rotating propellers were driven by a three-cylinder Brotherhood engine which was powered by a flask of air under 1,350 pounds of pressure. Subsequent models were fitted with a gyroscopic steering mechanism invented by the Austrian Ludwig Obry in 1895, and during the first decade of the 1900s range and speed were significantly increased by installation of an alcohol burner which heated the compressed air entering the engine, and later, by the introduction of the turbine drive.

Damage to Spanish cruisers in 1898 demonstrated that above-water launch tubes were extremely vulnerable to gunfire, and in 1899 the Department decided to remove them from unarmored cruisers and gunboats. After 1902 most new battleships and armored cruisers were fitted with improved 21-inch torpedoes and underwater launch tubes. While in these larger warships the torpedo was a weapon of opportunity, the fear of "torpedo water" kept battle fleets increasingly at stand-off ranges and thus exerted a powerful influence on gunnery. However, the torpedo would have to await perfection of a practical seagoing submarine in a subsequent era before it would see its maximum employment as a weapon of destruction.

By the mid-1890s, thirteen-inch-caliber guns like these aboard the Oregon *had become the standard for U.S. battleship main-battery ordnance.*

Battleship Guns

The introduction of smokeless powder in 1899–1900 permitted the Navy to reduce the caliber and weight of its new battleship main-battery guns while at the same time increasing their destructive power. These 12-inch rifles, photographed aboard the Mississippi in 1908, had a seventy-five-percent greater muzzle energy than the heavier 13-inch guns employed during the Spanish-American War. Their effective range of about nine thousand yards was more than double that of the older guns, and their firing rate of two rounds per minute represented a five-fold increase in efficiency.

Small Quick-Firing Guns

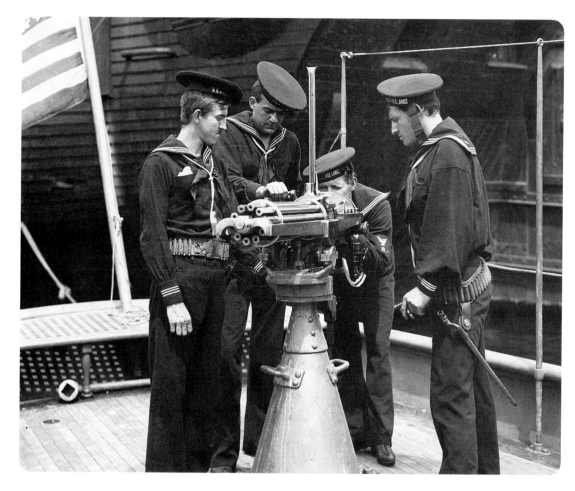

The secondary armament of nearly every warship included several machine guns, intended primarily for employment against personnel. The ten-barreled Gatling gun, right, had a firing rate of up to 1,200 rounds per minute. Although superseded and withdrawn from general fleet use during the 1890s, it was briefly recalled for service aboard converted craft as in this installation on the yacht Free Lance during the Spanish-American War.

After the mid-1890s, Colt machine guns like this one aboard the protected cruiser Cincinnati were adopted as the Navy's standard automatic weapon. The Colt had a firing rate of 400 rounds per minute and had the advantage of light weight, an important factor when carried in small boats and with landing parties.

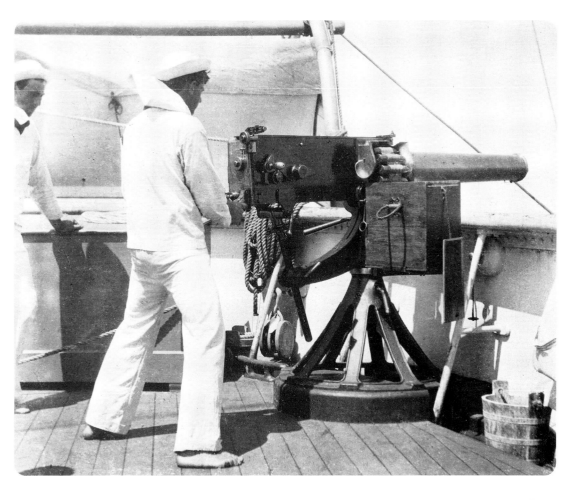

More powerful weapons were required for protection against torpedo boats. This Maxim 1-pounder, operated by a barefooted gunner aboard the training ship Hartford, could fire belt-fed cartridges at 200 rounds per minute but was almost as heavy as the much more destructive 6-pounder rapid-fire gun. Like the other weapons on these two pages it had a maximum range of about 2,000 yards.

One-, three-, and six-pounder rapid-fire guns were the most popular weapons for close-in work against unarmored vessels and torpedo boats. This Driggs-Schroeder one-pounder was installed aboard the refurbished Civil War monitor Nahant for harbor guard duty in 1898.

213

Guns Ashore

Although the steel forgings for the Navy's guns were produced by commercial firms, actual construction of most of its big breech-loading rifles was carried out at the Naval Gun Factory in Washington, D.C. Each gun basically consisted of an inner steel tube, a short outer jacket, and several hoops. First the forgings for the tube and jacket had to be turned to shape and bored out on giant lathes, an exacting and time-consuming process. Then the jacket was expanded by heating in a vertical pit furnace and, as photographed at left, carefully slipped over the tube. The outer surface of the assembly was again machined, the hoops shrunk into place, and the tube rebored to final tolerances. A rifling tool then cut the necessary grooves in the bore, as seen in progress above. Finally a breech mechanism was installed and the gun was ready for proof firing.

Target Practice

Beginning in 1903 great progress was achieved in U.S. naval gunnery as a result of the adoption of
"continuous-aim" firing and an emphasis on target practice. Here, sailors aboard the protected cruiser
Baltimore *operate one of the new 6-inch rapid-fire guns with which the ship was equipped in 1904.*
In this model the breech could be opened or closed by a single sweep of the operating lever.
A good eight-man crew could fire such a weapon eight times a minute for a short period.

Twice each year a fleet-wide firing competition was held. In this photograph, officers and gunners tally hits on a canvas target during spring "record" practice at Magdalena Bay, Mexico. During use the target was suspended above a wooden raft anchored at the apex of a 1,600-yard triangle marked by buoys. Each of the medium-caliber-gun crews was allowed twelve shots at the target as their ship steamed down the base of the triangle. By 1909 it was not unusual for some crews to place every shot through the target.

High Explosives

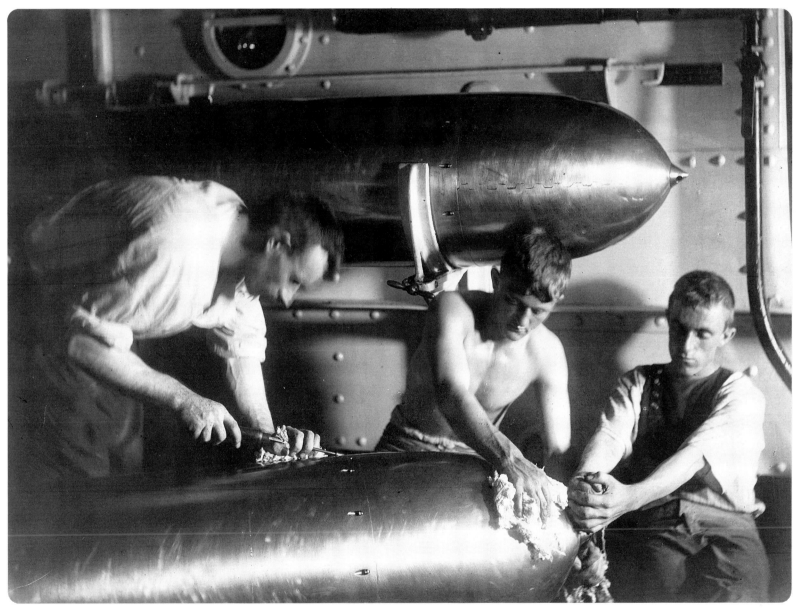

Thirteen-inch projectiles, like those being taken aboard the battleship Kearsarge *at left, were the largest-caliber shells used in the Steel Navy. Each weighed 1,100 pounds and contained a 50-pound bursting charge. Torpedoes were also carried aboard many warships and, while limited in range, packed a heavy punch. The eighteen-inch-diameter Whitehead model undergoing maintenance aboard the protected cruiser* Olympia, *above, weighed 836 pounds and was over eleven feet long. It had a range of almost one thousand yards at an average speed of twenty-six knots, and its 110-pound guncotton warhead could disable a battleship.*

Black coal smoke pours from the funnels of the new armored cruiser Pennsylvania *during trials under forced draft in 1905.*

Engineering and the Black Gang

To the Navy line officer of the 1870s and early 1880s, machinery in a warship consisted of the main engine, which was an auxiliary device for propelling the vessel when the wind was not right. This engine, unfortunately, had to have steam, which necessitated boilers. These in turn consumed expensive coal. The whole thing was an abominable nuisance. The drag of the propeller reduced speed when under sail; the boilers, engine, and fuel bunkers wasted great amounts of useful space; the stack emitted dirty smoke and dangerous sparks and got in the way of proper masts and rigging; and the coal dust was a plague. No major innovations in machinery had been introduced to U.S. warships since the Civil War. Engines and engineers were tolerated, but little more.

When plans were laid in 1883 for the Navy's first steel cruisers, the conservatism of the Second Advisory Board and the general limitations of U.S. naval shipbuilding practice led to a temporary continuation of traditional machinery design. The engines selected for the *Atlanta* and *Boston* were of the horizontal, back-acting, compound (two-stage) type, in which the high-pressure cylinder was driven by steam direct from the boilers and its exhaust in turn fed a pair of low-pressure cylinders. A system of valves and levers enabled the steam to drive each piston first to one end of its cylinder, then back—hence a "back-acting" engine. In order to keep the machinery safely below the waterline the cylinders had to be laid horizontally, because long piston rods and connecting rods were required to translate the reciprocating action of the pistons into the rotary motion of the propeller shaft. The mass of rods, cranks, journals, cams, levers, valves, and bearings required constant attention with oil can and wiping rag by oilers who dodged nimbly in and out among the fast-moving parts.

The British Admiral R. H. S. Bacon vividly described engine-room working conditions during this era: "When steaming at full speed in a man-of-war fitted with reciprocating engines, the engine room was always a glorified snipe-marsh; water lay on the floor plates and was splashed about everywhere; the officers often were clad in oilskins to avoid being wetted to the skin. The water was necessary to keep the bearings cool. Further, the noise was deafening; so much so that telephones were useless and even voice-pipes of doubtful value."

He might also have added that at high speed vibration so strained both hull and machinery that it was almost impossible to maintain full power for any extended period without suffering crippling breakdowns.

In the early boiler rooms sweating stokers shoveled coal ceaselessly into greedy furnaces beneath huge cylindrical boilers. The flames and hot gases rose through boiler tubes surrounded by water (hence, "fire-tubes") and ultimately out the smokepipe. The steam thus generated was delivered to the engines at pressures of about ninety pounds per square inch.

Steam engineering was afforded a more vital role in the construction of second- and third-generation U.S. steel warships. After 1887, when highly capable George W. Melville assumed the job of Engineer in Chief (an assignment that he held for the next sixteen years), developments took place with bewildering rapidity. The reciprocating engine was refined to three (triple-expansion) and even four (quadruple-expansion) stages, and sophisticated combinations of cylinders, linkages, and gears were devised to achieve greater efficiency and power. Horizontal and inclined cylinder engines yielded to compact vertical-cylinder designs, which were less subject to friction and wear, and by 1893 piston speeds were more than double those in ships of the Old Navy. Engines were soon producing about ten horsepower per ton of machinery, a fourfold increase in efficiency, and highly-tuned (and easily wrecked) torpedo boat plants even produced as much as forty horsepower per ton of machinery. Powerful twin-screw plants became the standard almost at the beginning of the Steel Navy era, but in the quest for ever greater speed, triple-screw warships were also built.

In boiler technology, demands for increased power led to

higher steam pressures and temperatures and to efforts to burn fuel more efficiently. To achieve faster combustion—and hence more rapid production of steam—forced draft was introduced. This could be accomplished by increasing the air pressure within the firebox alone, as was done experimentally in some gunboats, but the more practical solution was to pressurize the entire fireroom and thus avoid the escape of smoke and noxious gases from the furnace and ash pit. Forced draft necessitated the employment of large blowers driven by auxiliary steam engines, however, and these in turn introduced additional maintenance and repair problems. One-hundred-foot-high stacks in several warships of the 1890s represented a means of reducing forced-draft operation, since the hot gases rising up such long smokepipes produced a strong natural pressure differential.

An idea of the sophistication attained in U.S. Navy steam engineering by the mid-1890s may be derived from this contemporary description of the main propulsion plant of the new protected cruiser *Minneapolis:* "Her low-pressure piston, which is ninety-two inches in diameter, has an area of forty-six square feet, a very comfortable six-foot by eight-foot stateroom on board ship, and this piston has an initial load of one hundred tons, equal to the weight of three locomotives. The mean piston speed at maximum power will be eleven miles per hour, and the maximum speed sixteen miles an hour. The tips of the propeller blades will move through the water at the moderate rate of seventy-five miles an hour. The condenser tubes, if placed end to end, would form a tube thirty-three miles long, and if flattened out, would cover about two-thirds of an acre. The cooling water passed through these tubes will be equal to 36,000,000 gallons per day, enough to supply a large city with water. The main boilers, if placed end to end, would form a tunnel 156 feet long, and large enough for a train of cars to pass through. If divided up into rooms, they would supply a hotel with sixteen fair-sized bedrooms. The heating surface is equal to one and one-eighth acres. The grate surface, if arranged on one grate, would equal one small town lot of twenty feet front and seventy-seven feet depth. The boiler tubes, placed end to end, would be thirteen and one-half miles long."

A major breakthrough in U.S. steam plant development came at about the turn of the century with the general adoption of water-tube boilers. Construction of the "tubulous" or "express" boiler, as it was called, was almost directly the opposite to that of the less complex traditional fire-tube or "Scotch" boiler, since the feed water was carried through tubes in the combustion chamber instead of the other way around. This arrangement permitted employment of much higher steam pressures than with fire-tubes because the small-diameter tubing could be made much stronger than the boiler walls. The water-tube boiler was also lighter, took up less space, used less water, was easier to repair, worked better under forced draft, and was more efficient. Prototype tubulous boilers had been built even before the Civil War, and although technological advances made their formidable theoretical advantages practicable by about 1890, their use for several more years was largely restricted to steam plants for torpedo boats. After about 1900, however, most new U.S. warships incorporated the improved boilers, and steam working pressures quickly jumped to more than 250 pounds per square inch. A number of patented designs—differing mainly in the shape and arrangement of the tubes—came into use, each with its school of ardent advocates. The Babcock and Wilcox, Belleville, Durr, Mosher, Niclausse, Normand, Thornycroft, and Yarrow boilers all achieved prominence.

After a slow start, the use of auxiliary machinery in the Steel Navy also expanded with fantastic rapidity. Steam had been employed for training turrets aboard monitors and for running various auxiliary pumps as far back as the Civil War, but now it was also adopted for operating capstans, winches, ammunition and ash hoists, steering engines, ventilating fans, air compressors, dynamos, and even ice machines. The battleship *Indiana,* commissioned in 1895, boasted a total of eighty-six auxiliary steam engines of assorted types and sizes. Because the multitude of small steam engines was relatively inefficient, and due to losses from condensation, leakage, and friction, it was estimated that about twenty percent of a warship's steam went into running her auxiliaries.

Hydraulic systems (using distilled water as the operating medium) were sometimes employed for operating auxiliary machinery, especially in warships built by the Union Iron Works. These eliminated the overheating of closed compartments by steam engines and pipes, as well as the danger of scalding from ruptured steam lines. Pneumatic (compressed-air) auxiliaries were also used experimentally in such installations as the steering gear of the monitor *Terror,* and although these also avoided many of the problems associated with steam, they were very noisy and did not demonstrate a clear superiority.

The strongest impetus for shipboard auxiliary machinery came with the introduction of electricity. A brief demonstration of electric lighting was made aboard the old steam sloop *Brooklyn* in 1882, and the following year the *Trenton* was fitted with a steam-driven Edison dynamo and 238 electric lamps, making her the first naval vessel in the world to be so equipped. (Up to this time all lighting below decks had been by means of candles, oil lanterns, or deadlights in the overheads.) Similar plants were specified for the ABCD ships during their construction, and within a few years improved electrical systems, with their high efficiency and precise control,

Stokers feed a battleship's insatiable boilers in a photograph taken on board the Massachusetts *in about 1899. At full power ships of this class burned eight to twelve tons of coal per hour.*

were taking over many of the tasks formerly performed by steam auxiliaries. Competitive installations of steam and electrical turret-training machinery in the new armored cruiser *Brooklyn* in 1896 proved highly favorable to electricity, and thereafter electrical auxiliaries proliferated rapidly. The electrical equipment in the battleship *Kearsarge,* commissioned in 1900, included seven dynamos; 750 incandescent lights; four searchlights; two Ardois signaling sets; electric speed, helm, and steering transmitters and indicators; and fifty-five electric motors for powering the ship's winches, boat cranes, ventilating fans, gun-elevating and turret-turning gears, projectile ramming equipment, and ammunition hoists.

After the turn of the century engineering progress slowed somewhat. The major shipboard engineering development of the early twentieth century—the steam turbine—was not to achieve general acceptance until a later era. One major advance that was partially realized during this period, however, was the employment of liquid fuel for producing steam. Petroleum had been tried on board ship as early as 1867, and in 1892 interest was briefly revived when the Secretary of the Navy proposed that a torpedo boat be fitted for liquid-fuel operation. Although this idea was rejected at the time, on the specious grounds that the native supply of oil was unsuitable, by 1897 the experimental torpedo boat *Stiletto* had been so equipped, and in 1899 additional tests were conducted with the torpedo boat *Talbot.* About this time engineers recognized the importance of atomizing liquid fuel (it having previously been poured over the bed of coal or burned in an open pan under the boilers), and tests at the Washington Navy Yard demonstrated that steam could be produced much more rapidly and efficiently with oil than with coal. Several merchant auxiliaries were converted with great success, their fireroom crews being reduced by half. In 1902 the Secretary recommended that a third of the new torpedo boats and destroyers be built with liquid-fuel plants, but this proposal was not realized. Finally, in 1908 a landmark development was achieved with installation of the U.S. Navy's first large-scale oil-burning steam plant in the monitor *Wyoming.*

The Steel Navy was essentially a navy of coal, however, and "black diamonds" dominated its operation as thoroughly as their dust permeated its ships. A warship's endurance was limited by the size of her coal bunkers, and there was never enough room. Fleet commanders never knew what quality of fuel they would find in the next port or how they would have to get it aboard. Some coal burned beautifully and some formed huge clinkers. Some would hardly burn at all. Most smoked prodigiously, but none so much as the Japanese product. To keep the fleet in coal the Navy needed one special collier and one merchantman for every four fighting ships. "Coal passer" was a rating for which men had to be recruited and trained separately, so alien was it to the clean duties of the deck force.

All of the problems of coal were summed up in the evolution known as "coaling ship." This filthy process was the bane of every crew's existence and helped explain the long-standing nostalgia for sail among seamen. As one expert lamented, "Coaling causes more desertions from the Navy than any other feature of the service." In addition to its unpleasantness, coaling could be dangerous. During the Spanish-American War, ships off Cuba had to pull out of the blockade and find some sheltered cove where a collier could tie alongside. As the two ships banged together, coal was passed across in bags, dumped into little carts, wheeled along the deck to the round bunker scuttles, and dumped down chutes into the bunkers where dust-covered trimmers leveled and packed it into place. The captain of the battleship *Iowa,* after coaling from the *Justin,* noted with some satisfaction that "though we gave her some pretty hard knocks, no holes were punched in her side." He was disgusted with the collier *Sterling,* however, "for having sides like paper." The second-class battleship *Texas* couldn't coal at sea at all because her tremendous gun sponsons prevented colliers from coming alongside.

In such circumstances it was natural that Navy men dreamed of a decent method for coaling at sea. One inventor claimed that his proposed method would have the additional advantage of preventing coal passers from deserting, since they would be too far from land to get off the ship. In 1893 the Navy tested a rig between the protected cruiser *San Francisco* and the old *Kearsarge,* employing a 250-foot cable running from shear poles on the stern of the cruiser to a block on the foremast of the sloop, by which two-hundred-pound bags of coal could be trolleyed across. An improved version using a tensioned double span was tested aboard the collier *Marcellus* and battleship *Massachusetts* in 1899 and 1900, with considerable success. Many authorities felt that it was a mistake to burden warships with a lot of extra machinery, however, and instead recommended construction of specially designed coaling vessels. As a result the Navy laid down a dozen big colliers beginning with the *Vestal* in 1904, but most of these did not enter service until after 1910.

Coal remained an integral part of fleet operations well into a subsequent era. Two colliers were still on hand in 1940, and even during World War II a few coal-burning ships were pressed into service. Their crews must have cursed the black stuff just as heartily as their predecessors had done two generations earlier.

An electrician adjusts brushes on one of the battleship Oregon's *steam-driven dynamos. These provided electricity for shipboard lighting, searchlights, blowers, and ammunition hoists.*

Massive Power

Oilers and machinists in the protected cruiser Newark, *above, tend to one of their ship's 4,400-horsepower triple-expansion engines. The cylinder assemblies in this and other Steel Navy cruisers built during the 1880s had to be installed on their sides in order to fit under the protective deck. By the 1890s, however, engineers were able to produce vertical-cylinder engines—such as the 4,600-horsepower model in the armored cruiser* Brooklyn, *opposite— that were compact enough to fit below the protective armor. Because they were designed to have a relatively high piston speed and a short stroke, Navy engines were much more susceptible to vibration and wear at high speeds than were engines in merchant vessels, and a few hours at maximum power under battle conditions could virtually wreck a warship's machinery.*

Coal Dust Everywhere

Sailors in lighters alongside the second battleship Maine, *opposite, fill bags with "black diamonds" for hoisting aboard, while their begrimed counterparts on board the* Connecticut, *above, dump the disagreeable substance down their battleship's coal chutes. Coaling ship was an all-hands evolution, and once started was usually carried on nonstop, day and night, until the bunkers were full. Since the task was regarded as a drill, great efforts were made to attain record loading speed, and a good crew could handle more than one hundred tons per hour. The efficiency of a warship's engines varied in direct proportion to the quality of her coal, and that mined from the Pocahontas seam in West Virginia was generally considered the most desirable.*

Under Forced Draft

*Except for the supreme test of battle, the most critical
period in any warship's career came during her official
contract trials, when still in the hands of the builders.
Upon her engineering performance during a four-hour
speed run hinged not only the question of prompt
acceptance by the Navy Department, but also tens of
thousands of dollars in bonus payments or penalties,
depending on whether the ship exceeded or fell short of
the contract speed. Here the battleship Missouri steams
under forced draft during her four-hour trial off the
New England coast on 21 October 1903. To insure
maximum performance the builders manned the Missouri's
boiler and engine spaces with a force of 246 men (thirty-
four more than would be numbered in her entire
engineering department after entering commission) and
the battleship attained an average speed of 18.1454 knots,
slightly in excess of the requirement.*

With all available means of control at hand—wheel, engine telegraph, voice tubes, and messenger—a watch officer aboard the protected cruiser Newark *conns the ships under the practiced eye of his captain.*

Communications and Command

By the end of its first decade the New Navy had already made remarkable progress in the fields of naval construction, ordnance, and engineering, but in the area of communications it remained little changed from the days of sail. Although a network of transoceanic telegraph cables, begun in 1859, linked the major capitals and commercial centers of Europe and America, messages between the Navy's shore establishment and its commanders at sea still had to be transmitted at least part of the way by ship, a time-consuming and uncertain process.

The lack of rapid, reliable, long-range naval communications had a profound effect on command relationships; indeed it could be said to dictate them. Since commanders of ships beyond the sight of land were also beyond the control of their superiors, they simply had to be trusted to do what was right, and were of necessity given great latitude in the execution of their duties. Self-reliance, common sense, and a thorough knowledge of Navy Regulations and the laws of the sea were therefore prerequisites to command, and those officers selected to show the flag on distant stations had to be skilled leaders, tacticians, and diplomats, for in time of crisis higher authority back home would be unable to assist them with detailed instructions or advice.

At the same time, however, primitive internal shipboard and tactical communications tended to limit the degree of control which the fleet's captains and flag officers were able to exert over the increasingly complex operations of their own ships and squadrons. On board ship, simple mechanically operated gongs and bells were available for some control functions, but most information had to be transmitted by lung power alone over voice tubes which connected the bridge, engine room, and other key stations. Even the use of these was usually limited to the passing of simple and standardized commands, for as communications expert Lieutenant Albert P. Niblack explained it, "the voice gets confused and drowned amongst the several pipes, especially if the wind is blowing."

In time of battle the captain, watch officers, and helmsman were expected to squeeze themselves into a cramped armored conning tower where communications and visibility were at their very worst. The Sino-Japanese Battle of the Yalu in 1894 demonstrated that "a commanding officer, after a few moments, is half-blind and totally deaf," and to insure that vital orders would get through, relays of word-passers had to be stationed throughout the ship, some in vulnerable locations topside or in the unarmored superstructure. There was no provision at all for the admiral in charge of the force. "In the squadron I recently commanded . . . I expected to gain a large amount of glory, in the event of battle . . . by remaining outside the turret," declared Rear Admiral Richard Meade in 1895.

For daytime tactical ship-to-ship communications the Navy of the 1880s and early '90s relied primarily on a flag-hoist system of thirty signal flags and pennants. Although this method was basically sound—and similar to that still in use today—the clumsy general signal book used with it until after the turn of the century (containing 5,856 different signals of every description) was considered "beneath contempt" by some officers, so remote was it from the realities of command at sea. Night tactical communications were almost nonexistent. Lieutenant S. A. Staunton, signal officer for the new Squadron of Evolution in 1889, later recalled attempting "for half of the middle watch one night to send a short signal to a ship not a mile away . . . the ordinary torch, which at that time represented our total achievement in squadron night signaling, sputtered, threw turpentine, and repeatedly went out after the manner of its kind."

By about the mid-1890s, however, the pressing need for more effective ship and squadron control, along with progress in the employment of electricity at sea, led to a number of significant developments in naval communications. Lieutenant Bradley A. Fiske, one of the Navy's most brilliant and inventive officers, developed a whole family of electrical steering and engine telegraphs; speed, revolution, and direction indicators; and rangefinders; many of which were soon installed in the fleet's new warships. Telephones, installed experimentally aboard the cruiser *Philadelphia* in 1891, also quickly became standard shipboard equipment.

For the routine dissemination of orders to ships' crews, the traditional bugle call was to remain the keystone of communications throughout the era of the Steel Navy. So refined did this system eventually become that calling away the various types of ship's boats alone required twelve different bugle calls, and ninety-eight had to be learned for all of the routine events afloat and ashore.

Night communications between ships became much more effective early in the 1890s with general adoption of Ardois signaling, an idea borrowed from the French Navy. With this method, which employed five (later four) double electric lanterns suspended in a line from the masthead, characters were formed by combinations of red and white flashing lights. (Ardois lights may be seen hanging from the mast yardarm of the monitor *Miantonomoh* on page 92.) For longer-range communications the Very system, which used sequences of red and green flares fired from a pistol, was employed. Searchlights, intended primarily for illuminating targets, were occasionally used to send messages to ships over the horizon by directing their beams upward against the clouds, but line-of-sight "blinker" searchlight communication did not come into general use until about 1904.

Routine daytime communications over short distances were accomplished with the "wig-wag" code, which employed a single hand-held flag (see photograph on page 281). In 1907 the much faster two-flag semaphore system was also adopted, and to increase its effective range, signaling machines with large, flailing arms were devised. A four-arm masthead semaphore device, another Fiske invention, also enjoyed brief popularity just after the turn of the century. (One may be seen aboard the battleship *Massachusetts* on page 79.)

For many years there was considerable controversy within the Navy over the selection of the most efficient signal code. During the Civil War one devised by Army officer A. J. Meyer had been employed by both the Army and Navy, but in 1886 both services switched to the Continental Morse Code, and again in 1890 to the American Morse Code. Finally, in 1893–94 the Navy managed to secure adoption of a thirty-character modification of the Meyer code, known thereafter as the Army-Navy Code. This proved particularly versatile for shipboard use and formed the basis for the "wig-wag," four-arm semaphore, Ardois, and Very systems.

Naval operations during the Spanish-American War demonstrated that much improvement in communications was needed. Voice tubes were still deemed to be the most reliable means of internal communications, for telephones were found too weak to be heard above the noise of battle, and electrical devices were generally condemned as being "too delicate, difficult to keep in adjustment, and liable to be rendered unserviceable by the shock of large guns." An elaborate coastal signal network, numbering 193 stations manned by Naval Militiamen, and several homing pigeon stations, were hastily organized to warn of approaching Spanish warships, but these proved of little value and were soon disbanded. Long-distance communications during the war depended on a few vital underseas cables, often under foreign control and subject to enemy disruption. The vulnerability of such commercial lines was demonstrated when the Navy cut the Spanish cables into Cuba and the Philippines. As a result, after the war the collier *Nero* conducted a transpacific cable-route survey and the Government acquired several remote islands for cable stations to provide more secure communications between the United States and its new possessions.

It was the advent of Marconi wireless telegraphy in Europe during the late 1890s that really foreshadowed a new era in naval communications. In 1899 the Navy Department conducted a series of tests between temporary Marconi installations in the battleship *Massachusetts*, the cruiser *New York*, the torpedo boat *Porter*, and the Highlands, New Jersey, lighthouse station, during which messages were transmitted over ranges of up to thirty-five miles. In 1902 additional experiments were carried out at Washington, D.C., and Annapolis, Maryland, to choose the wireless best adapted to Navy use. Slaby-Arco apparatus (imported from Germany) was selected and in 1903 was installed in seven ships and at five shore stations. By the end of 1904 the Navy had fifty-nine wireless installations.

The value of the new medium was demonstrated during naval maneuvers off Maine in 1903, when the cruiser *Olympia*, acting as a scout, was able to alert the flagship *Kearsarge* by wireless in time for defending forces to intercept the attacking fleet. Wireless telegraphy also proved a great success during the world cruise of the Battle Fleet in 1907–09, with messages between ship and shore being sent over a thousand miles under favorable conditions. Radio was becoming an integral part of naval operations.

As in many other areas, the Steel Navy came into being with communications and command still attuned to the requirements of an earlier, less complex era. The period ended with the groundwork laid for near-instantaneous communications on a worldwide scale, but also with the seal of doom on the traditional absolute independence of naval commanders at sea and on distant stations.

This Slaby-Arco wireless telegraph apparatus, jury-rigged aboard the protected cruiser Baltimore, was one of seven sets installed in U.S. warships in 1903—thereby ushering in a new age of rapid naval communications.

Benjamin F. Tracy, Secretary of the Navy from 1889 to 1893, was one of several strong administrators who helped launch the Navy on its course towards control of the high seas.

Organization and the Shore Establishment

The yeast of change that began to transform the Navy during the 1880s had its effect on the organization and shore establishment as well as on ships and material. Developments in administration tended to be somewhat more sporadic than those affecting the fleet itself, however, for they were subject to the direct influence of powerful personalities and reflected the characteristics of successive Secretaries of the Navy, their assistants, chief advisers, and even Presidents.

Most major changes in the Navy's internal policies and organization were related to a continuing three-way struggle for power within the Department. On one side were the senior line officers—the "establishment"—whose views reflected the generally conservative attitudes of the seagoing forces. A second point of view was represented by the officers of the several staff corps, each with its own specialized area of interest, and seldom seeing eye to eye with its brothers except in a common determination to gain greater autonomy from the heavy-handed domination of the line. The third side was occupied by the civilian appointed officials—the secretaries—who exercised political control over the Navy Department. Subject to outside pressures from President, party, and Congress, they were also importuned by the internal naval factions and generally ended up more or less under the influence of one or another pressure group. The resulting interplay of forces as administrations changed and alliances were made and dissolved thus generated most of the organizational innovations achieved during the era of the Steel Navy.

The shore establishment during the early 1880s included nine large, but obsolete, navy yards: Portsmouth, Boston, New London, New York, Philadelphia, Washington, Norfolk, Pensacola and Mare Island. Smaller stations were also located at Newport, Annapolis, Port Royal, Key West, New Orleans, and Sackett's Harbor on Lake Erie.

The Navy Department itself during the eighties and early nineties consisted of a small, central staff and eight practically autonomous bureaus. Most important to the material development of the New Navy were the four so-called "manufacturing" bureaus, all of which came under the direction of a succession of able, though sometimes parochially strong-minded, chiefs. Responsibility for ships' hulls and structures belonged to the Bureau of Construction and Repair, headed by Chief Constructors Theodore D. Wilson, and later, Philip Hichborn. In the Bureau of Steam Engineering, which was responsible for ships' propulsion plants, successive counterparts to these officers were Engineers-in-Chief Charles H. Loring and George M. Melville. Both of these bureaus were "staff" in that they were headed and manned by officers of the Construction Corps and Steam Engineering Corps, respectively.

The powerful Bureau of Ordnance, in charge of providing the Navy's guns and ammunition, was headed consecutively by Commodores Montgomery Sicard, William M. Folger, and William T. Sampson. The fourth manufacturing bureau—Equipment and Recruiting—embraced a peculiar combination of functions including responsibility for anchors, sails, cordage, coal, fresh water, and other miscellany that had somehow escaped the cognizance of the bigger bureaus. Successive heads of this organization were Commodores Winfield Scott Schley, George Dewey, and French E. Chadwick. Both of these bureaus were controlled directly by line officers.

Three more branches dealt with problems farther removed from the seagoing needs of the Navy. The Bureau of Yards and Docks was responsible for the Navy's real estate, Provisions and Clothing for consumable supplies, and Medicine and Surgery for the health needs of the service. With the exception of Yards and Docks, which was for some years under the direction of line officers, these bureaus were headed by officers of the appropriate staff corps.

The final and most powerful branch was the Bureau of Navigation. Originally established as the scientifically-oriented supplier of charts and nautical almanacs, it soon gained control over all personnel assignments and fleet movements, thereby achieving domination over the other bureaus and offices of the Department. Its powerful chiefs—Commodores John Grimes Walker, and later, Francis M. Ramsay—usually had direct daily access to the office of the Secretary, and kept the reins of power firmly in the hands of the general line officers. Although widely respected as able and forceful individuals, these two men were also among the most unpopular officers in the Navy because of their autocratic ways and ability to make or break whomever they chose.

Nevertheless, the ultimate power to direct the policies of the Department lay in the hands of the various civilian secretaries. William H. Hunt (in office during 1881–82) succeeded in initiating development of the Steel Navy's first new ships, but was shunted aside before he could exert much influence on the administrative side of the Department's affairs. He did, however, establish a new Office of Intelligence to keep the Department informed of military developments abroad. Lieutenant Commander French E. Chadwick became the first, and for a time the only, U.S. naval attaché.

Hunt's replacement, William E. Chandler (Secretary during 1882–85), began to devote his attention to administration once he had overcome the difficulties of getting new ships authorized and under construction. Finding the number of yards and stations far in excess of the Navy's needs, he closed several of the least useful ones and began to concentrate the major shore operations at New York, Norfolk, and Mare Island. Reflecting President Chester A. Arthur's interest in eliminating the spoils system in government appointments, Chandler implemented the Pendleton Act, which established the civil service system in 1883, within the Navy Department. He also attempted to eliminate favoritism and the influence of cliques on the officer corps by breaking the Bureau of Navigation's stranglehold on personnel assignments and vesting this power in a small board of bureau chiefs. However this reform, made in 1884, was short-lived, being largely negated by Chandler's successor.

Probably the most far-reaching innovation during Chandler's administration was the establishment in 1884 of the Naval War College, a move long advocated by progressive officers under the leadership of Commodore Stephen B. Luce. Although principally concerned with the military education of senior officers, the college at Newport ultimately made its influence felt in nearly every sphere of the Navy's strategic and organizational thinking. Another, seemingly minor, change instituted in 1882 was the appointment of a librarian to keep the Department's growing collection of historical records and books in order. The man selected for the job was Professor James R. Soley of the Naval Academy. No mere custodian of books, however, Soley was destined to have a major influence on the expansion of the Navy.

The year 1885 saw a change in administration, with

Grover Cleveland entering the White House and William C. Whitney assuming the Navy Secretary's post (1885–89). Whitney, suspicious of political motivation in everything his predecessors had touched, turned to a new set of advisers when he took office. Relying heavily on the advice of Commodore Walker of the Bureau of Navigation, he rapidly became popular with the line faction, which regarded him as the "Prince of Secretaries." Old Admiral David Dixon Porter, however, wrote that Whitney was "completely hoodwinked by the bureaus and never had his own way at any time when he imagined himself master of the situation."

Although a progressive in many ways, Whitney seemed unable to accept the basic principles of sea-power strategy. Furthermore, he did not get on at all well with strategist Captain Alfred Thayer Mahan, who had succeeded Luce as president of the Naval War College in 1886. Apparently as the result of some complex service politics, Whitney allowed the independence of the institution to be undermined, a situation that led to the temporary closing of the school a few years later.

Secretary Whitney's chief administrative interest lay in reforming the business methods of the Department. When an inventory of material at the various navy yards turned up $20 million in excess supplies that had been hoarded by the separate bureaus, he determined to centralize the responsibility for purchasing and accounting in a single bureau. Unfortunately, his reorganization proposals were too sweeping to get through Congress and his administrative reforms were delayed while he undid everything started by the previous secretary before beginning with his own.

Whitney did succeed in regrouping some of the manufacturing jobs at the navy yards into a more efficient pattern, got the Navy's own facilities started in steel warship construction, converted the Washington Navy Yard into the Naval Gun Factory, and stimulated the development of U.S. sources of steel and armaments. Unfortunately, Whitney's deep interest in science sometimes led to an overemphasis on novel warship types of little lasting value.

Another development during the Whitney regime was the beginning of a naval reserve. In 1887 legislation was introduced in Congress to subsidize construction of mail steamers which could be converted into auxiliary cruisers in time of war, and to support the establishment of a reserve force to be recruited from the merchant service. Although the bills failed, several states, beginning with Massachusetts in 1888 and followed by New York, Pennsylvania, and Rhode Island, took up the initiative and created Naval Militias of their own.

The two terms of Grover Cleveland as President were interrupted by the administration of Benjamin Harrison,

Officers of the influential General Board, presided over by Admiral George Dewey (at the head of the table), assemble at the Naval War College in 1901 to consider matters of naval policy.

239

whose Secretary of the Navy (1889–93) was Benjamin F. Tracy. Beginning in 1890 Tracy was ably assisted by Professor Soley, the first appointee to the office of Assistant Secretary of the Navy since the late 1860s. An ardent supporter of the War College (and one of its chief lecturers), Soley played a leading role in revitalizing that institution despite continued opposition from the Bureau of Navigation.

Secretary Tracy tackled the problem of haphazard coordination between the various agencies involved in ship design and construction by appointing a Construction Board, consisting of the heads of the four manufacturing bureaus plus the Chief of Yards and Docks. Although not an ideal solution, Tracy's method of holding the bureau heads collectively responsible for the success of each new ship was a major improvement and resulted in some excellent war vessels.

In an effort to improve the "tumble-down condition" of his navy yards, Tracy proposed selling the excess stores and putting the proceeds to better use. He also reformed employment practices in the yards—over the protests of local politicians—by introducing a merit system for the selection of shop foremen and supervisors. Tracy added to the Navy's shore facilities, establishing a navy yard on Puget Sound; a new ordnance proving ground at Indian Head, Maryland; and an ammunition depot at Lake Denmark, New Jersey. Overseas, land was acquired for a naval station and coaling facility at Tutuila, Samoa. The Secretary also pushed work on new drydocks for the major yards, but most of these, for reasons of economy and expediency, were of timber construction and later proved to be of limited value.

Grover Cleveland's return to office brought former Congressman Hilary A. Herbert to the helm of the Navy Department (1893–97). Herbert came into office with a reputation as an enemy of the Naval War College and as a crony of the conservative Rear Admiral Francis Ramsay. Ramsay, chief of the Bureau of Navigation since 1889 and long a detractor of Captain Mahan, felt that "it is not the business of naval officers to write books." Blocked by Secretary Tracy in earlier efforts to remove Mahan from the War College, Ramsay now seized the opportunity to order him to sea duty in command of the protected cruiser *Chicago* (actually a most desirable assignment). Herbert allowed the orders to go through, but refused to downgrade the War College. After looking into both sides of the issue he became a convert to the theories of Mahan and his supporters, and from this time on the War College's position was secure.

U.S. naval expansion was temporarily interrupted during the early nineties by an economic depression, but in 1895 Secretary Herbert was able to initiate the resumption of battleship construction. He also made additional civil service reforms in the navy yards, and further refined the coordina-

tion of shipbuilding by giving the Bureau of Construction and Repair prime authority in this area, with responsibility for coordinating and approving design proposals initiated by the other bureaus. As a money-saving measure, Herbert instituted the practice of laying up ships in reserve with skeleton crews, and Secretary Tracy's speedy commerce raiders, the *Columbia* and *Minneapolis,* were thus put aside within a few years of their completion.

Development of the Naval Militias also received attention during this period. During Secretary Tracy's administration, in 1891, Congress had appropriated funds to equip the various state militias, and had granted subsidies for such commercial vessels as might be converted into auxiliaries in time of war. Under Herbert, in 1894, another act authorized the Department to loan older warships to the militias as training vessels. The rudiments of ships, men, materials, and training facilities were finally in existence to provide a viable naval reserve.

Naval expansion again accelerated following the election of imperialist William McKinley, whose Secretary of the Navy was John D. Long (1897–1902). Secretary Long brought in as his assistant "an interesting personality," Theodore Roosevelt, who in Long's words "worked indefatigably . . . was heart and soul in his work . . . his ardor sometimes went faster than the President or the Department approved."

During the first months of his administration, Long was principally occupied with the problems of the gathering war with Spain and with its prosecution once hostilities had begun. To provide central direction during the conflict the Secretary created an *ad hoc* Naval War Board with a flexible membership, whose duties were to evaluate military information, prepare strategic plans, and advise on the conduct of the war. The Board was dissolved immediately after the termination of hostilities, but its successful performance inspired long-time proponents of a strong general staff to increase pressure for establishment of such an organization. In response, Long organized a less-powerful General Board in 1900 to "insure efficient preparation of the fleet in case of war and for the naval defense of the coast." Presided over by Spanish-American War hero Admiral George Dewey, the Board was soon passing judgment on all matters of interest to the Navy. Although many functions were subsequently added by regulation, the General Board inexorably expanded its sphere of influence by virtue of the reputation and ability of the officers who served on it. Soon both Secretary Long and his new Assistant Secretary, Charles H. Darling, came to feel that the Board was encroaching on the civilian side of the Department's affairs as well as using its position to propagandize in favor of a general staff. Testifying before Congress after leaving office, in 1904, Darling complained

Battleships moor alongside the coal piers at the Norfolk Navy Yard, second-ranking U.S. Navy facility, in 1907.
The destroyer Stewart *is in the foreground and the receiving ship* Richmond *may be seen across the Elizabeth River.*

that the Board "has already invaded the province of civil administration and planted there its standard of conquest." But the General Board would continue to hold sway for many more years, until its unwieldy deliberations and often reactionary conclusions were found inadequate for the fast-moving changes of the 1930s.

Under Secretary Long many naval facilities were established, expanded, or improved. Even before the Spanish-American War, embarrassed by the necessity of sending the new battleship *Indiana* to Halifax for drydocking, he appointed a Drydock Board to determine what new facilities were needed. A similar Coaling Board was also established to review the need for fueling depots. Soon new drydocks were authorized for most major navy yards and stations. Originally specified to be of wood construction, they were redesigned in concrete and granite after a wooden dock at the New York yard suddenly collapsed. A steel floating drydock was also constructed for the station at New Orleans, another was brought from Cuba to Pensacola, and work was started on the mammoth *Dewey* drydock for use in the Philippines. The naval facilities at Portsmouth, Boston, League Island, and Pensacola—closed during earlier economy moves—were reopened, and new yards were introduced at Charleston and near Port Orchard on Puget Sound. Coaling stations were established at New London, Key West, and the Dry Tortugas; an ammunition depot at Iona Island near West Point; and overseas bases in the Philippines, on Guam, and later, at Guantanamo Bay, Cuba.

Although the state Naval Militias had rendered commendable service during the Spanish-American War, Long was convinced that "they are not to be considered in any sense a naval reserve capable of manning our seagoing fleet . . . a true naval reserve would have to be established under naval auspices alone . . . the dual character of the naval militia, owing as it does allegiance to the state maintaining it and the General Government, must place a limitation on the expec-

tations that the latter has concerning it." Secretary Long was unsuccessful in his attempts to establish a true national naval reserve, however, and thereafter did his best to strengthen the existing system by assigning the auxiliary cruiser *Prairie* to the full-time job of carrying militia units on training cruises. Long also improved the readiness of some of the Navy's older warships by holding them in reserve with half crews. In a test of this innovation in 1900, the battleships *Indiana* and *Massachusetts* were made materially ready for a three-month cruise within thirty hours of receiving the order for their activation. As in all postwar periods, however, the readiness of the reserve fleet and of the militias gradually declined.

When the redoubtable Theodore Roosevelt succeeded to the presidency in 1901, he brought with him many strong personal convictions concerning how the Navy Department should be run. Probably for this reason his five Secretaries of the Navy—William H. Moody, Paul Morton, Charles J. Bonaparte, Victor H. Metcalf, and Truman H. Newberry—tended to be less influential than their predecessors had been. Expansion continued apace, but the already-established organization of the Department was little modified.

Towards the very end of their regime, in January 1909, Roosevelt and Secretary Newberry attempted to push through a major innovation in the management of the navy yards by reorganizing their work under industrial managers. This plan, the product of converts to the emerging school of efficiency and industrial engineering, was technically sound but too far ahead of its time. Within the year most of the reforms had been undone by the more conservative George von L. Meyer, President William H. Taft's Secretary of the Navy. Although material progress after 1909 would continue at an accelerated rate, organizational changes would be minimal or even regressive until a shakeup would take place thirty years later under another President named Roosevelt.

The armored cruiser Maryland *inaugurates a new granite and concrete drydock at the Charlestown Navy Yard, Boston, in August 1905. The 750-foot-long dock was at that time the largest in the United States.*

Navy Yards

The Mare Island Navy Yard in California was for many years the Steel Navy's only major shore facility on the West Coast. Located just across from the town of Vallejo on an arm of San Francisco Bay, the yard was established in 1854. Here the monitor Monadnock, in gray war paint, enters Mare Island's granite drydock for a cleaning in April 1898, not long before her departure for the Philippines to augment Commodore Dewey's squadron.

In 1891 a second West Coast facility, the Puget Sound Naval Station, was established on a deep-water anchorage near the village of Bremerton, Washington. A large wooden drydock was completed there in 1896; the battleship Oregon, right, was the third vessel to be docked. Bremerton was still practically in the wilderness, however, and the yard grew at a very slow pace until after 1905.

A navy yard had existed at Philadelphia since 1801, but in 1871 its operations were moved across town to new facilities on League Island. The yard's fresh water basin on the Delaware River proved ideal for laying up old warships in reserve, an operation carried out there to this day. At left, a group of Civil War monitors, including the Nahant in the foreground, rusts away "in ordinary" some time in the 1890s.

Because conditions at the Navy's Mississippi River facility near New Orleans were unfavorable for excavation of a conventional graving dock, a 525-foot floating drydock was built for use there. Acceptance trials for the new dock, which was towed from Baltimore, Maryland, in 1902, included raising the 11,565-ton battleship Illinois, left. Pumps and other machinery for operating the dock were powered by boilers in its side walls.

The New York Navy Yard

The largest and most active U.S. Navy yard was located on the Brooklyn shore of New York's East River. Established in 1806, it had extensive shipbuilding and repair facilities, three drydocks, and a large naval hospital. Atlantic Fleet battleships in port in this 1903 view include the old Texas, *in the foreground; the* Kearsarge *and* Indiana, *mostly obscured just beyond her; and the* Alabama, *on the far side of the basin. The vessel at far right is the auxiliary cruiser* Buffalo, *employed at this time as a training ship for landsmen.*

247

"You don't need armor when you have men like mine."

Rear Admiral Robley D. Evans, 1908.

Men and Operations of the American Steel Navy

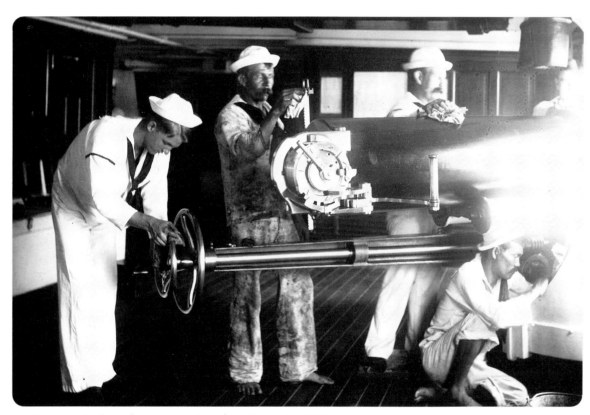

On the gun deck of the protected cruiser Olympia, *1899.*

Captain Francis A. Cook of the Brooklyn *poses with some of his officers. In addition to commissioned and warrant officers, the group includes several naval cadets, two Marines, and a chaplain.*

Officer Personnel and Training

The officer corps of the Old Navy had suffered mightily from the effects of long stagnation. Large numbers of new officers had been commissioned during and immediately after the Civil War and the subsequent gradual decline of the fleet had left them with fewer and fewer ships to serve in. Promotion was strictly by seniority, but advancement to the top positions was effectively blocked by the presence there of men who had achieved rapid promotion during the war and who had many more years to serve before reaching the age of mandatory retirement. Meanwhile, the Naval Academy continued to turn out more new officer candidates than there were vacancies for them. In 1882, with only thirty-one ships in service, there were 1,817 officers on active duty, one to every five seamen. Far too many had to be assigned to shore billets where duties were unchallenging if not downright trivial. Others sought sea duty with the Revenue and Lighthouse Services or the Coast Survey. Favoritism and the open solicitation of desirable orders were the rule of the day.

In legislation enacted into law in August 1882—which also included provisions for the creation of the New Navy—Congress attempted to cut back the swollen ranks of officers by reducing the authorized numbers in grade, curtailing the size of the Naval Academy, and limiting new appointments to the number of actual vacancies. This meat-axe approach reduced the rolls somewhat but further slowed down promotions and increased the age of command, and the personnel situation remained unsatisfactory for many more years.

An event of profound importance to the professional development of the Navy's officers occurred in 1884, however, when Secretary of the Navy William E. Chandler established the Naval War College at Newport, Rhode Island, on the recommendation of a few forward-looking officers. Despite dogged opposition from old-line traditionalists and some bitter personality clashes, the college gradually built up strength under Rear Admiral Stephen B. Luce and Captain Alfred T. Mahan. Although Mahan's opponents succeeded in ordering him to sea and even in shutting down the college in 1890 and 1891, the institution came to life with renewed vigor when one of its former instructors, Professor James R. Soley, became Assistant Secretary of the Navy under Benjamin F. Tracy in 1892. From then on it enjoyed a permanent staff and adequate facilities, growing in importance and imprinting its philosophy of rational study of military and political science on generations of senior officers.

In 1891 Secretary Tracy launched an investigation that identified the principal causes of officer personnel stagnation, but dissention within the service blocked immediate reform. Rivalry between the line and staff corps—especially the Engineer Corps—was growing more and more virulent. The grievances of the engineers dated back to 1869 when Vice Admiral David D. Porter high-handedly pushed through a series of measures downgrading the rank and status of the steam engineers and other staff corps. With the subsequent ascendancy of modern technology in the new ships of the Steel Navy, the engineers and constructors pressed for comparable recognition in the form of positive military rank in place of the old staff titles, and promotion opportunity equal to the line. The engineers were supported in many of their arguments by their professional counterparts in civilian life and ultimately, in 1897, by the outspoken Assistant Secretary of the Navy Theodore Roosevelt. In Roosevelt's view, the duties of a modern navy required that line and staff officers alike have a sound practical knowledge of science and engineering. "Every officer on a modern war vessel in reality has to be an engineer whether he wants to or not," he declared. "What is needed is one homogeneous body, all of whose members are trained for the efficient performance of the duties of the modern line officer."

A Naval Personnel Board reduced this philosophy to specific recommendations which, while delayed in Congress by the outbreak of war in 1898, were written into law in March of the next year. A general pay increase sweetened the pill for the old-liners, who were forced to grant positive rank to the staff officers and accept provisions for early retirement, both voluntary and forced if necessary. The rank of commodore was abolished to shorten the climb to flag rank. The Engineer Corps was amalgamated into the line, all naval cadets were henceforth to be trained in both deck and engineering assignments, and regular line officers were to stand normal tours of duty in the engineering department aboard ship. Officers of the former Engineer Corps who were above the rank of commander were designated for shore duty only, while others were given the option of taking up to two years to pass qualification examinations for line status, a change that many nevertheless elected not to make. The law also provided for a corps of 100 warrant machinists to take over a number of the routine engine room watch standing duties. The technical functions of ship and machinery design, however, were reserved for specialists selected from the line for advanced study. Beginning in 1901 a postgraduate course in naval construction was established at the Massachusetts Institute of Technology to replace previous training in Europe and at the Naval Academy, and in 1902 this was augmented by a similar postgraduate course in engineering at Annapolis.

Unfortunately, consolidation looked better on paper than it worked in fact. The dictum "every officer a fighting engineer" was not rigidly enforced, and junior officers were often excused from serving in engineering jobs. Others proved ill-prepared for their new duties, for as the Chief of the Bureau of Steam Engineering complained, "A man does not become at once a skilled engineer by assuming charge of machinery."

Other officer personnel shortcomings were overcome only slowly and with difficulty. Whereas a surplus of officers had been the problem during the early 1880s, just the opposite became the case two decades later when dozens of new warships were authorized and added to the rapidly expanding fleet. In 1900 Secretary of the Navy John D. Long warned that "the Department is seriously embarrassed by lack of necessary officers to properly man vessels required for immediate service," but corrective action was slow in coming and by 1902 the Navy was 577 officers short of the 1,600 allowed, with nearly 500 in addition to that number needed for new ships soon to be completed. As a result several older warships had to be placed in reserve with reduced complements in order to supply sufficient personnel to man new ones.

Age in command continued to be a nagging problem. In 1903, fifty-seven years of age was the average on taking command of a battleship, and it was not uncommon for senior officers to be incapacitated for duties afloat because of chronic illness. Even in 1908 the famous Rear Admiral Robley D. Evans was forced to relinquish command of the battle fleet on its world cruise because of rheumatism and stomach trouble. For many more years a seesaw struggle was waged between those who wanted to institute promotion by selection after a fixed time in grade, and those who would have preferred to speed up the flow of promotion by lowering the age of retirement.

In 1901 a long-standing barrier fell when Congress authorized the appointment of six new ensigns annually from the warrant officer ranks. While this number was so small as to be insignificant, the action was nevertheless a major breakthrough for the future advancement of enlisted men. A few years later another ancient tradition was breached with the authorization in 1908 of a female Nurse Corps.

The basic correction for officer deficiencies had to come ultimately from changes in the Naval Academy at Annapolis, where for years naval cadets had been trained along traditional lines, their classroom instruction leavened by annual seagoing cruises under sail and steam, and by local operational training in monitors and torpedo boats. As a first major step, the Academy's facilities, which had fallen into disrepair along with the rest of the Old Navy, were thoroughly rehabilitated between 1898 and 1907 with a $10 million building program.

But old traditions were not all easily shucked off. In 1903 the superintendent at Annapolis, Captain Willard H. Brownson, was forced to air some dirty linen when it was disclosed that "hazing of a serious character" had been carried out by midshipmen "in defiance not only of the orders of the Navy Department but also of the laws of Congress." This incident was followed by yet another public scandal in 1905 when a midshipman was killed in a fist fight. The authorities had to admit that such activities, while "highly objectionable and essentially unmilitary," were customs of long standing.

In 1902, when the officer shortage approached disaster proportions, Congress belatedly expanded the input to the Academy by extending the privilege of midshipman appointments to U.S. Senators, a prerogative previously limited to the President and members of the House of Representatives. The following year the number of appointments per Senator and Representative was increased from one to two, and by 1906 enrollment at Annapolis had grown to 879, nearly three times that at the turn of the century.

The famous round-the-world cruise long planned by President Theodore Roosevelt and carried out in 1907–09 was actually conceived as much as a training exercise as a show of force. For the first time new officers, new enlisted men, and new ships would be able to perform major fleet operations. Although the ships came home to face rapid technological obsolescence, the officers and men were on the way to being welded into a homogeneous force capable of leading and fighting a new Navy that would be second to none.

Disciples of sea power gather around Assistant Secretary of the Navy Theodore Roosevelt at the Naval War College in 1897. An ardent Navy advocate, Roosevelt became its most influential supporter when he succeeded to the presidency.

The Senior and the Junior

The officer complement aboard a typical Steel Navy battleship numbered about thirty and included the commanding and executive officers, navigator, four division and gunnery officers, signal officer, captain of the Marines and two assistants, chief engineer and four assistants, paymaster, surgeon and assistant surgeon, chaplain, several naval cadets, and a warrant boatswain, gunner, pay clerk, and carpenter.

With his faithful dog "Bob" at his side, Admiral of the Navy George Dewey enjoys a band concert on the quarterdeck of the flagship Olympia *soon after his triumphant return from Manila.*

Steely-eyed Captain Edwin Longnecker stands before the wheel of his new command, the ex-Brazilian cruiser New Orleans, *in 1899.*

Resplendent in whites, an officer of the Naval Militia called to active duty in 1898 stands watch as Officer of the Deck of the Civil War monitor Nahant.

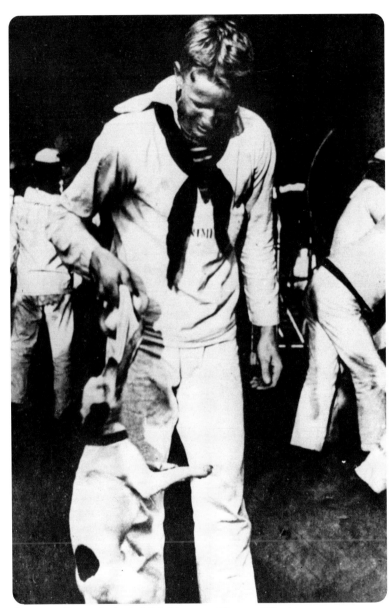

A future fleet admiral, Midshipman Chester Nimitz of the Class of 1905, gets a "chewing" from the ship's mascot during a Naval Academy summer cruise.

The Loneliness and Privilege of Command

Rear Admiral William M. Folger, commander of the Asiatic Station, and Commander Nathan Sargent, his chief of staff, savor after-dinner cigars in the admiral's cabin aboard the flagship Baltimore *in about 1906. The dictates of tradition and discipline required that commanders at sea remain aloof from their subordinates, and there was little social contact with the officers of the wardroom. On the opposite page, the ship's band, Marine detachment, and Officer of the Deck aboard the cruiser* New York *render honors as Rear Admiral Norman H. Farquhar, commander of the North Atlantic Station, departs for his flagship, the* Kearsarge, *anchored just astern. The climb to flag rank was a long and slow one: when this photograph was made in 1900 Admiral Farquhar had already completed some forty-five years of naval service.*

The Camaraderie of the Wardroom

*Officers of the old battleship Maine relax over cigars and table games in their paneled wardroom
in 1896. With fewer than 1,500 commissioned officers in the service, and with all sharing the common
bond of a Naval Academy background, the fleet's wardrooms had the congenial atmosphere of exclusive
social clubs. The day-to-day operation of each wardroom mess was the responsibility of an elected
treasurer or "mess caterer," and the officers paid for their own food. Until abolished by the Secretary
of the Navy in 1914, a "wine mess" of light wines and beer was an integral part of the wardroom scene.*

When ashore, officers of the Steel Navy moved among the upper strata of society, and life in port generally included a happy blend of receptions, dress balls, and genteel feminine companionship. Here, some of the Baltimore's officers demonstrate the workings of a 6-inch gun to a pretty visitor at Sydney, Australia, in 1906.

Future Officers and Gentlemen

The U.S. Naval Academy at Annapolis, Maryland, dated from 1845, when a naval school was established there by Secretary of the Navy George Bancroft. During the 1880s and '90s each graduating class numbered about thirty to fifty cadets, but soon after the turn of the century enrollment was doubled to meet the fleet's critical need for additional officers. In the photograph above, a platoon engages in competitive drill before a gallery of parasol-shaded visitors, while at right, naval cadets receive instruction in the basics of seamanship at a scale model of a full-rigged ship. (Between 1882 and 1902 students were called "naval cadets"; thereafter the traditional term "midshipman" was reinstated.)

Practical Work and
Social Graces

Professional studies during the four-year course at Annapolis were about equally divided between theoretical instruction and practical training. Subjects included seamanship, naval tactics, ordnance and gunnery, navigation, marine engineering, military and international law, and naval history. Practical work included such activities as small boat practice on the Severn River, at right, with old-fashioned muscle work at the oars and formation tactics in the steam launches.

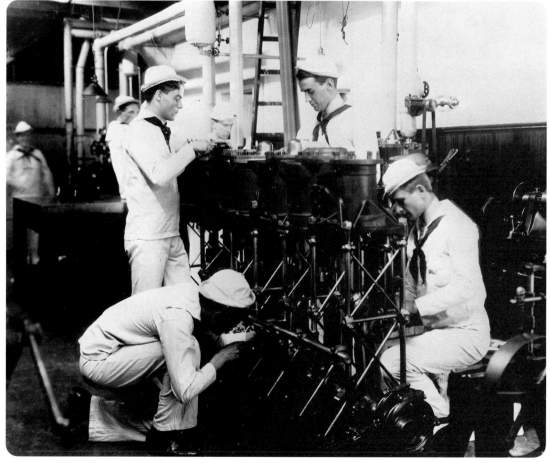

Until 1899, when the officers of the line and the Engineer Corps were amalgamated, engineer candidates devoted their fourth year at the Naval Academy to a specialized course of instruction; after 1899 all naval cadets received the same training. Facilities in the Department of Steam Engineering included this 100-horsepower, triple-expansion steam engine which was entirely designed and built by students.

The Naval Academy's rigorous course of study also embraced most of the arts and sciences, including English, French or Spanish, algebra, geometry, trigonometry, calculus, physics, and chemistry. Here cadets learn the mysteries of electricity in the physics laboratory.

Every aspect of a naval cadet's development was given due attention: at left young gentlemen practice their best manners at tea in the Superintendent's quarters. Following graduation, the cadets had to complete two additional years of practical training aboard ships of the fleet and pass a final examination before receiving their commissions as ensigns. During this period they were not permitted to marry.

Berth deck cooks aboard the battleship Oregon *pose with their simple utensils and chipped enamel coffee cups, kept clean with the aid of the "Gold Dust twins."*

Bluejackets of the Steel Navy

It took a long time for the ferment and excitement of building the new Steel Navy to filter down to the average bluejacket. While the new ships were gestating on the drawing boards and shipbuilders' stocks someone had to keep the Old Navy going, obsolete as it may have been. The enlisted men of the fleet were therefore oriented toward sail, smoothbore cannon, and wooden-walled ships long after the transition to steel was actually underway.

The bluejackets of the eighties were a polygot crew, enlisted from the seaports and merchant marines of half a hundred nations. Colorful old Admiral David D. Porter described them as "as fine a body of Germans, Huns, Norsemen, Gauls, Chinese and other outside barbarians as one could wish to see, softened down by time and civilization . . ." These "freelances," seasoned with a smattering of American boys rescued from "perdition" by the grace of the recruiting officer, had, in Porter's words, "no sentiment for our flag . . . They ship for money." Personnel turnover during the late 1880s ran to nearly sixty percent annually.

In an effort to improve the caliber of American seamen, the Navy had employed the apprentice system since 1875. Training started when a boy was between fourteen and eighteen years of age. Often a runaway from home, the aspiring seaman passed a cursory physical examination at the recruiting office, reported on board an unseaworthy old relic moored to a run-down pier in one of the moldering navy yards, and signed his articles of enlistment. In this ancient craft, known as a receiving ship or "guardo," the new apprentice drew his outfit of hammock, uniforms, and ditty box, and was put to work sweeping decks and polishing brass until a full draft of recruits had accumulated.

Then it was off to Coaster's Harbor Island at Newport, Rhode Island, and the old stationary training ship *New Hampshire* for classes in seamanship and gunnery as well as the traditional academic subjects suitable for a school of teenaged boys. Classroom work was spiced by drills in sail handling,

signaling, infantry tactics, and small boat handling. After about six months of shore training, the apprentice was transferred to the *Jamestown, Portsmouth,* or one of the other large sailing vessels of the apprentice training squadron. One year afloat, generally taken up by two long cruises to European or South American waters, completed the "school of the topman." Duty in one of the regular warships of the Steel Navy followed, until the apprentice reached the age of twenty-one, when he was discharged to reenlist as a seaman.

Unfortunately most did not ship over. Although there were more than a thousand apprentices under training in 1888, fewer than sixty graduates from the previous ten years of the program were still in the service. Of the entire enlisted force of 7,900, only forty-six percent were native born.

As steel warships began to enter the fleet the output of the sail training ships became less and less relevant to the needs of the service, but in spite of increased rumblings from officers of progressive inclinations, the old breed continued to have their way. Respected officers like Porter and Rear Admiral Stephen B. Luce maintained that a shift to schooling in machinery and ships of steel would produce a force of "deckhands" instead of "sailors." Others simply loved the ways of sail and resisted its decline almost instinctively. For all of its inefficiencies the apprentice system did gradually bring about a reversal in the proportions of native- and foreign-born sailors: by 1899 more than three-quarters of the bluejackets in the fleet were U.S. citizens.

Other factors also contributed to the appalling turnover in personnel. Men who found the Navy life not to their liking were frequently allowed to purchase an "ordinary discharge" after one year of service. For those who reenlisted faithfully until finally forced out of the Navy by old age or failing health, there was no provision whatever for retirement pay. An aged sailor's only hope for sustenance after discharge was to gain admission to the Old Sailor's Home in Philadelphia, but that institution always had more applicants than vacancies. The Military Retirement Act of 1885 granted pensions to retiring soldiers and Marines, but through an incredible oversight in Congress the Navy was left out, and it took until 1899 for new legislation to be passed granting sailors retirement pay after thirty years of naval service.

Another major source of dissatisfaction was the low regard in which enlisted men were held by the general populace. "No sailors or dogs allowed" was no joke, but rather was the general practice at restaurants, theaters, and hotels in most coastal cities. Not until 1906, when President Theodore Roosevelt lent his personal support to a courageous chief yeoman, Fred J. Buenzle, who had instituted legal suit in a test case against the proprietor of a Newport dance hall notorious for its discrimination against sailors, was public opinion finally mobilized in favor of the bluejacket and laws were passed making discrimination against Army or Navy personnel in uniform a misdemeanor.

It must be admitted that Jack often was a rough fellow who was inclined towards carousing and hell-raising on his rare visits ashore. Many sailors were so chronic in their misbehavior that they lived in a perpetual state of restriction broken only by shore liberty at least once every three months as mandated by Navy Regulations. Unfortunately, the social gap between old-line officers and seamen was so vast that little constructive attention was devoted to personnel problems. A natural result was that a high desertion rate added to the chronic personnel shortages. Despite the fact that deserters then could lose their citizenship for life, the desertion rate was more than fourteen percent in 1901 and almost as high for the next two years. A study of the desertion problem led to the interesting conclusion that a nine-percent rate was to be normally expected—one percent would leave on account of the poor food, another because of the crowded living conditions, three percent because of restricted opportunity for liberty ashore, and four percent by reason of the "restless spirit which is found in many of our young men."

As increasing numbers of new ships were completed and commissioned during the late 1890s, the need for crewmen caused pressures on the enlisted training system to increase inexorably. A new training station was authorized at Yerba Buena Island in San Francisco Bay, but this facility did not become operative until after the war with Spain. By 1899 the output of the apprentice training ships was so far behind the needs of the Navy that a parallel system was set up to bring older but inexperienced recruits in as "landsmen." A training station for landsmen was established at Norfolk and a squadron of five to seven ships was assigned to the new program in addition to a similar number for apprentices.

Nevertheless, by 1904 the situation had deteriorated to the point where the Navy was unable to man some of its new ships and drastic steps had to be taken. The training squadrons were abolished, the minimum age of enlistment was raised first to sixteen and then seventeen years, and the apprentice and landsman systems were combined into the basic arrangement that has continued to this day. Recruit training was concentrated at shore stations in Newport, Norfolk, and San Francisco, and a new facility at what is now Great Lakes, Illinois, was started. After four months of basic training "apprentice seamen" were examined, those who passed were advanced to ordinary seamen, and all future training was carried out "on the job" in regular ships of the active fleet. Only the lowly "coal passers," the entering rate of the engineering force, continued to be brought in separately for a few years before they too were integrated into the system. This group of sailors, described as a "class of men, in which beach combers are largely represented, as a temporary refuge from want and misery," continued to have a high desertion rate and attendant morale problems well into a later era.

Basic personnel corrective action had been so long delayed that the Navy had to struggle on for several more years with severe manpower shortages. In 1906, when the authorized enlisted strength was about 38,000, the actual number was 4,500 short of this figure. Major recruiting drives were organized in which traveling parties scoured the country and ships toured coastal and river areas. Not until 1908, for the first time in the history of the New Navy, was the authorized strength actually reached.

The growing technical complexity of the Steel Navy also required new emphasis on advanced training. Beginning in the 1890s the more promising second-cruise men had been sent to classes for gunners and artisans at the Naval Gun Factory in Washington, D.C., and later for training in diving, electricity, and torpedoes at the Torpedo Station in Newport. These schools were gradually improved and expanded. After the electrician rating was established in 1898 new schools were also set up at Boston, New York, and Mare Island, and in 1902 a new artificer's course was started in Norfolk. The big drive for improvement in target practice was supported by a practical course for gun captains aboard the monitor *Amphitrite*. A school for firemen was organized in the cruiser *Cincinnati*. Radioman and yeoman, even bandsman courses were instituted. Truly this was, in the words of Secretary of the Navy William H. Moody, "an era of training."

By 1909 the "bluff, jolly, illiterate, profane, and picturesque man-of-war's men of the old school" were disappearing fast, along with the old expertise in marlinspike seamanship. A new breed of "sea mechanics," as President Roosevelt called them, were to become the "highest type of sailormen" for the years ahead.

Apprentice boys, many of whom enlisted at the age of fourteen, assemble for a group portrait on the forward turret of the armored cruiser Brooklyn.

Jacks of All Trades

A typical Steel Navy battleship had a crew of about five hundred and was manned by five masters-at-arms, twenty-five gunner's mates, nine boatswain's mates, three quartermasters, eleven coxswains, ninety-five seamen, thirty-two ordinary seamen, thirty-seven landsmen, and sixty-four apprentices; three carpenter's mates, a sailmaker's mate, two painters, eighteen machinists, a boilermaker, a coppersmith, two blacksmiths, three plumbers, two shipwrights, six water tenders, eight oilers, thirty-eight firemen, and forty-two coal passers; five yeomen; an apothecary, a bugler, three stewards, six cooks, and thirteen mess attendants; four Marine sergeants, five corporals, fifty privates, a boy drummer and a fifer.

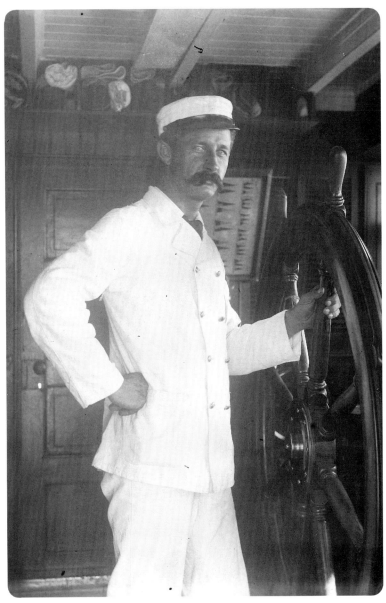

Proud Chief Quartermaster Rudolph C. Mehrtens stands at the wheel of the cruiser Olympia, *which he steered at the Battle of Manila Bay.*

A clean-shaven young gunner poses by the breech of one of the powerful new 8-inchers with which the cruiser Chicago *was refitted in 1898.*

Buglers like this sailor aboard the Olympia *were an indispensable part of every warship's complement in an era of primitive internal shipboard communications.*

The job of ship's tailor was as important as any in a Navy where the bluejacket's most prized possession was his "tailor-made" uniform.

Aboard the "Guardo"

A receiving ship or "guardo" was a permanent fixture at nearly every major naval station. Somewhat resembling a cross between a frigate and a cow barn, each served as a "floating hotel" for recruits and men awaiting reassignment. The New York Navy Yard's receiving ship, the Vermont, *above, was laid down at Boston in 1818 as a seventy-four-gun wooden sailing ship of the line, but lay uncompleted on the stocks for thirty years before finally being launched to clear the ways. During the Civil War she served as a depot vessel at Port Royal, South Carolina, and in 1865 was towed to New York, where she remained for more than thirty-five years.*

On the roofed-over upper deck of the Vermont *a draft of bluejackets awaits transfer to a seagoing* *warship. Seabags and rolled-up hammocks comprise their entire possessions. As many as three hundred* *men were frequently berthed aboard such a vessel, and because sanitation was impossible in such* *crowded conditions, sickness and disease often ran rampant. An outbreak of spinal meningitis in* *the* Vermont *in 1901 finally resulted in her being condemned and replaced by the steel cruiser* Columbia.

From Landsman to Man-of-War's Man

Diminishing numbers of enlistments by trained merchant seamen and rapidly expanding personnel requirements for the Steel Navy's new warships led to the inauguration of the "landsman-for-training" program in 1899, whereby men of ages twenty-one to twenty-six were enlisted for four years and given about six months of instruction aboard training vessels. In the photograph above, recruits—most of them in rough workingman's garb—are sworn in on the quarterdeck of the training ship Hartford. On the opposite page, the commanding officer of the Hartford inspects his new bluejackets. On the locker in the right foreground is the ship's pet goat. Extra wooden spars are lashed to the deck, and modern 6-pounder rapid-fire guns line the rail.

Going by the Blue Book

Under the strict discipline of shipboard routine new sailors quickly learned the Navy way of doing things. Every Sunday was the occasion for an exacting full-dress personnel inspection. Here, on the first Sunday of the month, landsmen aboard the Hartford *hear the solemn pronouncements and warnings of the "Articles for the Government of the Navy"—also known in irreverent bluejacket lingo as "Rocks and Shoals," or "Death and Worse Punishments."*

Sailors store their bedding in "nettings"—troughs in the spar deck railing—as part of the morning routine on board the cruiser San Francisco.

A Sailor's Life on Ship and Shore

Except for his apprentice or training cruise and brief lay-overs in decaying "guardos," Jack spent most of his enlistment on board seagoing warships if not actually at sea. He was blessed with little in the way of material possessions. His outfit consisted of a canvas hammock, mattress with two covers, a pair of white blankets; two suits of blues and three of whites, a grommet frame and two hat covers in each color, a watch cap, oilskins, a neckerchief, jackknife with lanyard, two suits of underwear, six pairs of socks, two pairs of shoes with blacking and a brush; a bowl, cup, and plate of white agate-wear; an iron knife, fork, and spoon; a small canvas bag for clothing, and a wooden "ditty box" for personal effects and trinkets. During daylight hours the hammock, mattress, and blankets—neatly rolled and lashed with seven turns of a manila line—were stowed in "nettings" on the upper or spar deck, while the clothing bag and ditty box were kept in racks on the gun deck.

It was said that the sailor was the only person who ate under the place where he slept and slept under the place where he ate. This riddle aptly described the multi-purpose use of the gun deck in ships of the period, both wood and steel. The crew was divided into "messes"—twenty-two in a large cruiser like the *Olympia*—each responsible for its own sustenance. Every man was allotted ration money of nine dollars per month. One member of each mess, usually someone who was "too small to be a shellman and too dumb to be anything else," served full-time as mess cook or "berth-deck slusher" for his shipmates, drawing provisions from the paymaster's storeroom and preparing and cooking them under the supervision of the ship's cook. At sea the rations ran heavily and monotonously to such easily preserved basics as beans, rice, "canned Willie" (corned beef), tinned mutton, salt pork, flour (usually made into a pudding or "duff"), ship's bread or hardtack, tea and coffee, and molasses for flavoring. Each month it was customary for the paymaster to "commute" one-quarter to one-half of the ration and turn the cash over to the individual mess cooks to do the best they could on the local market when in port. On the Asiatic Station they could do quite well.

Three times a day the crew lowered bare wooden tables and folding benches from their racks between the overhead deck beams, and the "belly robbers" dished out the simple fare, concocted into such sailors' delights as "dunderfunk," "lob dominion," "plum duff," "rope-yarn stew," "skillagalee," "slum," "slush," and "sea pie." As soon as the hungry sailors had "scoffed" down their meal, everything was cleaned and restowed as before. At night the bluejackets' hammocks were slung from numbered hooks on the overhead deck beams, under the stowed mess tables, high above the deck.

Each event in the daily routine was heralded by bugle call or boatswain's whistle. When the ship was in port the day began at 5:00 A.M. with "all hands, up all hammocks, roust out, lash and carry." After a quick mug of steaming "jamoke" (coffee), the barefooted sailors swept down the decks and hosed them off with sea water. At 7:30 each man drew a pail of fresh water at the scuttle butt (an amount that would have to last all day), washed himself, and sat down to breakfast. Colors were at 8:00, sick call at 8:45, and divisional quarters at 9:30. Various drills and evolutions, such as "clear ship for action" or "arm and away" then occupied the crew until retreat at 11:00, when Jack had an hour for mending his clothes and other personal business. Mess call at noon was followed by another session of instruction or drill until supper at 5:30 P.M. At 7:30 all hands mustered by the hammock nettings to draw their bedding and to hear a prayer by the chaplain. Taps were sounded at 9:00 P.M., by which time many sailors were already asleep in their "dream sacks."

The routine was sometimes varied with boat drills in the harbor, or when circumstances permitted, the landing force might be sent ashore for a few days of battalion drill. Pitching tents on some isolated island or beach, sandy bluejackets would struggle with unfamiliar evolutions involving heavy rifles and a light field gun or two.

Sunday morning was captain's inspection, with "General

Muster" on the third weekend of each month. At this awesome Special Full Dress ceremony, with the entire ship's complement drawn up in ranks, the paymaster's clerk called the complete muster roll starting with the chief master-at-arms, the senior enlisted man of the crew. As each bluejacket's name was called in turn he would salute, sing out his rate, march forward around the capstan and go below.

Sunday church services, conducted by the "sky-pilot," were attended by the officers as a matter of duty and by a faithful few of the crew as a matter of conviction. Hymns were sung to the accompaniment of a guitar or mandolin, or occasionally to a pump organ played by a lady volunteer from ashore. Some seamen were real authorities on the Scriptures, but most took little stock in religion. A few clung to superstitious beliefs in "Davy Jones," "Adamastor," and the "Flying Dutchman." A favorite legend was that whenever a sailor died at sea his soul rose up to inhabit the body of a white gull or albatross.

The crew was organized into two watch sections and at sea the schedule was watch-on and watch-off, around the clock. If the ship happened to leave port on an odd-numbered day of the month, the starboard section took the first underway watch, in accordance with a time-honored practice of the sea. Routine drills, general quarters, target practice, and cleaning duties kept the off-watch section from getting lazy.

Relaxation came after working hours in port and during the dog watch at sea. The four hours between 4:00 and 8:00 P.M. were divided into two short "dodge" or dog watches so that the crew would not have to stand the same cycle of duty day after day. During this time the men of the off-duty section were free to amuse themselves with games of "acey-deucy" and "Spanish pool" (a form of checkers), yarn-spinning by the old-timers, and with music and dancing. Some ships had a gramophone or pianola for the crew's amusement, and in the flagship the band played twice a day.

Nearly every ship had one or more mascots, which ranged from cats, dogs, and goats, to monkeys and parrots. The *Kentucky* was renowned for its pet bear, which crewmen would goad into roaring at strangers, while the *Oregon's* pride was "Dennis the pig," rescued from the *Cristobal Colon* at the Battle of Santiago. (Pig mascots were always named "Dennis.")

Jack loved all kinds of athletic amusements, with baseball, football, boxing, and swimming high on the list. Boat racing was the sport most closely associated with the Navy, however, and it was a great point of pride for a ship to have the speediest barge or whaleboat. On the Asiatic Station the champion ship became "Cock of the Station" and flew a purple flag emblazoned with a red rooster. As many as fourteen husky seamen manned the oars of each of the swift pulling-boats, and the grueling races were usually four miles straight-away, with the finish line at the squadron anchorage. All hands invariably wagered large sums on their ship's boat, and as much as $15,000 might be won or lost in a single race.

Holidays were always celebrated with skylarking and entertainment. Amateur minstrel and vaudeville shows were a great favorite, with the stage set up amidst elaborate decorations on the quarterdeck. If foreign men-of-war were in port there might be an exchange of visits, with each crew vying to outdo the other in lavishness. Christmas was the most nostalgic of holidays afloat. Small trees were hoisted to the trucks and rigged at the yardarms, and on the gun deck signal flags, bunting, and greens added a note of cheer. The swinging mess tables were heavy-laden with roast turkey, boiled ham, fruit of all kinds, nuts, sweet bread, plum pudding, and cakes. The more talented humorists in the mess regaled their shipmates with after-dinner speeches on such topics as "Reminiscences of the brig" and "What it is like to have money." Later the crew assembled on deck for three-legged and potato races, greased-pole climbing, pie-eating contests, and wrestling or boxing matches.

Many bluejackets turned their off-duty hours into extra pay, and chief among these were the amateur tailors found in every ship's crew. "Regulation" uniforms were available from the paymaster's storeroom, but Jack much preferred a "tailor-made" outfit with extra-wide trouser bottoms and lots of sewn fancy-work on the collar and pocket seams. A skilled "sheeny" could turn out one uniform a day on his "hurdy-gurdy," and for his efforts received five dollars—a respectable sum, considering that an ordinary seaman's pay was just twenty-four dollars per month. Other bluejackets specialized in hammering silver dollars flat and carving them into gleaming "buzzards" (eagles) for petty-officer sleeve emblems. Older hands skilled in the boatswain's art wove fancy ornamental "thrum mats" out of hemp, or braided white sennit lanyards decorated with hundreds of intricate knotted "Turk's heads." The ship's cook and the "Jack-o'-the-dust"—the paymaster's storeroom helper—made a tidy profit baking ten-cent pies from dried apples, flour, and lard "appropriated" from the crew's mess rations.

Every ship also had its own "bumboat man," or civilian merchant, who rowed out to the anchorage twice daily, after the noon and evening meals, with his stock of pies, cakes, candies, and tobacco. Sometimes a woman served as vendor and several of these became almost legendary characters, known throughout the fleet. "Old Kate" with her basket of fruit and notions was a fixture at the Washington Navy Yard for more than forty years, while Annie Daly, a young and pretty Brooklyn widow, catered sundries to the armored cruiser *New York* for several years and eventually married one of the crew.

Hard liquor was strictly forbidden on board ship. Navy

Side cleaners went over the side daily whenever the ship was in port; here a crew gets down to business on the battleship **Texas,** *which is still wearing her coat of Spanish War paint.*

Regulations permitted the sale of beer, however, and this commodity formed the bumboat man's principal stock in trade. Although no individual was permitted to purchase more than three bottles at a time, it was not unusual for a ship's crew to "splice the mainbrace" with eight or nine hundred bottles of the foamy stuff on a warm summer's day.

In spite of the renowned alcohol-detecting abilities of "Jimmy Legs," the ship's master-at-arms, the more incorrigible members of the crew frequently risked punishment by contriving to smuggle liquor aboard. Boat coxswains were notorious as "rum runners." Sailors were sometimes struck blind by improvised "man-of-war cocktails," and the abolition of prison irons on board ship was protested in the name of "the officer or man who has seen one or more members of his crew crazed and violent from the effects of West Indian 'rotgut' or other poison." As late as 1903 the commander of the Adriatic Squadron lamented that "a number of good men died during the year from drinking shellac mixed with wood alcohol."

Jack did not spend all of his time on board ship, to be sure. Shore leave was much loved but sparingly granted. Men were ranked in conduct classes based on their current behavior and past infractions of the rules. "First Class," limited to those with untarnished records for the last six months or more, entitled a bluejacket to full pay and all of the liberty rated by his watch. "Second Class," just one step down, rated liberty only once every two weeks and permitted the sailor to draw one-half his pay. "Fourth Class," where a majority of the crew often seemed to end up unless an amnesty was declared, was limited to the single leave every three months that was required by Navy Regulations, and one-quarter pay. When restrictions became too wearing a man might take his chances on leaving and returning by way of the anchor chain.

On reaching the pier a group of bluejackets would sometimes hold "tarpaulin muster" before taking off for the fleshpots, throwing all of their money into a neckerchief to be safeguarded by the most sober of the number until just enough was left to get the gang back to the ship. Then would follow roistering times in the waterfront dives, fist fights with sailors from other nations, police-baiting escapades, or visits to tattooing parlors where a man could be embellished from head to toe with multicolored designs, even to simulated carpet slippers on his feet.

In the ports of Japan there were opportunities for rickshaw rides to visit country temples and rest houses, or to hire bicycles for a more strenuous outing. A Salvation Army hotel in Yokohama and a Sailor's Home in Nagasaki (purchased by the men of the cruiser *Charleston*) provided clean and decent accommodations, in sharp contrast to the unsalubrious conditions prevailing on most waterfronts. In China the bluejacket was assailed by all of the degradations of a decaying empire—lepers dying at the city gates, opium dens, vice of every description, and beachcombers of all nationalities eager to steer the gullible youngsters to a fleecing. Other ports in Asia, South America, and Europe were often nearly as bad. In the United States the sailor was regarded as a pariah and was denied entrance to most decent establishments. His money was welcome, of course, in the saloons, dance halls, and brothels of such notorious districts as New York's Bowery and San Francisco's Barbary Coast.

The medicines available to "Microbes," the ship's doctor, were of little efficacy against many of the exotic diseases of the Orient or tropics that Jack was exposed to, let alone the ubiquitous venereal infections and common contagions. All too frequently the crew would be mustered to see one of their number depart "by the starboard gangway," forbidden to enlisted men in life. Turned over, it formed a polished chute for the burial at sea of a canvas-shrouded corpse.

"Seraphs don't wear blue jackets; bluejackets are not wearing wings," was an aphorism of the day. When Jack staggered back to his ship, it was with the knowledge that he would have to "face the stick" at captain's mast. Once a man was overleave he usually figured that he might as well prolong his fun to the bitter end, and nine days and twenty-three hours after becoming overdue he would turn himself in to the nearest ship or U.S. consul as a straggler, thereby avoiding the charge of desertion by an hour. While normal transgressions like straggling or returning to the ship "drunk and dirty" were not punished lightly—a few days in the "pie house" (ship's brig) were a sure reward—thieves were given "the book" if apprehended. The convicted offender would have his sentence read in front of the assembled crew, the hatband bearing his ship's name in gold would be ceremoniously stripped off, and he would be put ashore with his pay and meager belongings to fend for himself, disowned and disgraced.

In spite of all this, Navy life was not considered particularly hard. In comparison with the lot of the laboring man ashore, especially during recurrent depressions, it offered steady pay, regular meals, and security. Many seamen led a generally clean and sober life, learned skilled trades, advanced to responsible positions, and were in all respects a credit to their country. As Rear Admiral "Fighting Bob" Evans proudly declared, "You don't need armor when you have men like mine."

Midshipman idlers watch as the deck force rigs the battleship Indiana *for getting underway from her anchorage during a summer cruise out of* Annapolis.

All Hands on Deck

Young crewmen of the armored cruiser New York *give the forecastle a pre-breakfast scrubdown under the watchful eye of an old salt.*

New York *sailors limber up at calisthenics or "monkey drill" following morning quarters.*
Nearly every warship boasted at least one mascot, and a goat was the most popular choice.

*With the help of "scoojie moojie" (brightwork cleaner) and elbow grease, a young sailor on board
the cruiser* Cincinnati *polishes hoops on a fire bucket while his companion, seated on a ditty box,
overhauls the training and elevating gear of a 5-inch breech-loading rifle. Saturday morning was
"field day," devoted to giving the entire ship a thorough cleaning in preparation for Sunday inspection.*

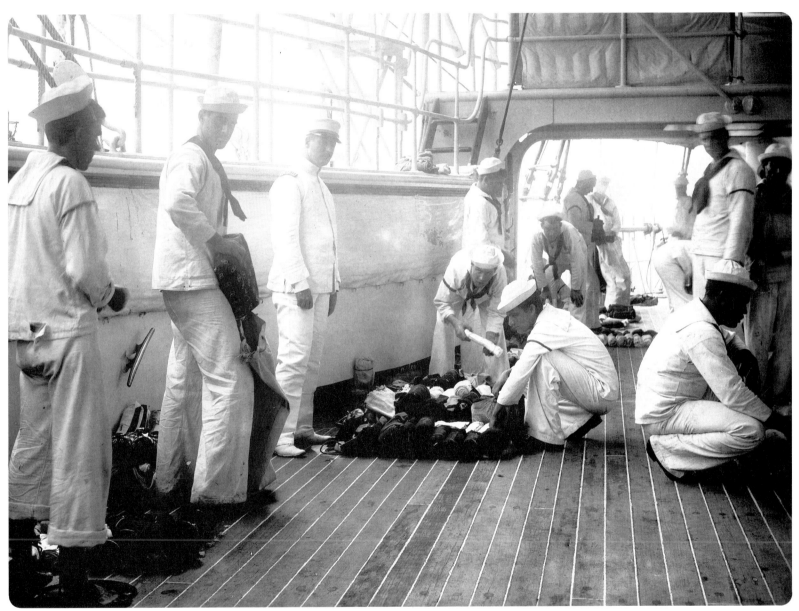

Hammock or bag inspection was usually conducted on alternate Wednesdays. Here bluejackets of the cruiser Olympia lay out their clothing, with each item neatly rolled and tied with clothes stops, to be carefully scrutinized by their division officer. Wednesday afternoon was always "rope-yarn Sunday," when Jack broke out his gear for mending and sewing, which the sailor at far left presumably has in mind.

Drills and More Drills

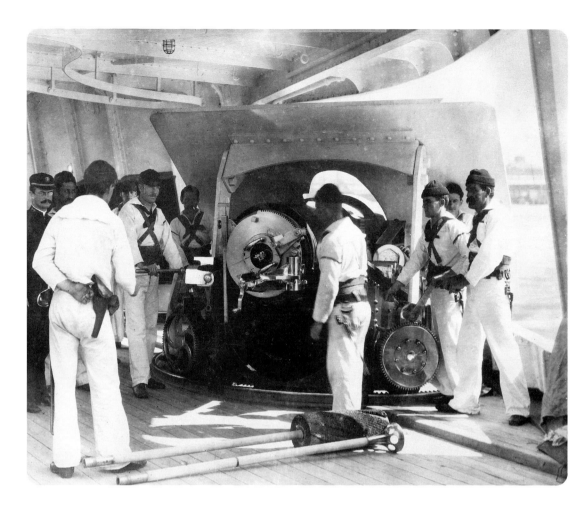

Cast loose and provide! Gunners on board the cruiser Chicago *stand by an 8-inch breech-loading rifle at battery drill. Dummy shells were usually employed for such practice, during which the men rehearsed loading and aiming procedures. The shipboard routine provided for two sessions of drilling daily, with different evolutions scheduled for every day of the week.*

New York *bluejackets engage in "single-stick" exercise with wooden swords. Cutlass drill, handed down to the Steel Navy from the age of sail, was employed mainly for physical fitness and for tradition's sake.*

An officer of the armored cruiser Brooklyn *unflinchingly directs his men at revolver drill. Other regular shipboard exercises included general quarters, fire quarters, abandon ship and collision drills, target practice, and signaling instruction.*

Boatloads of sailors from a Montgomery-*class cruiser exercise at "arm-and-away" drill, during which the naval battalion practiced shore landings with rifles and a few 3-inch field pieces. In addition to infantry and artillery, the landing party included "pioneers" for building fortifications, an ammunition party, a "commissariat," an ambulance party, a signal gang, buglers, and a color guard.*

287

Housekeeping Chores

Armed with "Ki-Yi" brushes and paymaster's bouquet (salt-water soap), sailors on the open gun deck of the cruiser Baltimore *work the cinders and coal dust out of their spare uniforms. "Scrub and wash clothes" was piped three or four mornings a week, and hammocks were scrubbed twice a month. Because fresh water was in short supply, the crew's wash was almost always done in sea water.*

While the berth deck slusher dishes out seconds, crewmen of the Olympia *enjoy a hearty meal by their guns. The enlisted force was organized into messes of about twenty-four men each, and one-fourth of the thirty-cents-per-man-per-day ration was usually paid to each mess in cash for fresh produce and such extras as mustard and "red lead." Occasionally one of the mess cooks would fall into the hands of the Philistines on the way to market and spend the money on whiskey instead, leaving his shipmates to exist on hard bread and coffee for the next four weeks. In 1902 the messing system was revolutionized when the Navy established the General Mess, under which all hands received a standard ration. Tapes sewn around the left sleeves of these men show they are in the port watch section.*

Ship's Work Is
Never Done

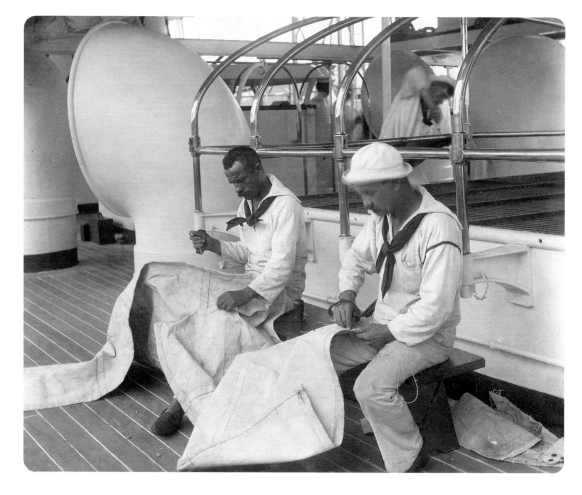

The age of sail was past, but the Steel Navy still needed sailmaker's mates to sew and repair canvas awnings, gun covers, targets, windsails (ventilators), clothing bags, hammocks, and sails for the ship's small boats. Here a pair of Olympia sailors apply palm and needle to a new hammock cloth, used to keep rain and spray out of the hammock nettings on the spar deck railings.

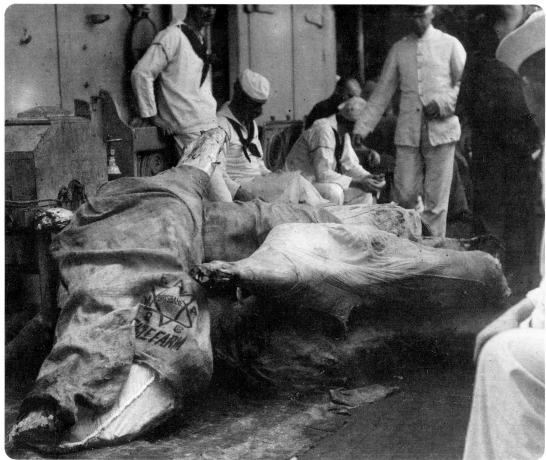

Fresh Australian beef, shipped from Brisbane to the Philippines by refrigerator ship, awaits disposition on board the Cincinnati. The development of modern refrigeration and the introduction of Navy supply ships during the late 1890s sounded the death knell for the infamous "harness cask" and its malodorous product, salt horse (beef preserved in brine).

"Underground savages" from the Cincinnati's black gang (engineering force) pay an unaccustomed visit topside to scrape scale from the evaporator tubes. The ship's steam-operated evaporators produced several tons of fresh water daily, but most of this was required to replenish feed water for the boilers.

A Cincinnati diver prepares to go overboard. Every warship had one or two gunner's mates qualified for such work and they were frequently called upon to scrape the propellers, remove barnacles from the injection strainers, check the hull plating for damage due to grounding, or recover lost practice torpedoes and anchors. For each hour spent underwater the diver received an extra $1.20 in pay.

291

Below Decks

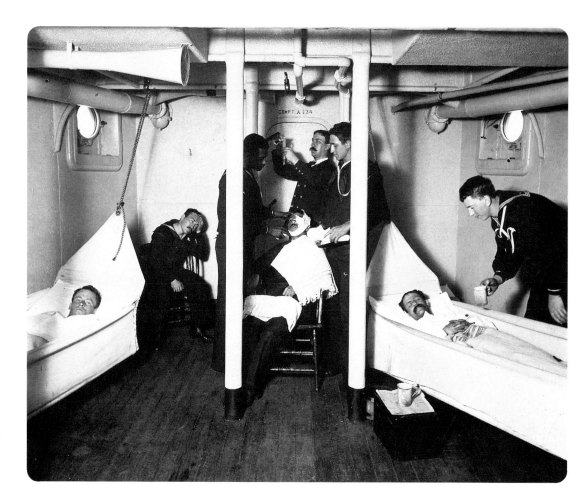

Sick call in the armored cruiser **Brooklyn:** *in an obviously staged scene, hospital apprentices patch up a bluejacket on the morning after the night before while the ship's pharmacist, in the background, blends a potion calculated to deaden another repentant celebrant's withdrawal symptoms.*

The **Brooklyn's** *paymaster was a busy man, for in addition to keeping track of the pay accounts he was responsible for purchasing the ship's provisions and supplies. Here his chief assistant, a warrant pay clerk, pores over the ledgers.*

The officers, of course, had separate cabins and dined over linen in the wardroom. Here an officer of a staff corps brushes up on his professional reading—perhaps the latest quarterly issue of the Naval Institute Proceedings—in his snug hardwood-paneled stateroom on board the cruiser Newark.

Rifles stood ready at all times in Marine country, as shown in this view on board the Brooklyn. The "spit kit," also kept within handy reach, was a necessary receptacle for tobacco chewers. Careless users had to swab the deck with their undershirts.

The Spirit and the Flesh

The "sky pilot," or ship's chaplain, pronounces benediction on crew and visitors during Sunday services on board the battleship Texas. *Younger members of the crew sometimes met during the week as shipboard chapters of the Christian Endeavor Society. The chaplain also served as an instructor and adviser to the ship's apprentice boys.*

While the bowler-hatted vendor stands by to reclaim empties, "Jimmy Legs" insures that sailors purchase only the au-thorized number of five-cent beers during an afternoon break on board the battleship Massachusetts. *When the ship put to sea the "bumboat man's" stock was sometimes locked in the brig for safekeeping by the obliging master-at-arms.*

Off Duty

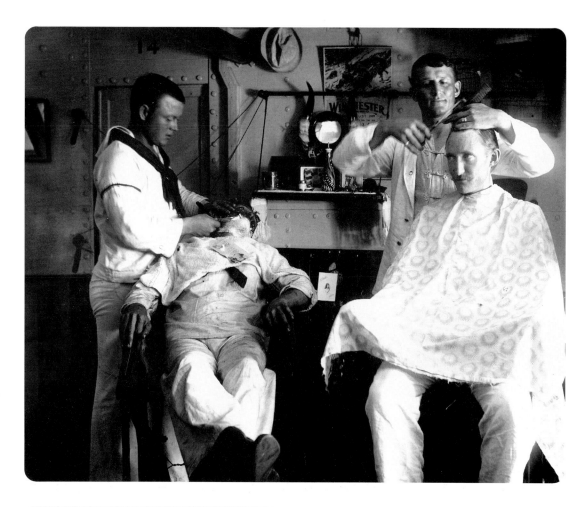

Jack's haircutting and shaving needs cost him fifty cents per month. Here Hunt and McDonald, tonsorial specialists on board the Olympia, hold forth at "No. 14 Larboard Avenue, Marine Country." Their chief competitor—as listed in advertisements in the Bounding Billow, the ship's newspaper—was E. C. Moore, "the musical barber," at "111 Dungaree Alley."

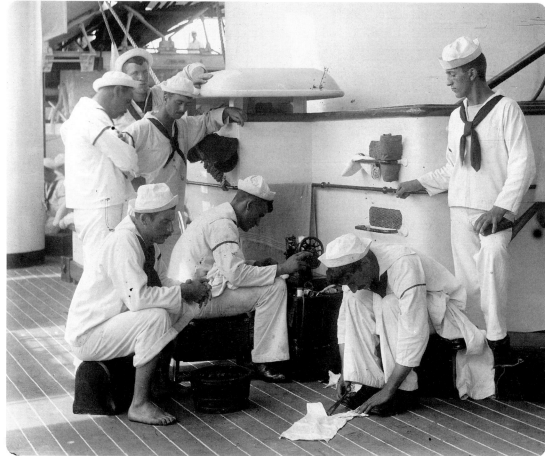

Every bluejacket's pride was his homeward bounder uniform, made to custom fit by one of the ship's amateur tailors. Here Olympia sailors watch a "sheeny" operate his "hurdy gurdy" while an assistant cuts out a jumper collar. The small hand-cranked sewing machines were preferred because they could be stowed out of the way in ditty box racks when not in use.

One collector of miscellaneous statistics found that fifty-four percent of Navy enlisted men were tattooed by their second enlistment. A number of sailors, like this artist on board the Olympia, were skilled with ink and needle. Because red and blue were the colors least likely to be toxic, they were the ones most employed. Subject matter ranged from patriotic and sacred designs to the profane. An anchor usually indicated service in the Atlantic, while a dragon was a souvenir of an Asiatic cruise.

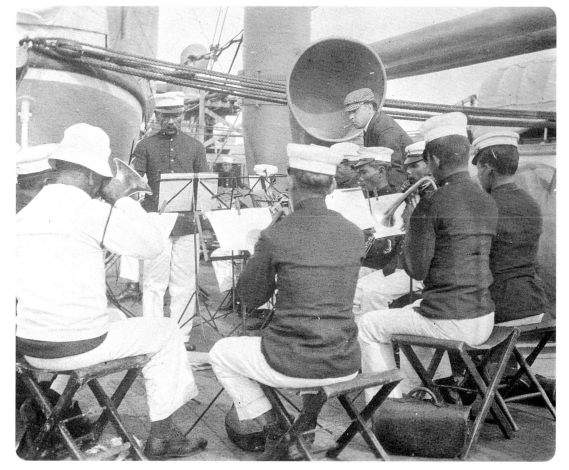

Flagships rated a ship's band, which played for the crew's enjoyment as well as for official functions and ceremonies. This group, on board the division flagship Rainbow on the Asiatic Station, was considered a very good one. One of the major "kicks" among Navy musicians was that they had to wear Marine uniforms, not having been assigned distinctive attire of their own.

Seeing the World

Although many bluejackets on shore liberty chose to become educated chiefly in the saloons, dance halls, and fleshpots common to most seaports, others were living testimony to the slogan, "Join the Navy and see the world." These petty officers having a souvenir picture taken by Egypt's Great Pyramid and Sphinx were from the cruiser Raleigh.

Any means of locomotion was fine as long as it got you there. This pony train of Marines and sailors from the cruiser Baltimore *was photographed at the Ming tombs north of Peking, China. Bicycling was another favorite form of bluejacket transportation when ashore in the Far East.*

A Long Way from Home

Mail-O! The Cincinnati's *chief master-at-arms distributes home-town newspapers, delivered to the*
Philippines by commercial steamer. The figure-eight knot on his sleeve is the badge of an ex-apprentice.
Mail call was a major event in the shipboard routine, for bluejackets on far stations were often away
from family and friends for an entire four-year enlistment. Even when in port, most of Jack's time
was spent on board ship; on the opposite page, Cincinnati *sailors pass the time staring at the horizon*
or pounding an ear on the forecastle deck.

Simple Pleasures

A boxing "smoker" was a favorite evening entertainment as well as an excellent means of settling minor differences. History has recorded that the winner of this match on the boat deck of the Oregon *was Gunner's Mate Third Class William "Sharkey" Smith.*

Going on 9:00 P.M. and bluejackets gather for a few yarns before climbing into their "dream sacks" on the crowded gun deck of the armored cruiser Brooklyn. *Mess tables are lashed up to the overhead, above hammocks.*

A landing party of Marines and bluejackets from the flagship Philadelphia *forms into marching order at Honolulu in 1895. U.S. intervention to keep order was commonplace during the years of Hawaiian independence.*

The Marines Have Landed

The 1880s found the U.S. Marine Corps a small, obscure service numbering fewer than three thousand officers and enlisted men. Headed by Colonel Charles G. McCawley, a veteran of the Mexican and Civil Wars, the force was widely dispersed among ships' detachments and barracks units, its duties a dichotomy of functions that made the Marine a darling of Congress but a sworn enemy to every bluejacket.

As an elite force of seaborne infantry the Corps distinguished itself in trouble spots around the world during the 1880s and '90s, protecting American lives, property, and interests wherever revolution or uprising threatened. In 1885, when revolution broke out in Panama (then a part of Colombia), two battalions of Marines were hastily dispatched to the isthmus from U.S. East Coast stations. Taking charge of the Panama Railroad, which had been halted by insurgents, the Marines soon had traffic moving again. Under Commander Bowman H. McCalla of the Navy, a force of Marines and bluejackets then neutralized Panama City until Colombian government troops arrived to reestablish control.

Thereafter Marines took part in U.S. military expeditions to Haiti (1888), Chile (1891), and Hawaii (1893), during anti-American disturbances in those countries. They were also sent to protect U.S. legations during revolutions in Argentina in 1890 and Nicaragua in 1894 and 1896, and were ordered to China and Korea on similar missions during the Sino-Japanese War of 1894.

These were years of activity and progress for the Marine Corps in the United States as well. Beginning in 1881, and continuing until 1897, all new Marine officers were recruited from among graduating cadets at the Naval Academy. When Colonel Charles Heywood became Marine Commandant in 1891 he instituted such reforms as a School of Application for newly commissioned officers, mandatory promotion examinations, and fitness reports. The Corps' spit-and-polish image was enhanced by the frequent presence of renowned bandmaster John Philip Sousa and the Marine Band at White House functions, and by 1894 the service had reached a peak of influence with a Marine instructor at the Naval War College, where Commodore Stephen Luce was a firm friend and supporter.

That same year, however, brought a major assault against the very existence of the Corps. The routine duties of the Marine on board ship had not been such as to make him beloved by either the enlisted men of the Navy or by many of its officers. When not engaged in quelling native uprisings on shore, the Marine's job was to assist in maintaining order on board ship. The average bluejacket viewed the "sailor's hitching post" as a guard to spy on him, to keep him away from storeroom and scuttlebutt, and to arrest him when he staggered aboard from a wild liberty. Although some old-line Navy officers considered the resulting animosity an effective aid to discipline, many others held exactly the opposite view. To make matters worse, the Corps had become understaffed and underpaid, its desertion rate was twelve percent annually, many of its personnel left something to be desired, and it had somewhat the reputation as a haven for officers who had run into trouble at the Naval Academy or who had political influence. The situation had all the potential of dynamite.

In the ferment of new ideas that marked the birth of the Steel Navy, one that had widespread appeal among certain "Young Turks" was the abolition of the Marine Corps. As early as 1890 Navy Lieutenant William F. Fullam had proposed such a course in a paper presented before the U.S. Naval Institute. In his view there was nothing in the Marines' guard and landing-force duties that sailors could not do better. In 1894 he renewed his agitation by proposing that the Marine detachment in his ship, the *Raleigh*, be reduced. This was backed by petitions circulated among the enlisted men of the fleet asking for the removal of the Marines. A bill was introduced in the Senate to transfer them to the Army as a Corps of Marine Artillery, and the redoubtable Captain Robley D. Evans requested that the Marine detachment be omitted from the complement of his new battleship, the *Indiana*. The Marines, however, were supported by Captain Henry C. Taylor, then president of the Naval War College, and by Secretary of the Navy Hilary A. Herbert. The latter not only disapproved Evans' request, but also spelled out the exact size of the detachment, prescribed its duties in detail, and emphasized that the Marines were an integral part of the ship's company and should man their own guns under their own officers.

The tenacious Fullam was not stilled by this temporary setback. In 1896, in another essay published in the Naval Institute *Proceedings,* he again urged the withdrawal of all Marines from sea duty. Other officers again rallied to his support. Congress reacted characteristically by increasing the authorized strength of the Marine Corps by thirty percent. Nevertheless, disaffection began to spread to Annapolis and for the first time—with the Classes of 1896 and 1897—the Academy failed to meet its quota of new officers for the Corps. In 1897 President William McKinley unwittingly offended the Navy by choosing a Marine captain as his naval aide. So deeply were feelings stirred that no naval officer would volunteer to serve as this man's assistant, and two refused orders to take the job that would normally have been considered a career plum. From 1898 to 1914 not a single Annapolis graduate entered the Marine Corps.

The Fullam forces also won a dangerous recruit in Assistant Navy Secretary Theodore Roosevelt, who generally supported their efforts to eliminate the Marines. The War with Spain gave the Corps a breather, however. Admiral Dewey was loud in their praise and Congress, impressed with their fighting achievements, authorized a further increase in the size of the Corps. Nevertheless, near the end of Roosevelt's term as President, the foes of the Marine Corps made their strongest bid and Rear Admiral John E. Pillsbury, Chief of the powerful Bureau of Navigation, wrote to the Secretary of the Navy that "the time has arrived when all Marine detachments should be removed from U.S. naval vessels. . . ." As described in Colonel Robert Heinl's comprehensive history of the Corps, to the anguished remonstrances of Marine supporters Roosevelt is said to have simply replied: "I know all about it—take them off!" Executive Order 969 of 12 November 1908 seemingly relegated Marines to guard and garrison duty ashore. The power of the Corps' image was convincingly demonstrated again, however, when Congress passed a rider with the 1909 appropriations bill requiring the retention of Marines in all battleships and armored cruisers. With this decisive victory the Marine Corps proved itself capable of thwarting any future attempts against its existence.

While fighting for its life on the home front, the Corps was far from idle abroad, engaging in a steady series of campaigns during the years following the Spanish-American War. Factional fighting at Samoa in 1899 led to intervention by a joint U.S.-British landing force, which ultimately brought about the partitioning of the islands between the United States and Germany. In 1903–04, the presence of a U.S. Marine force in Panama was instrumental in bluffing off the Colombian government long enough for the winning of Panamanian independence and President Roosevelt's cherished canal. Other campaigns and diplomatic missions placed the Marines ashore in Ethiopia, Honduras, Syria, Santo Domingo, Tangier, Korea, and Cuba. The high points of U.S. Marine operations during this period, however, came in China during the Boxer Rebellion and on the island of Samar during the Philippine Insurrection.

In May 1900, a small international force—including about fifty Marines from the U.S. warships *Oregon* and *Newark*—was rushed to Peking to protect the foreign legations from threatening mobs of Chinese. By late June the foreign settlement had been completely cut off and was taken under siege by rebellious "Boxers," members of a Chinese patriotic socity. As the Western world held its breath, the vastly outnumbered defenders fought off hordes of attackers bent on murdering every foreigner in the city. An eight-nation relief force was hastily organized and U.S. Marines were in the forefront of its subsequent operations, which included spirited fighting at Tientsin, a Boxer stronghold about ninety miles from Peking. Finally, in mid-August 1900 the expedition managed to break through and raise the siege.

Equally fierce fighting erupted during U.S. Marine operations against Philippine insurgents on Samar during 1901–02, when a battalion of Marines under Major L. W. T. Waller succeeded in locating and capturing the island's heavily defended guerrilla headquarters. Waller's men encountered even more harrowing going later during an attempt to cross the island for a telegraph-line survey. At one point the expedition's native carriers turned against the exhausted Marines and tried to murder them. Waller had the mutineers shot summarily, for which he was later court-martialed, but acquitted.

The development of modern amphibious warfare came long after the end of the Steel Navy era, but the Spanish-American War did produce a significant harbinger of the future when Marines were given their own transport, the 3,400-ton *Panther,* from which a special force assaulted and captured Guantanamo Bay in one of the war's major actions. After the war, landing forces were organized annually as a part of fleet exercises, using first the *Panther* and later the 6,000-ton *Dixie*. From these simple beginnings grew the Fleet Marine Force and the all-around amphibious capability that is the trademark of the U.S. Marine Corps today.

Marines from the second-class battleship Maine *board launches after shore maneuvers at Hampton Roads, Virginia, in 1897. The following February, twenty-eight Marines went down with their ship.*

Marines Afloat

With the precision and smartness that have characterized their Corps since 1775, pith-helmeted Marines of the protected cruiser San Francisco *present arms at a mid-1890s captain's inspection. In addition to manning guns of the secondary battery and providing honor guards for ceremonial functions, the "sea soldiers" served as orderlies to senior officers, as brig guards, and as deck sentinels.*

Marines aboard the battleship Massachusetts *break out their gear for kit inspection. Mess tables triced up to the overhead and numbered hammock hooks testify to the way these men ate and slept in the early steel warships.*

On Duty
Around the World

The Marine detail from the cruiser Charleston *lines up in winter garb in front of the U.S. legation in Seoul, Korea. This detachment was sent to protect American interests in the Hermit Kingdom during unrest occasioned by the Sino-Japanese War of 1894–95.*

The Marines distinguished themselves both afloat and ashore during the war with Spain. Here they raise the flag over Camp McCalla at newly captured Guantanamo Bay, Cuba, in June 1898. (Guantanamo was established as a permanent U.S. Navy base in 1903.) Relatively well trained, equipped for amphibious landings, and accustomed to taking care of themselves, the Marines fought hard and at the same time avoided many of the health hazards that decimated Army units during the war.

Marines man a Colt automatic machine gun behind an improvised barricade at the U.S. Consul's home in Apia, Samoa, in April 1899. These men from the cruiser Philadelphia *joined British Marines in suppressing a native uprising in what was then practically a British-American protectorate.*

The Marine legation guard in Peking musters with rifles and field rolls in about 1907. Although Marines won fame by holding the line against the Boxers in 1900, they were afterwards replaced by an Army company and did not return to Peking until 1905. The Marine Corps' presence in China finally ended in 1949.

Squadron and fleet-type operations developed rapidly after the turn of the century. Here, battleships of the Atlantic Fleet anchor off the New England coast during maneuvers in August 1906.

Fleet Operations and Foreign Ports

During the formative years of the 1880s, while plans for the Steel Navy were still being hammered out and the first ships were being erected on the shores of the Delaware, the wooden and iron vessels of the Old Navy carried on such operations as their limited numbers and feeble strength allowed. Administratively—and traditionally—the ships of the fleet were divided into five major groups: the North Atlantic Squadron, operating off of the U.S. East Coast and in the Caribbean; the South Atlantic Squadron, cruising along the east coast of South America; the European Squadron, in the Mediterranean; the Pacific Squadron (sometimes divided into North and South Pacific Squadrons), off the West Coast of the United States and Central and South America; and the Asiatic Squadron, in the Far East. From an operational standpoint, however, the Navy's few active cruising ships were widely scattered on the various stations and most of their activities were conducted singly and in relative isolation. The tactical employment of warships in concert was little practiced.

Arctic exploration was the favorite glamour assignment of this period. The *Jeannette* expedition under Lieutenant Commander George W. DeLong had sailed in 1879, and in the summer of 1881 the ship was crushed in the ice north of Siberia. The USS *Rodgers*, sent in search of the lost vessel, was destroyed by fire in the same general area. While survivors from these disasters were straggling back to civilization during 1882, Army Lieutenant Adolphus W. Greely was leading another expedition which became hopelessly stranded. A squadron of Navy ships under Commander Winfield S. Schley rescued the survivors in 1884.

Meanwhile, naval officers were busily engaged in promoting commerce or protecting life and property in widely separated parts of the world. In the first category was the mission of Commodore Robert W. Shufeldt in the *Swatara* to negotiate a treaty of trade and diplomatic recognition with the Hermit Kingdom of Korea, successfully completed in 1882.

Intervention of the other kind was accomplished by landing parties of sailors and Marines from U.S. warships at Egypt in 1882, Panama (then part of Colombia) in 1885, Korea in 1888, and Hawaii in 1889. In 1889 friction also began to build up in the kingdom of Samoa where British, German, and U.S. interests were all involved in various expansionist aims. The major U.S. objective, which later led to annexation of part of Samoa, was a coaling station for the Pacific Squadron. In March 1889 the situation was about to boil over as warships of the three nations confronted each other in the harbor of Apia. Nature, however, took charge in the form of a violent typhoon which wrecked most of the ships, including the U.S. vessels *Trenton*, *Vandalia*, and *Nipsic*.

The organization of the new steel warships *Atlanta*, *Boston*, *Chicago*, and *Yorktown* into the famous "Squadron of Evolution" in 1889 was indicative of a gradually reawakening interest in multiship operations in the U.S. Navy, and during the following decade warships on the North Atlantic Station were employed together in increasing numbers as their commanders developed the basic techniques of squadron cruising, tactics, and communications. Studies at the Naval War College, including experiments with the "Strategic War Game" under pioneer tactician William McCarty Little, also fostered the development of fleet doctrine.

U.S. Navy involvement overseas continued through the decade of the nineties in reaction to increasing unrest around the world. In 1890 landing parties were sent ashore to protect American interests in Argentina, and the next year saw a similar landing in Haiti. In 1893 Hawaii became the scene of trouble, and of more U.S. landings. Imperialism was at work as American residents overthrew Queen Liliuokalani and established a Hawaiian Republic, the first step towards union with the United States. Subsequent years brought Navy and Marine intervention in Brazil, Colombia, Nicaragua, Korea, and China.

The major incident during this period was the Chilean

war scare of 1891. During a civil war in August 1891 sailors and Marines from the new cruisers *Baltimore* and *San Francisco* were sent into Valparaiso to guard U.S. interests. Feeling ran high on the part of both Chilean factions, each of which interpreted the U.S. intervention as inimical to itself. Later Captain Winfield S. Schley injudiciously allowed a large liberty party to go ashore from the *Baltimore*. Local beverages were imbibed and insults traded until a mob killed two and injured several more bluejackets. Diplomatic relations deteriorated rapidly, and in January 1892 the U.S. Government delivered an ultimatum demanding an apology and reparations. The Navy Department, believing that war was imminent, made secret preparations for hostilities in which U.S. warships might well have come off second best, but Chile backed down and the crisis blew over.

In the Arctic, a detachment of older warships under Commander Robley D. Evans was kept busy between 1892 and 1894 patrolling the Bering Sea in an effort to halt the extermination of fur seals by foreign commercial vessels. In 1896 Lieutenant Robert E. Peary, on leave from the Navy, conducted the first of his many polar expeditions, which were finally to achieve success in 1909 with Peary's attainment of the North Pole.

Major ceremonial activities of the early 1890s included the return of inventor John Ericsson's body to Sweden aboard the cruiser *Baltimore* in 1891, and an international naval rendezvous and review at Hampton Roads and New York in 1893 in connection with the Columbian celebrations of that year.

Perils of the sea removed several old vessels from the Navy list, including the dispatch boat *Despatch* and tug *Triana* lost by grounding in 1891, and the famous Civil War sloop *Kearsarge* wrecked in the West Indies in 1894.

After the excitement and naval expansion of the Spanish-American War (discussed in the next chapter) came the aftermath of brushfire wars and rebellions. Much of the Asiatic Squadron was engaged in putting down the Philippine insurrection led by guerrilla general Emilio Aguinaldo. A number of small gunboats captured from Spain were pressed into service under the command of very junior officers to interdict rebel commerce, move troops and supplies, and provide fire support to the Army.

Action in the Philippines continued until 1906, but in 1900 the spotlight in the Far East shifted to China and international military operations to save the foreign legations at Peking from rebellious Boxers (as outlined in the previous chapter). Postwar trouble also erupted in Cuba, the Dominican Republic, Honduras, and in the Colombian province of Panama, where local proclivities toward revolution were further stimulated by U.S. pressures to obtain concessions for an isthmian canal. Uprisings in 1903 were accompanied by landings by U.S. Marines and seamen to preserve order and insure the success of the revolutionary forces, and subsequent Panamanian independence was followed by the signing of a treaty for the coveted canal.

Not all of the flag-showing was in Central and South America, however. In the Mediterranean, landing parties intervened in Syria in 1903 and in Morocco in 1904, while in the Far East additional landings were made in Korea to stabilize affairs during the Russo-Japanese War.

Humanitarian work by the Navy included aid at Martinique in 1903 after the devastating volcanic eruption of Mount Pelée, rescue and firefighting operations following the San Francisco earthquake and fire in 1906, and assistance to earthquake victims in Messina, Italy, in 1908.

In 1899 the Navy suffered its first loss of a steel warship by stranding when the cruiser *Charleston* piled up on an uncharted reef in the Philippines. The following year the auxiliary cruiser *Yosemite*, acting as station ship at the new U.S. possession of Guam, was blown to sea by a typhoon and sunk. Other Navy losses included the gunboat *Bennington*, decommissioned and sold after a boiler explosion at San Diego in 1905; the old wooden sailing vessel *Monongahela*, burned at Guantanamo Bay in 1908; and the tug *Nezinscot*, capsized and sunk off Cape Ann in 1909.

After the turn of the century the Navy began to concentrate its larger warships into active squadrons capable of combined operations. Most of the battleships were kept in the North Atlantic, while the new "armored cruiser squadron" operated off the U.S. West Coast. Annual fleetwide gunnery competition, squadron maneuvers, and battle practice were instituted. The trend towards consolidation was accelerated in 1905 when the European and South Atlantic Squadrons were abolished and their ships combined with those of the North Atlantic Squadron to form the new Atlantic Fleet.

Naval celebrations and reviews proliferated following the Spanish-American War. New York's spontaneous welcome to the returning Cuban blockading fleet in 1898 was followed by a Peace Jubilee in Philadelphia, and in 1899 both of these were eclipsed by a tumultuous celebration for returning war hero George Dewey. Another major event was the voyage of a squadron of warships to France in 1905 to bring the remains of naval hero John Paul Jones back to Annapolis. Much of the spring of 1907 was devoted to an impressive international naval review at the otherwise disappointing Jamestown Festival at Hampton Roads. The real scene stealer of the era, however, was the world cruise of the Great White Fleet. President Theodore Roosevelt's review of the returned fleet on 22 February 1909 rang the curtain down on an era of unprecedented naval activity.

Bluejackets from the cruiser Cincinnati *rig a 1-pounder rapid-fire gun on a railroad car during U.S. intervention in Panama in 1902.*

Foreign Ports

Service in each of the Navy's overseas squadrons had its own peculiar attractions. Cruises off Central and South America invariably included landings ashore to protect U.S. commercial and political interests during recurrent periods of civil unrest. Mediterranean duty in the European Squadron was regarded by officers as a "permanent yachting party." The most distant, independent— and interesting—operations of all were in the Asiatic Station. Flag-showing duty there included visits to such fabled and exotic ports as Amoy, Chefoo, Chemulpo, Nagasaki, Shanghai, Vladivostok, Woosung, and Yokohama. In the photograph above, the flag-bedecked cruiser Olympia *fires a salute in celebration of Washington's Birthday at the British crown colony of Hong Kong in February 1898, just a few weeks before her appointment with Montojo's squadron and destiny at Manila.*

U.S. naval operations on distant stations were complicated by a general lack of coaling stations, navy yards, and repair facilities. Even after the capture of the Cavite Navy Yard in the Philippines in 1898, ships of the Asiatic Squadron had to rely on commercial or foreign naval facilities for repairs that required drydocking. In the scene above, the armored cruiser New York *receives hull repairs at the Yokosuka Navy Yard through the courtesy of the Japanese Government, in October 1902. Also in port, at left, are the cruising gunboats* Annapolis *and* Princeton. *The arrival of the new "Dewey" floating drydock at Subic Bay in 1906 finally relieved Asiatic Squadron commanders of such embarrassing dependence on foreign facilities.*

Naval Disasters

*Several maritime disasters during the 1880s and 1890s served to hasten the end of the "Old Navy."
The most serious of these occurred in March 1889 at the harbor of Apia, Samoa, when a confrontation
between American, German, and British warships over the governing of the islands was interrupted
by one of the worst typhoons of the century. Three U.S. warships and three German vessels were
washed ashore, and nearly 150 lives were lost. Only the British cruiser* Calliope *was able to steam
to safety. In the photograph above, the U.S. flagship* Trenton *lies aground alongside the nearly
submerged sloop-of-war* Vandalia, *while the sloop-of-war* Nipsic, *successfully refloated, swings at anchor
beyond. The German warship* Adler *is lying on her beam ends in the distance. The improvised
shears were rigged to drag guns from the wrecked ships onto the beach.*

One of the Steel Navy's worst peacetime calamities occurred in San Diego, California, in July 1905 when a boiler in the gunboat Bennington *was charged with too much steam pressure and exploded, scalding to death more than sixty of the crew. Many more casualties were avoided when a courageous seaman sacrificed his life in order to slip the sinking ship's anchor, permitting her to be towed into shallow water. In the photograph above, made a few hours after the explosion, spectators watch as steam launches bring victims ashore from the grounded ship. Although later refloated, the* Bennington *was so badly damaged that she was never returned to naval service. In 1910 she was purchased by a sugar company and was thereafter employed for a number of years as a molasses barge in the Hawaiian Islands.*

In their hour of glory, gunners aboard the battleship Oregon *peer from a turret hatch after driving the last of Spanish Admiral Cervera's cruisers ashore at the Battle of Santiago on 3 July 1898.*

Remember the Maine!

It has become fashionable to view what statesman John Hay called the "splendid little war" as a classic case of trumped-up imperialism conceived by expansionist jingoes and delivered by the "yellow press." Contemporary accounts, however, stressed widespread popular sympathy for the Cuban rebels who were struggling for independence from Spain and relief from the repressive excesses of Governor Valeriano "Butcher" Weyler. By late 1897 feelings were running so high in both the United States and Spain that many viewed war as inevitable. Among these was Assistant Secretary of the Navy Theodore Roosevelt, who devoted his indefatigable energies to whipping the fleet into readiness.

With an eye to Spain's outpost of empire in the Philippines, Roosevelt quietly reinforced the U.S. Asiatic Squadron, and—using all of his political influence—secured the appointment of Civil War veteran George Dewey to command it. Meanwhile the armored warships of the North Atlantic Squadron were concentrated at Key West, Florida, "for maneuvers." Rioting in Havana in January 1898 stirred the U.S. Government to further activity, and President William McKinley ordered the second-class battleship *Maine* to Cuba in the fear that American citizens there were about to fall victim to anarchy. For three weeks the gleaming white and ochre-painted battleship lay quietly at an anchorage in Havana harbor while Captain Charles D. Sigsbee observed diplomatic punctilio with cool circumspection. Then, at 9:40 on the evening of 15 February, the seaport was jolted by two explosions and onlookers were horrified to see the *Maine* erupt in a column of flame. When her tangled wreckage settled into the muck of the harbor bottom a few minutes later, 251 of the crew were dead and most of the others injured. A U.S. Navy Court of Inquiry would later blame the catastrophe on the explosion of a submarine mine.

What followed was the deceptive lull before the storm. While anti-Spanish sentiment raged and diplomatic notes were exchanged, the Navy Department ordered additional supplies of ammunition and coal and scoured the shipyards of Europe for warships that might be purchased. Cruisers and gunboats were recalled from their distant stations and the battleship *Oregon* was ordered around South America from the Pacific. Passenger liners and freighters were acquired from the merchant marine, and yachts, tugs, and other miscellaneous craft were mobilized from their civilian pursuits. Members of the state Naval Militias were enlisted into service and a massive recruiting drive was initiated. In the Capitol, Congress quickly appropriated $50 million for national defense. President McKinley demanded that Spain agree to an armistice with the Cuban rebels and accept U.S. mediation. Spain refused. Her counter-proposals were ignored as Congress took the bit in its teeth with a resolution for Cuban independence and authorization for the President to bring it about. Spain severed relations, the Secretary of the Navy ordered the imposition of a naval blockade on Cuban ports, and on 25 April the United States declared war.

Although it was not realized at the time, the U.S. fleet outmatched its foe in every respect except numbers. Outwardly powerful, the Spanish squadrons were actually hollow shells of obsolete and ineffective ships manned by poorly trained crews. Spain's only battleship was temporarily inoperative, several new cruisers were still partially ungunned, and the entire fleet was in a wretched state of maintenance. U.S. military and civilian leaders alike, however, believed that they faced a superior adversary. Panicky delegations of citizens from U.S. East Coast ports demanded instant protection against imminent bombardment or invasion. The Navy was forced to split the armored ships of the North Atlantic Squadron between blockade and coastal defense operations, rendering both missions partially ineffective.

Meanwhile Commodore Dewey on board the *Olympia* prepared to strike first blood in the far Pacific, where Spanish Admiral Patricio Montojo y Pasaron guarded the Philippines with a squadron of cruisers and gunboats. Dewey's outfitting operations at Hong Kong were interrupted at the outbreak of war when his ships were ordered out of the neutral port, and he set up a temporary base at Mirs Bay on the China coast. Then, on 1 May the "little commodore" led his heterogeneous force (composed of the protected cruisers *Olympia, Baltimore, Boston,* and *Raleigh,* the gunboats *Concord* and *Petrel,* and the revenue cutter *McCulloch*) into Manila Bay and, in one of the most remarkable naval battles in U.S. history, blasted Montojo's entire squadron of seven warships to the bottom without the loss of a single American life.

Until the occupation of Manila by Army troops in August, Dewey blockaded the port with his squadron, reinforced by the protected cruiser *Charleston* and the lumbering monitors *Monterey* and *Monadnock.* Remaining operations in the Philippines consisted mainly of mop-up and salvage, livened by a tense stand-off with a squadron of semibelligerent German warships under Vice Admiral Otto von Diederichs.

In the Atlantic, divided command and split forces created initial confusion and inefficiency. Commodore Winfield S. Schley was put in command of a group of fast armored warships organized as the "Flying Squadron," but William T. Sampson, promoted to rear admiral over sixteen seniors including Schley, was given the main force of warships as commander of the North Atlantic Squadron. A third group of vessels was diverted to form the Northern Patrol Squadron under Commodore John A. Howell.

On 29 April a Spanish squadron consisting of the cruisers *Infanta Maria Teresa, Almirante Oquendo, Cristobal Colon,* and *Vizcaya,* and the destroyers *Furor, Pluton,* and *Terror,* all commanded by Admiral Pascual Cervera, departed the Cape Verde Islands enroute for the Caribbean and for most of the next month caused consternation as it successfully avoided detection by the U.S. fleet. Admiral Sampson took a force of battleships, cruisers, and slow-moving monitors on an expedition to Puerto Rico in hopes of intercepting Cervera, but found nothing and had to content himself with an ineffectual bombardment of San Juan's shore batteries. In mid-May the Flying Squadron was sent on a search along Cuba's southern coast and Commodore Schley fumbled around for ten days without success. On 1 June Sampson arrived off the south Cuban port of Santiago to find that Schley had finally boxed the enemy in, and the two squadrons were combined into a solid blockade, reinforced by such lighter ships as could be collected. On 3 June Assistant Naval Constructor Richmond P. Hobson and a crew of volunteers scuttled the collier *Merrimac* in the harbor entrance in a daring but unsuccessful attempt to bottle up the Spanish cruisers. Marines landed at Guantanamo Bay on 10 June and twelve days later the Army went ashore at Daiquiri to begin the investment of Santiago.

At 9:35 on the Sunday morning of 3 July, soon after Admiral Sampson had pulled the flagship *New York* out of the blockade ring off Santiago and headed east to confer with Army General William Shafter, the Spanish squadron emerged from Santiago in a spectacular dash for freedom. As Cervera's column of warships turned to starboard to hug the coast to the west, Commodore Schley in the armored cruiser *Brooklyn* moved to engage, and in a controversial maneuver swung sharply away from the enemy and across the bow of the onrushing battleship *Texas,* which had to back down hard to avert a collision. This incident, together with Schley's earlier vacillatory conduct, subsequently became the subject of a running feud between pro- and anti-Schley factions in the Navy. On that morning, however, the U.S. warships—led by the *Brooklyn* and the battleship *Oregon*—were too busy picking off the Spanish cruisers one by one while the converted yacht *Gloucester* blasted the destroyers *Fruor* and *Pluton.* At 1:20 P.M. the last Spanish cruiser, the *Cristobal Colon,* gave up and was run ashore fifty miles west of Santiago. As at Manila Bay, the carnage was strictly one-sided; only one American was killed while the Spaniards lost several hundred men and all six warships.

The U.S. Navy lost most of its seventeen killed and sixty-seven wounded during the war in minor skirmishes on the Cuban blockade line. Sharp battles were fought between U.S. warships and Spanish land forces and gunboats at Cardenas, Cienfuegos, Guantanamo, Manzanillo, Nipe, and Port Mariel. Several small Spanish warships were captured or salvaged, and a large number of merchant prizes were taken.

When intelligence reports disclosed that Spanish reinforcements under Admiral Manuel de la Cámara were en route to the Philippines via Suez in July, the Navy organized an Eastern Squadron to threaten the coast of Spain. This force never actually sailed, but its existence was enough to force the Spanish to recall their fleet to Cadiz. An armistice was signed on 12 August 1898, thus ending what Theodore Roosevelt is said to have called a "bully fight."

The war brought many profound changes to the Navy. Congress reacted to popular demand by approving a major program of fleet expansion, and this was accompanied by the improvement of shore facilities. New types of auxiliary ships and new applications of technology were stimulated. Changes in personnel and administrative policies were made, including a gradual evolution towards a unified command organization. The new popular respect for the Navy also led to higher morale in the fleet and to a better class of recruits, which in turn led to the reform of the training system.

Whatever one may think today of the political or moral justifications for the Spanish-American war, one thing is certain—it marked the coming of age of the United States Navy.

Marines and bluejackets from the flagship Olympia *march under New York City's Victory Arch, September 1899, climaxing a welcome-home celebration for Admiral of the Navy George Dewey, following the Spanish-American War.*

Prelude to War

Bloodshed and reported atrocities by Spain while attempting to put down an insurrection in Cuba in 1897 led to popular sympathy for the rebel cause in the United States, and to deteriorating relations between the U.S. and Spanish governments. Conditions in Cuba eventually grew so threatening that the second-class battleship Maine was sent there to protect American interests. At right, the Maine enters Havana Harbor on 25 January 1898 for her tense visit.

While moored to a buoy at Havana on the night of 15 February, the Maine was rocked by two tremendous explosions and quickly settled to the harbor bottom with three-quarters of her crew killed or drowned. Anti-Spanish sentiment in the United States reached a fever pitch, and four weeks of deliberations by a U.S. Navy Court of Inquiry led to the conclusion that the Maine had been destroyed "by the explosion of a submarine mine, which caused the partial explosion of two or more of her forward magazines."

During the early months of 1898 the Navy made hectic preparations for war. Mobilization efforts included the purchase of several merchant vessels for use as auxiliary cruisers. The former Morgan Line steamer El Norte, *being outfitted at left, was armed with 5-inch guns and recommissioned as the* Yankee *for patrol and blockade duty. Except for the commanding, executive, and navigating officers, she was manned entirely by members of the New York Naval Militia. By mid-1898 over a hundred vessels had been added to the fleet and more than twelve thousand new men enlisted into naval service.*

With the exception of the battleship Oregon, *all of the Navy's armored warships were attached to the North Atlantic Squadron at the time of the* Maine *disaster. The* Oregon's *subsequent race around South America to join the fleet off Cuba was one of the outstanding engineering achievements of the Steel Navy era. Here, crewmen secure the battleship's forecastle for heavy weather during the 66-day, 14,700-mile voyage.*

The Navy Fights on Two Fronts

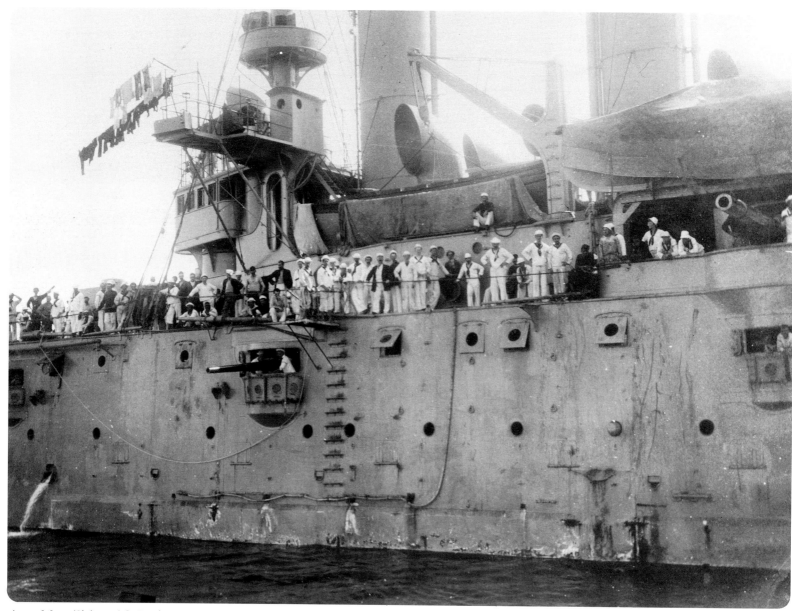

Actual hostilities with Spain commenced on 22 April 1898, when the North Atlantic Squadron under Rear Admiral William Sampson established a naval blockade of Havana and a portion of the north coast of Cuba. In the photograph above, Sampson's gray-painted flagship New York *lies off Key West, Florida, which served as the major U.S. support base for Caribbean operations. A wideranging search for a squadron of cruisers and destroyers under Spanish Admiral Pascual Cervera provided most of the excitement during the early weeks of the Cuban campaign. Cervera eluded detection and slipped into the south Cuban port of Santiago on 19 May, having steamed from the Cape Verde Islands off Africa via Martinique.*

The major naval action in the Pacific was Commodore George Dewey's smashing victory over Admiral Montojo at Manila Bay on 1 May. In a single morning Dewey's seven warships sank or burned eleven enemy vessels while sustaining only superficial damage. The Spaniards suffered nearly four hundred casualties; seven Americans were slightly wounded. The 950-ton Isla de Cuba, *seen above some time after the battle, was set afire by an American boarding party after being scuttled and abandoned in the shallows off Cavite. Like several other Spanish warships, she was later refloated, overhauled, and recommissioned in the U.S. Navy as a gunboat.*

Blockade and Battle

American warships finally located Cervera's squadron at Santiago late in May and on 1 June a tight naval blockade was established around the port. At right the battleship Oregon, almost obscured by the smoke of her own guns, fires at batteries guarding the harbor entrance during one of several shore bombardments conducted during the seven-week blockade. Beginning on 22 June, 17,000 Army troops were landed at the beaches of Daiquiri and Siboney for a land campaign against Santiago.

At 9:35 on the morning of 3 July the Spanish squadron of four cruisers and two destroyers emerged from Santiago in a futile dash for freedom. Within fifty minutes the destroyers Furor and Pluton were sunk and the cruisers Infanta Maria Teresa and Almirante Oquendo beached in flames. The cruiser Vizcaya lasted another hour before being overtaken and driven ashore fifteen miles west of Santiago. At right, crewmen aboard the battleship Iowa gather beneath silent guns to watch the sinking and burning Spanish ships.

The Cristobal Colon *was the fastest of the Spanish cruisers and succeeded in outdistancing all of the U.S. warships except the armored cruiser* Brooklyn *and the battleship* Oregon. *After a three-and-one-half-hour chase, however, the* Oregon *drew close enough to drop a 13-inch shell ahead of the* Colon *and she hauled down her battle flags and was run ashore. At left, jubilant* Oregon *crewmen cheer as the Spanish warship strikes her colors.*

In addition to numerous destructive shell hits, most of the Spanish warships suffered disastrous fires as a result of their wooden decks being set ablaze. At left, a towering explosion erupts from the Vizcaya *as flames reach her after magazine. A number of Spanish sailors were also lost by drowning or to sharks while trying to get ashore, and in all more than three hundred of Cervera's men were killed. In startling contrast, only one American was killed in the battle and one wounded.*

Total Victory

In the aftermath of battle, a member of a Navy salvage and inspection detail stands atop a scorched and silent turret on board the wrecked cruiser Vizcaya. A broken military mast and its fighting top lie askew at left. The subsequent surrender of Santiago's military garrison on 17 July was followed by an armistice between the United States and Spain on 12 August, and that by a formal treaty of peace in December. In accordance with the provisions of the peace treaty Spain gave up all sovereignty over Cuba, and the United States received the Philippines and the islands of Guam and Puerto Rico for a consideration of $20 million.

On board the presidential yacht Mayflower, *Theodore Roosevelt gives parting instructions to "Fighting Bob" Evans as the Battle Fleet prepares to depart Hampton Roads for the Pacific.*

The Great White Fleet

It is a common misconception that the memorable round the world cruise of the "Great White Fleet," as the United States Battle Fleet was popularly known between 1907 and 1909, was simply a saber-rattling show of force by the imperialistic Theodore Roosevelt. While it is true that the voyage served as a powerful instrument of international politics, demonstrating U.S. naval strength to the world and at the same time engendering good will during visits to the seaports of twenty-six countries, the cruise was equally important as a source of fleet training.

Ever since the formation of the Squadron of Evolution the U.S. fleet had been essentially a collection of small, isolated, and heterogeneous squadrons. Post-Spanish War construction programs promised for the first time to provide a battle line of ships that would be compatible in size, armament, speed, maneuverability, and cruising endurance. To those in a position to worry about such things, however, it was apparent that the Navy would have few officers with experience in commanding such a force. Nor were the hastily trained recruits and new Annapolis graduates that were entering the fleet in large numbers fully qualified for their future duties. New ships and new men would all need a thorough shaking down. It was in such a situation that Secretary of the Navy Victor H. Metcalf in 1907 revealed the administration's "plan long under consideration" to send the fleet from the Atlantic to the Pacific.

In December 1907 there gathered at Hampton Roads, Virginia, a fleet the likes of which the American people had never before seen—sixteen great battleships, none more than seven years in commission and some, like the *Kansas, Minnesota,* and *Vermont,* fresh from the builders. Commanding this armada—some 14,000 men strong—was Rear Admiral Robley D. Evans, an authentic war hero and sea dog of international reputation. Only a few days before sailing his force was officially designated as the Battle Fleet of the United States Navy. Evans himself was in charge of the first squadron of four battleships, and three more squadrons were headed by Rear Admirals William H. Emory, Charles M. Thomas, and Charles S. Sperry. (Ships comprising the four squadrons were the *Connecticut, Kansas, Louisiana,* and *Vermont; Georgia, New Jersey, Rhode Island,* and *Virginia; Maine, Minnesota, Missouri,* and *Ohio; Alabama, Illinois, Kearsarge,* and *Kentucky.*) A torpedo flotilla of six new destroyers and their tender *Arethusa* preceded the main force by a few days, while the repair ship *Panther,* supply ships *Culgoa* and *Glacier,* and converted yacht *Yankton* accompanied the battleships.

On 16 December the mighty line passed in review before President Roosevelt aboard the yacht *Mayflower* and took its departure, the flagship *Connecticut* in the lead. Soon after the battleships were at sea it was disclosed that following a short stay on the West Coast they would continue on around the world by way of Suez and the Mediterranean.

The first port of call was Port of Spain, Trinidad, where the crews celebrated Christmas with dinners of roast turkey and full trimmings, band concerts, boat races, deck sports, and visits ashore. The fun was followed by the drudgery of coaling ship, an evolution that was to be repeated many times during the cruise, for the battleships would consume a total of 430,000 tons of coal before their return to the East Coast. The next passage at sea was livened by informal New Year's celebrations and by "Crossing the Line" ceremonies at the equator. A nine-day call was made at beautiful Rio de Janeiro with official luncheons and parties for the officers and general liberty for the crews. South of Brazil the battleships exchanged twenty-one-gun salutes with warships of the Argentine Navy before entering the Strait of Magellan for a stop at bleak and chilly Punta Arenas, the southernmost town in the world. Continuing on through the straits in a dense fog, the fleet debouched safely into the Pacific and turned north. Off Valparaiso the battleships swept into the roadstead in column to render honors to the President of

Chile in passing and to be viewed by thousands of spectators dotting the hillsides. The next stop was Callao, Peru, from where many of the visitors were taken by train to Lima for parties, bullfights, and sightseeing trips into the high Andes.

The next pause, at remote Magdalena Bay in Mexico, was for business rather than pleasure, with a full month being devoted to semi-annual target practice. At this point Rear Admiral Evans, who had been suffering from rheumatism and stomach trouble the entire trip, left for a period of recuperation in the States. In mid-April the fleet arrived back in "God's Country" for good-will visits to San Diego, San Pedro, and Santa Barbara, with parades, flower shows, and popular festivities of all kinds. Evans rejoined the ships for a short cruise to San Francisco and another huge parade, but here illness finally forced him to relinquish his flag. Rear Admiral Thomas succeeded to command temporarily until he in turn was relieved by Rear Admiral Sperry.

During the next seven weeks the battleships visited northwest ports and entered navy yards for maintenance and drydocking. Then, on 7 July 1908 the reorganized Battle Fleet set sail from the Golden Gate on the next leg of its cruise. The *Alabama,* plagued by engineering problems, and the *Maine,* "the greatest coal eater in the fleet," were replaced by the *Nebraska* and *Wisconsin,* both of which had been built on the West Coast. The torpedo squadron was also detached to remain in the United States and the hospital ship *Relief* was assigned to the fleet's train of auxiliaries.

At Honolulu the sailors were treated to six days of luaus, leis, and dancing girls, not to mention surfriding canoes and a sailing regatta. From there the Battle Fleet headed straight across the South Pacific on its longest single leg, 3,850 miles, showing itself only at the sleepy port of Pago Pago in American Samoa. Aukland, New Zealand, was the next stop, where the visitors were entertained at horse races and officially welcomed with a Maori tribal war dance. Arriving at Sydney, Australia, the column of battleships was met by tens of thousands of spectators lining the shores "like thousands of wild birds on rocks and headlands" and by "cheers that did not abate for a week." Similar enthusiastic receptions were later received at Melbourne and Albany. After pausing off America's newest outpost of empire, Manila (then quarantined because of cholera), the fleet forged through a typhoon and into the North Pacific for a seven-day visit to Yokohama. Initial uneasiness, in light of recent tense relations with the land of the Rising Sun, quickly evaporated as the Japanese outdid themselves in entertaining their surprised guests. Turning southward again, one group of battleships returned to Manila while the rest visited Amoy on the China coast.

Most of November 1908 was spent at battle practice in the Philippines, where the fleet's gunners broke all previous records. Here the battleships exchanged a thousand men with vessels of the Asiatic station, and the *Glacier* and *Relief* were detached to remain in the Pacific. Steaming eastward across the Indian Ocean the fleet made a stop at Colombo, Ceylon, where the more adventurous sailors tried riding elephants while a special train carried others to the capital, Kandy. Then the ships filed through the Suez Canal and into the Mediterranean, where they split up for three weeks of flag-showing at Algiers, Athens, Beirut, Malta, Marseilles, Naples, Port Said, Salonica, Smyrna, Tangiers, Tripoli and Villefranche. The flagship *Connecticut* with the *Illinois* and *Culgoa* were pressed into relief work at Messina, Sicily, which had been devastated by an earthquake.

The Battle Fleet reformed at Gibraltar in February 1909 for the final leg across the Atlantic. It was met in mid-ocean by several of the remaining East Coast warships, and was welcomed home by President Roosevelt with another full dress review at Hampton Roads on Washington's Birthday, 1909.

The cruise around the world had served its purposes admirably. The United States had demonstrated that it was indeed a world power, and the Navy had achieved new-found respect at home and abroad. Inexperienced officers and men had been welded into a smoothly operating team by months of drill. Without fanfare, senior officers had been rotated through six changes of command in the course of which three battleship captains were fleeted up to division commander. Lieutenant Hutch I. Cone, who had been advanced from command of a destroyer to fleet engineering officer for the Pacific leg of the cruise, was promoted to Engineer-in-Chief of the Navy shortly after the fleet's return—from lieutenant to rear admiral in sixteen months. The Navy was really pushing its most able young officers to the top. Naval gunnery was at a peak of efficiency, squadron and fleet operational procedures had been honed to perfection, and the basics of a supply and repair force had been established.

While the press and public glowed in the light of the fleet's successes, the Navy's leaders quietly moved to correct its more basic deficiencies. The great white, buff, and gold battleships with their tall, straight funnels and towering military masts were undoubtedly impressive, but their peacetime rig was in sharp contrast to the sober, businesslike appearance of warships encountered overseas, whose grim efficiency clearly foreshadowed the coming struggles for world power. Soon after their return the U.S. battleships went into overhaul and when they emerged the gilded bow crests were gone, hulls had been streamlined by removing some of the angular and archaic forward sponsons, the old-fashioned military masts and fighting tops were replaced by cage masts with fire control platforms, and the Great White Fleet had donned a permanent coat of battleship gray.

Rear Admiral Charles S. Sperry, photographed with his aide and a U.S. consular official at Yokohama, commanded the fleet on the second half of its world-girdling cruise.

335

*At precise 400-yard intervals and a speed of ten knots, battleships of the Great White Fleet
steam in mighty array out of Hampton Roads, Virginia, on 16 December 1907.*

From the Atlantic to the Pacific

Officers and enlisted men haggle with native merchants at Port of Spain, Trinidad, the fleet's first stop. The Navy received a dispassionate reception at this British colony, whose residents seemed preoccupied with the local horse-racing season.

Neptunus Rex had one of his grandest days ever on 6 January 1908, when the Battle Fleet made the first of its six crossings of the equator and 12,500 landlubbers, pollywogs, and sea lawyers were initiated into the mysteries of the deep. In this scene on board the Vermont, shellbacks watch a pair of initiates tumble from semi-automatic chairs into the clutches of the Royal Bears while a third rookie endures the ministrations of the Royal Barber.

Visits to Rio de Janeiro, Punta Arenas, and Callao were followed by a month of gunnery exercises in Magdalena Bay, Mexico. With the exception of fishing, swimming, and baseball, the bleak and uninhabited bay offered few off-duty amusements. Here, bluejackets from the New Jersey enjoy a typically nautical pastime in one of their ship's specially rigged cutters.

The prize-winning crew of a 7-inch gun on board the Connecticut poses with its riddled target after practice at Magdalena Bay. With trophies, prize-money, and ship's reputation at stake, gunnery competition was spirited.

Through the Golden Gate

*Crowds of spectators, estimated at more than one million, watched from the hillsides of the Golden
Gate and the city of San Francisco as the Battle Fleet steamed majestically over the horizon, above,
and into San Francisco Bay on 6 May 1908. There the ships of the West Coast armored cruiser squadron
and their consorts combined with the battleships and torpedo flotilla to form an armada of forty-two
warships, the largest peacetime fleet ever assembled up to that time in American waters. Activities
during the two-week stay in San Francisco Bay included a naval review presided over by Secretary
of the Navy Victor H. Metcalf, two changes of command, a land parade featuring seventy-five hundred
bluejackets, and shipboard visiting, as seen aboard the battleship* New Jersey *on the opposite page.*

Westward Across
the Pacific

Before leaving the West Coast, several of the battleships visited the Puget Sound cities of Bellingham, Seattle, and Tacoma. Here, "Rodjestvensky," one of sixteen bear cubs presented to the fleet by the citizens of Aberdeen, Washington, gets a hosing down. The mascot later died at Manila.

On 7 July 1908, the Battle Fleet departed San Francisco Bay to begin the second segment of its voyage. Hawaiians showered the ships with fresh pineapples during a one-week visit to the islands of Maui and Oahu.

En route from Auckland, New Zealand, to Australia, the battleships ran into a typhoon. Here, the Georgia *shakes off a heavy sea. Later the fleet encountered an even worse storm north of the Philippines.*

"Sydney," a wallaby mascot added to the Connecticut's *growing menagerie by the citizens of Sydney, Australia, gets a friendly handshake. The fleet received a particularly warm welcome in Australia and more than two hundred bluejackets contrived to remain behind when the ships departed.*

343

The Exotic Orient

Relations between the United States and Japan had been deteriorating steadily since the end of the Russo-Japanese War, and the Battle Fleet's cordial reception at Yokohama was regarded as a triumph of diplomacy. Here, a contingent of bluejackets, carefully selected for good behavior and "sober habits," goes ashore for a garden party while an equally well-indoctrinated populace extends an enthusiastic welcome.

Half of the battleships spent a week at Amoy, where the Chinese had erected a $400,000 "Pleasure City" especially for the visiting Americans. The sailors were royally entertained with Chinese plays, gymnastic exhibitions, baseball games, banquets in nine large pavilions, and nightly displays of fireworks.

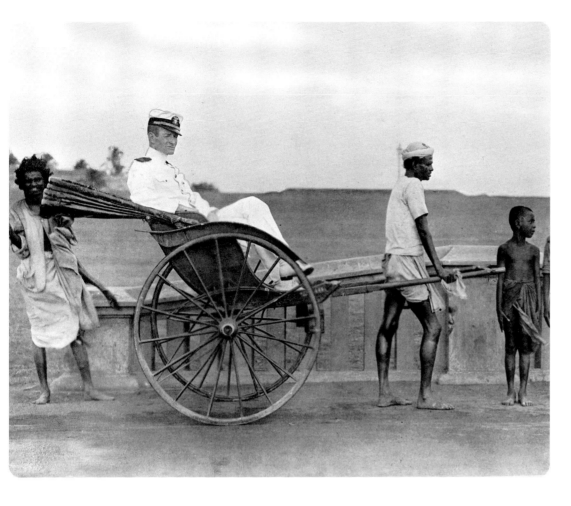

Lieutenant J. S. McCain of the flagship Connecticut *takes in the sights of Colombo, Ceylon, from a rickshaw. At this Indian Ocean port each sailor in the fleet was the recipient of one pound of tea from the plantations of Sir Thomas Lipton.*

Battleships ease their way through a sandy reach of the Suez Canal en route to the Mediterranean. Progress was briefly halted at one point when the Georgia *ran aground. Canal fees for the fleet totaled about $150,000. Once in the Mediterranean, the ships dispersed for visits to a dozen European and North African ports.*

The Fleet Returns—An Era Ends

On 22 February 1909 the Connecticut *led the Battle Fleet back into Hampton Roads to successfully conclude "the most stupendous task ever attempted by any naval power," having visited six continents and steamed 42,227 miles in 434 days. On board the flagship officers and bluejackets crowded together with little regard for rank to see and hear their champion, "Teddy" Roosevelt, welcome them home with a rousing speech. A few days later the President's last term in office ended and the Great White Fleet broke up to be transformed from gala white and gilt into the somber grays of the dreadnought era.*

*Men of a signal detail gaze across three-quarters of a century of time
as they haul down their admiral's flag aboard the* Brooklyn.

Epilogue

The return of the Great White Fleet to Hampton Roads in February 1909 marked the end of an era. Theodore Roosevelt, one of the men most responsible for the creation of the modern Navy, was a lame-duck President when he received the salutes of his admirals on board the *Mayflower*. The tide of U.S. imperialism had nearly reached high slack. Instances of high-handed gunboat diplomacy would still occur in Central America and the Caribbean, but there were already stirrings of withdrawal from the responsibilities and burdens of empire. Across the Atlantic, gathering war clouds cast their shadows over Europe and Asia—Balkan hatreds were being fanned into flame, and an Anglo-German naval race was hurtling the great powers toward a collision.

New breakthroughs in technology were making existing fleets obsolescent in almost every respect: oil would soon begin to drive out coal, the turbine would replace the reciprocating engine, electricity was assuming ever more important roles aboard ship, the wireless was undermining the time-honored independence of commanders at sea, and scientific fire control was supplanting traditional methods of gunnery. Every major seafaring nation had committed itself to the all-big-gun dreadnought battleship, and submarine and aerial warfare would soon move onto the high seas.

But during the preceding quarter-century the architects of the Steel Navy had performed their jobs well. From a twelfth-rate position the U.S. Navy had been built up into a serious adversary to any fleet, excepting perhaps the mighty battle line of Great Britain. Its ships—soundly constructed, heavily armed, and well commanded—would hold the line until a new generation of warships would be ready to fight.

Although the Steel Navy's ships were to be relegated to secondary roles during World War I and the majority of them would go to the scrappers during the decade to follow, a number were destined to continue on for many additional years in humble but nevertheless useful service. The battleship *Illinois* (renamed *Prairie State*) served as a Naval Reserve headquarters until the mid-1950s and the *Kearsarge,* converted into a craneship, lasted nearly as long. The famed *Oregon,* preserved for many years as a relic, was stripped during an overzealous World War II scrap drive and used as a dynamite storage barge, finally to be dismantled in 1956.

The old protected cruiser *Chicago* (renamed *Alton*) was employed as a barracks ship at Pearl Harbor until 1935, and the *Boston* (renamed *Despatch*) served until 1946 as a receiving ship on San Francisco Bay. The *Baltimore* and the *San Francisco* (renamed *Yosemite*) were converted into minelayers and were not scrapped until the beginning of the Second World War. The hulk of the long-lived armored cruiser *New York* (renamed first *Saratoga* and then *Rochester*) was scuttled at Subic Bay late in 1941 to avoid capture by the Japanese. Another armored cruiser, the *Washington* (renamed *Seattle*), was used as a receiving ship until 1946.

The gunboats *Dubuque* and *Paducah* served during World War II as patrol and gunnery training ships, and the *Wheeling,* converted into a floating barracks, lasted until 1946. The hull of the *Nashville,* long out of naval service, was used as a lumber barge until being broken up in 1957. The monitor *Wyoming* (renamed *Cheyenne*) served with the Naval Reserve for many years, finally being scrapped in 1939, while the older *Amphitrite,* sold in 1920, was employed until 1951 as the hull of a floating hotel. Three destroyers, the *Truxtun, Whipple,* and *Worden,* had civilian careers lasting until the mid-1950s in the guise of banana boats.

Today, of the nearly 150 warships of the American Steel Navy, but a single example remains. On board the famous protected cruiser *Olympia,* berthed at Philadelphia, visitors still wander across decks once trod by Dewey and the heroes of Manila Bay. And on the West Coast a dwindling muster of the fourteen thousand officers and enlisted men who took the Navy's battleships around the world still gather once a year, under the auspices of the Great White Fleet Association, to celebrate the memory of a fleet that is no more.

Farewell to friends, farewell to foes,
Farewell each kind relation,
I'm going to cross the raging main,
Bound for a foreign station,
While I cross the raging main,
The Stars and Stripes I will sustain,
And I'll think of my love when I'm far, far away,
And I'll think of my love when I'm far, far at sea.
An old Navy song.

Appendixes

Bluejackets man the San Francisco's *six-oared captain's gig, circa 1895.*

Personalities
of the
American
Steel Navy

FRANCIS TIFFANY BOWLES 1858–1927

Second-ranking member of the Naval Academy class of 1879, Bowles later attended the Royal Naval College at Greenwich, England, where he was awarded an advanced degree in naval architecture. He served as secretary of the Second Naval Advisory Board in 1882, and is generally credited with the designs of the *Atlanta* and *Boston*. Later he supervised construction of the Navy's first battleship, the *Texas*. Bowles was head of the construction department at the Brooklyn Navy Yard in 1895–1901, and as a rear admiral in 1901–03 was chief of the Bureau of Construction and Repair. In 1903 he left the Navy to become president of the Fore River Shipbuilding Company.

Bowles had a major influence on the design of the Steel Navy's warships, starting with the ABCD ships.

FRENCH ENSOR CHADWICK 1844–1919

A member of the Naval Academy class of 1864, Chadwick saw brief Civil War service. After a normal career in the Old Navy he was stationed in London in 1883–89 as the first U.S. naval attaché. He headed the expanded Office of Naval Intelligence in 1892–93 and was chief of the Bureau of Equipment in 1893–97. He commanded the armored cruiser *New York* in 1897–98 and was also chief of staff to Admiral William Sampson during the Spanish-American War. Chadwick was president of the Naval War College in 1900–03, and commanded the South Atlantic Squadron before retiring as a rear admiral in 1906.

A member of the progressive faction of younger officers, Chadwick filled a number of key posts during the development of the Steel Navy. Chadwick's influence was also felt through his writings on naval intelligence, diplomacy, history, and science.

WILLIAM EATON CHANDLER 1835–1917

A lawyer and a journalist, Chandler had a long and active career in state and national politics. He was solicitor and judge-advocate of the Navy under Lincoln and Assistant Secretary of the Treasury in 1865–67. He served as Secretary of the Navy under President Chester Arthur in 1882–85, and as a member of the Senate in 1887–1901.

An aggressive and industrious Secretary, Chandler took up where his predecessor William Hunt had left off and got the first steel warships under construction. His awarding of the ABCD-ship contracts to a political crony, John Roach, laid the Navy open to charges of corruption which, although apparently unmerited, delayed the shipbuilding program and blackened the early reputation of these ships.

CHARLES EDGAR CLARK 1843–1922

An 1863 graduate of the Naval Academy, Clark saw Civil War action at Mobile Bay. His later service included varied shore and afloat assignments, including command of the sloop *Ranger* on a survey of the Mexican and Central American coasts in 1883–86. Clark commanded the battleship *Oregon* during the Spanish-American War, and retired as a rear admiral in 1905.

One of the Steel Navy's outstanding sea captains, Clark is best remembered for his war service aboard the *Oregon*. His ship's 14,000-mile dash around the Horn to the Caribbean was hailed as a masterpiece of planning and discipline, and Clark's policy of keeping fires under all boilers during the Santiago blockade enabled the *Oregon* to take a leading role in the destruction of the Spanish cruisers.

CHARLES HENRY CRAMP 1828–1913

Scion of an old Philadelphia shipbuilding family, Cramp succeeded to the presidency of his father's yard, William Cramp and Sons, in 1879. He was a pioneer in naval construction and engine design, and promoted a native shipbuilding capacity and a strong merchant marine. His company, in which four brothers and six sons also served, was the chief competitor of John Roach and was the prime beneficiary of Roach's downfall. In addition to producing many U.S. merchant and war vessels, Cramp built warships for the Russian, Turkish, and Japanese navies. He retired in 1903.

Under Cramp's direction, his yard became the leading shipbuilder for the U.S. Navy, turning out such well-known warships as the *Indiana, Massachusetts, Iowa, Alabama, Maine, New York, Brooklyn,* and *Columbia.*

GEORGE DEWEY 1837–1917

A member of the Naval Academy class of 1858, Dewey saw much action in the Civil War. He commanded the flagship *Pensacola* in 1886–88, was chief of the Bureau of Equipment in 1888–93, and headed the influential Board of Inspection and Survey in 1896–98. Dewey commanded the Asiatic Squadron during the Spanish-American War, and Congress revived the rank of Admiral of the Navy especially for him in 1899. He served as president of the General Board from its creation in 1900 until his death in 1917.

Dewey's resounding victory over the Spanish Admiral Montojo at Manila in 1898 rocketed him to lasting fame and he became the best-known officer of the Steel Navy. His prestige and force of character subsequently assured Dewey of great influence over the direction of the Navy for many years.

ROBLEY DUNGLISON EVANS 1846–1912

An 1863 graduate of the Naval Academy, Evans was seriously wounded during a heroic assault on Fort Fisher in 1865. Progressively advancing in rank, in 1881 he served as a member of the First Naval Advisory Board. As captain of the gunboat *Yorktown* in 1891, Evans won recognition for skilled handling of a crisis with Chile. His later commands included the armored cruiser *New York* and battleships *Indiana* and *Iowa,* the latter at the Battle of Santiago. As a rear admiral in 1907–08, Evans commanded the Battle Fleet on its cruise from Hampton Roads to the West Coast, at which point he was forced by ill health to retire.

With his able leadership, colorful personality, and spectacular career, "Fighting Bob" Evans was one of the most admired officers in the Steel Navy, as well as a major contributor to its technological development.

BRADLEY ALLEN FISKE 1854–1942

Second-ranking graduate of the Naval Academy class of 1874, Fiske became one of the Navy's leading experts on electricity. He saw extensive sea duty, helped install the ordnance in the *Atlanta* and *Boston,* and was navigator aboard the gunboat *Petrel* at the Battle of Manila Bay. As a member of the Naval Wireless Telegraph Board in 1904–05, he was instrumental in introducing radio to the fleet. Fiske commanded several warships, served on the General Board in 1910–11, and as Aide for Operations held the senior Navy office in 1913. He retired as a rear admiral in 1916.

A prolific inventor, Fiske held sixty patents and was responsible for many of the devices that revolutionized naval warfare, including a rangefinder, telescopic gun sight, stadimeter, and electric interior communications apparatus.

HILARY ABNER HERBERT 1834–1919

A native of South Carolina, Herbert entered law practice in 1856. During the Civil War he served as an officer in the Confederate Army until wounded in 1864. Later he returned to law, entered politics, and served in Congress during 1877–93. He was Secretary of the Navy under President Grover Cleveland in 1893–97.

As chairman of the House Committee on Naval Appropriations in the early 1880s, Herbert was instrumental in obtaining funds for building the Steel Navy. As Secretary he became a convert to the doctrines of Mahan. Although ship construction lagged during the first years of his tenure and he allowed political influence to reestablish itself to some extent in the Navy yards, by the time he left his post the fleet had risen to fifth place among the world's navies.

PHILIP HICHBORN 1839–1910

As a youth Hichborn studied naval architecture and served as an apprentice shipwright at Charlestown, Massachusetts. Later he worked at Mare Island, California, where in 1869 he was appointed an assistant naval constructor. He served as a member of the First Naval Advisory Board in 1881 and was sent to Europe in 1884 to report on naval progress abroad. In 1893, following several years of duty in Washington, D.C., Hichborn was appointed Chief Constructor of the Navy. From then until 1901 he presided over construction of the Navy's warships.

Hichborn was the author of many technical papers and is credited with several inventions, including the balanced turret. He was probably the man most responsible for the progress achieved in the designs of warships for the Steel Navy.

RICHMOND PEARSON HOBSON 1870–1937

At the Naval Academy Hobson was placed "in Coventry" for reporting the delinquencies of his fellows, but nevertheless graduated at the top of the class of 1889. He chose duty in the Construction Corps, where as a junior officer during the Spanish-American War he was put in command of the collier *Merrimac* in a heroic attempt to block the channel at Santiago. Although the scuttling attempt failed and Hobson and his men were captured, he returned home at war's end a popular hero and was promoted directly to captain. A progressive and a man of strict moral principles, Hobson resigned in 1903 to better promote such diverse causes as U.S. naval supremacy and the prohibition of alcohol. He served in Congress in 1907–15. In 1933 Congress belatedly awarded Hobson the Medal of Honor for his war exploits.

JOHN PHILIP HOLLAND 1841–1914

Born in Ireland, Holland served for a number of years as a teacher in the order of Christian Brothers before emigrating to the United States in 1873. During 1878–85 he designed and built a succession of small submarines which were financed in part by the revolutionary Irish Fenian Brotherhood. He also submitted several designs to the Navy Department and finally in 1895 received the first U.S. Navy contract for a submarine. This boat, the *Plunger*, was never completed, but a smaller boat designed and financed independently by Holland, and embodying most of the characteristics of modern submarines, was purchased by the Navy in 1900 (USS *Holland*). Holland himself later lost control of his company, which ultimately grew to become the Electric Boat Company, the principal U.S. builder of submarines.

WILLIAM HENRY HUNT 1823–1884

Entering law practice in Louisiana in 1844, Hunt was a Union sympathizer during the Civil War but was nevertheless forced to serve in the Confederate Army. He entered politics during the Reconstruction and in 1881 was appointed Secretary of the Navy under James Garfield. Soon afterwards, however, the President was assassinated, and his successor, Chester Arthur, paid off a political debt by replacing Hunt and shifting him to the post of Minister to Russia.

Despite his short tenure as head of the Navy Department, Hunt deserves the title of Father of the Steel Navy. It was he who moved Congress and the Administration to undertake the program that was to lead to the design and construction of the ABCD ships, and ultimately to the renaissance of the Navy.

JOHN DAVIS LONG 1838–1915

A Harvard-educated lawyer, Long served as governor of Massachusetts in 1880–82 and in Congress during 1883–89. He held the post of Secretary of the Navy under President William McKinley from 1897 to 1902. Following his retirement from politics, Long continued to write extensively on naval affairs and in support of social and political reforms.

Long's policy as Secretary of the Navy was to delegate authority, and since he had good officers in all the key positions and the energetic Theodore Roosevelt as his assistant, his administration was successful. Although he was an unspectacular leader, Long ably guided the Navy through the Spanish-American War and thereafter launched it on a course of unprecedented expansion.

STEPHEN BLEECKER LUCE 1827–1917

Appointed a midshipman in 1841, Luce saw extensive service during the Civil War, and as a faculty member at the Naval Academy wrote an important text on seamanship. During the 1870s he served as Commandant of Midshipmen at the Naval Academy, established and helped administer the Navy's apprentice training program, and helped form the U.S. Naval Institute. In 1884 he became the first president of the Naval War College at Newport, Rhode Island. Luce retired as a rear admiral in 1889 but returned to Newport for special duty from 1901 to 1910.

A scholar and a prolific writer, Luce was a lifetime advocate of better training. Because of his tireless efforts to establish and maintain the Naval War College, he is recognized as the father of that institution.

ALFRED THAYER MAHAN 1840–1914

Second-ranking member of the Naval Academy class of 1859, Mahan served on blockade duty during the Civil War and in routine assignments until 1885. Summoned by Commodore Stephen Luce to lecture at the new Naval War College that year, he succeeded to its presidency in 1886–89 and 1892–93. In 1890 he published *The Influence of Sea Power Upon History, 1660–1783,* the first of many writings that would make him world famous. Mahan was forced to leave the War College to command the flagship *Chicago* in 1893–95, and retired as a captain in 1896. He was recalled in 1898 to sit on the Spanish War Board, and in 1899 served as a delegate to the Hague Peace Conference. In 1906 he was promoted to rear admiral, retired.

Mahan was at first more highly regarded abroad than in America, but is today everywhere recognized as the major prophet of sea power.

GEORGE WALLACE MELVILLE 1841–1912

Entering the Steam Engineering Corps from civilian life in 1861, Melville saw much duty in the Civil War and received a number of commendations. Between 1873 and 1884 he served as chief engineer on three expeditions to the Arctic and in 1881 commanded the only party to reach safety when DeLong's *Jeannette* was lost following two years in the ice. In 1887 he was promoted over forty-four senior officers to head the Bureau of Steam Engineering, a position he held until retiring as a rear admiral in 1903.

During his tenure as engineer-in-chief, Melville supervised the engineering design of 120 ships and introduced water-tube boilers, vertical and multiple expansion engines, and triple screws. A progressive administrator, he is justly credited as the principal creator of machinery for the Steel Navy.

DAVID DIXON PORTER 1813–1891

Porter entered the Navy as a midshipman in 1829. He was a Civil War naval hero and was promoted to rear admiral in 1862. He became superintendent of the Naval Academy in 1865 and instituted many reforms in its training methods. In 1869 Porter became virtual head of the Navy under ineffectual Secretary Adolph Borie, and in 1870 succeeded David Farragut as Admiral of the Navy. From 1877 until his death he remained influential as head of the Board of Inspection.

A complex man—arbitrary, opinionated, and mercurial—Porter worked tirelessly to upgrade the caliber of naval personnel, but remained always a strong advocate of sail. Although he supported construction of a new Navy, he imposed some of his old-fashioned concepts and prejudices upon the designs of its first ships.

FRANCIS MUNROE RAMSAY 1835–1914

An 1856 graduate of the Naval Academy, Ramsay rose to command during the Civil War and compiled a notable combat record. He was superintendent of the Naval Academy during 1881–86, becoming known as a strict disciplinarian. In 1889 he was named chief of the powerful Bureau of Navigation, where he held sway over officer personnel assignments and promotions until his retirement as a rear admiral in 1897. Ramsay had little use for such activities as the Naval War College and made many efforts to detach Captain Mahan from his lectures and writings for sea duty. Although he was conservative and autocratic, he was respected by his contemporaries. Secretary of the Navy Hilary Herbert considered Ramsay "more upright and just-minded" than any other officer of his acquaintance.

JOHN ROACH 1813–1887

A poverty-stricken Irish immigrant, Roach learned the trade of iron molder and laboriously established himself in the iron works business. Civil War profits enabled him to expand into ship construction, and between 1872 and 1886 the Roach shipyard built 126 iron-hulled ships. In 1883 he won the contracts for the first warships of the Steel Navy, the *Atlanta, Boston, Chicago,* and *Dolphin,* but two years later his political ties brought down the vengeance of the incoming Democratic administration, led by Secretary of the Navy William Whitney. The reputation of Roach's workmanship was blackened, his contracts were voided, and he was forced into receivership. Broken and discouraged, Roach died before his cruisers were completed, but the ABCD ships' long and honorable service careers ultimately vindicated him.

JOHN RODGERS 1812–1882

Son of the elder commodore of the same name, Rodgers was appointed a midshipman in 1828 and served his junior years in the age of sail. He was a monitor and ironclad captain during the Civil War and in 1865–66 commanded a squadron, including the original monitor *Monadnock,* that steamed around Cape Horn to San Francisco. Later commands included the Boston and Mare Island Navy yards, the Asiatic Squadron, and the Naval Observatory. In 1881 Rear Admiral Rodgers presided over the first steps toward creation of a new Navy as head of the First Naval Advisory Board.

Rodgers was a progressive in an era when tradition's grip was strong. Although he did not live to see any of the new ships that he had recommended, he must be numbered among the true progenitors of the Steel Navy.

THEODORE ROOSEVELT 1858–1919

A wealthy Harvard graduate, Roosevelt made a name during the early 1890s as a civil service reformer and as New York City police commissioner. He was an aggressive Assistant Secretary of the Navy in 1897–98, and became a hero during the Spanish-American War as a colonel in the Rough Riders. He was governor of New York in 1899–1901, and became Vice President in 1901. McKinley's assassination in 1901 catapulted him to the Presidency, an office he held until 1909.

The very example of the strenuous life, Roosevelt personally dominated the Navy Department. He built the fleet into a first-class force and flexed its muscles on the world cruise of 1907–09. Roosevelt regarded the Navy as the right arm of national expansion and was one of the principal shapers of its destiny.

WILLIAM THOMAS SAMPSON 1840–1902

Graduating at the top of the Naval Academy class of 1861, Sampson saw action during the Civil War and routine sea and shore duty thereafter. He was superintendent of the Naval Academy in 1886–90 and chief of the Bureau of Ordnance in 1893–97. He commanded the battleship *Iowa* in 1897 and was president of the *Maine* Board of Inquiry in 1898. During the Spanish-American War, Sampson was given command of the important North Atlantic Blockading Squadron. In 1899 he assumed command of the Boston Navy Yard, where he died as a rear admiral.

Sampson grew with the Steel Navy, held the right jobs at the right times, and was an effective commander at war. He had the misfortune of being out of range when the Spaniards sortied at Santiago, but to most historians, remains the true architect of that victory.

355

WINFIELD SCOTT SCHLEY 1839–1911

An 1860 graduate of the Naval Academy, Schley saw action during the Civil War and on a punitive expedition to Korea in 1871. He commanded the Greely relief expedition in 1884, and as captain of the protected cruiser *Baltimore* in 1891 became involved in a crisis with Chile. Schley was captain of the armored cruiser *New York* in 1895–97 and was commander of the Flying Squadron during the Spanish-American War. He retired as a rear admiral in 1901.

Although Schley was subordinate to Sampson off Cuba, he was in tactical command at the Battle of Santiago and received popular credit for the victory. In 1901 controversy erupted over his war conduct and Schley requested a Court of Inquiry, the judgment of which was generally critical of him.

MONTGOMERY SICARD 1836–1900

An 1855 graduate of the Naval Academy, Sicard rose to command of a gunboat in the Civil War. While on duty at the Naval Academy, Brooklyn Navy Yard, and at Washington, D.C., during the next decade he became the Navy's leading authority on naval ordnance. As captain of the steamer *Saginaw* in 1870 he lost his ship on a remote reef in the Pacific. Sicard co-authored a text on gunnery in 1880 and served as chief of the Bureau of Ordnance during 1881–91. He commanded the North Atlantic Squadron in 1897–98, but was forced by ill health to relinquish command on the eve of the Spanish-American War. He retired as a rear admiral in 1898.

One of the prime architects of the Steel Navy, Sicard was largely responsible for the development of the modern ordnance used in its ships.

CHARLES DWIGHT SIGSBEE 1845–1923

An 1863 graduate of the Naval Academy, Sigsbee saw combat in the Civil War. During the 1870s he commanded the steamer *Blake* on a survey of the Gulf of Mexico, invented several important deep-sea sounding and sampling devices, and wrote a book on the subject. He headed the Navy Hydrographic Office in 1893–97. As captain of the battleship *Maine* in 1898, Sigsbee was acclaimed for cool handling of the disaster that befell his ship. He commanded the auxiliary cruiser *Saint Paul* during the Spanish-American War and held several fleet commands before retiring as a rear admiral in 1907.

Sigsbee's role in oceanography was better recognized abroad than in the U.S., and his career would probably have remained one of obscure competence had it not been for the loss of the USS *Maine.*

WILLIAM SOWDEN SIMS 1858–1936

An 1880 graduate of the Naval Academy, Sims acquired an extensive knowledge of foreign naval progress while in the Asiatic Fleet and as naval attaché in Paris in 1897–1900. He served as inspector of target practice during 1902–09, and also was aide to President Roosevelt in 1907–09. As a commander in 1909 Sims became the first officer below captain to command a battleship. He was commander of U.S. naval forces in European waters during World War I and retired as a full admiral in 1922.

A tireless crusader for naval reform, Sims made both friends and enemies with his many reports and criticisms of naval gunnery, ship design, and organizational deficiencies. His major contribution to the Steel Navy was the revolution in gunnery in 1902–09.

JAMES RUSSELL SOLEY 1850–1911

A graduate of Harvard, Soley accepted an appointment as an instructor at the Naval Academy in 1871. In 1876 he was commissioned in the Navy's corps of professors of mathematics, continuing at the academy until 1890 and rising to the relative rank of commander. Soley also served as Navy Department librarian, supervised publication of voluminous official naval records of the Civil War, and lectured at the Naval War College, where he became one of the influential group around Mahan. He served as Assistant Secretary of the Navy to Benjamin Tracy in 1890–93.

A prolific writer on naval history, Soley was one of the major movers in the rapid expansion of the Navy during the early 1890s, and was an important contributor to its rise in the affections of the American people during that decade.

HENRY CLAY TAYLOR 1845–1904

A graduate of the Naval Academy class of 1863, Taylor saw some service during the Civil War and rose gradually through the ranks of the Old Navy. In 1893, as a captain, he was chosen to succeed Mahan as president of the Naval War College, a position that he held until 1896. Taylor commanded the battleship *Indiana* during the Spanish-American War, and became chief of the Bureau of Navigation in 1902. He retired as a rear admiral in 1902.

Taylor was a particularly strong advocate of strategic planning. At the War College he made war gaming a permanent part of the curriculum and had his student officers practice tactical maneuvers in steam launches as a way of teaching them to avoid "visionary formations." His proposal for creation of a general staff organization led to creation of the influential General Board in 1900.

BENJAMIN FRANKLIN TRACY 1830–1915

A lawyer and district attorney from New York, Tracy served during the Civil War as a colonel in the New York Volunteers and was later awarded the Medal of Honor. Following the war he returned to law practice, but through his association with the head of the Republican organization in New York was named Secretary of the Navy during the Benjamin Harrison administration in 1889–93.

Tracy was the first Secretary of the Navy to embrace the sea-power doctrines of Mahan and his associates and he put them into effect with great efficiency. He obtained authorization for the Navy's first real battleships, and under his administration the fleet was built into a well-rounded force backed by efficient facilities ashore and a sound organization.

RICHARD WAINWRIGHT 1849–1926

An 1868 graduate of the Naval Academy, Wainwright saw varied duty as a junior officer at sea, at the Hydrographic Office, in the Bureau of Navigation, at the Naval Academy, and in the Office of Naval Intelligence. He was executive officer of the battleship *Maine* when she was sunk in 1898, and commanded the converted yacht *Gloucester* during the Spanish-American War. He was superintendent at the Naval Academy in 1900–02. Wainwright commanded a division of battleships during the world cruise of the Great White Fleet in 1907–09, and retired as a rear admiral in 1911.

A dedicated officer, Wainwright's greatest fame lay in his exemplary conduct during the *Maine* disaster, and in his exploits as captain of the *Gloucester* against the torpedo boats *Pluton* and *Furor* at the Battle of Santiago.

JOHN GRIMES WALKER 1835–1907

Top graduate of the Naval Academy class of 1856, Walker served with distinction under Admiral Porter during the Civil War and thereafter. During 1881–89 he held the influential assignment of chief of the Bureau of Navigation, and in 1889 assumed command of the new Squadron of Evolution. Walker subsequently commanded the South Atlantic, North Atlantic, and Pacific Squadrons before retiring as a commodore in 1897.

Rigid, conservative, and authoritarian, Walker was one of the most disliked men in the Navy. Although he was considered an anti-intellectual, his effectiveness as an administrator and as a commander afloat was valuable to the Steel Navy during its time of greatest transition.

WILLIAM COLLINS WHITNEY 1841–1904

Born to wealth and married into riches, Whitney entered law practice in 1865 after attending Yale and the Harvard Law School. He moved into politics as a corporation counsel and multiplied his wealth as a streetcar magnate. Whitney served as Secretary of the Navy during the second term of Grover Cleveland in 1885–89.

Whitney introduced the second generation of steel warships to the fleet, but his greatest contributions were in the areas of administrative reform. He was regarded as "prince of the Secretaries" by many senior officers of the day, possibly in part because of his often letting the traditional line faction have its way in the internal struggles of the era. He is especially remembered for his harsh criticism of John Roach and the ABCD ships.

OTHER NOTABLE PERSONALITIES

President Theodore Roosevelt kept a firm grip on the helm of the Navy Department, and although the five men who served him as Secretary of the Navy were strong men in their own right, they were allowed little scope for originality. Roosevelt's first Secretary, WILLIAM H. MOODY (who held office during 1902–04), was a lawyer from Massachusetts who was ultimately elevated to the Supreme Court. The second, PAUL MORTON (1904–05), was a railroad man. His earlier dealings ran him afoul of the Interstate Commerce Commission and he resigned to enter the insurance business. He was succeeded by CHARLES J. BONAPARTE (1905–06), a colorful political reformer and grandnephew of Napoleon Bonaparte, who soon moved on to the Attorney Generalship. VICTOR H. METCALF (1906–08), was a California lawyer and politician who ably administered the Department for two years. The last of the five was TRUMAN H. NEWBERRY (1908–09), a railroad tycoon with a Navy background and extensive industrial experience. Newberry, who had learned a great deal as Assistant Secretary, initiated some sweeping management reforms during his tenure, but his concepts, too far ahead of their time, were largely negated by his conservative subordinates and political successors.

Several officers merit special mention for their roles in the development of the Navy's first steel warships. ROBERT W. SHUFELDT headed the Second Naval Advisory Board which hammered out the details of the ABCD ships in 1883. As heads of their respective bureaus, THEODORE D. WILSON (Chief Constructor in 1882–93) and CHARLES H. LORING (Engineer-in-Chief in 1884–87) were directly involved in the design and construction of the new ships. DANIEL AMMEN, an influential holdover from the Old Navy, pressed Congress endlessly in favor of a fleet of rams. His persistence was probably the principal reason for the construction of the useless *Katahdin*.

Ordnance pioneers included WILLIAM M FOLGER, chief of the Bureau of Ordnance in 1890–93, and RICHARD W. MEADE, commander of the Washington Navy Yard gun factory in 1887–90. LEWIS A. KIMBERLY organized and conducted the competitive tests of armor plate under direct gunfire that led to the rapid improvement of armor in the early 1890s. An Army officer, EDMUND L. G. ZALINSKI, briefly achieved prominence with his development of the pneumatic dynamite gun in the 1880s, as did Navy officer JOHN A. HOWELL, inventor of a flywheel-driven torpedo.

ALBERT P. NIBLACK was one of the most prolific idea-men among the Navy's younger officers during the 1890s. His writings, appearing principally in the U.S. Naval Institute *Proceedings*, influenced progress in a number of areas including strategy, tactics, ship design, and organization. Naval Academy professor PHILIP R. ALGER achieved much the same role in the field of ordnance.

Nearly all of the officers commanding major warships during the Spanish-American War received a share of glory. In addition to those already mentioned, these included FRANCIS A. COOK, captain of Commodore Schley's flagship *Brooklyn*, and JOHN W. PHILIP, captain of the battleship *Texas*. The captain of Commodore Dewey's flagship *Olympia*, CHARLES V. GRIDLEY, ably conned his ship at Manila in spite of serious illness.

Much of the responsibility for command during the Great White Fleet's voyage around South America in 1907–08 fell on CHARLES M. THOMAS after Robley D. Evans fell ill. Thomas formally assumed command of the battleships for a brief period on the West Coast and died soon thereafter from the strain. CHARLES S. SPERRY ably commanded the fleet during the second half of its world cruise.

Chief Yeoman FRED J. BUENZLE was possibly the most influential enlisted man in the Steel Navy. As editor of a series of enlisted-men's magazines during 1901–09, he sought and achieved higher standards in the fleet and greater respect for the uniform ashore.

357

Anatomy of an Indiana-Class Battleship, Circa 1898

Inboard Profile and Sections by Arthur D. Baker III, based on plans in the National Archives
and information in contemporary volumes of the *Journal of the American Society of Naval Engineers.*
Scale: 1 inch = 19⅓ feet. The inboard profile does not show all 269 compartments in the ship,
since only those spaces bisected by or directly adjacent to the centerline can be depicted. The two
cross-sections on the opposite page suggest the number of additional compartments located outboard
of the centerline.

Decks
A Main Deck
B Berth Deck
C Orlop Deck
D Platform
E Hold

After Spaces
1 After Torpedo Room
2 Captain's Cabin
3 Officers' State Rooms
4 Passageway; Store Rooms to Port & Starboard
5 Steering Engine Room
6 13-Inch Powder Magazine
7 Rudder
8 After Trimming Tanks
9 8-Inch Powder Magazine

After Ordnance Spaces
10 13-Inch Turret
11 Barbette Enclosure; Wardroom Spaces to Port & Starboard
12 Access Trunk; 13-Inch Powder Magazines to Port & Starboard
13 Ammunition Handling Room; 13-Inch Shell Rooms to Port & Starboard
14 8-Inch Shell Room
15 Turret Turning Machinery

Superstructure
16 Superstructure Deck, with 14 6-Pounder Rapid-Fire Guns
17 After Bridge Deck, with 2 6-Pounder Rapid-Fire Guns
18 Rangefinder Platform
19 After Searchlights
20 Magnetic Compass Platform
21 Boat Cranes, Port & Starboard
22 Forward Searchlights
23 Military Mast
24 Fighting Tops, with 4 Machine Guns
25 Rangefinder Platform
26 Navigation Bridge
27 Pilot House
28 Armored Conning Tower
29 Emergency Steering Station; 8-Inch Turrets to Port & Starboard
30 After Stack
31 Forward Stack
32 8-Inch Turrets, Port & Starboard
33 Executive Officer's Office
34 6-Inch Rifles, Port & Starboard
35 Ship's Galley; 6-Pounder Rapid-Fire Guns to Port & Starboard
36 6-Inch Rifles, Port & Starboard

Midships Spaces
37 Wardroom Pantry
38 Engine Room Ventilation Hatch; Torpedo Tubes to Port & Starboard
39 Auxiliary Boiler
40 Boiler Room Uptake; Wash Rooms to Port & Starboard
41 Auxiliary Boiler
42 Boiler Room Uptake; Refrigerating Spaces to Port & Starboard
43 Torpedo Tubes, Port & Starboard
44 Ship's Brig
45 Engine Rooms, Port & Starboard
46 After Firerooms, Port & Starboard; Coal Bunkers Outboard of Fire Rooms
47 After Boilers, Port & Starboard
48 Dynamo Room
49 Coal Bunker
50 Forward Firerooms, Port & Starboard; Coal Bunkers Outboard of Firerooms
51 Forward Boilers, Port & Starboard
52 Hydraulic Room
53 Coal Bunker

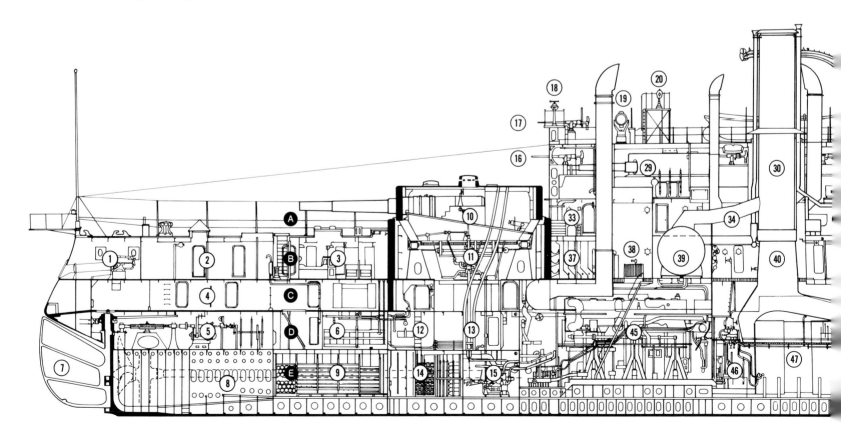

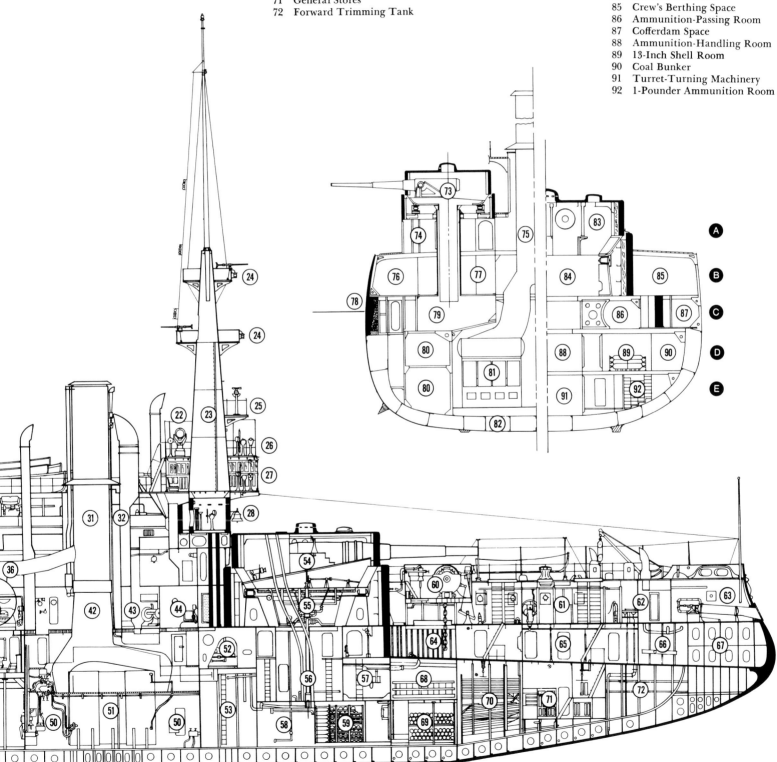

Forward Ordnance Spaces
54 13-Inch Turret
55 Barbette Enclosure; Crew's Berthing to Port & Starboard
56 Ammunition Handling Room; 13-Inch Shell Rooms to Port & Starboard
57 Access Trunk; 13-Inch Powder Magazines to Port & Starboard
58 Turret-Turning Machinery
59 8-Inch Shell Room

Forward Spaces
60 Anchor Windlass
61 Crew's Berthing Space
62 Sick Bay
63 Forward Torpedo Room
64 Chain Locker
65 Passageway; Bread Room & Stores to Port & Starboard
66 Paint Locker
67 Water-Excluding Material
68 13-Inch Powder Magazine; Stores to Port & Starboard
69 8-Inch Powder Magazine
70 Hold
71 General Stores
72 Forward Trimming Tank

Section Through Forward Stack
73 8-Inch Turret
74 Crew's Head
75 Forward Stack
76 Coal Bunker
77 Passageway
78 18-Inch Armor Belt
79 Turret-Turning Machinery
80 Coal Bunkers
81 Forward Boiler Room
82 Double Bottom

Section Through Forward Turret
83 13-Inch Turret
84 Barbette Enclosure
85 Crew's Berthing Space
86 Ammunition-Passing Room
87 Cofferdam Space
88 Ammunition-Handling Room
89 13-Inch Shell Room
90 Coal Bunker
91 Turret-Turning Machinery
92 1-Pounder Ammunition Room

Major Classes of Warships in the United States Navy, 1883-1909

Data based on material in reports of the Chief of the Bureau of Construction and Repair, from the *Annual Report of the Secretary of the Navy* for the years 1883–1909, and from *Ships' Data, U.S. Naval Vessels,* various years.

Wherever possible, the information quoted is for warships as first commissioned. For uniformity, the vessel having the lowest hull number in any class has been designated the name-ship for that class.

"Normal" displacement indicates a vessel fully equipped and ready for sea, with two-thirds supply of ammunition, stores, and fuel.

The speed and indicated horsepower quoted are the averages obtained during the official four-hour acceptance trial.

Warship complements quoted should be considered approximate, as these frequently varied from ship to ship within a class, or from year to year in a ship.

Warship profiles by Arthur D. Baker III, based on plans in the National Archives and in contemporary volumes of the *Transactions of the Society of Naval Architects and Marine Engineers* and the *Journal of the American Society of Naval Engineers.*

The scale for all profiles is 1:750 (1 inch = 62.5 feet).

Special Class Vessels

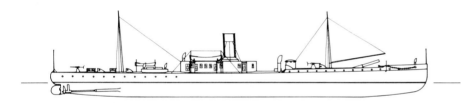

Vesuvius (Dynamite Cruiser)

Length on Load Waterline:	252 feet, 4 inches
Extreme Breadth:	26 feet, 6⅜ inches
Mean Draft:	10 feet, 7½ inches
Normal Displacement:	929 tons
Armament:	3 15-inch pneumatic dynamite guns
	3 3-pounders
Watertight Deck:	³⁄₁₆ inch (slopes); ³⁄₁₆ inch (flats)
Engines:	twin-screw, vertical triple-expansion
Performance:	21.42 knots; 3,795 indicated horsepower
Complement:	6 officers; 64 enlisted men

USS *Vesuvius*
Built by William Cramp & Sons, Philadelphia, Pa.
Authorized 3 August 1886.
Commissioned 7 June 1890.
Served as experimental torpedo tender 1905–1921.
Sold 19 April 1922.

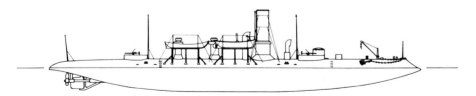

Katahdin (Harbor Defense Ram)

Length on Load Waterline:	250 feet, 9 inches
Extreme Breadth:	43 feet, 5 inches
Mean Draft:	15 feet
Normal Displacement:	2,155 tons
Armament:	4 6-pounders
Maximum Armor Thickness:	6 inches (sides)
Engines:	twin-screw, horizontal triple-expansion
Performance:	16.11 knots; 5,068 indicated horsepower
Complement:	7 officers; 90 enlisted men

USS *Katahdin*
Built by Bath Iron Works, Bath, Me.
Authorized 2 March 1889.
Commissioned 20 February 1896.
Stricken 9 July 1909, designated *Ballistic Experimental Target A*.
Sunk as a gunnery target at Rappahannock Spit, Virginia, in September 1909.

Second-Class Battleships

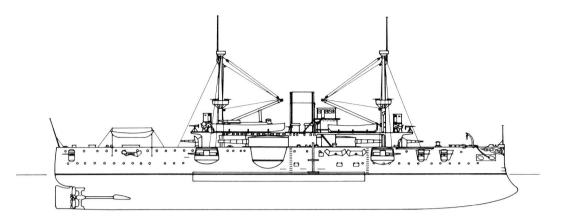

Texas

Length on Load Waterline:	301 feet, 4 inches
Extreme Breadth:	64 feet, 1 inch
Mean Draft:	22 feet, 6 inches
Normal Displacement:	6,315 tons
Armament:	2 12-inch, 35-caliber breech-loading rifles
	6 6-inch, 40-caliber breech-loading rifles
	12 6-pdr.; 6 1-pdr.; 4 37-mm.; 2 Gatlings
Torpedo Tubes:	4 18-inch, Whitehead above-surface tubes
Maximum Armor Thickness:	12 inches (sides); 12 inches (turrets)
Engines:	twin-screw, vertical triple-expansion
Performance:	17.8 knots; 8,610 indicated horsepower
Complement:	30 officers; 362 enlisted men

USS Texas

Built at Norfolk Navy Yard, Portsmouth, Va.
Authorized 3 August 1886.
Commissioned 15 August 1895.
Renamed *San Marcos* 18 February 1911.
Sunk as an experimental gunnery target
in Chesapeake Bay, 11 October 1911.

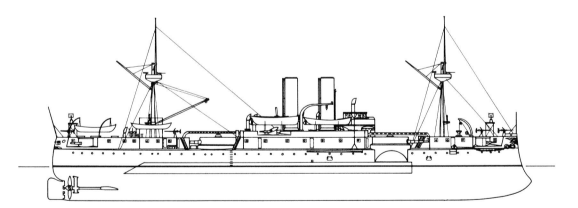

Maine

Length on Load Waterline:	318 feet
Extreme Breadth:	57 feet
Mean Draft:	21 feet, 6 inches
Normal Displacement:	6,682 tons
Armament:	4 10-inch, 35-caliber breech-loading rifles
	6 6-inch, 40-caliber breech-loading rifles
	7 6-pounders; 8 1-pounders; 4 Gatlings
Torpedo Tubes:	4 18-inch, Whitehead above-surface tubes
Maximum Armor Thickness:	12 inches (sides); 8 inches (turrets)
Engines:	twin-screw, vertical triple-expansion
Performance:	17.45 knots; 9,293 indicated horsepower
Complement:	31 officers; 343 enlisted men

USS Maine

Built at New York Navy Yard, Brooklyn, N.Y.
Authorized 3 August 1886.
Originally classified Armored Cruiser No. 1.
Commissioned as a battleship 17 September 1895.
Sunk by an explosion of undetermined origin
in Havana Harbor, 15 February 1898.
Refloated 2 February 1912.
Towed to sea and scuttled 16 March 1912.

Battleships

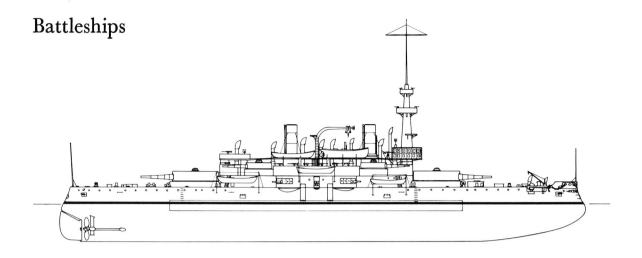

Indiana Class   Coast Battleships Nos. 1–3

Length on Load Waterline:	348 feet
Extreme Breadth:	69 feet, 3 inches
Mean Draft:	24 feet
Normal Displacement:	10,288 tons
Armament:	4 13-inch, 35-caliber breech-loading rifles
	8 8-inch, 35-caliber breech-loading rifles
	4 6-inch, 40-caliber breech-loading rifles
	20 6-pounders; 6 1-pounders; 4 Gatlings
Torpedo Tubes:	6 18-inch, Whitehead above-surface tubes
Maximum Armor Thickness:	18 inches (sides); 15 inches (turrets)
Engines:	twin-screw, vertical triple-expansion
Performance (Indiana):	15.55 knots; 9,738 indicated horsepower
Complement:	32 officers; 441 enlisted men

USS Indiana

William Cramp & Sons, Philadelphia.
Authorized 30 June 1890.
Commissioned 20 November 1895.
Renamed *Coast Battleship No. 1*
   29 March 1919.
Sunk as an experimental bombing
   target, 1 November 1920.

USS Massachusetts

William Cramp & Sons, Philadelphia.
Authorized 30 June 1890.
Commissioned 10 June 1896.
Renamed *Coast Battleship No. 2*
   29 March 1919.
Sunk as a target for shore batteries
   at Pensacola, Florida,
   22 November 1920.

USS Oregon

Union Iron Works, San Francisco,
   Calif.
Authorized 30 June 1890.
Commissioned 15 July 1896.
Demilitarized 4 January 1924 and
   reclassified IX-22.
Loaned to State of Oregon as naval
   relic, 15 June 1925.
Recalled by Presidential order
   26 October 1942.
Partially scrapped; used as a
   dynamite barge at Guam.
Sold 15 March 1956; scrapped in
   Japan.

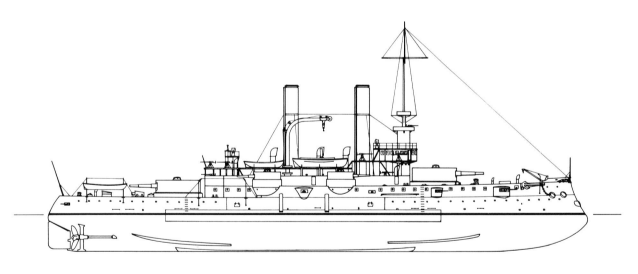

Iowa

Length on Load Waterline:	360 feet
Extreme Breadth:	72 feet, 2½ inches
Mean Draft:	24 feet
Normal Displacement:	11,340 tons
Armament:	4 12-inch, 35-caliber breech-loading rifles
	8 8-inch, 35-caliber breech-loading rifles
	6 4-inch, 40-caliber rapid-fire guns
	20 6-pounders; 4 1-pounders; 4 .30-cal.
Torpedo Tubes:	4 14-inch, Howell above-surface tubes
Maximum Armor Thickness:	14 inches (sides); 15 inches (turrets)
Engines:	twin-screw, vertical triple-expansion
Performance:	17.09 knots; 12,105 indicated horsepower
Complement:	36 officers; 469 enlisted men

USS Iowa   Coast Battleship No. 4

Built by William Cramp & Sons, Philadelphia, Pa.
Authorized 19 July 1892.
Commissioned 16 June 1897.
Renamed *Coast Battleship No. 4* 30 April 1919.
Unclassified, IX-6.
Sunk as a radio-controlled target ship during fleet battle practice off Panama,
   23 March 1923.

Battleships

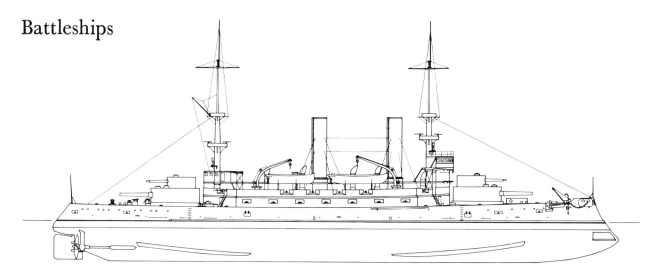

Kearsarge Class

Length on Load Waterline:	368 feet
Extreme Breadth:	72 feet, 2½ inches
Mean Draft:	23 feet, 6 inches
Normal Displacement:	11,540 tons
Armament:	4 13-inch, 35-caliber breech-loading rifles
	4 8-inch, 35-caliber breech-loading rifles
	14 5-inch, 40-caliber rapid-fire guns
	20 6-pounders; 8 1-pounders; 4 .30-cal.
Torpedo Tubes:	4 18-inch, Whitehead above-surface tubes
Maximum Armor Thickness:	16½ inches (sides); 17 inches (turrets)
Engines:	twin-screw, vertical triple-expansion
Performance (*Kearsarge*):	18.82 knots; 11,954 indicated horsepower
Complement:	38 officers; 548 enlisted men

USS *Kearsarge* Coast Battleship No. 5

Built by Newport News S.B. & D.D. Co., Newport News, Va.
Authorized 2 March 1895.
Commissioned 20 February 1900.
Unclassified, IX-16.
Designated AB-1 5 August 1920 and converted into a floating shipyard crane.
Renamed Crane Ship No. 1 6 November 1941.
Stricken 22 June 1955.

USS *Kentucky* Coast Battleship No. 6

Built by Newport News S.B. & D.D. Co., Newport News, Va.
Authorized 2 March 1895.
Commissioned 15 May 1900.
Sold 23 January 1924.

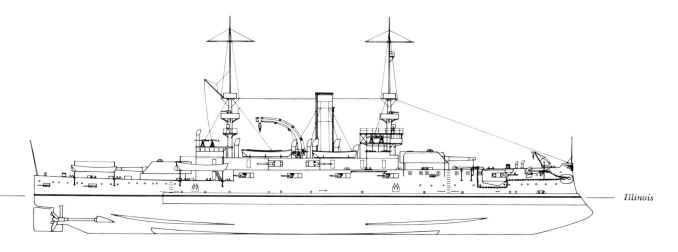

Illinois

Illinois Class   Coast Battleships Nos. 7–9

Length on Load Waterline:	368 feet
Extreme Breadth:	72 feet, 2½ inches
Mean Draft:	23 feet, 6 inches
Normal Displacement:	11,565 tons
Armament:	4 13-inch, 35-caliber breech-loading rifles
	14 6-inch, 40-caliber rapid-fire guns
	16 6-pounders; 6 1-pounders; 4 .30-cal.
Torpedo Tubes:	4 18-inch, Whitehead above-surface tubes
Maximum Armor Thickness:	16½ inches (sides); 14 inches (turrets)
Engines:	twin-screw, vertical triple-expansion
Performance (*Illinois*):	17.45 knots; 12,898 indicated horsepower
Complement:	40 officers; 496 enlisted men

USS *Illinois*

Built by Newport News S.B. & D.D. Co., Newport News, Va.
Authorized 10 June 1896.
Commissioned 16 September 1901.
Served as a Naval Militia and Naval Reserve drill ship in New York 1921–1955.
Reclassified IX-15.
Renamed *Prairie State* 8 January 1941.
Sold 18 May 1956.

USS *Alabama*

Built by William Cramp & Sons, Philadelphia, Pa.
Authorized 10 June 1896.
Commissioned 16 October 1900.
Sunk as an experimental bombing target, 27 September 1921.

USS *Wisconsin*

Built by Union Iron Works, San Francisco, Cal.
Authorized 10 June 1896.
Commissioned 4 February 1901.
Sold 26 January 1922.

Battleships

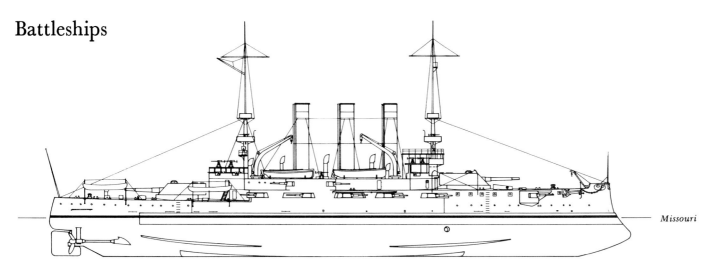

Missouri

Maine Class   Coast Battleships Nos. 10–12

Length on Load Waterline:	388 feet
Extreme Breadth:	72 feet, 2½ inches
Mean Draft:	23 feet, 6 inches
Normal Displacement:	12,370 tons
Armament:	4 12-inch, 40-caliber breech-loading rifles
	16 6-inch, 50-caliber rapid-fire guns
	6 3-inch; 8 3-pdr.; 6 1-pdr.; 2 .30-cal.
Torpedo Tubes:	2 18-inch, submerged tubes
Maximum Armor Thickness:	11 inches (sides); 12 inches (turrets)
Engines:	twin-screw, vertical triple-expansion
Performance (*Maine*):	18.00 knots; 15,603 indicated horsepower
Complement:	34 officers; 614 enlisted men

USS *Maine*

Built by William Cramp & Sons, Philadelphia, Pa.
Authorized 4 May 1898.
Commissioned 29 December 1902.
Sold 26 January 1922.

USS *Missouri*

Built by Newport News S.B. & D.D.
Co., Newport News, Va.
Authorized 4 May 1898.
Commissioned 1 December 1903.
Sold 26 January 1922.

USS *Ohio*

Built by Union Iron Works, San Francisco, Cal.
Authorized 4 May 1898.
Commissioned 4 October 1904.
Sold 24 March 1923.

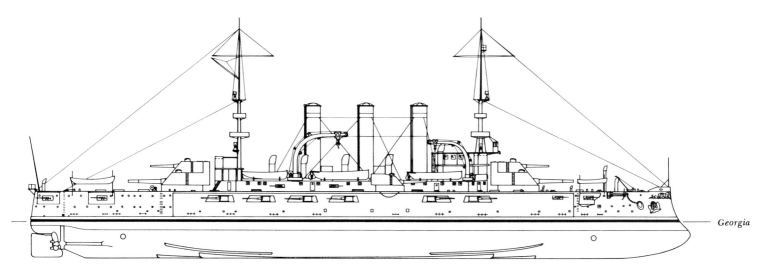

Georgia

Virginia Class   Coast Battleships Nos. 13–15*

Length on Load Waterline:	435 feet
Extreme Breadth:	76 feet, 2½ inches
Mean Draft:	23 feet, 9 inches
Normal Displacement:	14,948 tons
Armament:	4 12-inch, 40-caliber breech-loading rifles
	8 8-inch, 45-caliber breech-loading rifles
	12 6-inch; 50-caliber rapid-fire guns
	12 3-inch; 12 3-pounders; 2 .30-cal.
Torpedo Tubes:	4 21-inch, submerged tubes
Maximum Armor Thickness:	11 inches (sides); 12 inches (turrets)
Engines:	twin-screw, vertical triple-expansion
Performance (*Virginia*):	19.01 knots; 22,841 indicated horsepower
Complement:	40 officers; 772 enlisted men

USS *Virginia*

Newport News S.B. & D.D. Co.,
Newport News, Va.
Authorized 3 March 1899.
Commissioned 7 May 1906.
Stricken 12 July 1922.
Sunk as a target 5 September 1923.

USS *Nebraska*

Moran Brothers, Seattle, Wash.
Authorized 3 March 1899.
Commissioned 1 July 1907.
Sold 30 November 1923.

USS *Georgia*

Bath Iron Works, Bath, Me.
Authorized 3 March 1899.
Commissioned 24 September 1906.
Sold 1 November 1923.

USS *New Jersey*

Fore River S.B. Co., Quincy, Mass.
Authorized 7 June 1900.
Commissioned 12 May 1906.
Stricken 12 July 1922.
Sunk as a target 5 September 1923.

USS *Rhode Island*

Fore River S.B. Co., Quincy, Mass.
Authorized 7 June 1900.
Commissioned 19 February 1906.
Sold 1 November 1923.

* USS *New Jersey*, Battleship No. 16, and USS *Rhode Island*, Battleship
No. 17, although of the same class, were not designated Coast Battleships.

Battleships

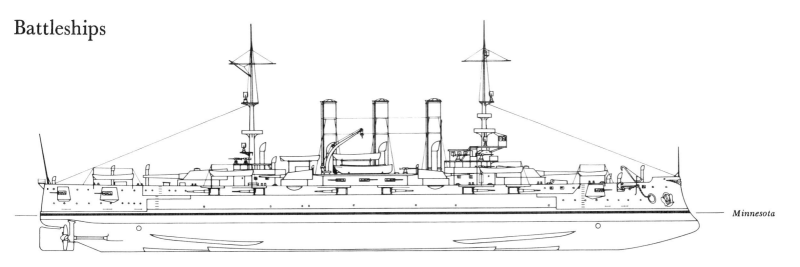

Minnesota

Connecticut Class   Battleships Nos. 18–22 & 25

Length on Load Waterline:	450 feet
Extreme Breadth:	76 feet, 10 inches
Mean Draft:	24 feet, 6 inches
Normal Displacement:	16,000 tons
Armament:	4 12-inch, 45-caliber breech-loading rifles
	8 8-inch, 45-caliber breech-loading rifles
	12 7-inch, 45-caliber rapid-fire guns
	20 3-inch; 12 3-pdr.; 4 1-pdr.; 6 .30-cal.
Torpedo Tubes:	4 21-inch, submerged tubes
Maximum Armor Thickness:*	11 inches (sides); 12 inches (turrets)
Engines:	twin-screw, vertical triple-expansion
Performance (*Connecticut*):	18.78 knots; 16,500 indicated horsepower
Complement:	41 officers; 855 enlisted men

* 9-inch main belts in *Vermont*, *Kansas*, *Minnesota*, and *New Hampshire*.

USS *Connecticut*
New York Navy Yard, Brooklyn, N.Y.
Authorized 1 July 1902.
Commissioned 29 September 1906.
Sold 1 November 1923.

USS *Louisiana*
Newport News S.B. & D.D. Co.,
  Newport News, Va.
Authorized 1 July 1902.
Commissioned 2 June 1906.
Sold 1 November 1923.

USS *Vermont*
Fore River S. B. Co., Quincy, Mass.
Authorized 3 March 1903.
Commissioned 4 March 1907.
Sold 30 November 1923.

USS *Kansas*
New York Shipbuilding Co.,
  Camden, N.J.
Authorized 3 March 1903.
Commissioned 18 April 1907.
Stricken 24 August 1923.

USS *Minnesota*
Newport News S.B. & D.D. Co.,
  Newport News, Va.
Authorized 3 March 1903.
Commissioned 9 March 1907.
Stricken 1 December 1921.

USS *New Hampshire*
New York Shipbuilding Co.,
  Camden, N.J.
Authorized 27 April 1904.
Commissioned 19 March 1908.
Sold 1 November 1923.

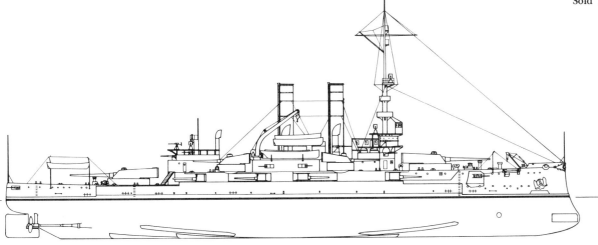

Mississippi Class

Length on Load Waterline:	375 feet
Extreme Breadth:	77 feet
Mean Draft:	24 feet, 8 inches
Normal Displacement:	13,000 tons
Armament:	4 12-inch, 45-caliber breech-loading rifles
	8 8-inch, 45-caliber breech-loading rifles
	8 7-inch, 45-caliber rapid-fire guns
	12 3-inch; 6 3-pdr.; 2 1-pdr.; 6 .30-cal.
Torpedo Tubes:	2 21-inch, submerged tubes
Maximum Armor Thickness:	9 inches (sides); 12 inches (turrets)
Engines:	twin-screw, vertical triple-expansion
Performance (*Mississippi*):	17.11 knots; 13,607 indicated horsepower
Complement:	34 officers; 673 enlisted men

USS *Mississippi*   Battleship No. 23
Built by William Cramp & Sons, Philadelphia, Pa.
Authorized 3 March 1903.
Commissioned 1 February 1908.
Stricken 21 July 1914.
Sold to Greece 30 July 1914.
Renamed *Lemnos*.
Sunk by German bombers at Salamis Harbor, Greece, 10 April 1941.

USS *Idaho*   Battleship No. 24
Built by William Cramp & Sons, Philadelphia, Pa.
Authorized 3 March 1903.
Commissioned 1 April 1908.
Stricken 21 July 1914.
Sold to Greece 30 July 1914.
Renamed *Kilkis*.
Sunk by German bombers at Salamis Harbor, Greece, 10 April 1941.

Monitors

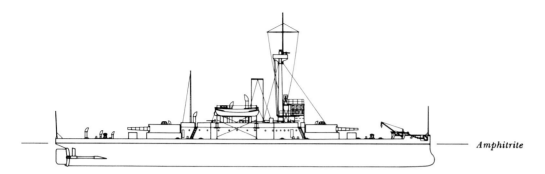

Amphitrite

Amphitrite Class

Length on Load Waterline:	259 feet, 6 inches
Extreme Breadth:	55 feet, 10 inches
Mean Draft:	14 feet, 6 inches
Normal Displacement:	3,990 tons
Armament:*	4 10-inch, 30-caliber breech-loading rifles
	2 4-inch, 40-caliber rapid-fire guns
	2 6-pdr.; 2 3-pdr.; 2 1-pdr.; 2 37-mm.
Maximum Armor Thickness:*	9 inches (sides); 7½ inches (turrets)
Engines:†	twin-screw, inclined compound
Performance (*Amphitrite*):	10.5 knots; 1,600 indicated horsepower
Complement:	26 officers, 145 enlisted men

* *Miantonomoh* had 2 10-inch, 30-caliber and 2 10-inch, 35-caliber breech-loading rifles. *Miantonomoh* and *Terror* had 7-inch armor on sides, 11½-inch armor on turrets, no barbettes, and no 4-inch guns.

† *Monadnock* had twin-screw, horizontal triple-expansion engines, providing 12 knots speed at 3,000 indicated horsepower.

USS *Amphitrite*

Partially constructed by Harlan & Hollingsworth, Wilmington, Del.
Laid down circa 1874.
Launched 7 June 1883.
Completed at Norfolk Navy Yard.
Commissioned 23 April 1895.
Served as a Naval Militia training ship 1910–1917.
Sold 3 January 1920.
Converted into a 75-room floating hotel for use at Beaufort, S.C., and Fort Lauderdale, Fla.
Scrapped in 1951.

USS *Miantonomoh*

Partially constructed by John Roach & Sons, Chester, Pa.
Laid down circa 1874.
Launched 5 December 1876.
Completed at New York Navy Yard.
Commissioned 27 October 1891.
Stricken 3 December 1915 and employed as a gunnery target.
Hulk sold 26 January 1922.

USS *Monadnock*

Partially constructed by Continental Iron Works, Vallejo, Cal.
Laid down circa 1874.
Launched 19 September 1883.
Completed at Mare Island Navy Yard.
Commissioned 20 February 1896.
Stricken 2 February 1923.

USS *Terror*

Partially constructed by William Cramp & Sons, Philadelphia, Pa.
Laid down circa 1874.
Launched 24 March 1883.
Completed at New York Navy Yard.
Commissioned 15 April 1896.
Stricken 15 December 1915 and employed as a gunnery target.
Hulk sold 10 March 1921.

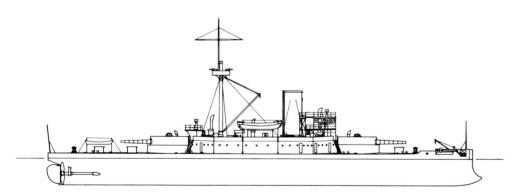

Puritan

Length on Load Waterline:	289 feet, 6 inches
Extreme Breadth:	60 feet, 1½ inches
Mean Draft:	18 feet
Normal Displacement:	6,060 tons
Armament:	4 12-inch, 35-caliber breech-loading rifles
	6 4-inch, 40-caliber rapid-fire guns
	6 6-pounders; 2 1-pounders; 2 37-mm.
Maximum Armor Thickness:	14 inches (sides); 8 inches (turrets)
Engines:	twin-screw, horizontal compound
Performance:	12.4 knots; 3,700 indicated horsepower
Complement:	22 officers; 208 enlisted men

USS *Puritan*

Partially constructed by John Roach and Sons, Chester, Pa.
Laid down circa 1874.
Launched 6 December 1882.
Completed at New York Navy Yard.
Commissioned 10 December 1896.
Stricken 27 February 1913 and employed as a gunnery target.
Hulk sold 26 January 1922.

Monitors

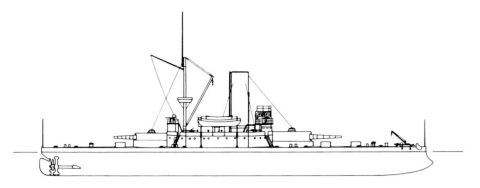

Monterey

Length on Load Waterline:	256 feet
Extreme Breadth:	59 feet
Mean Draft:	14 feet, 10 inches
Normal Displacement:	4,084 tons
Armament:	2 12-inch, 35-caliber breech-loading rifles
	2 10-inch, 30-caliber breech-loading rifles
	6 6-pounders; 4 1-pounders; 2 Gatlings
Maximum Armor Thickness:	13 inches (sides); 8 inches (forward turret)
Engines:	twin-screw, vertical triple-expansion
Performance:	13.6 knots; 5,244 indicated horsepower
Complement:	19 officers; 172 enlisted men

USS *Monterey*

Built by Union Iron Works, San Francisco, Cal.
Authorized 3 March 1887.
Commissioned 13 February 1893.
Sold 25 February 1922.

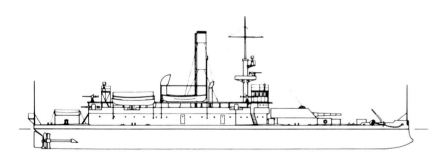

Arkansas Class

Length on Load Waterline:	252 feet
Extreme Breadth:	50 feet
Mean Draft:	12 feet, 6 inches
Normal Displacement:	3,200 tons
Armament:	2 12-inch, 40-caliber breech-loading rifles
	4 4-inch, 50-caliber rapid-fire guns
Maximum Armor Thickness:	11 inches (sides); 10 inches (turrets)
Engines:	twin-screw, vertical triple-expansion
Performance (*Arkansas*):	12.03 knots; 1,739 indicated horsepower
Complement:	13 officers; 135 enlisted men

USS *Arkansas*   Monitor No. 7

Built by Newport News S.B. & D.D.
  Co., Newport News Va.
Authorized 4 May 1898.
Commissioned 28 October 1902.
Renamed *Ozark* 2 March 1909.
Sold 26 January 1922.

USS *Nevada*   Monitor No. 8

Built by Bath Iron Works, Bath, Me.
Authorized 4 May 1898.
Named changed from *Connecticut*
  during construction.
Commissioned 5 March 1903.
Renamed *Tonopah* 2 March 1909.
Sold 26 January 1922.

USS *Florida*   Monitor No. 9

Built by Lewis Nixon, Elizabethport,
  N.J.
Authorized 4 May 1898.
Commissioned 18 June 1903.
Renamed *Tallahassee* 20 June 1908.
Sold 25 July 1922.

USS *Wyoming* Monitor No. 10

Built by Union Iron Works, San Fran-
  cisco, Cal.
Authorized 4 May 1898.
Commissioned 8 December 1902.
Renamed *Cheyenne* 1 January 1909.
Served as a Naval Reserve training
  ship 1920–1926.
Unclassified IX-4.
Stricken 25 January 1937.
Sold 20 April 1939.

Armored Cruisers

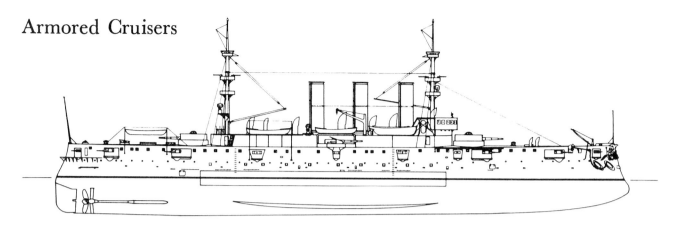

New York

Length on Load Waterline:	380 feet, 6½ inches
Extreme Breadth:	64 feet, 10 inches
Mean Draft:	23 feet, 3½ inches
Normal Displacement:	8,200 tons
Armament:	6 8-inch, 35-caliber breech-loading rifles
	12 4-inch, 40-caliber rapid-fire guns
	8 6-pounders; 4 1-pounders; 4 Gatlings
Torpedo Tubes:	3 18-inch, Whitehead above-surface tubes
Maximum Armor Thickness:	4 inches (sides); 5½ inches (turrets)
Machinery:	twin-screw, with 4 vertical triple-expansion engines
Performance:	21 knots; 17,401 indicated horsepower
Complement:	40 officers; 526 enlisted men

USS *New York*   Armored Cruiser No. 2*

Built by William Cramp & Sons, Philadelphia, Pa.
Authorized 7 September 1888.
Commissioned 1 August 1893.
Renamed *Saratoga* 16 February 1911.
Renamed *Rochester* 1 December 1917.
Reclassified CA-2 17 July 1920.
Stricken 28 October 1938.
Scuttled in Subic Bay, Philippines, 24 December 1941.

* USS *Maine* originally designated Armored Cruiser No. 1.

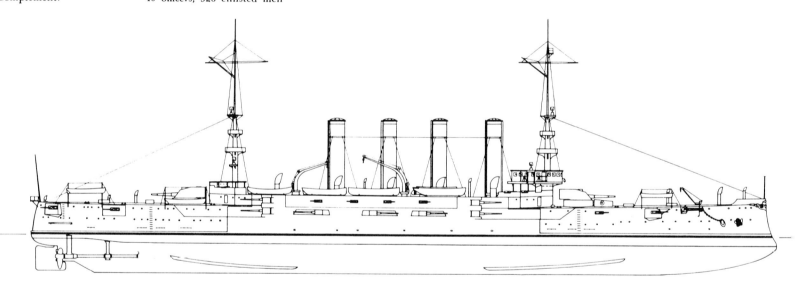

Pennsylvania Class   Armored Cruisers Nos. 4–9

Length on Load Waterline:	502 feet
Extreme Breadth:	69 feet, 6½ inches
Mean Draft:	24 feet, 1 inch
Normal Displacement:	13,680 tons
Armament:	4 8-inch, 40-caliber breech-loading rifles *
	14 6-inch, 50-caliber rapid-fire guns
	18 3-inch; 12 3-pdr; 4 1-pdr; 6 .30 cal.
Torpedo Tubes:	2 18-inch, submerged tubes
Maximum Armor Thickness:	6 inches (sides); 6½ inches (turrets)
Engines:	twin-screw, vertical triple-expansion
Performance (*Pennsylvania*):	22.44 knots; 28,600 indicated horsepower
Complement:	41 officers; 791 enlisted men

* Replaced by 8-inch, 45-caliber guns after about 1909.

USS *Pennsylvania*

William Cramp & Sons, Philadelphia.
Authorized 3 March 1899.
Commissioned 9 March 1905.
Renamed *Pittsburg* 27 August 1912.
Stricken 28 October 1931 and
  employed as a bombing target.

USS *West Virginia*

Newport News S.B. & D.D. Co.
Authorized 3 March 1899.
Commissioned 23 February 1905.
Renamed *Huntington* 11 November
  1916.
Stricken 12 March 1930.

USS *California*

Union Iron Works, San Francisco.
Authorized 3 March 1899.
Commissioned 1 August 1907.
Renamed *San Diego* 1 September 1914.
Sunk by a German mine 19 July 1918.

USS *Colorado*

William Cramp & Sons, Philadelphia.
Authorized 7 June 1900.
Commissioned 19 January 1905.
Renamed *Pueblo* 9 November 1916.
Stricken 21 February 1930.

USS *Maryland*

Newport News S.B. & D.D. Co.
Authorized 7 June 1900.
Commissioned 18 April 1905.
Renamed *Frederick* 9 November
  1916.
Stricken 13 November 1929.

USS *South Dakota*

Union Iron Works, San Francisco.
Authorized 7 June 1900.
Commissioned 27 January 1908.
Renamed *Huron* 7 June 1920.
Stricken 15 November 1929.

Armored Cruisers

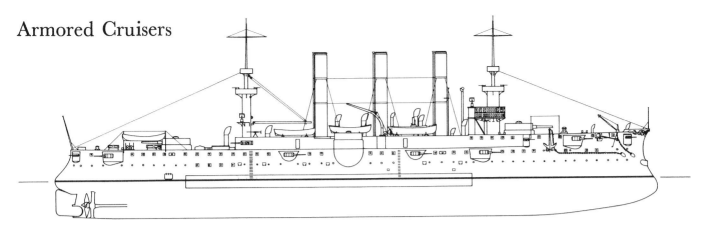

Brooklyn

Length on Load Waterline:	400 feet, 6 inches
Extreme Breadth:	64 feet, 8¼ inches
Mean Draft:	24 feet
Normal Displacement:	9,215 tons
Armament:	8 8-inch, 35-caliber breech-loading rifles
	12 5-inch, 40-caliber rapid-fire guns
	12 6-pounders; 4 1-pounders; 4 Gatlings
Torpedo Tubes:	4 18-inch, Whitehead above-surface tubes
Maximum Armor Thickness:	3 inches (sides); 5½ inches (turrets)
Machinery:	twin-screw, with 4 vertical triple-expansion engines
Performance:	21.91 knots; 18,769 indicated horsepower
Complement:	46 officers; 470 enlisted men

USS *Brooklyn* Armored Cruiser No. 3

Built by William Cramp & Sons, Philadelphia, Pa.
Authorized 19 July 1892.
Commissioned 1 December 1896.
Reclassified CA-3 17 July 1920.
Sold 20 December 1921.

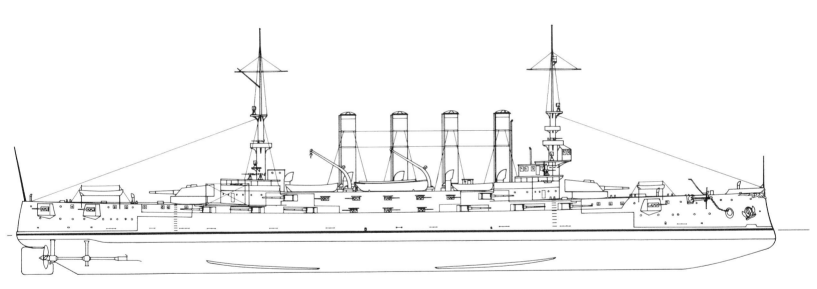

Tennessee Class Armored Cruisers Nos. 10–13

Length on Load Waterline:	502 feet
Extreme Breadth:	72 feet, 10½ inches
Mean Draft:	25 feet
Normal Displacement:	14,500 tons
Armament:	4 10-inch, 40-caliber breech-loading rifles
	16 6-inch, 50-caliber rapid-fire guns
	22 3-inch; 12 3-pdr.; 2 1-pdr.; 6 .30-cal.
Torpedo Tubes:	4 21-inch, submerged tubes
Maximum Armor Thickness:	5 inches (sides); 9 inches (turrets)
Engines:	twin-screw, vertical triple expansion
Performance (*Tennessee*):	22.16 knots; 26,963 indicated horsepower
Complement:	40 officers; 874 enlisted men

USS *Tennessee*

Built by William Cramp & Sons, Philadelphia, Pa.
Authorized 1 July 1902.
Commissioned 17 July 1906.
Renamed *Memphis* 25 May 1916.
Washed ashore by seismic wave near Santo Domingo, 29 August 1916.

USS *Washington*

Built by New York Shipbuilding Co., Camden, N.J.
Authorized 1 July 1902.
Commissioned 7 August 1906.
Renamed *Seattle* 9 November 1916.
Reclassified CA-11 17 July 1920.
Served at New York 1927–1946.
Reclassified IX-39 1 July 1931.
Stricken 19 July 1946.

USS *North Carolina*

Built by Newport News S.B. & D.D. Co., Newport News, Va.
Authorized 27 April 1904.
Commissioned 7 May 1908.
Renamed *Charlotte* 7 June 1920.
Reclassified CA-12 17 July 1920.
Stricken 15 July 1930.

USS *Montana*

Built by Newport News S.B. & D.D. Co., Newport News, Va.
Authorized 27 April 1904.
Commissioned 21 July 1908.
Renamed *Missoula* 7 June 1920.
Reclassified CA-13 17 July 1920.
Stricken 15 July 1930.

Protected Cruisers

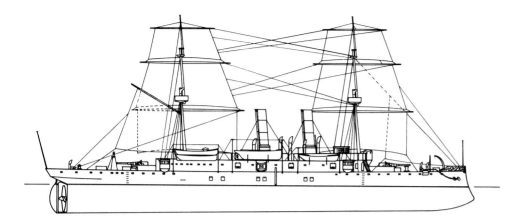

Atlanta Class

Length on Load Waterline:	270 feet, 3 inches
Extreme Breadth:	42 feet
Mean Draft:	17 feet
Normal Displacement:	3,189 tons
Armament:	2 8-inch, 30-caliber breech-loading rifles
	6 6-inch, 30-caliber breech-loading rifles
	2 6-pdr.; 2 3-pdr.; 2 1-pdr.; 2 47-mm.; 2 37-mm
Torpedo Tubes:	none
Protective Deck:	1½ inches (slopes); 1½ inches (flats)
Auxiliary Sail Rig:	brig; 10,400 square feet of sail
Engine:	single-screw, horizontal compound
Performance (*Atlanta*):	15.60 knots; 4,030 indicated horsepower
Complement:	19 officers; 265 enlisted men

USS *Atlanta*

Built by John Roach & Sons, Chester, Pa.
Authorized 3 March 1883.
Commissioned 19 July 1886.
Served as a barracks ship at Norfolk and Charleston 1905–1912.
Stricken 24 April 1912.

USS *Boston*

Built by John Roach & Sons, Chester, Pa.
Authorized 3 March 1883.
Commissioned 2 May 1887.
Served as a receiving ship in San Francisco Bay 1918–1946.
Renamed *Despatch* 9 August 1940, reclassified IX-2.
Towed to sea and scuttled 8 April 1946.

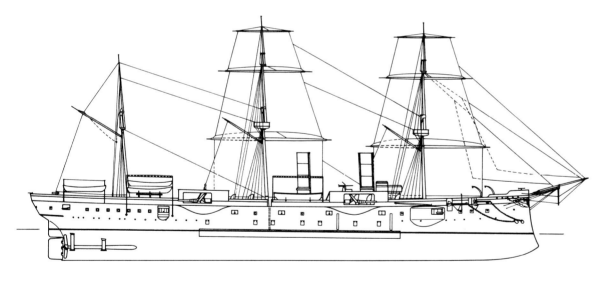

Chicago

Length on Load Waterline:	325 feet
Extreme Breadth:	48 feet, 2 inches
Mean Draft:	19 feet
Normal Displacement:	4,500 tons
Armament:	4 8-inch, 30-caliber breech-loading rifles
	8 6-inch, 30-caliber breech-loading rifles
	2 5-inch, 30-caliber breech-loading rifles
	2 6-pdr.; 2 1-pdr.; 4 47-mm.; 2 37-mm.;
	2 Gatlings
Torpedo Tubes:	none
Protective Deck:	1½ inches (slopes); 1½ inches (flats)
Auxiliary Sail Rig:	bark; 14,880 square feet of sail
Engines:	twin-screw, compound overhead beam
Performance:	15.33 knots; 5,084 indicated horsepower
Complement:	33 officers; 376 enlisted men

USS *Chicago*

Built by John Roach & Sons, Chester, Pa.
Authorized 3 March 1883.
Commissioned 17 April 1889.
Reclassified CA-14 17 July 1920.
Reclassified CL-14 8 August 1921.
Served as barracks ship at Pearl Harbor 1923–1935.
Renamed *Alton* 16 July 1928 and reclassified IX-5.
Sold 15 May 1936.
Foundered at sea while under tow 8 July 1936.

Protected Cruisers

Newark

Length on Load Waterline:	310 feet
Extreme Breadth:	49 feet, 2 inches
Mean Draft:	18 feet, 9 inches
Normal Displacement:	4,083 tons
Armament:	12 6-inch, 30-caliber breech-loading rifles
	4 6-pdr.; 4 3-pdr.; 2 1-pdr.; 2 37-mm.
Torpedo Tubes:	openings for 6 14-inch, above-surface tubes
Protective Deck:	3 inches (slopes); 2 inches (flats)
Auxiliary Sail Rig:	bark; 11,932 square feet of sail
Engines:	twin-screw, horizontal triple-expansion
Performance:	19.00 knots; 8,869 indicated horsepower
Complement:	34 officers; 350 enlisted men

USS *Newark*   Cruiser No. 1

Built by William Cramp & Sons, Philadelphia, Pa.
Authorized 3 March 1885.
Commissioned 2 February 1891.
Stricken 26 June 1913 and transferred to Public Health Service.
Returned to Navy temporarily 1918–1919.
Returned to Navy 7 July 1926.
Sold 7 September 1926.

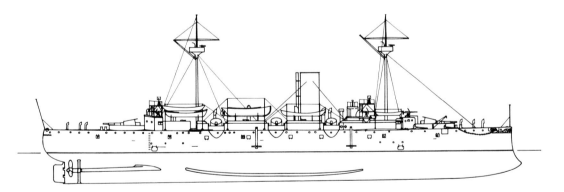

Charleston

Length on Load Waterline:	312 feet
Extreme Breadth:	46 feet
Mean Draft:	19 feet, 7 inches
Normal Displacement:	4,040 tons
Armament:*	2 8-inch, 35-caliber breech-loading rifles
	6 6-inch, 30-caliber breech-loading rifles
	4 6-pdr.; 2 3-pdr.; 2 1-pdr.; 4 37-mm.; 2 Gatlings
Torpedo Tubes:	openings for 4 14-inch, above-surface tubes
Protective Deck:	3 inches (slopes); 2 inches (flats)
Engines:	twin-screw, horizontal compound
Performance:	18.21 knots; 6,666 indicated horsepower
Complement:	20 officers; 280 enlisted men

* Due to unavailability of 8-inch guns at time of ship's completion, temporarily outfitted with 10 6-inch rifles.

USS *Charleston*   Cruiser No. 2

Built by Union Iron Works, San Francisco, Cal.
Authorized 3 March 1885.
Commissioned 26 December 1889.
Wrecked on uncharted reef near Camiguin Island, Philippines, 2 November 1899.

Protected Cruisers

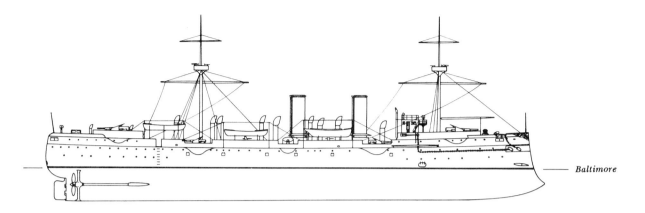

Baltimore

USS *Baltimore*   Cruiser No. 3

Length on Load Waterline:	327 feet, 6 inches
Extreme Breadth:	48 feet, 6 inches
Mean Draft:	20 feet, 6 inches
Normal Displacement:	4,600 tons
Armament:	4 8-inch, 35-caliber breech-loading rifles
	6 6-inch, 30-caliber breech-loading rifles
	4 6-pdr.; 2 3-pdr.; 2 1-pdr.; 4 37-mm.
Torpedo Tubes:	openings for 5 14-inch, above-surface tubes
Protective Deck:	4 inches (slopes); 2½ inches (flats)
Rig:	two military masts
Engines:	twin-screw, horizontal triple-expansion
Performance:	19.58 knots; 10,064 indicated horsepower
Complement:	36 officers; 350 enlisted men

Built by William Cramp & Sons, Philadelphia, Pa.
Authorized 3 August 1886.
Commissioned 7 January 1890.
Converted to a minelayer in 1913–1914.
Reclassified CM-1 17 July 1920.
Lay inactive at Pearl Harbor 1922–1942.
Sold 16 February 1942.

USS *Philadelphia*   Cruiser No. 4

Length on Load Waterline:	327 feet, 6 inches
Extreme Breadth:	48 feet, 6 inches
Mean Draft:	19 feet, 2½ inches
Normal Displacement:	4,324 tons
Armament:	12 6-inch, 30-caliber breech-loading rifles
	4 6-pdr.; 4 3-pdr.; 2 1-pdr.; 3 37-mm.
Torpedo Tubes:	openings for 4 14-inch, above-surface tubes
Protective Deck:	4 inches (slopes); 2½ inches (flats)
Auxiliary Sail Rig:	three-masted schooner
Engines:	twin-screw, horizontal triple-expansion
Performance:	19.68 knots; 8,814 indicated horsepower
Complement:	34 officers; 350 enlisted men

Built by William Cramp & Sons, Philadelphia, Pa.
Authorized 3 March 1887.
Commissioned 28 July 1890.
Served as a receiving ship at Bremerton, 1910–1926.
Unclassified, IX-24.
Stricken 24 November 1926.

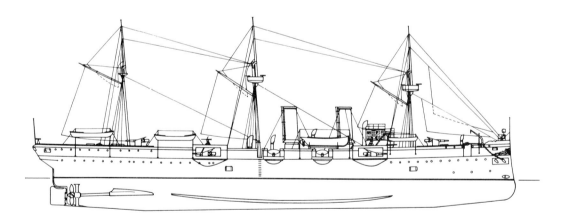

San Francisco

Length on Load Waterline:	310 feet
Extreme Breadth:	49 feet, 2 inches
Mean Draft:	18 feet, 9 inches
Normal Displacement:	4,083 tons
Armament:	12 6-inch, 30-caliber breech-loading rifles
	4 6-pdr.; 4 3-pdr.; 2 1-pdr.; 3 37-mm.
Torpedo Tubes:	openings for 6 14-inch, above-surface tubes
Auxiliary Sail Rig:	three-masted schooner
Engines:	twin-screw, horizontal triple-expansion
Performance:	19.52 knots; 9,913 indicated horsepower
Complement:	34 officers; 350 enlisted men

USS *San Francisco*   Cruiser No. 5

Built by the Union Iron Works, San Francisco, Cal.
Authorized 3 March 1887.
Commissioned 15 November 1890.
Converted into a minelayer in 1916.
Reclassified CM-2 17 July 1920.
Renamed *Yosemite* 1 January 1931.
Stricken 8 June 1937.

Protected Cruisers

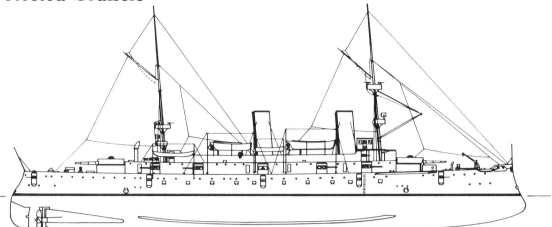

Olympia

Length on Load Waterline:	340 feet
Extreme Breadth:	53 feet, 0⅝ inches
Mean Draft:	21 feet, 6 inches
Normal Displacement:	5,870 tons
Armament:	4 8-inch, 35-caliber breech-loading rifles
	10 5-inch, 40-caliber rapid-fire guns
	14 6-pounders; 6 1-pounders; 4 Gatlings
Torpedo Tubes:	6 18-inch, Whitehead above-surface tubes
Protective Deck:	4¾ inches (slopes); 2 inches (flats)
Auxiliary Sail Rig:	two-masted schooner
Engines:	twin-screw, vertical triple-expansion
Performance:	21.69 knots; 17,313 indicated horsepower
Complement:	33 officers; 395 enlisted men

USS *Olympia* Cruiser No. 6

Built by Union Iron Works, San Francisco, Cal.
Authorized 7 September 1888.
Commissioned 5 February 1895.
Reclassified CA-15 17 July 1920.
Reclassified CL-15 8 August 1921.
Reclassified IX-40 June 1931, and thereafter maintained as a
  naval relic.
Released to Cruiser *Olympia* Association 11 September 1957.
Restored and maintained as a naval shrine and museum at Philadelphia.

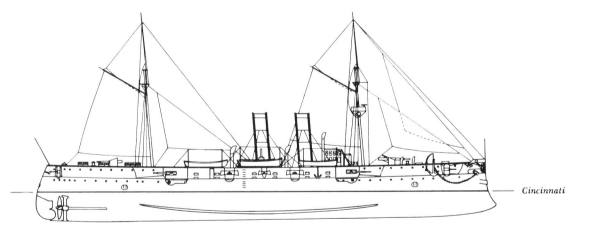

Cincinnati

Cincinnati Class

Length on Load Waterline:	300 feet
Extreme Breadth:	42 feet
Mean Draft:	18 feet
Normal Displacement:	3,213 tons
Armament:	1 6-inch, 40-caliber rapid-fire gun
	10 5-inch, 40-caliber rapid-fire guns
	8 6-pounders; 4 1-pounders; 2 Gatlings
Torpedo Tubes:	4 above-surface tubes
Protective Deck:	2½ inches (slopes); 1 inch (flats)
Auxiliary Sail Rig:	two-masted schooner
Engines:	twin-screw, vertical triple-expansion
Performance (estimated):	19 knots; 10,000 indicated horsepower
Complement:	20 officers; 292 enlisted men

USS *Cincinnati* Cruiser No. 7

Built at New York Navy Yard, Brooklyn, N.Y.
Authorized 7 September 1888.
Commissioned 16 June 1894.
Sold 5 August 1921.

USS *Raleigh* Cruiser No. 8

Built at Norfolk Navy Yard, Portsmouth, Va.
Authorized 7 September 1888.
Commissioned 17 April 1894.
Sold 5 August 1921.

Protected Cruisers

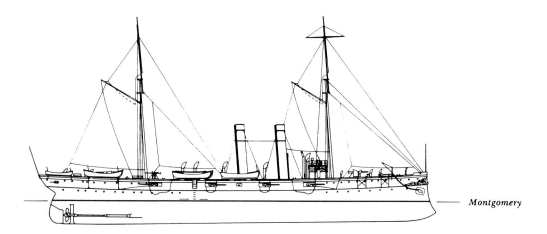

Montgomery

Montgomery Class ("Unprotected" Cruisers)

Length on Load Waterline:	257 feet
Extreme Breadth:	37 feet
Mean Draft:	14 feet, 7 inches
Normal Displacement:	2,094 tons
Armament:*	2 6-inch, 40-caliber rapid-fire guns
	8 5-inch, 40-caliber rapid-fire guns
	6 6-pounders; 2 1-pounders; 2 Gatlings
Torpedo Tubes:	3 above-surface tubes
Watertight Deck:	7/16 inches (slopes); 5/16 inches (flats)
Auxiliary Sail Rig:	two-masted schooner
Engines:	twin-screw, vertical triple-expansion
Performance (*Montgomery*):	19.05 knots; 5,527 indicated horsepower
Complement:	20 officers; 254 enlisted men

* Almost immediately reduced to 9 5-inch, 40-caliber rapid-fire guns to improve ships' stability.

USS *Montgomery* Cruiser No. 9

Built by Columbian Iron Works, Baltimore, Md.
Authorized 7 September 1888.
Commissioned 21 June 1894.
Renamed *Anniston* 14 March 1918.
Stricken 25 August 1919.

USS *Detroit* Cruiser No. 10

Built by Columbian Iron Works, Baltimore, Md.
Authorized 7 September 1888.
Commissioned 20 July 1893.
Stricken 12 July 1910.

USS *Marblehead* Cruiser No. 11

Built by City Point Works, Boston, Mass.
Authorized 7 September 1888.
Commissioned 2 April 1894.
Reclassified PG-27 17 July 1920.
Sold 5 August 1921.

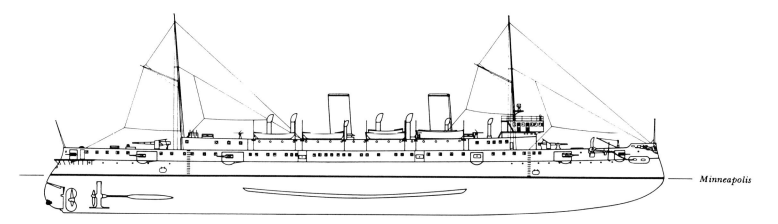

Minneapolis

Columbia Class

Length on Load Waterline:	412 feet
Extreme Breadth:	58 feet, 2¼ inches
Mean Draft:	22 feet, 6½ inches
Normal Displacement:	7,375 tons
Armament:	1 8-inch, 40-caliber breech-loading rifle
	2 6-inch, 40-caliber rapid-fire guns
	8 4-inch, 40-caliber rapid fire guns
	12 6-pounders; 4 1-pounders; 4 Gatlings
Torpedo Tubes:	4 14-inch, Whitehead above-surface tubes
Protective Deck:	4 inches (slopes); 2½ inches (flats)
Auxiliary Sail Rig:	two-masted schooner
Engines:*	triple-screw, vertical triple-expansion
Performance (*Columbia*):	22.8 knots; 18,509 indicated horsepower
Complement:	30 officers; 429 enlisted men

* Four stacks aboard *Columbia;* two aboard *Minneapolis.*

USS *Columbia* Cruiser No. 12

Built by William Cramp & Sons, Philadelphia, Pa.
Authorized 30 June 1890.
Commissioned 23 April 1894.
Reclassified CA-16 17 July 1920.
Renamed *Old Columbia* 17 November 1921.
Sold 26 January 1922.

USS *Minneapolis* Cruiser No. 13

Built by William Cramp & Sons, Philadelphia, Pa.
Authorized 2 March 1891.
Commissioned 13 December 1894.
Reclassified CA-17 17 July 1920.
Sold 5 August 1921.

Protected Cruisers

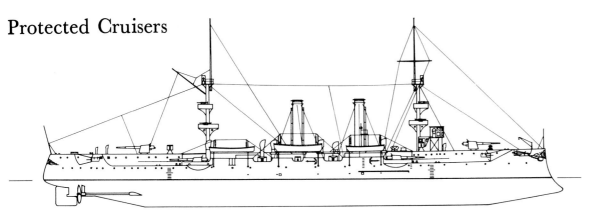

New Orleans Class

Length on Load Waterline:	346 feet
Extreme Breadth:	43 feet, 9 inches
Mean Draft:	16 feet, $10\frac{1}{3}$ inches
Normal Displacement:	3,437 tons
Armament:	6 6-inch, 50-caliber rapid-fire guns
	4 4.7-inch, 50-caliber rapid-fire guns
	10 6-pdr.; 4 1-pdr.; 4 .30-cal.
Torpedo Tubes:	3 18-inch, Whitehead above-surface tubes
Protective Deck:	3 inches (slopes); $1\frac{1}{4}$ inches (flats)
Engines:	twin-screw, vertical inverted triple-expansion
Performance (estimated):	20 knots; 7,500 indicated horsepower
Complement:	24 officers; 383 enlisted men

USS *New Orleans* (ex-Brazilian *Amazonas*)

Built by Sir W. G. Armstrong, Whitworth & Co., Elswick Yard,
    Newcastle-on-Tyne, England.
Purchased from Brazil 16 March 1898.
Commissioned 18 March 1898 as USS *Amazonas*.
Renamed USS *New Orleans* 15 April 1898.
Reclassified PG-34 17 July 1920 and CL-22 8 August 1921.
Stricken 13 November 1929.

USS *Albany* (ex-Brazilian *Almirante Abreu*)

Built by Sir W. G. Armstrong, Whitworth & Co., Elswick Yard,
    Newcastle-on-Tyne, England.
Purchased 16 March 1898, while under construction.
Commissioned 29 May 1900.
Reclassified PG-36 17 July 1920 and CL-23 8 August 1921.
Stricken 13 November 1929.

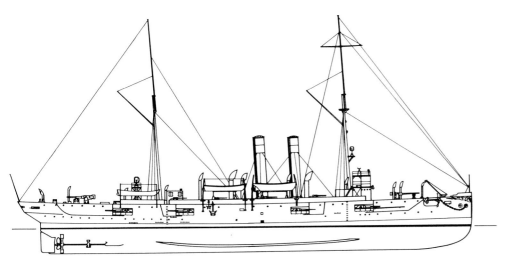

Denver Class (Sheathed Protected Cruisers)

Length on Load Waterline:	292 feet
Extreme Breadth:	44 feet, $0\frac{1}{2}$ inches
Mean Draft:	15 feet, 9 inches
Normal Displacement:	3,191 tons
Armament:	10 5-inch, 50-caliber rapid-fire guns
	8 6-pdr.. 2 1-pdr.; 4 .30-cal.
Torpedo Tubes:	none
Protective Deck:	2 inches (slopes); $\frac{1}{2}$ inch (flats)
Auxiliary Sail Rig:	two-masted schooner
Engines:	twin-screw, vertical triple-expansion
Performance (*Denver*):	16.75 knots; 6,135 indicated horsepower
Complement:	19 officers; 308 enlisted men

USS *Denver* Cruiser No. 14
Neafie & Levy, Philadelphia, Pa.
Authorized 3 March 1899.
Commissioned 17 May 1904.
Reclassified PG-28, then CL-16.
Stricken 12 March 1931.

USS *Des Moines* Cruiser No. 15
Fore River S. & E. Co., Quincy, Mass.
Authorized 3 March 1899.
Commissioned 5 March 1904.
Reclassified PG-29, then CL-17.
Stricken 13 December 1929.

USS *Chattanooga* Cruiser No. 16
Crescent Shipyard, Elizabethport, N.J.
Completed at New York Navy Yard.
Authorized 3 March 1899.
Commissioned 11 October 1904.
Reclassified PG-30, then CL-18.
Stricken 13 December 1929.

USS *Galveston* Cruiser No. 17
William R. Trigg Co., Richmond, Va.
Completed at Norfolk Navy Yard.
Authorized 3 March 1899.
Commissioned 15 February 1905.
Reclassified PG-31, then CL-19.
Stricken 1 November 1930.

USS *Tacoma* Cruiser No. 18
Union Iron Works, San Francisco.
Authorized 3 March 1899.
Commissioned 30 January 1904.
Reclassified PG-32, then CL-20.
Wrecked off Mexico 16 January 1924.

USS *Cleveland* Cruiser No. 19
Bath Iron Works, Bath, Me.
Authorized 3 March 1899.
Commissioned 2 November 1903.
Reclassified PG-33, then CL-21.
Stricken 13 December 1929.

Semi-Armored Cruisers

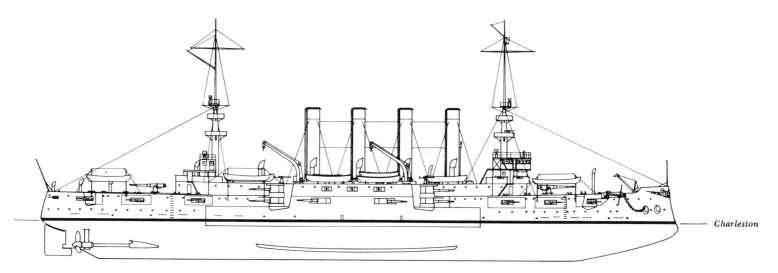

Charleston

St. Louis Class

Length on Load Waterline:	424 feet
Extreme Breadth:	66 feet
Mean Draft:	22 feet, 6 inches
Normal Displacement:	9,700 tons
Armament:	14 6-inch, 50-caliber rapid-fire guns
	18 3-inch; 12 3-pdr.; 8 1-pdr.; 4 .30-cal.
Torpedo Tubes:	none
Maximum Armor Thickness:	4 inches (sides); no turrets
Engines:	twin-screw; vertical triple-expansion
Performance (*St. Louis*):	22.13 knots; 27,264 indicated horsepower
Complement:	36 officers; 627 enlisted men

USS *St. Louis* Cruiser No. 20
Neafie & Levy, Philadelphia, Pa.
Authorized 7 June 1900.
Commissioned 18 August 1906.
Reclassified CA-18 17 July 1920.
Stricken 20 March 1930.

USS *Milwaukee* Cruiser No. 21
Union Iron Works, San Francisco, Cal.
Authorized 7 June 1900.
Commissioned 11 December 1906.
Stranded off Eureka, Calif., 13 January 1917.
Hulk sold 5 August 1919.

USS *Charleston* Cruiser No. 22
Newport News S.B. & D.D. Co., Newport News, Va.
Authorized 7 June 1900.
Commissioned 17 October 1905.
Reclassified CA-19 17 July 1920.
Stricken 25 November 1929.

Gunboats

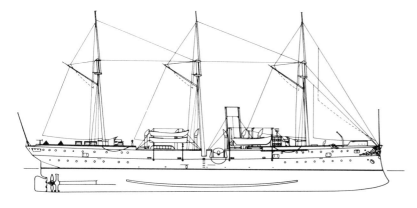

Yorktown Class

Length on Load Waterline:	230 feet
Extreme Breadth:	36 feet
Mean Draft:	14 feet
Normal Displacement:	1,710 tons
Main Armament:	6 6-inch, 30-caliber breech-loading rifles
	2 6-pdr.; 2 3-pdr.; 1 1-pdr.; 2 37-mm.; 2 Gatlings
Torpedo Tubes:	openings for 6 above-surface tubes
Watertight Deck:	⅜ inches (slopes); ⅜ inches (flats)
Auxiliary Sail Rig:	three-masted schooner
Engines:	twin-screw, horizontal triple-expansion
Performance (*Yorktown*):	16.14 knots; 3,660 indicated horsepower
Complement:	14 officers; 178 enlisted men

USS *Yorktown* Gunboat No. 1
William Cramp & Sons, Philadelphia, Pa.
Authorized 3 March 1885.
Commissioned 23 April 1889.
Sold 30 September 1921.

USS *Concord* Gunboat No. 3
N. F. Palmer, Jr., & Co., Chester, Pa.
Authorized 3 March 1887.
Commissioned 14 February 1891.
Transferred to Treasury Dept. 15 June 1914.
Employed as a quarantine vessel on the Columbia River 1914–1929.
Returned to Navy 19 March 1929.
Sold 28 June 1929.

USS *Bennington* Gunboat No. 4
N. F. Palmer, Jr., & Co., Chester, Pa.
Authorized 3 March 1887.
Commissioned 20 June 1891.
Wrecked by boiler explosion at San Diego, Cal., 21 July 1905.
Stricken 10 September 1910.

Gunboats

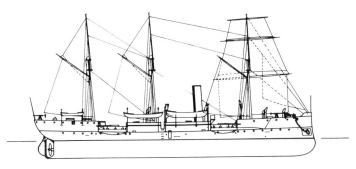

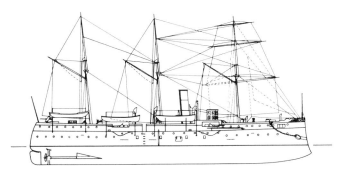

Petrel

Length on Load Waterline:	176 feet, 3 inches
Extreme Breadth:	31 feet
Mean Draft:	11 feet, 7 inches
Normal Displacement:	892 tons
Main Armament:	4 6-inch, 30-caliber breech-loading rifles
	2 3-pdr.; 1 1-pdr.; 2 37-mm.; 2 Gatlings
Torpedo Tubes:	none
Watertight Deck:	⅜ inch (slopes); ⁵⁄₁₆ inch (flats)
Auxiliary Sail Rig:	barkentine; 4,850 square feet of sail
Engine:	single-screw, horizontal compound
Performance:	11.55 knots; 1,045 indicated horsepower
Complement:	10 officers; 122 enlisted men

USS *Petrel*   Gunboat No. 2
Built by Columbia Iron Works, Baltimore, Md.
Authorized 3 March 1885.
Commissioned 10 December 1889.
Sold 1 November 1920.

Bancroft

Length on Load Waterline:	187 feet, 6 inches
Extreme Breadth:	32 feet
Mean Draft:	11 feet, 6 inches
Normal Displacement:	839 tons
Main Armament:	4 4-inch, 40-caliber rapid-fire guns
	2 6-pdr.; 2 3-pdr.; 1 1-pdr.; 1 37-mm.; 1 Gatling
Torpedo Tubes:	2 above-surface tubes
Watertight Deck:	⁵⁄₁₆ inch (slopes); ¼ inch (flats)
Auxiliary Sail Rig:	barkentine
Engines:	twin-screw, vertical triple-expansion
Performance:	14.37 knots; 1,213 indicated horsepower
Complement:	10 officers; 120 enlisted men

USS *Bancroft*   (Naval Academy Practice Vessel)
Built by Moore & Sons, Elizabethport, N.J.
Authorized 7 September 1888.
Commissioned 3 March 1893.
Employed as a gunboat after 1896.
Transferred to Revenue Cutter Service 30 June 1906.
Renamed *Itasca*.
Scrapped in 1922.

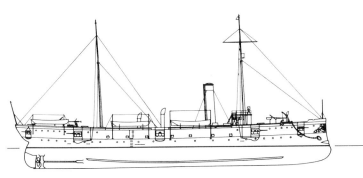

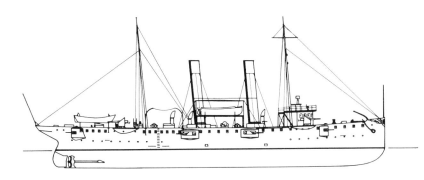

Machias Class

Length on Load Waterline:	204 feet *
Extreme Breadth:	32 feet, 1½ inches
Mean Draft:	12 feet
Normal Displacement:	1,177 tons
Armament:	8 4-inch, 40-caliber rapid-fire guns
	4 6-pounders; 2 1-pounders; 2 Gatlings
Torpedo Tubes:	opening for 1 above-surface tube
Watertight Deck:	⅜ inch (slopes); ⁵⁄₁₆ inch (flats)
Auxiliary Sail Rig:	two-masted schooner
Engines:	twin-screw, vertical triple-expansion
Performance (*Machias*):	15.46 knots; 1,873 indicated horsepower
Complement:	11 officers; 143 enlisted men

* Lengthened from 190 feet after completion to improve stability.

USS *Machias*   Gunboat No. 5
Built by Bath Iron Works, Bath, Me.
Authorized 2 March 1889.
Commissioned 20 July 1893.
Sold 29 October 1920 to Mexico.
Renamed *Agua Prieta*.
Sold by Mexican Navy in 1935.

USS *Castine*   Gunboat No. 6
Built by Bath Iron Works, Bath, Me.
Authorized 2 March 1889.
Commissioned 22 October 1894.
Sold 5 August 1921.

Nashville

Length on Load Waterline:	220 feet
Extreme Breadth:	38 feet, 1½ inches
Mean Draft:	11 feet
Normal Displacement:	1,371 tons
Armament:	8 4-inch, 40-caliber rapid-fire guns
	4 6-pounders; 2 1-pounders; 2 .30-cal.
Torpedo Tubes:	none
Watertight Deck:	⅜ inch (slopes); ⁵⁄₁₆ inch (flats)
Auxiliary Sail Rig:	two-masted schooner, pole masts
Engines:	twin-screw, vertical quadruple-expansion
Performance:	16.30 knots; 2,536 indicated horsepower
Complement:	11 officers; 165 enlisted men

USS *Nashville*   Gunboat No. 7
Built by Newport News S.B. & D.D. Co., Newport News, Va.
Authorized 3 March 1893.
Commissioned 19 August 1897.
Sold 20 October 1921.
Converted into a lumber barge and renamed *Richmond Cedar Works No. 4*.
Scrapped in 1957.

Gunboats

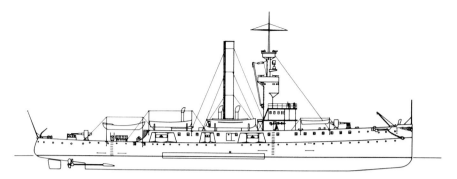

Wilmington Class

Length on Load Waterline:	250 feet, 9 inches
Extreme Breadth:	40 feet, 0¹¹⁄₁₆ inches
Mean Draft:	9 feet
Normal Displacement:	1,397 tons
Armament:	8 4-inch, 40-caliber rapid-fire guns
	4 6-pounders; 4 1-pounders; 4 .30-cal.
Torpedo Tubes:	none
Watertight Deck:	⅜ inch (slopes); ⁵⁄₁₆ inch (flats)
Engines:	twin-screw, vertical triple-expansion
Performance (Wilmington):	15.08 knots; 1,894 indicated horsepower
Complement:	10 officers; 165 enlisted men

USS *Wilmington* Gunboat No. 8

Built by Newport News S.B. & D.D.
  Co., Newport News, Va.
Authorized 3 March 1893.
Commissioned 13 May 1897.
Reclassified IX-30 26 June 1922.
Renamed *Dover* 17 February 1941.
Sold 30 December 1946.

USS *Helena* Gunboat No. 9

Built by Newport News S.B. & D.D.
  Co., Newport News, Va.
Authorized 3 March 1893.
Commissioned 8 July 1897.
Stricken 27 May 1932.

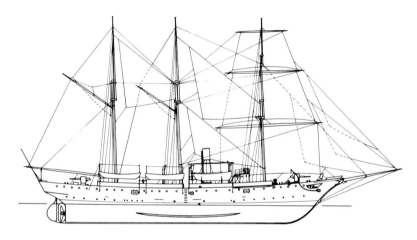

Annapolis Class

Length on Load Waterline:	168 feet
Extreme Breadth:	36 feet
Mean Draft:	12 feet
Normal Displacement:	1,000 tons
Armament:	6 4-inch, 40-caliber rapid-fire guns
	4 6-pounders; 2 1-pounders; 1 .30-cal.
Torpedo Tubes:	none
Auxiliary Sail Rig:	barkentine; 11,253 square feet of sail
Engine:	single-screw, vertical triple-expansion
Performance (Annapolis):	13.17 knots; 1,227 indicated horsepower
Complement:	11 officers; 124 enlisted men

USS *Annapolis* Gunboat No. 10

Built by Lewis Nixon, Elizabethport,
  N.J.
Authorized 2 March 1895.
Commissioned 20 July 1897.
Reclassified IX-1 1 July 1921.
Served as a schoolship for the State
  of Pennsylvania 1920–1940.
Transferred to Maritime Commission
  11 April 1940 for disposal.
Converted into a merchant vessel
  and renamed *Keystone State*.
Scrapped in 1950.

USS *Vicksburg* Gunboat No. 11

Built by Bath Iron Works, Bath, Me.
Authorized 2 March 1895.
Commissioned 23 October 1897.
Transferred to Coast Guard
  2 May 1921 and renamed
  Alexander Hamilton.
Renamed *Beta*.
Sold March 1946.

USS *Newport* Gunboat No. 12

Built by Bath Iron Works, Bath, Me.
Authorized 2 March 1895.
Commissioned 5 October 1897.
Served as a Naval Militia training
  ship 1907–1931.
Reclassified IX-19 1 July 1921.
Stricken 12 October 1931.
Transferred to city of Aberdeen,
  Wash., 14 May 1934 for use as a
  training ship.

USS *Princeton* Gunboat No. 13

Built by J. H. Dialogue & Son,
  Camden, N.J.
Authorized 2 March 1895.
Commissioned 27 May 1898.
Sold 13 November 1919.

Gunboats

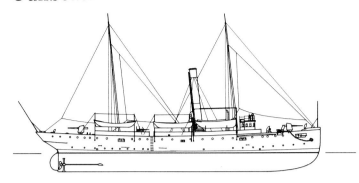

Wheeling Class   Gunboats Nos. 14 & 15

Length on Load Waterline:	174 feet
Extreme Breadth:	34 feet
Mean Draft:	12 feet
Normal Displacement:	1,000 tons
Armament:	6 4-inch, 40-caliber rapid-fire guns
	4 6-pounders; 2 1-pounders; 1 .30-cal.
Torpedo Tubes:	none
Auxiliary Sail Rig:	two-masted schooner
Engines:	twin-screw, vertical triple-expansion
Performance (*Wheeling*):	12.88 knots; 1,081 indicated horsepower
Complement:	11 officers; 129 enlisted men

Dubuque Class   Gunboats Nos. 17 & 18

Length on Load Waterline:	174 feet
Extreme Breadth:	35 feet
Mean Draft:	12 feet, 3 inches
Normal Displacement:	1,085 tons
Armament:	6 4-inch, 40-caliber rapid-fire guns
	4 6-pounders; 2 1-pounders; 2 .30-cal.
Torpedo Tubes:	none
Auxiliary Sail Rig:	two-masted schooner
Engines:	twin-screw, vertical triple-expansion
Performance (*Dubuque*):	12.90 knots; 1,193 indicated horsepower
Complement:	9 officers; 153 enlisted men

USS *Wheeling*
Union Iron Works, San Francisco,
Cal.
Authorized 2 March 1895.
Commissioned 10 August 1897.
Reclassified IX-28 1 July 1921.
Served as a berthing ship 1941–
1946.
Sold 5 October 1946.

USS *Marietta*
Union Iron Works, San Francisco,
Cal.
Authorized 2 March 1895.
Commissioned 1 September 1897.
Sold 25 March 1920.

USS *Dubuque*
Gas Engine & Power Co. & Chas.
L. Seabury & Co. Consolidated,
Morris Heights, N.Y.
Authorized 1 July 1902.
Commissioned 3 June 1905.
Reclassified IX-9 24 April 1922.
Reclassified AG-6 1920.
Reclassified PG-17 4 November
1940.
Served as a gunnery training ship
1941–1945.
Transferred to Maritime Com-
mission for disposal 19 Dec-
ember 1945.

USS *Paducah*
Gas Engine & Power Co. & Chas.
L. Seabury & Co. Consolidated,
Morris Heights, N.Y.
Authorized 1 July 1902.
Commissioned 2 September 1905.
Reclassified AG-7 1920.
Reclassified IX-23 24 April 1922.
Reclassified PG-18 4 November
1940.
Served as a training ship during
World War II.
Sold by Maritime Commission
19 December 1946.
Scrapped in 1949.

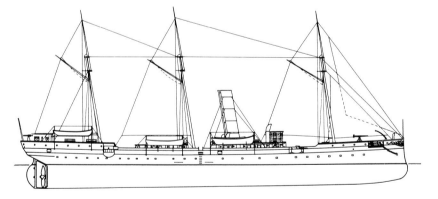

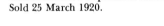

Dolphin (Dispatch Vessel)

Length on Load Waterline:	240 feet
Extreme Breadth:	32 feet
Mean Draft:	14 feet, 3 inches
Normal Displacement:	1,485 tons
Armament:	1 6-inch, 30-caliber breech-loading rifle *
	2 6-pounders; 4 47-mm.; 2 Gatlings
Torpedo Tubes:	none
Auxiliary Sail Rig:	three-masted schooner
Engine:	single-screw, vertical compound
Performance:	15.50 knots; 2,240 indicated horsepower
Complement:	10 officers; 80 enlisted men

* Soon replaced by 2 4-inch breech-loading rifles.

USS *Dolphin*
Built by John Roach & Sons, Chester, Pa.
Authorized 3 March 1883.
Commissioned 8 December 1885.
Reclassified PG-24 in 1920.
Sold 25 February 1922 to Mexican Navy.
Renamed *Plan de Guadalupe*.
Scrapped in 1925–1926.

Torpedo Boats

Cushing

Foote

No.	Name	Length on Load-Waterline	Displacement	Torpedo Tubes	Armament	Complement	Trial Speed (*Estimated)	Builder	Date Authorized (* Purchase)	Date Commissioned
	Stiletto	88½ feet	31 tons	2 Howell	None	1 off., 5 enl.	18.22 kts.	Herreshoff Mfg. Co.	3 March 1887*	
1	Cushing	138¾ feet	105 tons	3 Whitehead	3 1-pdr.	2 off., 20 enl.	22.50 kts.	Herreshoff Mfg. Co.	3 August 1886	22 April 1890
2	Ericsson	149½ feet	120 tons	3 Whitehead	4 1-pdr.	2 off., 20 enl.	24 kts.*	Iowa Iron Works	30 June 1890	18 February 1897
3	Foote	160 feet	142 tons	3 Whitehead	3 1-pdr.	2 off., 21 enl.	24.53 kts.	Columbian Iron Works	26 July 1894	7 August 1897
4	Rodgers	160 feet	142 tons	3 Whitehead	3 1-pdr.	2 off., 21 enl.	24.49 kts.	Columbian Iron Works	26 July 1894	2 April 1898
5	Winslow	160 feet	142 tons	3 Whitehead	3 1-pdr.	2 off., 21 enl.	24.82 kts.	Columbian Iron Works	26 July 1894	29 December 1897
6	Porter	175 feet	165 tons	3 Whitehead	4 1-pdr.	2 off., 28 enl.	28.63 kts.	Herreshoff Mfg. Co.	2 March 1895	20 February 1897
7	Du Pont	175 feet	165 tons	3 Whitehead	4 1-pdr.	2 off., 28 enl.	28.58 kts.	Herreshoff Mfg. Co.	2 March 1895	23 September 1897
8	Rowan	170 feet	210 tons	3 Whitehead	4 1-pdr.	2 off., 28 enl.	27.07 kts.	Moran Bros. Co.	2 March 1895	1 April 1899
9	Dahlgren	147 feet	146 tons	2 Whitehead	4 1-pdr.	2 off., 26 enl.	30.00 kts.	Bath Iron Works	10 June 1896	16 June 1900
10	Craven	147 feet	146 tons	2 Whitehead	4 1-pdr.	2 off., 26 enl.	30 kts.*	Bath Iron Works	10 June 1896	9 June 1900
11	Farragut	213½ feet	279 tons	2 Whitehead	4 1-pdr.	2 off., 60 enl.	30.13 kts.	Union Iron Works	10 June 1896	22 March 1899
12	Davis	146 feet	154 tons	3 Whitehead	3 1-pdr.	2 off., 21 enl.	23.41 kts.	Wolff & Zwicker	10 June 1896	10 May 1899
13	Fox	146 feet	154 tons	3 Whitehead	3 1-pdr.	2 off., 21 enl.	23.13 kts.	Wolff & Zwicker	10 June 1896	8 July 1899
14	Morris	138¼ feet	105 tons	3 Whitehead	4 1-pdr.	2 off., 23 en.	24.00 kts.	Herreshoff Mfg. Co.	10 June 1896	11 May 1898
15	Talbot	99½ feet	46 tons	2 Whitehead	1 1-pdr.	2 off., 13 enl.	21.15 kts.	Herreshoff Mfg. Co.	10 June 1896	4 April 1898
16	Gwin	99½ feet	46 tons	2 Whitehead	1 1-pdr.	2 off., 13 enl.	20.88 kts.	Herreshoff Mfg. Co.	10 June 1896	4 April 1898
17	MacKenzie	99¼ feet	65 tons	2 Whitehead	1 1-pdr.	2 off., 13 enl.	20.11 kts.	Chas. Hillman Co.	10 June 1896	1 May 1899
18	McKee	99¼ feet	65 tons	2 Whitehead	2 1-pdr.	2 off., 13 enl.	19.82 kts.	Columbian Iron Works	10 June 1896	16 May 1898
19	Stringham	225 feet	340 tons	2 Whitehead	4 6-pdr.	3 off., 56 enl.	30 kts.*	Harlan & Hollingsworth	3 March 1897	7 November 1905
20	Goldsborough	198 feet	255 tons	2 Whitehead	4 6-pdr.	3 off., 53 enl.	30 kts.*	Wolf & Zwicker	3 March 1897	9 April 1908
21	Bailey	205 feet	280 tons	2 Whitehead	4 6-pdr.	3 off., 53 enl.	30.20 kts.	Gas Engine & Power Co.	3 March 1897	10 June 1901
22	Somers	149¼ feet	150 tons	2 Whitehead	4 1-pdr.	2 off., 21 enl.	17.5 kts.*	Schichau Works, Germany	1898*	28 March 1898
23	Manley	60⅔ feet	30 tons			1 off., 5 enl.	17 kts.*	Yarrow, England	13 April 1898*	not commissioned
24	Bagley	157 feet	175 tons	3 Whitehead	3 1-pdr.	2 off., 26 enl.	29.15 kts.	Bath Iron Works	4 May 1898	18 October 1901
25	Barney	157 feet	175 tons	3 Whitehead	3 1-pdr.	2 off., 26 enl.	29.04 kts.	Bath Iron Works	4 May 1898	21 October 1901
26	Biddle	157 feet	175 tons	3 Whitehead	3 1-pdr.	2 off., 26 enl.	28.57 kts.	Bath Iron Works	4 May 1898	26 October 1901
27	Blakely	175 feet	196 tons	3 Whitehead	3 1-pdr.	2 off., 26 enl.	26.00 kts.	Lawley & Sons	4 May 1898	27 December 1904
28	De Long	175 feet	262 tons	3 Whitehead	3 1-pdr.	2 off., 26 enl.	25.52 kts.	Lawley & Sons	4 May 1898	27 October 1902
29	Nicholson	175 feet	218 tons	3 Whitehead	3 1-pdr.	2 off., 26 enl.	25.74 kts.	Lewis Nixon	4 May 1898	10 January 1905
30	O'Brien	175 feet	220 tons	3 Whitehead	3 1-pdr.	2 off., 26 enl.	25.00 kts.	Lewis Nixon	4 May 1898	15 July 1905
31	Shubrick	175 feet	200 tons	3 Whitehead	3 1-pdr.	2 off., 26 enl.	26.07 kts.	Wm. R. Trigg Co.	4 May 1898	25 September 1905
32	Stockton	175 feet	200 tons	3 Whitehead	3 1-pdr.	2 off., 26 enl.	25.79 kts.	Wm. R. Trigg Co.	4 May 1898	16 November 1902
33	Thornton	175 feet	200 tons	3 Whitehead	3 1-pdr.	2 off., 26 enl.	24.88 kts.	Wm. R. Trigg Co.	4 May 1898	9 June 1902
34	Tingey	175 feet	165 tons	3 Whitehead	3 1-pdr.	2 off., 26 enl.	24.94 kts.	Columbian Iron Works	4 May 1898	7 January 1904
35	Wilkes	175 feet	165 tons	3 Whitehead	3 1-pdr.	2 off., 26 enl.	25.99 kts.	Gas Engine & Power Co.	4 May 1898	18 September 1902

Submarines

Holland

Adder

No.*	Name	Length Overall	Surface Displ.	Submerged Displ.	Torpedo Tubes	Complement	Surface Speed*	Subm. Speed*	Builder	Date Authorized	Date Commissioned
	Holland	53 ft., 11 in.	64 tons	74 tons	1 18-inch	1 off., 6 enl.	8 kts.	5 kts.	Crescent Shipyard*	3 March 1899	12 October 1900
A-1	Plunger	63 ft., 10 in.	107 tons	122.5 tons	1 18-inch	1 off., 6 enl.	8 kts.	7 kts.	Crescent Shipyard*	3 March 1899	19 September 1903
A-2	Adder	63 ft., 10 in.	107 tons	122.5 tons	1 18-inch	1 off., 6 enl.	8 kts.	7 kts.	Crescent Shipyard*	7 June 1900	12 January 1903
A-3	Grampus	63 ft., 10 in.	107 tons	125 tons	1 18-inch	1 off., 6 enl.	8 kts.	7 kts.	Union Iron Works*	7 June 1900	28 May 1903
A-4	Moccasin	63 ft., 10 in.	107 tons	122.5 tons	1 18-inch	1 off., 6 enl.	8 kts.	7 kts.	Crescent Shipyard*	7 June 1900	17 January 1903
A-5	Pike	63 ft., 10 in.	107 tons	125 tons	1 18-inch	1 off., 6 enl.	8 kts.	7 kts.	Union Iron Works*	7 June 1900	28 May 1903
A-6	Porpoise	63 ft., 10 in.	107 tons	122.5 tons	1 18-inch	1 off., 6 enl.	8 kts.	7 kts.	Crescent Shipyard*	7 June 1900	19 September 1903
A-7	Shark	63 ft., 10 in.	107 tons	122.5 tons	1 18-inch	1 off., 6 enl.	8 kts.	7 kts.	Crescent Shipyard*	7 June 1900	19 September 1903
B-1	Viper	82 ft., 5 in.	145 tons	173 tons	2 18-inch	1 off., 9 enl.	9 kts.	8 kts.	Fore River S.B. Co.**	27 April 1904	18 October 1907
B-2	Cuttlefish	82 ft., 5 in.	145 tons	173 tons	2 18-inch	1 off., 9 enl.	9 kts.	8 kts.	Fore River S.B. Co.**	27 April 1904	18 October 1907
B-3	Tarantula	82 ft., 5 in.	145 tons	173 tons	2 18-inch	1 off., 9 enl.	9 kts.	8 kts.	Fore River S.B. Co.**	27 April 1904	3 December 1907
C-1	Octopus	105 ft., 4 in.	238 tons	275 tons	2 18-inch	1 off., 14 enl.	10.5 kts.	9 kts.	Fore River S.B. Co.**	27 April 1904	30 June 1908

* Class letters and numbers assigned November 17, 1911.

* Contract speeds   * For J. P. Holland T. B. Co.

** For Electric Boat Co.

Torpedo Boat Destroyers

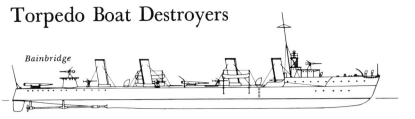

Bainbridge

Destroyers Nos. 1–5 & 10–13

Length on Load Waterline:	240 feet, 6¼ inches
Extreme Breadth:	23 feet, 7¼ inches
Mean Draft:	6 feet, 6 inches
Normal Displacement:	420 tons
Torpedo Tubes:	2 18-inch, Whitehead tubes
Armament:	2 3-inch rapid-fire guns
	5 6-pounder rapid-fire guns
Engines:	twin-screw, vertical inverted triple-expansion
Performance (*Bainbridge*):	28.45 knots; 8,000 indicated horsepower
Complement:	3 officers; 69 enlisted men

USS *Bainbridge*   Torpedo Boat Destroyer No. 1
Built by Neafie & Levy, Philadelphia, Pa.
Authorized 4 May 1898.
Commissioned 24 November 1902.
Sold 3 January 1920.

USS *Barry*   Torpedo Boat Destroyer No. 2
Built by Neafie & Levy, Philadelphia, Pa.
Authorized 4 May 1898.
Commissioned 24 November 1902.
Sold 3 January 1920.

USS *Chauncey*   Torpedo Boat Destroyer No. 3
Built by Neafie & Levy, Philadelphia, Pa.
Authorized 4 May 1898.
Commissioned 20 November 1902.
Sunk following collision with British merchantman SS *Rose* off Gibraltar,
   19 November 1917.

USS *Dale*   Torpedo Boat Destroyer No. 4
Built by William R. Trigg Co., Richmond, Va.
Authorized 4 May 1898.
Commissioned 24 October 1902.
Sold 3 January 1920.

USS *Decatur*   Torpedo Boat Destroyer No. 5
Built by William R. Trigg Co., Richmond, Va.
Authorized 4 May 1898.
Commissioned 19 May 1902.
Sold 3 January 1920.

USS *Paul Jones*   Torpedo Boat Destroyer No. 10
Built by Union Iron Works, San Francisco, Cal.
Authorized 4 May 1898.
Commissioned 19 July 1902.
Sold 3 January 1920.

USS *Perry*   Torpedo Boat Destroyer No. 11
Built by Union Iron Works, San Francisco, Cal.
Authorized 4 May 1898.
Commissioned 4 September 1902.
Sold 3 January 1920.

USS *Preble*   Torpedo Boat Destroyer No. 12
Built by Union Iron Works, San Francisco, Cal.
Authorized 4 May 1898.
Commissioned 21 June 1902.
Sold 3 January 1920.

USS *Stewart*   Torpedo Boat Destroyer No. 13
Built by Gas Engine & Power Co. & Chas. L. Seabury & Co., Consolidated,
   Morris Heights, N.Y.
Authorized 4 May 1898.
Commissioned 17 December 1902.
Sold 3 January 1920.

Destroyers Nos. 6 & 7

Length on Load Waterline:	238 feet, 9 inches
Extreme Breadth:	24 feet, 6 inches
Mean Draft:	6 feet
Normal Displacement:	408 tons
Torpedo Tubes:	2 18-inch, Whitehead tubes
Armament:	2 3-inch rapid-fire guns
	5 6-pounder rapid-fire guns
Engines:	twin-screw, vertical inverted triple-expansion
Performance (*Hopkins*):	29.02 knots; 7,200 indicated horsepower
Complement:	3 officers; 69 enlisted men

USS *Hopkins*   Torpedo Boat Destroyer No. 6
Built by Harlan & Hollingsworth, Wilmington, Del.
Authorized 4 May 1898.
Commissioned 23 September 1903.
Sold 7 September 1920.

USS *Hull*   Torpedo Boat Destroyer No. 7
Built by Harlan & Hollingsworth, Wilmington, Del.
Authorized 4 May 1898.
Commissioned 20 May 1903.
Sold 3 January 1920.

Destroyers Nos. 8 & 9

Length on Load Waterline:	240 feet, 7 inches
Extreme Breadth:	22 feet, 3 inches
Mean Draft:	6 feet, 9 inches
Normal Displacement:	446 tons
Torpedo Tubes:	2 18-inch, Whitehead tubes
Armament:	2 3-inch rapid-fire guns
	5 6-pounder rapid-fire guns
Engines:	twin-screw, vertical inverted triple-expansion
Performance (*Lawrence*):	28.41 knots; 6,375 indicated horsepower
Complement:	3 officers; 69 enlisted men

USS *Lawrence*   Torpedo Boat Destroyer No. 8
Built by Fore River Engine Co., East Braintree, Mass.
Authorized 4 May 1898.
Commissioned 14 April 1903.
Sold 3 January 1920.

USS *Macdonough*   Torpedo Boat Destroyer No. 9
Built by Fore River Engine Co., East Braintree, Mass.
Authorized 4 May 1898.
Commissioned 5 September 1903.
Sold 10 March 1920.

Destroyers Nos. 14–16

Length on Load Waterline:	248 feet
Extreme Breadth:	23 feet, 3 inches
Mean Draft:	6 feet
Normal Displacement:	433 tons
Torpedo Tubes:	2 18-inch, Whitehead tubes
Armament:	2 3-inch rapid-fire guns
	6 6-pounder rapid-fire guns
Engines:	twin-screw, vertical inverted triple-expansion
Performance (*Truxtun*):	29.58 knots; 8,300 indicated horsepower
Complement:	3 officers, 69 enlisted men

USS *Truxtun*   Torpedo Boat Destroyer No. 14
Built by Maryland Steel Co., Sparrows Pt., Md.
Authorized 4 May 1898.
Commissioned 11 September 1902.
Sold 3 January 1920.
Employed as a banana boat from 1920 until the 1950s.

USS *Whipple*   Torpedo Boat Destroyer No. 15
Built by Maryland Steel Co., Sparrows Pt., Md.
Authorized 4 May 1898.
Commissioned 21 October 1902.
Sold 3 January 1920.
Employed as a banana boat from 1920 until the 1950s.

USS *Worden*   Torpedo Boat Destroyer No. 16
Built by Maryland Steel Co., Sparrows Pt., Md.
Authorized 4 May 1898.
Commissioned 31 December 1902.
Sold 3 January 1920.
Employed as a banana boat from 1920 until the 1950s.

Vessels of the United States Navy, 1 January 1900

* Spanish-American War Purchases
† Former Spanish Vessels (captured, salvaged, or transferred from War Department)

Name	Type	Condition or Station
Abarenda*	Collier	Samoan Islands.
Accomac*	Steam Tug	Havana.
Active*	Steam Tug	Mare Island.
Adams	Wooden Steam Vessel	Training Ship. Pacific Coast.
Aileen*	Converted Yacht	Naval Militia. New York
Alabama	Battleship	Building. Cramp Shipyard.
Albany*	Protected Cruiser	Building. Armstrong Co., England.
Albay†	Small Gunboat	Asiatic Station.
Alert	Iron Steam Vessel	Out of Commission. Mare Island.
Alexander*	Collier	Out of Commission. Norfolk.
Alice*	Steam Tug	Norfolk.
Alliance	Wooden Steam Vessel	Training Ship. Atlantic Coast.
Alvarado†	Small Gunboat	Out of Commission. Portsmouth.
Amphitrite	Monitor	Training Ship. North Atlantic.
Annapolis	Composite Gunboat	Out of Commission. Annapolis.
Apache*	Steam Tug	Norfolk.
Arayat†	Small Gunboat	Repairing. Cavite.
Arethusa*	Tank Steamer	Out of Commission. League Island.
Arkansas	Monitor	Building. Newport News.
Atlanta	Protected Cruiser	Out of Commission. New York.
Badger*	Auxiliary Cruiser	Out of Commission. Mare Island.
Bagley	Torpedo Boat	Building. Bath Iron Works.
Bailey	Torpedo Boat	Building. Gas Engine & Power Co.
Bainbridge	T.B. Destroyer	Building. Neafie & Levy Works.
Baltimore	Protected Cruiser	Asiatic Station.
Bancroft	Gunboat	Out of Commission. Boston.
Barcelo†	Small Gunboat	Out of Commission. Cavite.
Barney	Torpedo Boat	Building. Bath Iron Works.
Barry	T.B. Destroyer	Building. Neafie & Levy Works.
Belusan†	Small Gunboat	Out of Commission. Cavite.
Bennington	Gunboat	Asiatic Station.
Biddle	Torpedo Boat	Building. Bath Iron Works.
Blakely	Torpedo Boat	Building. Bath Iron Works.
Boston	Protected Cruiser	Out of Commission. Mare Island.
Brooklyn	Armored Cruiser	Asiatic Station.
Brutus*	Collier	Asiatic Station.
Buffalo*	Auxiliary Cruiser	Out of Commission. New York.
Caesar*	Collier	North Atlantic Station.
Calamianes†	Small Gunboat	Repairing. Cavite.
Callao†	Small Gunboat	Asiatic Station.
Canonicus	Monitor	Laid Up. League Island.
Castine	Gunboat	Asiatic Station.
Catskill	Monitor	Laid Up. League Island.
Celtic*	Refrigerator Ship	Asiatic Station.
Charleston	Protected Cruiser	Wrecked in Philippines.
Chattanooga	Protected Cruiser	Building. Crescent Shipyard.
Chauncey	T.B. Destroyer	Building. Neafie & Levy Works.
Chesapeake	Training Ship	Building. Bath Iron Works.
Chicago	Protected Cruiser	South Atlantic Station.
Chickasaw*	Steam Tug	Out of Commission. Port Royal.
Choctaw*	Steam Tug	Newport.
Cincinnati	Protected Cruiser	Out of Commission. New York.
Cleveland	Sheathed Cruiser	Building. Bath Iron Works.
Columbia	Protected Cruiser	Out of Commission. League Island.
Concord	Gunboat	Asiatic Station.
Connecticut	Monitor	Building. Bath Iron Works.
Constellation	Wooden Sailing Vessel	Training Ship. Newport.
Constitution	Wooden Sailing Vessel	Out of Commission. Boston.
Craven	Torpedo Boat	Building. Bath Iron Works.
Culgoa*	Refrigerator Ship	Asiatic Station.
Cushing	Torpedo Boat	Out of Commission. New York.
Dahlgren	Torpedo Boat	Building. Bath Iron Works.
Dale	T.B. Destroyer	Building. William R. Trigg Co.
Dale	Wooden Sailing Vessel	Naval Militia. Maryland.
Davis	Torpedo Boat	Mare Island.
Decatur	T.B. Destroyer	Building. William R. Trigg Co.
De Long	Torpedo Boat	Building. Fore River Engine Co.
Denver	Sheathed Cruiser	Building. Neafie & Levy Works.
Des Moines	Protected Cruiser	Building. Fore River Co.
Detroit	Unprotected Cruiser	North Atlantic Station.
Dixie*	Auxiliary Cruiser	Training Ship. North Atlantic.
Dolphin	Dispatch Boat	Special Duty. North Atlantic.
Don Juan de Austria†	Gunboat	Rebuilding. Hong Kong.
Dorothea*	Converted Yacht	Out of Commission. Norfolk.
Du Pont	Torpedo Boat	Newport.
Eagle*	Converted Yacht	North Atlantic Station.
Elcano†	Small Gunboat	Repairing. Cavite.
Elfrida*	Converted Yacht	Naval Militia. Connecticut.
Enterprise	Wooden Steam Vessel	Training Ship. Massachusetts.
Ericsson	Torpedo Boat	Out of Commission. New York.
Essex	Wooden Steam Vessel	Training Ship. North Atlantic.
Farragut	Torpedo Boat	Mare Island.
Fern	Wooden Steam Vessel	Naval Militia. Washington, D.C.
Florida	Monitor	Building. Lewis Nixon Co.
Foote	Torpedo Boat	Out of Commission. New York.
Fortune	Steam Tug	Newport.
Fox	Torpedo Boat	Mare Island.
Franklin	Wooden Steam Vessel	Receiving Ship. Norfolk.
Frolic*	Converted Yacht	Out of Commission. Norfolk.
Galveston	Sheathed Cruiser	Building. William R. Trigg Co.
Gardoqui†	Small Gunboat	Asiatic Station.
Glacier*	Refrigerator Ship	Asiatic Station.
Gloucester*	Converted Yacht	Annapolis.
Goldsborough	Torpedo Boat	Building. Wolf & Zwicker Co.
Gwin	Torpedo Boat	Annapolis.
Hannibal*	Collier	Out of Commission. Norfolk.
Hartford	Wooden Steam Vessel	Training Ship. Pacific Coast.
Hawk*	Converted Yacht	Out of Commission. Norfolk.
Helena	Light-Draft Gunboat	Asiatic Station.
Hercules*	Steam Tug	Port Royal.
Hist*	Converted Yacht	Out of Commission. Norfolk.
Hopkins	T.B. Destroyer	Building. Harlan & Hollingsworth.
Hornet*	Converted Yacht	Naval Militia. North Carolina.
Hull	T.B. Destroyer	Building. Harlan & Hollingsworth.
Huntress*	Converted Yacht	Naval Militia. New Jersey.
Illinois	Battleship	Building. Newport News.
Inca*	Converted Yacht	Naval Militia. Massachusetts.
Independence	Wooden Sailing Vessel	Receiving Ship. Mare Island.
Indiana	Battleship	Repairing. New York.
Iona†	Steam Tug	Cavite.
Iowa	Battleship	Pacific Station.
Iris*	Distilling Ship	Asiatic Station.
Iroquois	Wooden Steam Vessel	Marine Hospital Service.
Iroquois*	Steam Tug	Honolulu.
Isla de Cuba†	Gunboat	Repairing. Hong Kong.
Isla de Luzon†	Gunboat	Repairing. Hong Kong.
Iwana	Steam Tug	Boston.
Jamestown	Wooden Sailing Vessel	Marine Hospital Service.
Jason	Monitor	Laid Up. League Island.
Justin*	Collier	Out of Commission. Mare Island.
Katahdin	Armored Ram	Out of Commission. League Island.
Kearsarge	Battleship	Building. Newport News.
Kentucky	Battleship	Building. Newport News.
Lancaster	Wooden Steam Vessel	Training Ship. North Atlantic.
Lawrence	T.B. Destroyer	Building. Fore River Engine Co.
Lebanon*	Collier	Out of Commission. Norfolk.
Lehigh	Monitor	Laid Up. League Island.
Leonidas*	Collier	Out of Commission. League Island.
Leyden	Steam Tug	Newport.
Leyte†	Small Gunboat	Out of Commission. Cavite.
Macdonough	T.B. Destroyer	Building. Fore River Engine Co.
Machias	Gunboat	North Atlantic Station.
MacKenzie	Torpedo Boat	Out of Commission. Newport.
Mahopac	Monitor	Laid Up. League Island.
Maine	Battleship	Building. Cramp Shipyard.
Manhattan	Monitor	Laid Up. League Island.
Manila†	Transport	Asiatic Station.
Manileno†	Small Gunboat	Repairing. Cavite.

Name	Type	Condition or Station
Manly* or Manley*	Torpedo Boat	Out of Commission. Annapolis.
Marblehead	Unprotected Cruiser	Pacific Station.
Marcellus*	Collier	Out of Commission. New York.
Marietta	Composite Gunboat	En route to Asiatic Station.
Marion	Wooden Steam Vessel	Naval Militia. California.
Marivelest	Small Gunboat	Asiatic Station.
Massachusetts	Battleship	Repairing. New York.
Massasoit*	Steam Tug	Key West.
Mayflower	Converted Yacht	Out of Commission. New York.
McKee	Torpedo Boat	Out of Commission. New York.
Miantonomoh	Monitor	Out of Commission. League Island.
Michigan	Iron Steam Vessel	Great Lakes.
Mindanao†	Gunboat	Rebuilding. Cavite.
Mindoro†	Small Gunboat	Asiatic Station.
Minneapolis	Protected Cruiser	Out of Commission. League Island.
Minnesota	Wooden Steam Vessel	Naval Militia. Massachusetts.
Missouri	Battleship	Building. Newport News.
Modoc*	Steam Tug	League Island.
Mohawk*	Steam Tug	Norfolk.
Mohican	Wooden Steam Vessel	Out of Commission. Mare Island.
Monadnock	Monitor	Asiatic Station.
Monocacy	Iron Steam Vessel	Asiatic Station.
Monongahela	Wooden Sailing Vessel	Training Ship. North Atlantic.
Montauk	Monitor	Laid Up. League Island.
Monterey	Monitor	Asiatic Station.
Montgomery	Unprotected Cruiser	South Atlantic Station.
Morris	Torpedo Boat	Newport.
Nahant	Monitor	Laid Up. League Island.
Nanshan*	Collier	Asiatic Station.
Nantucket	Monitor	Laid Up. Port Royal.
Narkeeta	Steam Tug	New York.
Nashville	Light-Draft Gunboat	Asiatic Station.
Nero*	Collier	Cable Survey. Pacific.
Newark	Protected Cruiser	Asiatic Station.
New Hampshire	Wooden Sailing Vessel	Naval Militia. New York.
New Orleans*	Protected Cruiser	Asiatic Station.
Newport	Composite Gunboat	Out of Commission. Norfolk.
New York	Armored Cruiser	North Atlantic Station.
Nezinscot*	Steam Tug	Out of Commission. Norfolk.
Nicholson	Torpedo Boat	Building. Crescent Ship Yard.
Nina	Steam Tug	New York.
Nipsic	Wooden Steam Vessel	Out of Commission. Bremerton.
O'Brien	Torpedo Boat	Building. Crescent Ship Yard.
Ohio	Battleship	Building. Union Iron Works.
Olympia	Protected Cruiser	Out of Commission. Boston.
Omaha	Wooden Steam Vessel	Marine Hospital Service.
Oneida*	Converted Yacht	Out of Commission. Norfolk.
Oregon	Battleship	Asiatic Station.
Osceola*	Steam Tug	New York.
Pampanga†	Small Gunboat	Asiatic Station.
Panay†	Small Gunboat	Asiatic Station.
Panther*	Auxiliary Cruiser	Out of Commission. League Island.
Paragua†	Small Gunboat	Asiatic Station.
Paul Jones	T.B. Destroyer	Building. Union Iron Works.
Pawnee*	Steam Tug	New York.
Pawtucket	Steam Tug	Bremerton.
Penacook	Steam Tug	Port Royal.
Pensacola	Wooden Steam Vessel	Receiving Ship. San Francisco.
Peoria*	Auxiliary Gunboat	Out of Commission. Boston.
Perry	T.B. Destroyer	Building. Union Iron Works.
Petrel	Gunboat	Asiatic Station.
Petrelito†	Steam Tug	Asiatic Station.
Philadelphia	Protected Cruiser	Pacific Station.
Pinta	Iron Steam Vessel	Naval Militia. California.
Piscataqua*	Steam Tug	Portsmouth.
Plunger	Submarine T.B.	Building. Columbian Iron Works.
Pompey*	Collier	Out of Commission. League Island.
Pontiac*	Steam Tug	Boston.
Porter	Torpedo Boat	North Atlantic Station.
Portsmouth	Wooden Sailing Vessel	Naval Militia. New Jersey.
Potomac*	Steam Tug	North Atlantic Station.
Powhatan	Steam Tug	Marine Hospital Service.
Prairie*	Auxiliary Cruiser	North Atlantic Station.
Preble	T.B. Destroyer	Building. Union Iron Works.
Princeton	Composite Gunboat	Asiatic Station.
Puritan	Monitor	Out of Commission. Annapolis.
Rainbow*	Distilling Ship	Out of Commission. New York.
Raleigh	Protected Cruiser	Out of Commission. Portsmouth.
Ranger	Iron Steam Vessel	Pacific Station.
Rapido†	Steam Tug	Asiatic Station.
Reina Mercedes†	Unprotected Cruiser	Out of Commission. Norfolk.
Resolute*	Transport	Out of Commission. Philadelphia.
Restless*	Converted Yacht	Out of Commission. New York.
Richmond	Wooden Steam Vessel	Receiving Ship. League Island.
Rodgers	Torpedo Boat	Out of Commission. New York.
Rowan	Torpedo Boat	Out of Commission. Bremerton.
Samar†	Small Gunboat	Asiatic Station.
Samoset	Steam Tug	League Island.
Sandoval†	Small Gunboat	Out of Commission. Portsmouth.
San Francisco	Protected Cruiser	Out of Commission. Norfolk.
Saratoga	Wooden Sailing Vessel	School Ship. Pennsylvania.
Saturn*	Collier	Out of Commission. Norfolk.
Scindia*	Collier	Pacific Station.
Scorpion*	Converted Yacht	North Atlantic Station.
Sebago	Steam Tug	Pensacola.
Seminole*	Steam Tug	Out of Commission. Boston.
Shearwater*	Converted Yacht	Naval Militia. Pennsylvania.
Shubrick	Torpedo Boat	Building. William R. Trigg Co.
Sioux*	Steam Tug	Norfolk.
Siren*	Converted Yacht	Naval Militia. Virginia.
Solace*	Hospital Ship	Asiatic Station.
Somers*	Torpedo Boat	Out of Commission. New York.
Southery*	Collier	Out of Commission. Norfolk.
Standish	Steam Tug	Annapolis.
Sterling*	Collier	Out of Commission. Boston.
Stewart	T.B. Destroyer	Building. Gas Engine & Power Co.
Stiletto	Torpedo Boat	Newport.
St. Louis	Wooden Sailing Vessel	Naval Militia. Pennsylvania.
St. Mary's	Wooden Sailing Vessel	School Ship. New York.
Stockton	Torpedo Boat	Building. William R. Trigg Co.
Stranger*	Converted Yacht	Naval Militia. Louisiana.
Stringham	Torpedo Boat	Building. Harlan & Hollingsworth.
Supply*	Supply Ship	Out of Commission. New York.
Sureste†	Steam Tug	Asiatic Station.
Sylph*	Converted Yacht	Special Duty. Washington, D.C.
Sylvia*	Converted Yacht	Naval Militia. Maryland.
Tacoma	Sheathed Cruiser	Building. Union Iron Works.
Tacoma*	Steam Tug	Pensacola.
Talbot	Torpedo Boat	Norfolk.
Tecumseh*	Steam Tug	Washington, D.C.
Terror	Monitor	Out of Commission. Norfolk.
Texas	Battleship	North Atlantic Station.
Thornton	Torpedo Boat	Building. William R. Trigg Co.
Tingey	Torpedo Boat	Building. Colonial Iron Works.
Topeka*	Gunboat	Out of Commission. Boston.
Traffic	Steam Tug	New York.
Triton	Steam Tug	Norfolk.
Truxtun	T.B. Destroyer	Building. Maryland Steel Co.
Unadilla	Steam Tug	Mare Island.
Uncas*	Steam Tug	San Juan.
Urdaneta†	Small Gunboat	Asiatic Station.
Vasco†	Small Gunboat	Asiatic Station.
Vermont	Wooden Sailing Ship	Receiving Ship. New York.
Vesuvius	Dynamite Cruiser	Out of Commission. Boston.
Vicksburg	Composite Gunboat	Out of Commission. Boston.
Vigilant*	Steam Tug	San Francisco.
Vixen*	Converted Yacht	North Atlantic Station.
Waban*	Steam Tug	Port Royal.
Wabash	Wooden Steam Vessel	Receiving Ship. Boston.
Wahneta	Steam Tug	Norfolk.
Wasp*	Converted Yacht	Out of Commission. Norfolk.
Wheeling	Composite Gunboat	Asiatic Station.
Whipple	T.B. Destroyer	Building. Maryland Steel Co.
Wilkes	Torpedo Boat	Building. Gas Engine & Power Co.
Wilmington	Light-Draft Gunboat	South Atlantic Station.
Winslow	Torpedo Boat	Out of Commission. New York.
Wisconsin	Battleship	Building. Union Iron Works.
Wompatuck	Steam Tug	New York.
Worden	T.B. Destroyer	Building. Maryland Steel Co.
Wyoming	Monitor	Building. Union Iron Works.
Yankee*	Auxiliary Cruiser	Out of Commission. League Island.
Yankton*	Converted Yacht	North Atlantic Station.
Yantic	Wooden Steam Vessel	Naval Militia. Michigan.
Yorktown	Gunboat	Asiatic Station.
Yosemite*	Auxiliary Cruiser	Station Ship. Guam.
Zafiro*	Supply Ship	Asiatic Station.

Main-Battery Ordnance and Torpedoes in the United States Navy, 1883-1909

Based on information in the 1894–1910 editions of the *Text Book of Ordnance and Gunnery* and the 1902–1904 editions of the *Bluejacket's Manual*.

Gun	Length	Model	Year Intro.	Weight of Projectile	Weight of Service Charge	Muzzle Velocity	Employment
13-Inch	35 calibers	Mark I	1895	1,100 pounds	550 pounds (brown)	2,100 feet per second	*Indiana* class
13-Inch	35 calibers	Mark II	1900	1,100 pounds	295 pounds (smokeless)	2,300 feet per second	*Kearsarge* and *Illinois* classes
12-Inch	35 calibers	Mark I	1893	850 pounds	425 pounds (brown)	2,100 feet per second	*Monterey, Texas, Puritan*
12-Inch	35 calibers	Mark II	1897	850 pounds	425 pounds (brown)	2,100 feet per second	*Iowa*
12-Inch	40 calibers	Mark III	1902	850 pounds	370 pounds (smokeless)	2,800 feet per second	*Maine* and *Arkansas* classes
12-Inch	40 calibers	Mark IV	1906	870 pounds	305 pounds (smokeless)	2,600 feet per second	*Virginia* class
12-Inch	45 calibers	Mark V	1906	870 pounds	305 pounds (smokeless)	2,700 feet per second	*Connecticut* and *Mississippi* classes
10-Inch	30 calibers	Mark I	1891	500 pounds	225–240 pounds (brown)	2,000 feet per second	*Miantonomoh*
10-Inch	35 calibers	Mark I	1891	500 pounds	225–240 pounds (brown)	2,080 feet per second	*Miantonomoh*
10-Inch	30 calibers	Mark II	1893	500 pounds	225–240 pounds (brown)	2,000 feet per second	*Amphitrite* class, *Monterey*
10-Inch	35 calibers	Mark II	1895	500 pounds	225–240 pounds (brown)	2,080 feet per second	*Maine* (first)
10-Inch	40 calibers	Mark III	1906	510 pounds	207.5 pounds (smokeless)	2,700 feet per second	*Tennessee* class
8-Inch	30 calibers	Mark I	1886	250 pounds	105–115 pounds (brown)	2,000 feet per second	*Atlanta* class
8-Inch	30 calibers	Mark II	1889	250 pounds	105–115 pounds (brown)	2,000 feet per second	*Chicago*
8-Inch	35 calibers	Mark III	1889	250 pounds	105–115 pounds (brown)	2,080 feet per second	*Charleston, Olympia, New York, Brooklyn, Indiana*
8-Inch	40 calibers	Mark III	1894	250 pounds	105–115 pounds (brown)	2,150 feet per second	*Columbia* class
8-Inch	35 calibers	Mark IV	1900	250 pounds	63 pounds (smokeless)	2,300 feet per second	*Kearsarge* class
8-Inch	40 calibers	Mark V	1905	250 pounds	115 pounds (smokeless)	2,700 feet per second	*Pennsylvania* class
8-Inch	45 calibers	Mark VI	1906	250 pounds	98.5 pounds (smokeless)	2,750 feet per second	*Virginia, Connecticut,* and *Mississippi* classes
7-Inch	45 calibers	Mark I	1902	165 pounds	74 pounds (smokeless)	2,900 feet per second	Experimental prototype
7-Inch	45 calibers	Mark II	1906	165 pounds	58 pounds (smokeless)	2,700 feet per second	*Connecticut* and *Mississippi* classes
6-Inch	30 calibers	Mark I	1884	100 pounds	50 pounds (brown)	2,000 feet per second	Experimental prototype
6-Inch	30 calibers	Mark II	1886	100 pounds	45–48 pounds (brown)	2,000 feet per second	*Atlanta* class, *Chicago*
6-Inch	30 calibers	Mark III	1889	100 pounds	44–47 pounds (brown)	2,000 feet per second	*Charleston, San Francisco, Yorktown, Indiana*
6-Inch	35 calibers	Mark III	1894	100 pounds	44–47 pounds (brown)	2,080 feet per second	*Texas, Minneapolis* class
6-Inch	40 calibers	Mark III	1894	100 pounds	44–47 pounds (brown)	2,150 feet per second	*Columbia* and *Cincinnati* classes
6-Inch	50 calibers	Mark VIII	1902	105 pounds	37 pounds (smokeless)	2,800 feet per second	*Pennsylvania, Tennessee,* and *St. Louis* classes
5-Inch	30 calibers	Mark I	1889	60 pounds	26–29 pounds (brown)	2,000 feet per second	*Chicago*
5-Inch	40 calibers	Mark II	1893	50 pounds	28–30 pounds (brown)	2,250 feet per second	*Olympia, Brooklyn, Cincinnati, Montgomery*
5-Inch	50 calibers	Mark VI	1904	60 pounds	27 pounds (smokeless)	2,900 feet per second	*Denver* class

Torpedo	Year Intro.	Length	Diameter	Weight of Torpedo	Weight of Warhead	Air-Flask Pressure	Range and Speed
Howell	1893	11 feet, 2 inches	14.2 inches	518 pounds	100 pounds		600 yards at 18 knots
Whitehead	1893	11 feet, 8 inches	17.7 inches	836 pounds	110 pounds	1,350 pounds per square inch	800 yards at 26 knots
Whitehead	1895	16 feet, 5 inches	17.7 inches	1,161 pounds	220 pounds	1,350 pounds per square inch	850 yards at 28 knots
Bliss-Leavitt	1905	16 feet, 5 inches	17.7 inches		132 pounds	2,250 pounds per square inch	3,500 yards at 28 knots
Bliss-Leavitt	1905	16 feet, 5 inches	21 inches		300 pounds	2,250 pounds per square inch	3,500 yards at 36 knots

The maximum effective range for Steel Navy guns varied from about 5,000 yards for 5-inch rifles to about 9,000 yards for the later 12-inch rifles. Brown or "cocoa" powder was introduced as the standard propellant in about 1884, replacing traditional black powder. Between 1898 and 1900 the Navy shifted to improved smokeless powder.

Propellers on the Howell torpedo were driven by a 130-pound flywheel spinning at 10,000 r.p.m. In the Whitehead torpedoes a three-cylinder engine operating on compressed air was employed. The Bliss-Leavitt models used a turbine drive, and the air was superheated by an alcohol burner.

Enlisted Rates and Pay in the U.S. Navy, 1902

As listed in the *Bluejacket's Manual,* 1902 edition. Pay indicated is per month.

Chief Petty Officers

Seaman Branch		Artificer Branch		Special Branch	
Chief Master-at-Arms	$65	Chief Machinist	$70	Chief Commissary Steward	$70
Chief Boatswain's Mate	50	Chief Electrician	60	Chief Yeoman	60
Chief Gunner's Mate	50	Chief Carpenter's Mate	50	Hospital Steward	60
Chief Gun Captain	50			Commissary Steward	60
Chief Quartermaster	50			Bandmaster	52

Petty Officers, First Class

Seaman Branch		Artificer Branch		Special Branch	
Master-at-Arms, first class	$40	Boilermaker	$65	Yeoman, first class	$40
Boatswain's Mate, first class	40	Machinist, first class	55	First Musician	36
Gunner's Mate, first class	40	Shipfitter, first class	55		
Gun Captain, first class	40	Coppersmith	55		
Quartermaster, first class	40	Electrician, first class	50		
		Blacksmith	50		
		Plumber	45		
		Sailmaker's Mate	40		
		Carpenter's Mate, first class	40		
		Water Tender	40		
		Painter	40		

Petty Officers, Second Class

Seaman Branch		Artificer Branch		Special Branch	
Master-at-Arms, second class	$35	Machinist, second class	$40	Yeoman, second class	$35
Boatswain's Mate, second class	35	Electrician, second class	40		
Gunner's Mate, second class	35	Shipfitter, second class	40		
Gun Captain, second class	35	Oiler	37		
Quartermaster, second class	35	Carpenter's Mate, second class	35		
		Printer	35		
		Painter	35		

Petty Officers, Third Class

Seaman Branch		Artificer Branch		Special Branch	
Master-at-Arms, third class	$30	Carpenter's Mate, third class	$30	Yeoman, third class	$30
Coxswain	30	Electrician, third class	30	Hospital Apprentice, first class	30
Gunner's Mate, third class	30	Painter	30		
Quartermaster, third class	30				

Seamen, First Class

Seaman Branch		Artificer Branch		Special Branch	
Seaman Gunner	$26	Fireman, first class	$35	Musician, first class	$32
Seaman	24				
Apprentice, first class	21				

Seamen, Second Class

Seaman Branch		Artificer Branch		Special Branch	
Ordinary Seaman	$19	Fireman, second class	$30	Musician, second class	$30
Apprentice, second class	15	Shipwright	25	Bugler	30
				Hospital Apprentice	20

Seamen, Third Class

Seaman Branch		Artificer Branch		Special Branch	
Landsman	$16	Coal Passer	$22		
Apprentice, third class	9				

Daily Shipboard Routine in the United States Navy, 1902

As described in *The Bluejacket's Manual,* 1902 edition.

PORT ROUTINE

4:00 A.M.	Call ship's cook (earlier if necessary).
4:45	Anchor watch trice up hammock cloths: call hammock stowers, boatswain's mate and music: mates of deck.
5:00	Reveille, call "All hands": fifteen minutes to clear deck of hammocks: coffee: light smoking lamp.
5:20	Pipe sweepers.
5:30	Turn to: clear up decks: execute morning orders and routine: hoist ashes: call warrant officers.
5:45	Market boat.
6:00	Day men report to the officer of the deck: side cleaners over the side.
6:30	Serve out fresh water: fill distributing tanks.
6:50	Trice up hammock cloths.
7:00	Up all hammocks.
7:20	Mess gear: light smoking lamp: coxswains report boats ready.
7:30	Breakfast: shift into the uniform of the day.
8:00	Colors: lower running boats.
8:15	Turn to: bright-work: out smoking lamp: pipe sweepers: inspect running crews.
8:45	Sick call.
9:00	Spread awnings: flemish down gear.
9:15	Clear up decks for quarters: down towels and wash deck gear: pipe sweepers.
9:25	Officer's call: report decks ready for quarters.
9:30	Quarters. First drill period: inspection of berth deck, mess gear, and storerooms. When first drill period is over, reports and requests at mast. Extra-duty men to work when not at drill. Saturdays, weather permitting, up all bags.
10:30	Second drill period.
11:00	Retreat from drill.
11:30	Inspect dinner: if still up and dry, down wash clothes: up ditty boxes: pipe sweepers.
11:45	Mess gear: light smoking lamp.
Noon	Dinner (emergencies alone interfere with this).
1:00 P.M.	Turn to: out smoking lamp: down ditty boxes: pipe sweepers: special requests to the executive officer.
1:30	Provision call: extra-duty men at work when not at drill: drill call.
2:00	Drill retreat: pipe sweepers.
3:00	Pipe sweepers.
4:00	Knock off work: pipe sweepers.
4:30	Pipe sweepers: clear up for quarters: lay up gear.
4:55	Officers' call.
5:00	Quarters.
5:20	Spread mess gear.
5:30	Supper: shift into blue.
6:00	Turn to: pipe sweepers: coal and water steamers: fill distributing tanks.
Sunset	Retreat: ceremony prescribed to be carefully observed. When ceremony is ended hoist boats: up wash deck gear: see fire hose coupled. Scrub clothes Sunday, Tuesday, and Thursday.
6:25	Wardroom dinner call.
7:30	Hammocks: lights in hold, orlop, and storerooms to be reported out not later than 7:30. Mate of splinter deck see that water-tight doors and hatches are closed for the night.
8:00	Warrant officers and storeroom keepers report.
8:55	First call: out smoking lamp: down ditty boxes.
9:00	Tattoo: inspection of all decks. Silence. Muster anchor watch. Pipe down. Taps.
10:00	Lights in wardroom and steerage to be extinguished.

SEA ROUTINE

3:00 A.M.	Call ship's cook.
3:50	Call the watch: relieve the wheel and lookouts.
4:00	Relieve the watch: light smoking lamp.
4:30	Turn to: out smoking lamp: pipe sweepers: clear up the decks: wash clothes.
5:00	Call idlers and day men.
5:15	Trice up clothes lines: execute morning orders.
Sunrise	Take in running lights: station masthead lookout.
6:30	Hoist ashes.
6:50	Trice up six bell hammock cloths.
7:00	Up all hammocks: serve out washing water.
7:20	Mess gear: watch below: light smoking lamp.
7:30	Breakfast: watch below: clean deck bright-work.
7:50	Mess gear: watch on deck.
8:00	Relieve the watch: breakfast.
8:30	Turn to: out smoking lamp: clean bright-work.
9:00	Sick call.
9:15	Clear up deck: down towel lines: stow away ditty boxes and cleaning gear: pipe sweepers.
9:25	Officers' call. Report decks ready for quarters.
9:30	Quarters: after which drills and exercises as per routine.
10:00	Relieve wheel and lookouts.
10:30	Retreat from drill: "Extra-duty call": pipe sweepers: hoist ashes.
11:30	Clean up decks: pipe sweepers.
11:50	Mess gear: watch below: light smoking lamp.
Noon	Dinner: watch below.
12:20	Mess gear: watch on deck.
12:30	Relieve the watch: dinner.
1:00 P.M.	Turn to: out smoking lamp: pipe sweepers: start work about the deck.
1:30	Serve out provisions: drill call.
2:00	Hoist ashes: relieve the wheel and lookout.
2:15	Retreat from drill: pipe sweepers: "Extra-duty call."
2:30	Instruction of landsmen: hoist ashes.
3:30	Pipe sweepers.
4:00	Relieve the watch.
4:30	Pipe sweepers: clear up decks: knock-off all work.
4:55	Officers' call.
5:00	Evening quarters: close water-tight doors.
5:20	Mess gear: watch below: light smoking lamp.
5:30	Supper: watch below: pipe sweepers.
5:50	Mess gear: watch on deck.
6:00	Relieve watch: supper: relieve wheel and lookouts: life-boats and life-buoys reported ready.
6:30	Turn to: pipe sweepers: hoist ashes.
Sunset	Set deck lookouts: running lights: get up wash deck gear.
7:30	Hammocks: mate of splinter-deck see water-tight doors and hatches closed.
8:00	Relieve the watch, wheel and lookouts: out smoking lamp. Warrant officers and store-room keepers report.

A Brief Glossary of Nautical Expressions and Slang

Adapted from material in *The American Battleship in Commission; Naval Customs, Traditions and Usage; Patterson's Illustrated Nautical Encyclopedia; Tales of a Cruise;* and *Three Years Behind the Guns.*

Beach Comber   One found idling around the wharves and saloons of seaports; a drifter.

Big Ticket   An honorable discharge.

Binnacle List   The list of men excused from duty due to illness.

Blue Book   U.S. Navy Regulations.

Bluejacket or *Jack*   The universal name for a sailor.

Bob or *Straight Kick*   A dishonorable discharge.

Bolo Man   A warrant officer.

Boston   The Navy prison at Boston, Massachusetts.

Breaking It   Remaining overtime on shore liberty.

Bumboat Man   A seafaring peddler catering to the enlisted men.

Burgoo   A mixture of molasses and broken biscuits or hardtack.

Canned Willie   Canned corned beef.

Charlie Noble   The galley smokestack.

Cheese Knife   An officer's sword.

Cock of the Station   That ship having the champion boat-racing crew.

Coming Up Through the Hawse-Hole   Earning an officer's commission via the enlisted ranks.

Corking Mat   A rectangular strip of canvas laid on the deck, upon which to take a noontime nap.

Crow or *Buzzard*   A petty officer's rating badge.

Cum Shaw   Obtaining something for nothing; a gratuity.

Dead Soldier   An empty bottle.

Ditty Box   A small wooden box with a hinged lid, issued to each sailor for his trinkets and personal items.

Dog   A bottle of whiskey.

Dog Watch   One of the two-hour watches between 4:00 and 8:00 P.M., employed to rotate the watch schedule.

Down For A Chance   Going before the commanding officer at mast.

Draws More Water   One who receives more pay.

Dream Sack   The sailor's hammock.

Duff or *Plum Duff*   A pudding made from a paste of flour, water, and raisins, and considered a delicacy.

Dynamo Buster   The ship's electrician.

First Luff   The ship's executive officer, or first lieutenant.

Ghost Walking   Payday.

Going Down Hill   An enlistment that is over one-half completed.

Greaser or *Under Ground Savage*   A member of the engineer's force.

Guardo   A receiving ship at a navy yard or station.

Hammock Ladder   "That which a rookie desires on his first experience with a hammock, and for which he inquires diligently."

Holystone   A sandstone brick, used for scrubbing the wooden deck.

Homeward-Bounder Clothing   A bluejacket-tailored uniform, with as much fancy-work as the regulations will allow.

Hurdy Gurdy   A small, hand-operated sewing machine.

Idler   A member of the ship's company who does not stand watch, such as a cook, yeoman, or musician.

Jack-o'-the-Dust   The paymaster's storeroom keeper, in charge of issuing uniforms and other shipboard needs.

Jaw-Bone   Credit.

Jimmock or *Jamoke*   Navy coffee, also known as *Java.*

Jimmy Legs   The master-at-arms, in charge of maintaining discipline.

Jump   To desert from the service.

Ki Yi   A scrubbing brush.

Lose the Number of One's Mess   To die.

Lucky Bag   A locker where articles found adrift by the master-at-arms are kept until redeemed by their owners.

Mailo   Mail is aboard and ready for distribution.

Man-of-War Cocktail   A potent drink usually composed of condensed milk, alcohol, hot water, eggs, sugar, and nutmeg.

Microbes   The ship's doctor.

Monkey Drill   Calisthenics.

Mud Hook   The ship's anchor.

Mustang   An officer who entered the Navy through the merchant service instead of via the Naval Academy.

On the Books   Money due on the paymaster's books.

Paymaster's Bouquet   Salt-water soap; a soap made from coconut oil which makes a good lather when used with salt water.

Pie House or *Pie Wagon*   The ship's brig.

Ping Pong   Sub-caliber target practice, employing .22-caliber rifles and targets attached to the ship's guns.

Plank Owner   One who has served aboard a ship so long that probably only death or retirement will remove him.

Pound Your Ear   To take a nap on the deck.

Politician   One with a talent for holding down easy details.

Prayer Book or *Testament*   A small holystone.

Punk   Bread.

Red Lead   Catsup served out by the commissary.

Regulation   Clothing issued by the paymaster's storekeeper without regard to fit.

Rocks And Shoals   The Articles for the Government of the Navy, read monthly to all hands.

Rope-Yarn Sunday   Wednesday afternoon, devoted to the care and mending of uniforms.

Sailor's Hitching Post   A Marine.

Salt Horse   Salt beef preserved in barrels of brine.

Scoffer   One endowed with an unusually hearty appetite.

Scoojie-Moojie   Brightwork cleaner.

Scuttle Butt   The ship's fresh water tap or fountain.

Sea Lawyer   An argumentative sailor; one who thinks he knows more about Navy Regulations than the captain.

Sea Pie   A dish of fish and vegetables served between several layers of pie crusts.

Sheeney   A sailor owning a small sewing machine and doing tailor work for profit during his off-duty hours.

Show a Leg   The master-at-arms' exhortation upon rousing the crew from their hammocks at reveille.

Six for Five   A popular loan, of five dollars for thirty days, with a dollar's interest.

Single Stick   A hickory sword used for cutlass drill.

Six Months and a Bob   Six months' confinement and a dishonorable discharge.

Sky Pilot   The ship's chaplain.

Sloper   A sailor hailing from the West Coast of the U.S.

Slum   A Navy stew of doubtful origin.

Slusher or *Belly-Robber*   A berth-deck cook.

Smoking Lamp   A lamp used to light the sailor's pipe, and to indicate the hours during which smoking is permitted.

Snowdigger   A sailor hailing from the East Coast of the U.S.

Spit Kid or *Spit Kit*   A sea-going cuspidor.

Stick   Captain's mast, at which erring sailors appear before the commanding officer for judgment.

Stone Frigate   A Navy prison ashore.

Straggler   A sailor who turns himself in within ten days after being absent without leave.

Sundowner   An officer who is an unreasonably harsh disciplinarian.

Swallow the Anchor   To retire and move ashore.

Swallow the Blue Book   To continually quote Navy Regulations.

Swankie   A drink made of vinegar, molasses, and water.

Tell It to a Marine   A reply to a doubtful or exaggerated statement.

Thirty and Three   A sentence of thirty days' confinement and the loss of three months' pay.

Trimmer   A sailor who works overtime with a purpose apparent to his shipmates; an apple-polisher.

Yellow Jack   Yellow fever.

Young Gentleman   A midshipman from the Naval Academy.

Bibliography

GENERAL REFERENCES

American Society of Naval Engineers Journal. Washington, D.C., 1889–

Beehler, W. H. "The United States Navy." *Brassey's Naval Annual* (1899): 90–122.

Bennett, Frank M. *The Steam Navy of the United States.* Pittsburg: W. T. Nicholson, 1896.

Heinl, Robert Debs, Jr. *Soldiers of the Sea.* Annapolis: U.S. Naval Institute, 1962.

Herrick, Walter R., Jr. *The American Naval Revolution.* Baton Rouge: Louisiana State University Press, 1966.

Hovgaard, William. *Modern History of Warships.* London: E. & F. N. Spon, 1920.

Jane's Fighting Ships. London: Various publishers, 1898–

Paullin, Charles Oscar. *Paullin's History of Naval Administration, 1775–1911.* Annapolis: U.S. Naval Institute, 1968.

Reed, Edward J. and Edward Simpson. *Modern Ships of War.* New York: Harper and Brothers, 1888.

"Special Navy Supplement." *Scientific American Supplement* XLV (April 30, 1898): 1–40

"Special Navy Issue—Development of the United States Navy Since the Spanish War." *Scientific American* LXXXV (1901): 373–90.

"Special Navy Issue—Ten Years of the United States Navy." *Scientific American* XCVII (1907): 405–36.

Transactions of the Society of Naval Architects and Marine Engineers. New York, Vol. I, 1893–

United States Naval Institute Proceedings. Annapolis, Vol. I, 1874–

U.S. Navy Department. *Annual Report of the Secretary of the Navy.* Washington, D.C., 1880–1909.

U.S. Navy. *Dictionary of American Naval Fighting Ships.* Vol I–V. Washington: Government Printing Office, 1959–1971.

BIOGRAPHIES AND AUTOBIOGRAPHIES

Buenzle, Fred J. *Bluejacket: An Autobiography.* New York: W. W. Norton, 1939.

Clark, Charles E. *My Fifty Years in the Navy.* Boston: Little, Brown, 1917.

Dewey, George. *Autobiography of George Dewey, Admiral of the Navy.* New York: Scribner's, 1913.

Evans, Robley D. *A Sailor's Log.* New York: Appleton, 1901.

———. *An Admiral's Log.* New York: Appleton, 1910.

Fiske, Bradley A. *From Midshipman to Rear Admiral.* New York: Century, 1919.

Gleaves, Albert. *Life and Letters of Rear Admiral Stephen B. Luce, U.S. Navy, Founder of the Naval War College.* New York: Putnam's, 1925.

Morison, Elting E. *Admiral Sims and the Modern American Navy.* Boston: Houghton Mifflin, 1942.

Morris, Richard Knowles. *John P. Holland, 1841–1914.* Annapolis: U.S. Naval Institute, 1966.

Puleston, William D. *Mahan: The Life and Work of Captain Alfred Thayer Mahan, U.S.N.* New Haven: Yale University Press, 1939.

Schroeder, Seaton. *A Half-Century of Naval Service.* New York: Appleton, 1922.

Swann, Leonard Alexander, Jr. *John Roach, Maritime Entrepreneur.* Annapolis: U.S. Naval Institute, 1965.

Yarnell, Harry E. *Admiral Richard Wainwright and the United States Fleet.* Washington: Government Printing Office, 1962.

WARSHIPS

Bowles, Francis T. "Remarks on the New Designs of Naval Vessels." *Transactions of the Society of Naval Architects and Marine Engineers* X (1902): 273–87.

Hichborn, Philip. "Recent Designs of Vessels for the U.S. Navy." *Transactions of the Society of Naval Architects and Marine Engineers* III (1895): 159–83.

———. "Designs of the New Vessels for the U.S. Navy." *Transactions of the Society of Naval Architects and Marine Engineers* VI (1898): 115–38.

———. "Recent Designs of Battleships and Cruisers for the U.S. Navy. *Transactions of the Society of Naval Architects and Marine Engineers* VIII (1900): 261–78.

Reuterdahl, Henry. "The Needs of Our Navy." *McClure's Magazine* XXX (1908): 251–63.

Wilson, Theodore D. "Steel Ships of the United States Navy." *Transactions of the Society of Naval Architects and Marine Engineers* I (1893): 116–139.

BATTLESHIPS

Crank, R. K. "The U.S. Battleship *Louisiana.*" *Journal of the American Society of Naval Engineers* XVIII (1906): 171–226.

Gardiner, C. A. "The U.S. Battleship *Virginia.*" *Journal of the American Society of Naval Engineers* XVII (1905): 1113–32.

Hall, Harry. "Contract Trial of the U.S. Coast-Line Battleship *Indiana.*" *Journal of the American Society of Naval Engineers* VII (1895): 637–66.

Hichborn, Philip. "The New Battleships." *Transactions of the Society of Naval Architects and Marine Engineers* IV (1896): 73–92.

———. "Some Notes on the Speed Trials and Experience in Commission of Our New Battleships." *Transactions of the Society of Naval Architects and Marine Engineers* V (1897): 135–50.

Kinkaid, T. W. "Contract Trial of the Machinery of the USS *Texas.*" *Journal of the American Society of Naval Engineers* VIII (1896): 82–86.

Mahony, D. S. "The U.S. Battleship *Maine.*" *Journal of the American Society of Naval Engineers* XIV (1902): 1123–34.

Morley, A. W. "Contract Trial of the U.S. Armored Cruiser *Maine.*" *Journal of the American Society of Naval Engineers* VII (1895): 1–29.

Pickrell, James M. "Contract Trial of the U.S. Seagoing Battleship *Iowa.*" *Journal of the American Society of Naval Engineers* IX (1897): 453–80.

———. "Contract Trial of the U.S. Seagoing Battleship *Illinois.*" *Journal of the American Society of Naval Engineers* XIII (1901): 559–85.

Price, Claude B. "Contract Trial of the U.S. Seagoing Battleship *Kearsarge.*" *Journal of the American Society of Naval Engineers* XI (1899): 823–50.

"Report of the Board of Construction on Designs of the New Battleships." *Journal of the American Society of Naval Engineers* XIII (1901): 734–67.

Strauss, Joseph. "The Turrets of the New Battleships." *U.S. Naval Institute Proceedings* XXI (1895): 772–77.

"U.S. Battleships *Mississippi* and *Idaho.*" *Journal of the American Society of Naval Engineers* XX (1908): 134–147.

MONITORS

Bennett, Frank M. "Reconstructed American Monitors." *Journal of the American Society of Naval Engineers* IX (1897): 525–48.

Gage, Howard and Emil Theiss. "The Contract Trial of the USS *Monterey.*" *Journal of the American Society of Naval Engineers* V (1893): 115–37.

Kinkaid, T. W. "The USS *Terror* and the Pneumatic System as Applied to the Guns, Turrets, and Rudder." *Journal of the American Society of Naval Engineers* IX (1897): 14–28.

Mallory, C. K. "Description and Trials of the U.S. Monitor *Arkansas.*" *Journal of the American Society of Naval Engineers* XIV (1902): 1172–85.

ARMORED CRUISERS

Anderson, M. A. and E. R. Freeman. "The Contract Trial of the USS *New York.*" *Journal of the American Society of Naval Engineers* V (1893): 613–35.

Herbert, W. C. "Contract Trial of the U.S. Armored Cruiser *Brooklyn.*" *Journal of the American Society of Naval Engineers* VIII (1896): 741–62.

Kenney, Lewis H. "The USS *Pennsylvania.*" *Journal of the American Society of Naval Engineers* XVII (1905): 1–41.

———. "The U.S. Armored Cruiser *Tennessee.*" *Journal of the American Society of Naval Engineers* XVIII (1906): 386–464.

PROTECTED CRUISERS

Bowles, Francis T. "Our New Cruisers." *U.S. Naval Institute Proceedings* IX (1883): 595–626.

Carney, R. E. "Contract Trial of the USS *Olympia.*" *Journal of the American Society of Naval Engineers* VI (1894): 241–58.

McFarland, Walter M. and Harold P. Norton. "Contractor's Full-Power Forced-Draft Trial of the USS *Baltimore.*" *Journal of the American Society of Naval Engineers* I (1889): 337–44.

Melville, George W. "U.S. Triple-Screw Cruisers *Columbia* and *Minneapolis.*" *Transactions of the Society of Naval Architects and Marine Engineers* II (1894): 95–148.

Naumann, W. H. "The USS *Denver.*" *Journal of the American Society of Naval Engineers* XVI (1904): 67–94.

Reed, M. E. "Description and Official Trial of the USS *Charleston.*" *Journal of the American Society of Naval Engineers* XVII (1905): 754–805.

Warburton, Edgar T. "Contract Trial of the USS *Charleston.*" *Journal of the American Society of Naval Engineers* I (1889): 310–29.

———. "Contract Trial of the USS *San Francisco.*" *Journal of the American Society of Naval Engineers* II (1890): 537–50.

MISCELLANEOUS TYPES

Bieg, F. C. "Contract and Screw Trials of the USS *Katahdin.*" *Journal of the American Society of Naval Engineers* VIII (1896): 1–18.

Clark, Francis E. "The Last Years of the Sail Navy." *The American Neptune* XX (April 1960): 134–45.

Gibbons, William G. "The Marine Ram as Designed by Rear Admiral Daniel Ammen, U.S.N." *U.S. Naval Institute Proceedings* VIII (1882): 209–19.

Jackson, R. H. "Torpedo Craft and Employment." *U.S. Naval Institute Proceedings* XXVI (1900): 1–45.

Kennon, John W. "USS *Vesuvius.*" *U.S. Naval Institute Proceedings* LXXX (February 1954): 182–90.

Magoun, H. A. "U.S. Torpedo Boat Destroyers *Truxtun, Whipple,* and *Worden.*" *Journal of the American Society of Naval Engineers* XV (1903): 393–403.

Magruder, P. H. "Naval Academy Practice Ships." *U.S. Naval Institute Proceedings* LX (May 1934): 623–32.

Potter, David. " 'Old Half-Seas Under': Experiences in the U.S. Ram *Katahdin* during the War with Spain." *U.S. Naval Institute Proceedings* LCVIII (January 1942): 57–69.

Stephens, W. P. "The Steam Yacht as a Naval Auxiliary." *Transactions of the Society of Naval Architects and Marine Engineers* VI (1898): 89–112.

White, William R. "Official Trials of the Submarine Boats *Adder* and *Moccasin.*" *Journal of the American Society of Naval Engineers* XV (1903): 39–58.

Woodward, J. J. "Recent Light Draught Gunboats for the U.S. Navy." *Transactions of the Society of Naval Architects and Marine Engineers* II (1894): 285–95.

ORDNANCE

Alger, Philip R. "Naval Ordnance." *U.S. Naval Institute Proceedings* XX (1894): 573–97.

———. "Development of Ordnance and Armor in the Immediate Past and Future." *U.S. Naval Institute Proceedings* XXII (1896): 777–93.

———. "Improvements in Ordnance and Armor in the Recent Past and Future." *U.S. Naval Institute Proceedings* XXIII (1897): 125–40.

———. "Ordnance and Armor." *U.S. Naval Institute Proceedings* XXVII (1901): 529–50.

———. "Gunnery in Our Navy." *U.S. Naval Institute Proceedings* Prize Essay Supplement (1903): 1–70.

"Army and Coast Defense Supplement." *The Scientific American Supplement* XLVI (1898): 18798–846.

Dyer, Francis John. "Marksmanship in the Navy." *The World's Work* XVI (1908): 9768–78.

Eberle, Edward W. *Gun and Torpedo Drills for the United States Navy.* Annapolis: U.S. Naval Institute, 1900.

Gleaves, Albert. "Training Gunners in the United States Navy." *The World's Work* VIII (1904): 4895–903.

Gleaves, Albert and E. W. Very. "The Howell Torpedo." *U.S. Naval Institute Proceedings* XXI (1895): 124–29.

Ingersoll, R. R. *Text-Book of Ordnance and Gunnery.* Annapolis: U.S. Naval Institute, 1899.

O'Neil, Charles. "The Development of Modern Ordnance and Armor in the United States." *Transactions of the Society of Naval Architects and Marine Engineers* X (1902): 235–71.

Rodgers, T. S. "The Navy Six-Inch Breech-Loading Rifle." *U.S. Naval Institute Proceedings* XII (1886): 77–90.

Sears, W. J. "A General Description of the Whitehead Torpedo." *U.S. Naval Institute Proceedings* XXII (1896): 803–08.

Zalinski, E. L. "The Naval Uses of the Pneumatic Torpedo Gun." *U.S. Naval Institute Proceedings* XIV (1888): 9–56.

ENGINEERING

Hollis, Ira N. "Coal Endurance and Machinery of the New Cruisers." *Journal of the American Society of Naval Engineers.*" IV (1892): 637–756.

Fiske, Bradley A. "Electricity in Naval Life." *U.S. Naval Institute Proceedings* XXII (1896): 323–428.

McFarland, W. M. "The Modern Marine Engine, Boiler, Etc." *Journal of the American Society of Naval Engineers* VI (1894): 647–701.

———. "Notes on the Machinery of the New Vessels of the United States Navy." *Transactions of the Society of Naval Architects and Marine Engineers* I (1893): 140–75.

———. "Causes for the Adoption of Water-Tube Boilers in the United States Navy." *Transactions of the Society of Naval Architects and Marine Engineers* VII (1899): 19–40.

Miller, Spencer. "Coaling Vessels at Sea." *Transactions of the Society of Naval Architects and Marine Engineers* VII (1899): 1–18.

Greene, S. Dana. "Electricity on Shipboard." *Transactions of the Society of Naval Architects and Marine Engineers* II (1894): 51–68.

COMMUNICATIONS AND COMMAND

Howeth, L. S. *History of Communications-Electronics in the United States Navy.* Washington, D.C.: Government Printing Office, 1963.

Niblack, A. P. "Proposed Day, Night, and Fog Signals for the Navy, with a Brief Description of the Ardois Night System." *U.S. Naval Institute Proceedings* XVII (1891): 253–63.

———. "Naval Signaling." *U.S. Naval Institute Proceedings* XVIII (1892): 431–89.

———. "The Signal Question Once More." *U.S. Naval Institute Proceedings* XXVIII (1902): 553–63.

———. "Tactical Considerations Involved in Warship Design." *Transactions of the Society of Naval Architects and Marine Engineers* III (1895): 149–58.

PERSONNEL AND LIFE IN THE NAVY

Abbey, William and Charles House, ed. *Tales of A Cruise: Souvenir of the Cruise of the United States Monitor Florida.* 1906.

Beyer, Thomas. *The American Battleship in Commission.* Chicago: Laird and Lee, 1906.

Buenzle, Fred J., ed. *Our Naval Apprentice.* Newport: Vol I–III, April 1901–May 1904.

———. *The Bluejacket.* In *Army and Navy Life.* New York: Vol XII–XIV, May 1908–January 1909.

Gleaves, Albert. "The New Navy at Work." *The World's Work* V (1903): 3059–81.

Henderson, W. J. "A War-Ship Community." *Scribner's Magazine* XXIV (1898): 285–95.

Luce, Stephen B. "Naval Training." *U.S. Naval Institute Proceedings* XVI (1890): 367–430.

McLean, Ridley. *The Bluejacket's Manual.* Annapolis: U.S. Naval Institute, 1902, 1904.

Niblack, Albert P. "The Enlistment, Training, and Organization of Crews for Our New Ships." *U.S. Naval Institute Proceedings* XVII (1891): 3–50.

Quinlan, Michael, ed. *Ocean Wave.* Published at intervals aboard the USS *San Francisco,* 1893–94.

Tisdale, L. G. *Three Years Behind the Guns.* New York: The Century Co., 1908.

Young, L. S., ed. *The Bounding Billow.* Published at intervals aboard the USS *Olympia,* 1895–98.

Zogbaum, Rufus Fairchild. "With Uncle Sam's Bluejackets Afloat." *Scribner's Magazine* VIII (1890): 267–83.

SPANISH-AMERICAN WAR

Calkins, Carlos G. "Historical and Professional Notes on the Naval Campaign of Manila Bay in 1898." *U.S. Naval Institute Proceedings* XXV (1899): 267–321.

Chadwick, French E. *The Relations of the United States and Spain: The Spanish-American War.* New York: Scribner's, 1911.

Clark, G. S. "Naval Aspects of the Spanish-American War." *Brassey's Naval Annual.* Portsmouth, J. Griffin, 1899.

Eberle, Edward W. "The *Oregon's* Great Voyage." *Century Magazine* LVIII (1898–99): 912–24.

Farenholt, A. "Incidents of the Voyage of the USS *Charleston* to Manila in 1898." *U.S. Naval Institute Proceedings* L (1924): 753–70.

Hobson, Richmond P. *The Sinking of the Merrimac.* New York: Century, 1899.

Offley, C. N. "The Work of the *Oregon* During the Spanish-American War." *Journal of the American Society of Naval Engineers* XV (1903): 1144–62.

Sampson, William T. "The Atlantic Fleet in the Spanish War." *Century Magazine* LVII (1899): 886–913.

Sigsbee, Charles D. *The Maine; An Account of Her Destruction in Havana Harbor.* New York: Century, 1899.

"The Story of the Captains. Personal Narratives of the Naval Engagements Near Santiago de Cuba, July 3, 1898." *Century Magazine* LVIII (1899) : 51–118.

U.S. Navy. *Naval Operations of the War With Spain: Appendix to the Report of the Chief of the Bureau of Navigation.* Washington, D.C.: G.P.O., 1898.

WORLD CRUISE OF THE WHITE FLEET

Around the World with the Fleet, 1907–1909; A Pictorial Log of the Cruise. Annapolis: U.S. Naval Institute, 1929.

Jones, Robert D. *With the American Fleet from the Atlantic to the Pacific.* Seattle: Harrison Pub. Co., 1908.

Mathews, Franklin. *With the Battle Fleet; Cruise of the U.S. Atlantic Fleet from Hampton Roads to the Golden Gate.* New York: B. W. Huebsch, 1909.

———. *Back to Hampton Roads; Cruise of the U.S. Atlantic Fleet from San Francisco to Hampton Roads.* New York: B. W. Huebsch, 1909.

Miller, Roman J. *Pictorial Log of the Battle Fleet Cruise Around the World.* Chicago: A. C. McClurg, 1909.

Acknowledgments and Credits

Photographs appearing in the *American Steel Navy* have been assembled through the generous cooperation of the following organizations and individuals:

Brown Brothers, New York: Harry Collins, Jr.
Culver Pictures, New York: Audrey Kapelsohn, Corrin Meadows
Imperial War Museum, London: J. F. Golding
Library of Congress, Washington: Virginia Daiker, Donald C. Holmes, Milton Kaplan, Jerald Maddox, Renata Shaw
Mariners Museum, Newport News: John L. Lochhead, William T. Radcliffe
National Archives, Washington: Walter R. McNutt, James Moore, Paul White
National Maritime Museum, Greenwich: George A. Osbon
Naval Historical Display Center, Washington: Captain Shelby Gass, Lieutenant (j.g.) Philip Strub
Naval Historical Foundation, Washington: Vice Admiral W. S. DeLany, Lieutenant Mal Collet
Naval History Division, U.S. Navy, Washington: Charles R. Haberlein, Agnes F. Hoover, Samuel L. Morison
Peabody Museum of Salem: Philip Chadwick Foster Smith
San Francisco Maritime Museum: Mathilda Dring, Albert Harmon
Smithsonian Institution, Washington: Philip K. Lundeberg
Society for the Preservation of New England Antiquities, Boston: E. Florence Addison
Staten Island Historical Society: Raymond C. Fingado
Submarine Library and Museum, New London: Theda Bassett
Title Insurance and Trust Company, San Diego: Larry Booth
U.S. Marine Corps Museum, Quantico: Richard A. Long, Charles A. Wood
U.S. Naval Academy Library, Annapolis: Patrick F. Clausey, Margaret Peterson
U.S. Naval Academy Museum, Annapolis: Joseph C. Bruzek, James Cheevers
Washington State Historical Society, Olympia: Anna M. Ibbotson
Hugh Allen, Robert A. Dawes, Charles A. Focht, Alfred W. Harris, Neville T. Kirk, Jack Moore, Harry L. Pence, John Perry, James T. O'Reilly, Roland R. Riggs, Theodore Roscoe, Robert F. Sumrall

A surprising number of photographs—possibly 25,000—documenting the era of the American Steel Navy have been preserved by various institutions. The two major collections, both in Washington, D.C., are in the National Archives and the Library of Congress. The National Archives collection was originally assembled by the Navy's Bureau of Construction and Repair and consists of approximately 10,000 glass negatives. In general, these plates document construction of the Navy's warships and activities at navy yards, and are primarily the work of anonymous photographers. The major related collection in the Library of Congress, known as the "Detroit Collection," numbers about 2,500 glass negatives of naval scenes. This material, which once comprised part of the stock of the Detroit Publishing Company, headed by noted frontier photographer William Henry Jackson, is particularly rich in documentation of life aboard the Navy's warships. The majority of the photographs in *The American Steel Navy* are from contact prints of 8 x 10-inch and 11 x 14-inch plates in these two collections.

Several outstanding photographers specialized in photographing U.S. Navy activities during the period 1883–1909. Probably the two most talented and well-known of these were E. H. Hart and Enrique Muller, both of New York. The bulk of the naval scenes in the Detroit Collection are attributed to Hart. Most of Muller's negatives are unfortunately lost to history, although a few are in private hands and in the National Archives. Other leading navy-oriented photographers of the day, whose work has been largely preserved, included Nathaniel Stebbins of Boston, Asahel Curtis of Seattle, and Frank H. Child of Newport. The Stebbins negatives have been saved by the Society for the Preservation of New England Antiquities, those of Curtis by the Washington State Historical Society, and many of Child's by the National Archives. A number of excellent shipboard scenes depicting life aboard the protected cruiser *Olympia* were the work of a woman, Frances Benjamin Johnston, and these are in the Library of Congress. Additional maritime photographers of the day, whose work has been preserved to a lesser degree, included J. S. Johnston, A. Loeffler, H. G. Peabody, and William H. Rau.

A final valuable source of naval photographs has been a number of personal albums compiled by officers and enlisted men serving in the Navy at the turn of the century. Although many of these collections have come to light, it is hoped that publication of this volume will lead to the discovery of more such material.

Where known, the photographers have been listed in the photographic credits.

Page	Photographer and Source
i	Bureau of Ships Collection, National Archives
ii–iii	By William H. Rau: U.S. Naval Academy Library
iv	Eldredge Collection, The Mariners Museum
vii	U.S. Naval Academy Museum
viii	U.S. Naval Institute
x	Collection of Charles A. Focht
1–2	Naval Historical Foundation
5	U.S. Naval Academy Museum
6	Peabody Museum of Salem
7	By George Barrie: Library of Congress
8–9	By E. H. Hart: U.S. Naval Institute
11	By Frank H. Child: National Archives
12	Detroit Collection, Library of Congress
15	By Nathaniel L. Stebbins: Soc. Pres. New Eng. Ant.
17	Collection of Neville T. Kirk
18	By E. H. Hart: U.S. Naval Academy Library
19	Gould Collection: National Maritime Museum
20–21	By E. H. Hart: Naval History Division, U.S. Navy
22–23	By E. H. Hart: U.S. Naval Academy Library
24–30	Detroit Collection, Library of Congress
33	Naval History Division, U.S. Navy
34	By E. H. Hart: The Mariners Museum
35	By E. H. Hart: Library of Congress
36	Detroit Collection, Library of Congress
37	Bureau of Ships Collection, National Archives
38	Naval History Division, U.S. Navy
41	By Hart and Child: The Mariners Museum
42	By Nathaniel L. Stebbins: Soc. Pres. New Eng. Ant.
43	By Nathaniel L. Stebbins: U.S. Naval Academy Library
44	Detroit Collection, Library of Congress
45	By Asahel Curtis: Washington State Historical Society
46	By Nathaniel L. Stebbins: Soc. Pres. New Eng. Ant.
49–50	By E. H. Hart: Library of Congress
51	Detroit Collection, Library of Congress
52	By Nathaniel L. Stebbins: Soc. Pres. New Eng. Ant.
53	Detroit Collection, Library of Congress
54	Collection of Neville T. Kirk
57	Detroit Collection, Library of Congress
58	Bureau of Ships Collection, National Archives
59	By Frances Benjamin Johnston: Library of Congress
60	Bureau of Ships Collection, National Archives
61	By J. S. Johnston: Brown Brothers
62	Detroit Collection, Library of Congress
63	Gould Collection, National Maritime Museum, U.S. Naval Institute
64	U.S. Naval Academy Museum
67–71	Bureau of Ships Collection, National Archives
72	Detroit Collection, Library of Congress. Bureau of Ships Collection, National Archives
73	By H. G. Peabody: Peabody Museum of Salem
74–75	Detroit Collection, Library of Congress
76	By William H. Rau: U.S. Naval Institute
79	Bureau of Ships Collection, National Archives
80	Detroit Collection, Library of Congress. U.S. Naval Institute
81	San Francisco Maritime Museum
82–85	Detroit Collection, Library of Congress
86–87	Bureau of Ships Collection, National Archives
88	The Mariners Museum
90–91	Detroit Collection, Library of Congress
92	By Frank H. Child: National Archives
95	San Francisco Maritime Museum
96	Detroit Collection, Library of Congress
97–98	Bureau of Ships Collection, National Archives
99	Naval History Division, U.S. Navy
100	San Francisco Maritime Museum
102	By Frank H. Child: National Archives
105	Bureau of Ships Collection, National Archives
106	Detroit Collection, Library of Congress
107	U.S. Naval Academy Library
108	By Frank H. Child: National Archives
109–110	Bureau of Ships Collection, National Archives
112	Both Detroit Collection, Library of Congress
113	Bureau of Ships Collection, National Archives

INDEX

The index cites only those ships mentioned within the text. See pages 382–383 for a complete listing of vessels in the United States Navy as of 1 January 1900.
Italicized page numbers refer to pages on which photos appear.

At the smoking lamp: lighting up on board the protected cruiser
Olympia *in 1899.*

The Naval Institute Press is the book-publishing arm of the U.S. Naval Institute, a private, nonprofit professional society for members of the sea services and civilians who share an interest in naval and maritime affairs. Established in 1873 at the U.S. Naval Academy in Annapolis, Maryland, where its offices remain today, the Naval Institute has more than 100,000 members worldwide.

Members of the Naval Institute receive the influential monthly naval magazine *Proceedings* and substantial discounts on fine nautical prints, ships and aircraft photos, and subscriptions to the Institute's recently inaugurated quarterly, *Naval History.* They also have access to the transcripts of the Institute's Oral History Program and may attend any of the Institute-sponsored seminars regularly offered around the country.

The book-publishing program, begun in 1898 with basic guides to naval practices, has broadened its scope in recent years to include books of more general interest. Now the Naval Institute Press publishes more than forty new titles each year, ranging from how-to books on boating and navigation to battle histories, biographies, ship guides, and novels. Institute members receive discounts on the Press's more than 300 books.

For a free catalog describing books currently available and for further information about U.S. Naval Institute membership, please write to:

Membership Department
U.S. Naval Institute
Annapolis, Maryland 21402

or call, toll-free, 800-233-USNI.